How Far the Promised Land?

How Far the Promised Land?

WORLD AFFAIRS AND THE
AMERICAN CIVIL RIGHTS
MOVEMENT FROM THE
FIRST WORLD WAR TO VIETNAM

Jonathan Rosenberg

PRINCETON UNIVERSITY PRESS

PRINCETON AND OXFORD

Library of Congress Cataloging-in-Publication Data

Rosenberg, Jonathan, 1958–
How far the promised land? : world affairs and the American civil rights
movement from the First World War to Vietnam / Jonathan Rosenberg.
p.   cm.
Includes bibliographical references and index.
ISBN-13: 978-0-691-00706-9 (cl : alk. paper)
ISBN-10: 0-691-00706-3 (cl : alk. paper)
1. African Americans—Civil rights—History—20th century. 2. Civil
rights movements—United States—History—20th century. 3. African
Americans—Politics and government—20th century. 4. African American
leadership—History—20th century. 5. Civil rights workers—United States—
History—20th century. 6. Political activists—United States—History—20th
century. 7. Internationalism—History—20th century. 8. United States—Race
relations—Political aspects—History—20th century. 9. United States—Foreign
relations—20th century. 10. World politics—20th century. I. Title.

E185.61.R8155 2006
323.1196′073′00904—dc22   2005048749

This book has been composed in Sabon

Printed on acid-free paper. ∞

pup.princeton.edu

Printed in the United States of America

1   3   5   7   9   10   8   6   4   2

*To my mother
and to the memory of my father*

CONTENTS

ILLUSTRATIONS

ACKNOWLEDGMENTS

THIS BOOK began as a dissertation at Harvard University under the direction of Akira Iriye and Ernest R. May, who were interested, from early on, in an unconventional topic, which they encouraged me to explore as fully as I could. Time and again, they provided acute insights into the link between overseas and domestic developments and offered important suggestions about the larger international context in which the civil rights struggle developed. The standard that Professors Iriye and May have set in their own work over several decades is at once inspiring and daunting, and I am grateful for their encouragement and erudition.

For a number of years, James Goodman undoubtedly heard far too much about the link between civil rights and world affairs. But prior to demonstrating such estimable patience, Jim unwittingly provided the intellectual catalyst for this subject when he offered me a summer research job researching the black press in the 1930s as he worked to complete his first book. What I saw in those newspapers was tremendously exciting, and that experience set this project in motion. Thus, Jim was present at the work's creation and encouraged me to pursue it. Had it not been for that summer position, I would not have contemplated writing this book. It is a pleasure to thank Jim for his guidance—and for the job.

Numerous colleagues and friends have read portions of the work, listened to me discuss it (endlessly perhaps), and offered a great deal of constructive advice on how best to proceed. I am genuinely pleased to thank the following people for their willingness to provide substantive comments, tactful criticisms, friendly suggestions, and, now and then, a few words of encouragement: Mark Baker, Rick Belsky, Andrew Erdmann, Ellen Fitzpatrick, Brett Flehinger, Marc Gallicchio, Frank Gavin, Stewart Hoffman, Max Holland, Christopher Hurd, Zachary Karabell, Thomas Knock, Erin Mahan, Tarek Masoud, Bernadette McCauley, John T. McGreevy, Jeff Moran, Michael Pak, Andrew Port, David Purvin, Mark Rose, Neal Rosendorf, and Jerry Sweeney. While some hold academic positions, others work outside the academy. Whether they know it or not, they all helped me to complete this book.

During the past several years, I presented portions of the work at several conferences and seminars, and benefited from the perceptive comments that many wonderful scholars sent my way. It is a pleasure to thank Carol Anderson, Brian Balogh, David Blight, James Campbell, John W. Chambers, John Milton Cooper, Frank Costigliola, Mary Dudziak, Cary Fraser, John Lewis Gaddis, Cheryl Greenberg, Matthew Holden, James

Kloppenberg, Michael Krenn, Walter LaFeber, Melvyn Leffler, Sidney Milkis, Frank Ninkovich, Richard Pells, and Brenda Gayle Plummer. Their willingness to share their knowledge of twentieth-century American and international history has been enormously helpful.

Several people deserve special thanks for the great care with which they read the entire manuscript. Inordinately generous with their time, these devoted souls offered numerous suggestions, both substantive and stylistic: Daniel Gross, K.C. Johnson, Paul Mitchinson, Thomas Noer, and Jack Salzman. Each supplied constructive comments in an effort to help improve the manuscript, and even as I wisely incorporated many of their suggestions, I foolishly ignored some of what they had to say. At least a couple of these conscientious readers will no doubt remind me of this for years to come and wonder how I could have possibly neglected to listen to every bit of advice they offered.

Over a number of years, I received generous assistance from several sources, which helped me to complete this volume. I wish to thank the PSC-CUNY Research Awards Program; the Kittredge Foundation; the Charles Warren Center in American History, Harvard University; the Department of History, Harvard University; and the Mark DeWolfe Howe Fund. In addition, as I researched this book, the reference staff at Harvard's Widener Library was exceedingly helpful on countless occasions. More recently, the staff at the New York Public Library, especially Linden Anderson and Tom Lisanti, provided efficient and courteous assistance in helping me to obtain the photographs that are included in these pages. Credit for the photographs goes to the Photographs and Prints Division of the Schomburgh Center for Research in Black Culture, The New York Public Library, the Astor, Lenox and Tilden Foundations. I also wish to thank the Crisis Publishing Company, the publisher of the magazine of the National Association for the Advancement of Colored People, for the use of the November 1918 cover of *The Crisis*, which graces the front cover of this volume.

My editor at Princeton University Press, Brigitta van Rheinberg, has been extraordinarily helpful in a multitude of ways as I worked to complete this book. Brigitta is not only a perspicacious and sensitive reader, but she also possesses an abundance of patience. I am genuinely grateful for both sets of attributes. I must also express my gratitude for the kindness Brigitta demonstrated when a family crisis sprang up just as I was preparing to submit the manuscript to the Press. Her thoughtfulness helped ease my worries during a difficult time. Let me also thank Jill Harris and Alison Kalett, who helped guide the manuscript through the production process, and Beth Gianfagna, who meticulously copyedited it.

Since 2001, I have had the good fortune to call the history department at Hunter College of the City University of New York my professional home. An institution with a diverse, hard-working, and altogether interesting student body, Hunter is an unusually rewarding environment in which to teach American history. The department of history, which is expertly chaired by Barbara Welter, is composed of a marvelous group of people, who are stimulating, collegial, and, quite simply, great fun to be around. Indeed, the faculty and staff make coming to the office a pleasure, and I genuinely enjoy spending time on the fifteenth floor of Hunter West.

My most profound thanks are reserved for my family, whose sustained love and support have long been a source of inspiration and strength. My wife, Jane, and our children, James and Isobel, have enriched my life in more ways than I can count or even fully comprehend. Like the families of many authors, mine has endured far too many afternoons, evenings, and weekends away from spouse and parent, who, in a mad desire to complete the Great Work, was not nearly as attentive to their concerns as he should have been. While I am quite sure that I did not always tell them so, the swirl of family excitement, which at times seemed a distraction, made the solitary enterprise of conducting research and writing infinitely more meaningful than it would otherwise have been.

Finally, I lovingly dedicate this book to my mother and to the memory of my father, who, together, awakened in me a passion for asking questions, seeking answers, and reflecting upon consequential events, foreign and domestic. To their children, my parents conveyed the notion that beyond the walls of our house in the suburbs was a fascinating world ripe for exploration. But as they often reminded us, it was a world in need of improvement. Throughout my childhood, my mother and father decried the persistence of injustice and inequality in America and around the world, and asserted that if the United States, in particular, was to become a truly just society, it was essential for all Americans, including their three children, to lead lives founded on tolerance, compassion, and political commitment. It saddens me that I cannot present a copy of this book to both my parents, but its existence is a testament to their deepest convictions.

How Far the Promised Land?

COLOR-CONSCIOUS INTERNATIONALISM AND THE

TWENTIETH-CENTURY STRUGGLE

> The nightmare is over. The world awakes. The long, hor-
> rible years of dreadful night are passed. Behold the sun!
> We have dreamed! . . . And now suddenly we awake! It
> is done. We are sane. We are alive.

WITH THE END of the First World War, this hymn to peace appeared in the pages of the December 1918 issue of *The Crisis*, the monthly organ of the National Association for the Advancement of Colored People. That same month, just three weeks after the armistice was signed, the author of those hopeful lines, W.E.B. Du Bois, was on his way to France, where statesmen would gather to forge the postwar order. Representing the NAACP, America's leading race reformer would remain in Europe for more than three months on a mission possessed of both domestic and international implications. Du Bois, who was involved in a variety of efforts to ameliorate the plight of peoples of color at home and abroad, would write later that he had gone to Paris in the belief that "the destinies of mankind" were centered there.[1]

As he crossed the Atlantic on the *Orizaba*, Du Bois shared a cabin with Lester Walton, a leading black journalist, and Robert R. Moton, who had succeeded Booker T. Washington at Tuskegee Institute. The vessel carried the press corps that would cover the peace conference and according to philanthropist George Foster Peabody, who was also on board, it was fortunate Du Bois and Moton were traveling together, for this would allow them to "map out . . . a program" and advance the "single-minded-cooperation of the colored people in this great crisis period . . . when the future of the colored races is of so great moment."[2] Guided by three objectives on his foreign mission, Du Bois would gather material for a proposed history of black Americans in the Great War, act as the special representative of *The Crisis*, and represent the NAACP in an effort to aid the cause of black peoples throughout the world. He would play a key role at the Pan-African Congress, which would meet in Paris and seek, in part, to influence the diplomatic discussions over the disposition of the former German colonies in Africa, an issue world leaders would address in the French capital. This was no assignment for the faint of heart. But Du Bois was blessed with supreme confidence in his ability to transform world affairs, and he reached Paris believing in the transcendent importance of his mission. In this respect, he was not unlike another American who would soon arrive in France: the president of the United States.[3]

Indeed, just days before both men left for Europe, Du Bois penned an illuminating letter to Woodrow Wilson, which suggests the importance race leaders attached to the peace conference. Identifying an interconnection between developments in Paris and in the United States, Du Bois noted that race reform leaders would not hesitate to link international and domestic matters to advance their reform aims. He claimed the American race question was "intimately related to the import of the international conferences" and wrote of potential American vulnerability at Paris to charges of racial discrimination in the United States, which might lead to an "indictment of inconsistency." The reformer noted that America, which denied democratic privileges to "more than twelve million souls," was seeking to provide leadership at a conference that aimed to democratize states that had long withheld equal rights from their inhabitants. If the United States continued to deny some of its own citizens these rights, it would be "a libel on our civilization." Asserting that blacks had "earned as much consideration as most of the smaller nations whose liberties and rights" were to be safeguarded by the international agreement, Du Bois told Wilson that America "owes to the world the solution of her race problem," which should be resolved "by the same impartial and righteous judgement that is to be applied to other peoples." While the president did not respond to Du Bois's letter, it testifies to the race leader's conviction that the peace conference was supremely important in the context of the domestic struggle for racial justice. And it suggests the extent to which he believed the international gathering could help the campaign at home.[4]

Du Bois's European journey and his views on the significance of the peace conference point to the focus of this study, which explores the interconnection between world affairs and the most important reform movement in twentieth-century American history, the African-American freedom struggle. More specifically, the work is an inquiry into why American race reform leaders found world affairs so engaging and how they incorporated their understanding of a variety of international developments into their domestic reform campaign. It is equally important to understand the way the reformers perceived American actions on the international stage from World War I to the Vietnam War, and the manner in which they responded to the country's emerging preeminence in world politics. In examining the reformers' response to international developments and American actions overseas, I consider a variety of narratives that are typically presented in different books written by different historians, and I explore the interplay between the black freedom struggle, international affairs, and America's changing role in the world.[5]

Among the reform leaders who figure prominently in the work are W.E.B. Du Bois, James Weldon Johnson, Joel Spingarn, Mary White Ovington, William Pickens, Walter White, Mary McLeod Bethune, A. Philip Randolph, Roy Wilkins, Ralph Bunche, and Martin Luther King, Jr. A cosmopolitan group of men and women, black and white, these were central figures in the struggle for racial justice, who toiled to end discrimination in education, voting, housing, transportation, and employment. If some occasionally subscribed to a radical perspective, by and large, these individuals were not seeking the fundamental transformation of the American political and economic order. Although such leaders were working, in a real sense, to achieve radical change, they were mainly traditional figures in the history of modern American race reform and represented the movement's mainstream.

In addition to considering the views of reform leaders, I focus closely on the National Association for the Advancement of Colored People, which played a crucial role in the unfolding campaign for racial justice. Indeed, much of the study traces how the association and its leadership responded to global developments and American actions in world politics throughout the twentieth century.[6] While I examine the NAACP, I also consider the worldviews of figures in other civil rights organizations, including the National Urban League, the National Negro Congress, the March on Washington Movement, and later, the Congress of Racial Equality, the Southern Christian Leadership Conference, and the Student Nonviolent Coordinating Committee.

Although my focus is largely on top-level reformers and the organizations in which they served, I am mindful of the trend away from "top-down" studies of the movement in favor of more grass-roots approaches. To be sure, such work continues to enrich our understanding of the struggle, but I would suggest that during much of the twentieth century, a considerable amount of the movement's energy and direction came from above. From World War I through the mid-1950s, top leaders and organizations like the NAACP played a critical role in the reform effort by generating support among black Americans and by persuading the American people their cause was just. And of course, such leaders spearheaded the attack on Jim Crow in the judicial and legislative spheres. Moreover, to the extent that world affairs informed the struggle, such matters were likely more significant to national rather than local figures, who were more concerned with the day-to-day challenges of sustaining the reform enterprise, often in small and inhospitable environments.[7]

Perhaps it is surprising that the men and women I have chosen to study—those devoted to building a more just society in the United

States—would have found the world beyond America so engaging. Surely, such leaders were occupied with the daunting challenges of the reform enterprise, with publicizing the inequities of race relations in America and convincing their fellow citizens to abolish institutionalized racial oppression. One might imagine that scrutinizing, reflecting, speaking, and writing on events overseas would have weakened the reformers' efforts to effect change in the United States. But they did precisely this, and over many decades, the movement's leaders demonstrated an extraordinary interest in global affairs and made their understanding of the world central to the message they presented to their followers, the nation, and the international community. In speeches, articles, columns, editorials, lectures, petitions, conferences, essays, books, letters, and travel accounts, the race reformers focused intently on overseas affairs and America's place in the world, and they made such matters a key part of their crusade. They did so to energize their supporters and to clarify, legitimize, and strengthen the aims of their struggle to policymakers and the American people. The reformers were convinced, in short, that developments abroad could provide traction for the cause.

This keen interest in the world points to an important theme I shall develop in this study, namely, that numerous mainstream race reform leaders were internationalists, who shared some of the ideas and values embraced by American internationalists throughout the twentieth century. One historian has written that the internationalists were nearly all old-stock Protestants descended from English forebears, but I would suggest that the race reformers' worldview was not dissimilar from that of this traditional group, although the race leaders' understanding of the world was very much their own.[8]

Scholars have found it difficult to agree on the precise meaning of the term *internationalism*, and have established a variety of taxonomies in order to elucidate the concept. Still, a belief in the practicability of cooperation (economic, social, or cultural) among the world's peoples and a belief in the possibility of constructing a more pacific world order that could render war less likely or even obsolete have been among the core ideas embraced by nearly all internationalists. Moreover, most internationalists have believed that some type of international organization, for example, the League of Nations or the United Nations, was needed to help create and sustain global comity. Another tenet of the internationalist creed has suggested that the United States has a special mission in the world, the achievement of which would enable humanity to construct a more cooperative global order.[9] In important respects, the race reform leaders subscribed to such ideas and supported the development of organizations like the League and the United Nations, believing transnational cooperation and the abolition of war were desirable and attainable goals.

And surprisingly, many race reformers were persuaded that the United States had a unique role to play in the world, although as we shall see, for the reformers this was a more complicated matter.

If there were points of convergence between the race reformers' understanding of the world and that of the traditional internationalists, there were also significant areas of difference. The race reformers' worldview, which I have chosen to call color-conscious internationalism, combined the familiar with the novel and represented a bold departure from traditional internationalist thought. One objective of this study is to delineate the course of color-conscious internationalism, for to understand the history of the civil rights campaign, it is necessary to consider how the movement's leading figures viewed twentieth-century global affairs and America's changing role in the world.

Color-conscious internationalism comprised three key characteristics. First was the conviction that transnational institutions such as the League of Nations and the United Nations had a critical role to play not just in world politics but also in the domestic realm. In the international sphere, such institutions would be instrumental in helping to dismantle imperial rule in the developing world and, by contributing to the cause of self-determination, would foster a more just global order. In the domestic sphere, the reformers believed the League and the United Nations could help abolish institutionalized racial oppression in two ways: first, by compelling the United States to apply the provisions of the League or United Nations charters to American domestic society; and second, by serving as useful arenas in which race reform leaders could marshal world public opinion against America's discriminatory racial practices. The race reformers were hopeful that such organizations could contribute to the reconfiguration of race relations in the United States, which would help to create a more just society.[10]

A second aspect of color-conscious internationalism concerned the notion that America—despite its domestic shortcomings—had a critical role to play in helping to shape world politics, the ultimate outcome of which would be a global order that was less oppressive and more democratic. But for the United States to assume the mantle of world leadership and to help humanity reach this exalted plane, the race reformers insisted that America had to reform its domestic social relations, race relations, especially. To become the world's reformer, the United States had first to democratize its domestic social and political institutions—to harmonize them with its self-proclaimed global aspirations—for it was not possible, to use the famous phrase, "to make the world safe for democracy" as long as America itself was not genuinely democratic. The race reformers thus identified a tension between America's willingness to assume a world leadership role, a posture many supported, and the persistence of domestic racial oppression. This tension would inform the way many civil rights leaders viewed the activities of the United States on the international stage throughout the twentieth century.

A third component of color-conscious internationalism flowed from the idea, embraced by most traditional internationalists, that it was desirable to work toward cooperation among peoples and that such cooperation could transcend national boundaries. Sondra Herman has written of the internationalist impulse to help increase "the sense of human unity," while Warren Kuehl writes of the internationalists' desire to "heighten an awareness" of such unity.[11] This belief in the possibility of worldwide cooperation and transnational unity lay at the very heart of color-conscious internationalism, though for the race reformers the notion was not quite so expansive. The unity in which the race reformers believed was the unity of the downtrodden. Oppressed peoples of color throughout the world—whether in Africa, Asia, or the United States—were bound together by the reality of their subordinate status, interconnected by a shared lack of autonomy. For race reform leaders, the domestic campaign was inseparable from the worldwide struggle against racial oppression, and it was in this way that the internationalist belief in the unity of humanity and in transnational cooperation achieved meaning. Throughout the twentieth century, civil rights leaders identified themselves as part of a global reform project, and as part of this "imagined community" of reformers they wedded their domestic aims to the aspirations of those working to liberate peoples of color around the world.[12] For the men and women animated by the idea of color-conscious internationalism, freedom was indivisible.

I have suggested that color-conscious internationalism powerfully informed how American race reformers viewed the world and that throughout the twentieth century they placed their understanding of international affairs at the center of their reform message. In exploring that message, this study rests on sources derived from the public record the movement produced, a record typically encountered by large numbers of people in a variety of settings. Not surprisingly, as the reformers presented their message to different audiences, their aims varied considerably. An NAACP official speaking before the United States Congress had objectives different from a reformer addressing the NAACP's annual conference, for example. Likewise, the objectives of Du Bois, writing in the black press, differed from those that drove Walter White when he was speaking to a national radio audience. The work considers the importance of such distinctions as the reformers articulated their message in myriad settings: in addresses at annual conferences; in sermons, books, pamphlets, and essays; and in the columns and editorials published in newspapers, journals, and magazines.[13] Private correspondence is included, particularly when it illuminates the reformers' perceptions of foreign developments.

One of the key sources is the NAACP's monthly publication, *The Crisis*. The association's journal, which Du Bois established in 1910, serves as a superb lens through which to view a broad range of issues related to race reform in America. From the outset, Du Bois believed the monthly would be essential for the movement's success, asserting that his creation, in its words, pictures, manner, and "conception of life," would be crucial for training reformers and potential reformers.[14] As a source for understanding the unfolding struggle for justice, *The Crisis* is unsurpassed. And in establishing an unambiguous connection between overseas developments and domestic reform, it consistently articulated the reformers' distinctive brand of internationalism, which it conveyed to hundreds of thousands of devoted readers throughout the twentieth century.

The work is divided into eight chapters and includes a prelude and a postlude. Following the prelude, which briefly considers the significance of World War I for the race reform campaign, the first two chapters examine the war and its immediate aftermath, a period in which the American president had repeatedly told his fellow citizens that they were involved in a conflict that would enable humanity to establish a more just and democratic world, an effort America was uniquely suited to lead. Listening closely to Woodrow Wilson, the race reformers appropriated and reconfigured his language, infusing their message for change with Wilsonian rhetoric, in an effort to get the country to grant to black Americans the freedom—the self-determination—the president told his people they were fighting for overseas. The notion that the war and race reform were inextricably connected pervaded the discourse of reform in the black press, magazines, speeches, and sermons. Reform leaders transformed the president's rhetoric on the superiority of democratic institutions, the oppression of ethnic minorities, and the necessity for a League of Nations—language Wilson had used to rally the nation in war—and deployed such ideas to rally the black population at home and to legitimize their program for change. If the president could use the grammar of right and justice to convince the country it was worth dying for democracy overseas, the activists asserted, it was right and just to create a genuine democracy in the United States.

During the interwar years, the focus of chapters 3 and 4, the outside world continued to attract the reformers' gaze. The international disarmament impulse was of particular interest during the 1920s, as were developments in the Soviet Union, which some reformers saw as an emerging egalitarian society and even a possible model for reconfiguring American race relations. The reformers were also fascinated by Gandhi's activities and tactics in India, a reflection of their growing interest in the stirrings against empire in the developing world. During the 1930s, the reformers were intently interested in European fascism and were energized by developments in Ethiopia, which Italy invaded in 1935, and moved by the civil war in Spain. The emergence of Nazism provides an especially compelling story in this period, as the reformers consistently linked the horrific developments in Hitler's Germany to life in the Jim Crow South. They hoped such an analogy would clarify the character of American race prejudice and thus legitimize the reform movement in the minds of their fellow citizens.[15]

Chapter 5 considers World War II, a watershed in the struggle for racial justice, after which it would become impossible to shunt the civil rights debate to one side of the national agenda. The race activists persistently equated the global battle against tyranny with their domestic struggle against racial oppression, and the fact that ideas about race were supremely important in the European and Pacific theaters made it easy to use the conflict to serve the domestic cause.[16] As the race reformers argued throughout the war, because America had assumed a leading role in sweeping German and Japanese racialism from the world stage, it was imperative to sweep Jim Crow from the domestic scene.[17] The war defined the contours of the movement in these years, and the reformers used it effectively to help their cause by setting the opportunities and dangers inherent in the world crisis before their supporters, policymakers, and the American people. This approach would yield tangible gains, and these achievements, which the reformers believed were milestones in their struggle, are attributable in part to the reformers' deft use of the war as a lever with which to effect change.

If World War II powerfully influenced the movement, the postwar years presented the reformers with distinctive challenges and opportunities. With victory in 1945, there was a sense that race relations had reached a new juncture, and reform leaders continued to seize upon world affairs as they had for many years, placing the momentous events of the postwar era at the center of their quest. Chapter 6 examines the period from 1945 to 1950, when, in the wake of the war, the movement assumed an increasingly global character. Civil rights leaders determinedly equated their domestic struggle with the freedom campaigns that peoples of color were waging in Asia and Africa, recognizing little distinction between the aspirations of colonial peoples and those of black Americans. In addition, the reformers manifested a keen interest in the activities of the United Nations, believing the institution had a role to play in helping the oppressed in the developing world and in abolishing domestic racial oppression. The emerging East-West antagonism would also become a key concern for the reformers, given the questions it raised about what many saw as a struggle between democracy and tyranny.

Throughout the 1950s, as I trace in chapter 7, the Cold War and decolonization remained the key international considerations of the race reformers, and they made both of these epochal developments central to their message. As was common in these years, many mainstream reformers viewed the Cold War as a struggle between two ways of life and believed the conflict could help them persuade their fellow citizens to construct a genuine democracy in the United States. If by the late 1940s the American government had taken the lead in working to quash the perceived global threat of Soviet Communism, the reformers pointed time and again to the inconsistency between fighting tyranny abroad and tolerating segregation at home. Mainstream reformers did not doubt that America had a leadership role to play in the world. But to do so effectively, they asserted, the country had to get its own house in order. At the same time, the liberation campaigns waged by peoples of color were of particular moment to reform leaders, who pointed to the parallels between their domestic exertions and the efforts of the oppressed throughout the world. Significantly, the reformers wedded North-South to East-West concerns, arguing repeatedly that the United States needed to end domestic racial persecution if it wished to command the loyalty of peoples of color in the developing world, a goal they claimed was vital during the Cold War.

The final chapter briefly considers the movement during the 1960s and suggests the divisive effect the Vietnam War wrought on the civil rights campaign. Many, but not all, reformers came to argue that American brutality overseas was merely an extension of American brutality at home, a perspective that tested severely the tenets of color-conscious internationalism. United States policies in southeast Asia, which opened fissures throughout American society, proved no less problematic for those seeking justice for African Americans. The book concludes with a short postlude that ponders the relationship between world affairs and the domestic freedom struggle.

During the fifty years examined in this work, the ebb and flow of America's international engagement informed how civil rights leaders sought to use foreign affairs to serve their cause. When the United States was at war, the reformers worked to translate American belligerency into concrete achievements such as the democratization of military service, officer training, and defense industry employment. But when the United States was not an active belligerent overseas, the reformers deployed international developments in a more purely rhetorical fashion—to fortify, clarify, and legitimize their message. This approach is especially important for understanding how the movement's leaders responded to events after 1945, as the United States energetically pursued its foreign policy aims throughout the world.

The way the reformers responded to overseas affairs may have been supple, but a consistent theme throughout these years concerned their conviction that it was necessary to highlight the gap that separated America's historic belief in the sanctity of democracy, freedom, and equality from the historic reality of racial oppression in the United States. Throughout this fifty-year period, the race reformers spoke forcefully about the disjunction between the nation's professed commitment to democratic ideals and the institutionalized oppression of black Americans, and they consistently invoked America's deeply rooted ideology of freedom to fortify their cause.[18] The race activists chided America for not living up to its promise, particularly at those moments when the nation entered the maelstrom of world politics and engaged in actions that American leaders inevitably characterized as efforts to defend democratic values.

The persistent tendency among presidents and policymakers to portray the United States as the international defender of democratic ideals calls forth another of the book's themes, namely, the correlation between the emergence of American globalism and progress achieved on the civil rights front. American activism in the world, particularly as it developed during and after World War II, contributed to the movement's postwar success, and the chapters that follow point to the interconnection between these two signal developments in twentieth-century American history: the quest for racial justice and the increasing global preeminence of the United States. The reformers' strategy of trying to turn overseas affairs to their advantage became most powerful when the United States began to play a leading role in world politics, especially after 1940. For then, American policymakers began to recognize that Jim Crow was expensive and that the cost would be drawn on America's international account. And later, as the United States became more deeply engaged overseas, the reformers' argument that domestic racial oppression exposed the country to grave risks in a perilous world became a trenchant rhetorical device, and the strategy of incorporating international matters into the civil rights campaign became considerably more effective than it had been earlier. At a time when national insecurity was becoming the order of the day, the reformers asserted repeatedly that the nation's failure to create a genuine democracy at home would diminish America's global influence and endanger its well-being. In using the East-West conflict to prod the nation into building a more just society, the movement's leaders conjoined the language of reform with the concerns of the emerging national security state.

Something of a hybrid, the book does not fit easily into any obvious field or subfield. Part of the ongoing effort to enrich our understanding of the history of the United States in the world, the project has been informed by the work of scholars interested in reconceptualizing United

States international history, especially by those drawn to what has come to be called the cultural approach to that field. One of the pioneers of this approach to international history, Akira Iriye, has written that there is "no definition of culture that is completely satisfactory to students of international affairs." This point suggests a related observation, namely, that there is no definition of the cultural approach to United States international history that is completely satisfactory either. According to Iriye, one characteristic of the approach is that it considers world affairs "in terms of dreams, aspirations, and other manifestations of human consciousness."[19] With this in mind, I have sought to examine how a group of committed reformers perceived and interpreted global developments and incorporated such matters into their campaign in an effort to help realize their dreams and aspirations at home. The aim of the book, then, unlike that of other important works on civil rights and world affairs, is to explore the distinctive internationalism that was central to the crusade for racial justice in twentieth-century America.[20]

It should be noted that I do not consider how black Americans influenced foreign policy, nor is the state, the centrality of which is typically a defining characteristic of works of foreign relations history, my primary focus. The subjects under consideration, civil rights organizations and those who headed them, are nonstate actors, and though the state plays an important part in the story (the movement's leaders were responding to state actions and working to reform state-sanctioned oppression), it is not the fundamental object of inquiry.[21] Instead, I have sought to probe the perceptions and ideals of a group of American reformers and to understand, as Iriye has written, how "local forces integrate themselves into a global situation," or more pertinently, into changing global situations.[22] This local-global nexus is especially salient when one considers the extent to which civil rights leaders conceived of their movement as part of a worldwide crusade to liberate peoples of color.

While my primary objective is to illuminate the interconnection between overseas developments and domestic race reform, the book points to a broader phenomenon in American history, namely, the extent to which world affairs have interacted powerfully with domestic life. Although it has become a commonplace to observe that the United States has had a profound impact on the twentieth-century world, it is worth remembering that throughout American history, the world has had a profound impact on America. Indeed, one of the lineaments of American history is the considerable influence global developments have had on the contours of the nation's political, social, cultural, economic, and intellectual life, and this study, which stands at the point where domestic and international developments intersect, suggests, I hope, that this historical and historiographic marchland is worth exploring.[23]

A final (introductory) word concerns the historical bricks and mortar out of which this book is constructed. A distinguished scholar has noted that the work is based mainly on rhetoric, and to be sure, one of my primary aims is to examine the reformers' language as it unfolded over the course of the twentieth century. In considering reform movements, one must look closely at the way reform leaders frame their message, for this is how they seek to gain support for their agenda. Those working to advance the campaign for racial justice in America were convinced that to achieve their aims it was essential to articulate a powerful message that would catalyze support for their program and persuade the American people their cause was right. According to one reformer, it was necessary to gain public acceptance of the movement's goals and to present a message that would help change public attitudes on racial matters. This objective, he said, was "the basic public relations task" of the struggle.[24] The material out of which reformers fashion a language of persuasion—how they shape their message, what they choose to emphasize, and why—is thus integral to the reform enterprise. And such language is the means reformers use to realize tangible ends such as the passage of legislation or victory in the courtroom. Persuasive language is closely related, moreover, to the preeminent goal on the reform agenda: the transformation of beliefs and values that allows for social progress.[25]

With this in mind, it might be helpful to imagine civil rights leaders sealed off completely from any awareness of world affairs during the fifty years covered here. Such leaders would have headed a movement altogether different from the campaign that actually unfolded and framed a fundamentally different message. The race reformers would have explained the character of American race relations in different terms, sought to inspire their supporters differently, and tried to persuade the American people and policymakers that their cause was just in ways other than they did. The content of the reform journals and countless opinion pieces in the black press would have been different, as would the focus of innumerable speeches, conferences, and meetings. One cannot say how the movement would have sounded, what arguments the reformers would have made, or how they would have framed their program for domestic change. But they would, necessarily, have done so differently. The reformers' strategy of incorporating their unique understanding of the world into their message profoundly affected the tone, the trajectory, and, finally, the momentum of race reform in these years. That the movement's leaders made global developments central to their struggle makes it imperative to understand how and why they did so.

PART I

World War I and the Peace Settlement

"YOURS FOR WORLD DEMOCRACY"
Journeys to Paris

ON THE MORNING of December 4, 1918, thousands gathered on the Manhattan waterfront to watch President Woodrow Wilson set sail for France. Five destroyers from the Atlantic Torpedo Flotilla escorted the president's ship, the *George Washington*, out of the harbor toward the open sea. Small craft of every description circled in the waters around the great ship, and military planes circled in the sky above. Standing on the ship's bridge with his wife, Edith, at his side, the president waved and tipped his hat again and again to the adoring crowd. Aboard the *George Washington* were scores of aides and advisers, who, with their president, had high hopes of transforming the practice of international relations and improving the condition of the world's peoples. The mood was festive. With the Great War over and America triumphant, the president was off to Europe to reconstruct the world.

After more than four years of carnage, it was a hopeful moment at home and abroad. In a letter to Wilson, the brother of the president's first wife expressed these sentiments:

> You carry overseas with you the hearts and hopes and dreams . . . of millions of your fellow Americans. Your vision of the new world that should spring from the ashes of the old is all that has made the war tolerable. . . . Nothing but a new world is worth the purchase price of the war, and . . . you have the vision to glimpse it and the power to realize it in action.[1]

When the *George Washington* reached the French coast on December 13, the welcome was as spectacular as the departure had been nine days before. The sun shone brightly on a tranquil sea, and as the ship neared Brest, a fleet of American warships welcomed the president. Twenty-one gun salutes erupted, and French warships soon joined the flotilla, firing salutes of their own. Batteries on shore added to the din, as did the military bands, which blared forth "The Star-Spangled Banner" and "La Marseillaise." The atmosphere remained festive when President and Mrs. Wilson came ashore early in the afternoon. Thousands cheered, French and American troops presented arms as Wilson passed, and the seven-year-old daughter of the mayor of Brest presented the First Lady with a bouquet. Above the motorcade hung printed signs: "Hail the Champion of the Rights of Man. Honor to the Apostle of International Justice. Honor and Welcome to the Founder of the Society of Nations."[2] From Brest the presidential entourage headed to Paris, where the scene was, if anything, even more delirious. The largest crowds the war-weary capital had ever seen greeted the American leader, lining the streets and filling the rooftops. Georges Clemenceau, the French premier, remembered the scene: "I do not think there has been anything like it in the history of the world."[3] Later that day, the American president spoke at a luncheon given by President Raymond Poincaré of France, giving voice to the hopeful dreams and noble aspirations that had vitalized the crowds in New York, Brest, and Paris:

> From the first the thought of the people of the United States turned toward something more than the mere winning of this war. It turned to the establishment of the eternal principles of right and justice. [The war] must be won in such a way and the questions raised by it settled in such a way as to insure the future peace of the world and lay the foundation for the freedom and happiness of its many peoples and nations.[4]

Such language, a perfect expression of what would later be called "Wilsonianism," was capable of exciting the hearts of peoples throughout the world, not least of all in America.

Little more than four months after the president had sailed for Europe, in late April 1919, another American, William Monroe Trotter of Boston, headed to the peace conference in Paris. The Harvard-educated Trotter was already a legendary figure among African Americans, owing largely to his earlier actions as a race reformer, which had included highly publicized confrontations with Booker T. Washington and Woodrow Wilson. Trotter, who was chairman of the National Equal Rights League, a black-run civil rights organization, and editor of the Boston *Guardian*, believed the peace conference would provide an appropriate setting to advance the cause of race reform. With the cry of democracy and self-determination in the air, humanity seemed ready at last to address the claims of oppressed peoples. Trotter believed his presence in Paris to be essential, for that was where statesmen had convened to rebuild the world.[5] The French capital would serve as a grand stage from which to make his demands for reform; in Paris, Trotter could tell the world about the plight of black America.

But the American government proved uncooperative. Asserting that the French government would oppose the reformers' activities, the State Department denied passports to Trotter and several other black Americans who had hoped to join him on his mission. Trotter was not easily stymied, however; passport or not, he was determined to attend the conference. In disguise, Trotter managed to gain a seaman's passport, and after a six-week search, he secured a job as second cook on the *Yarmouth*, a small freighter bound for Le Havre. Unlike the grand presidential voyage four months earlier, no ships escorted Trotter's vessel toward the open sea, nor did any meet the *Yarmouth* on the other side of the Atlantic. Upon reaching the French coast, the crew was kept aboard ship for several days. Trotter, claiming he had to mail a letter, jumped ship, hopped a train the next morning, and headed for the French capital. Shabbily dressed, hungry, and with little money, he reached Paris later that day. Although no band was there to welcome him, Trotter would shortly become something of a celebrity in a city filled with important people.

Trotter settled down in Paris, and for several weeks he bombarded the French and foreign press, along with many delegates to the conference (including Woodrow Wilson) with letters, memoranda, and pleas, all in the name of "letting the world know that the Negro race wants full liberty and equality of rights, as the fruit of the world war." Trotter broadened the idea of Wilsonian internationalism, reworking the concept of self-determination to include peoples beyond the frontiers of Europe's ancient states. In Wilsonian language, he described African Americans as "an ethnical minority denied equal rights" and declared, "We are asking that we be accorded only what every one else has."[6]

While in Paris, Trotter tried to meet with Wilson and his aide Edward House, neither of whom was inclined to confer with the race activist. In late May, Trotter sent the president an open letter, which was published in the French press and which the Associated Press cabled back to the United States. Reflecting a characteristic theme found in many of the race reformers' writings in these years, Trotter's letter asserted that the struggle abroad was linked inextricably to the struggle at home. Written in response to an incident in which a white mob had dragged a black man from a Missouri courthouse and lynched him, the letter pointed to Wilson's Memorial Day address (delivered the day before Trotter penned his letter) in which the president had spoken of the brave American boys who had been sent to France to die for democracy. Trotter reminded the president that many of the dead were young black men and wondered if Wilson was prepared to work for justice in the United States. Trotter asked if these "lads . . . gallant and loyal . . . [had] died in vain." Was the president willing to "grant to their kin and race at home protection of right and life in the world peace agreement?" And finally, Trotter asked if Wilson was prepared to "send a special message to Congress recommending that lynching be made a crime against the Federal Government." He closed with the phrase, "Yours for world democracy."[7]

William Trotter's trip to Paris, however quixotic, is significant because it suggests how race reformers understood the war and the peace settlement. At the same time, Trotter's adventure reflected the conviction that animated race activists in these years. Believing strongly that the war and the peace could help ameliorate the condition of blacks in America, they sought to use overseas events to realize this aim. Most race reformers came to see the war and the peace as laden with opportunity and thought the war, by providing African Americans with a chance to serve their country, would help improve the status of the black population. Beyond providing the black soldier with an opportunity to serve, the war presented the reformers with an additional reason for optimism. The terms Woodrow Wilson used to frame the war and the peace—specifically, his conviction that American belligerency and peacemaking would allow the United States to construct a stable international order, which would rest on a commitment to democratic governance and self-determination under the aegis of the League of Nations—proved especially meaningful to the movement's leaders, who sought to construct a domestic order founded on the principles of justice and equality. The reformers deepened the meaning of Wilsonian internationalism, and, reworking the president's ideas, applied his emphasis on democracy and self-determination to the domestic aspirations of black Americans. Throughout these years, race activists drew comparisons between the struggle abroad and the one at home, and tailored the rhetoric of race reform to fit the shape of Wilsonianism. Just as Woodrow Wilson hoped the war could help America remake the world, race reform leaders believed the war and the unique character of the peace settlement could help advance the campaign for racial justice in America. And indeed, the war and the peace would have what economists describe as a "multiplier effect" on the movement, increasing its energy, as well as the number of people committed to working for racial progress. But that is to get ahead of the story.

One

"LET US BE TRUE TO OUR MISSION"
Race Reform and the World War

SOME TEN YEARS before Woodrow Wilson and William Trotter journeyed to Paris, in the summer of 1908, racial violence rocked Springfield, Illinois, the city where Abraham Lincoln had lived and was buried. White mobs terrorized the black district, burning homes, lynching two black citizens, and interfering with the work of firemen. Half a dozen blacks and whites were killed, and more than fifty people were wounded in the chaos. Black residents in the thousands fled the city, and more than four thousand members of the state militia were called in to help put down the violence whites had visited on the black population. To many in Springfield's white community, the episode was attributable not to white racism and hatred, but to the deficiencies of the city's black residents, specifically, their "misconduct, general inferiority, [and] unfitness for free institutions." A more enlightened observer spoke critically of Springfield's white population, contending that they hoped black residents would simply leave the city.[1]

As a direct consequence of this ignoble event, the National Association for the Advancement of Colored People was established in 1909, and while several organizations were toiling to improve the plight of black Americans, the association rather quickly became the nation's preeminent race reform group.[2] More broadly, the NAACP was the product of the reform impulse of the Progressive period. Its founders and leaders, mainly whites in the association's early days, were upper-middle-class professionals devoted to addressing the social and political challenges of a country transformed by industrialization, urbanization, and immigration. Lawyers, ministers, journalists, educators, and settlement workers, the NAACP's founders possessed a deep commitment to political and social reform, and while not a monolithic group, they were united in the belief that their organization could create a more just society by helping the country overcome racial oppression.[3] Their conviction that the nation's black population deserved inclusion in the American democracy distinguished them from the vast majority of white Americans of their generation. If these mainly white activists were not untainted by racism—and most white reformers at this time did not see blacks as their equals—they remained a remarkable collection of individuals whose attitudes toward black Americans and race relations were enlightened by the standards of the early twentieth century.[4]

A key figure among the Progressive activists who helped found the NAACP was Oswald Garrison Villard. Born into an extraordinary family in 1872, Villard followed in the footsteps of his forebears, mixing journalism and social activism in an effort to help build a more just society.[5] Speaking at the NAACP's founding in 1909, Villard articulated his personal commitment to racial justice and that of the infant organization:

> [I]n this era of organized publicity and of combinations of capital and brains in every field . . . the white friends of the negro [sic] and the negro himself should fall in line with the times and use the very best tools for his defence and his advancement. . . . At heart the great masses are sound on every question—if we can but get the facts before them. . . . If our plan seems a counsel of perfection, let us in truth hitch our wagons to a star and devote our lives, if necessary, to its realization. . . . [We] shall bring home to the heart of every man . . . the existence of gross injustice and oppression in this land of the free and the home of the brave.[6]

Villard worked indefatigably for race reform, and his unwavering commitment to racial justice, exemplified by his frequent speeches at NAACP meetings and elsewhere, along with his editorials in the *New York Post* and the *Nation* on behalf of the cause, kept the issue before the American public. At the fourth annual conference in 1912, Villard described the organization's aims, asserting that it existed "to combat the spirit of persecution and prejudice which confronts the colored people of this land. . . . It [seeks] equality of opportunity, equality at the ballot box, equality in the courts of the land." While he would later achieve renown as a critic of American foreign policy, Villard maintained a deep interest in race reform and remained a determined foe of racial injustice throughout his life.[7]

Another leader in the association's early years was Mary White Ovington, who possessed an unsurpassed devotion to race reform. Born three days before Lincoln was shot, Ovington would listen to the voice of Frederick Douglass and live on into the presidency of Harry Truman. During this remarkable life, she witnessed epochal changes in the state of American race relations, which, in her determined and quietly effective way, she helped make possible. An archetypical Progressive, Ovington attended Radcliffe College in the early 1890s and by mid-decade had become active in the settlement house movement in Brooklyn. In 1900, she toured London's East End slums and shortly thereafter began to study employment and housing problems in black Manhattan. From the NAACP's founding until the 1940s, Ovington was a key player in the association, serving, writes one biographer, as a "minister-without-portfolio" who articulated policy, raised money, helped create new branches, and acted as a "buoyant spirit of tenacity in the face of persistent racism."[8] Holding a variety of positions in the organization, Ovington was adept at smoothing the sometimes choppy waters of its internal politics and displayed considerable altruism by drawing no salary from the association during most of her tenure.[9] In reflecting upon her commitment to the movement, Villard would observe that "she had been fired with a desire to aid the Negro . . . to [whom] she had given the greater part of her life with an unselfishness . . . [and] a sweetness of spirit."[10]

A crucial figure in the NAACP's crusade was Moorfield Storey of Boston, a Harvard-trained lawyer, who had been born in Massachusetts in 1845 into a family deeply committed to racial justice. Given his background, Storey seemed almost predestined to devote himself to the race reform campaign. Though he was one of the country's premier corporate lawyers, he would serve as NAACP president from 1910 until his death in 1929.[11] Storey's reasons for joining the NAACP were similar to those held by most race reformers early in the century. "I felt the Negroes were being badly treated, denied the equal chance that every human being ought to have, denied justice in the courts, that their lives were at the mercy of the mob in large parts of the country, and . . . something ought to be done against it."[12] Like many of his fellow reformers, Storey hoped the NAACP could remedy this situation, and in 1911, he outlined his vision of the organization's goals in language heard often from the association's white leadership in its early years. The NAACP aimed "to smooth the path of the Negro race upward, and create a public opinion which will frown upon discrimination against their property rights, which will endeavor to see that they get in the courts the same justice that is given to their white neighbors. . . . We want to make race prejudice if we can as unfashionable as it is now fashionable."[13] In his concern for justice, his benevolent paternalism, and his desire to transform popular social attitudes, Storey exemplifies perfectly the Progressive mindset of the early-twentieth-century race reformer.

Joel Elias Spingarn was another central figure in the NAACP's formative years. Born in New York City in 1875, this son of Jewish immigrants would devote enormous energy to the race reform campaign for almost thirty years, and, with his brother Arthur, would play a critical part in the domestic cause. After earning his doctorate from Columbia University in 1899, Spingarn accepted a position in the Department of Comparative Literature there and soon became a leader in the field of literary criticism. In 1911, he was dismissed by university president Nicholas Murray Butler, as a result of a celebrated dispute concerning a colleague.[14] If there was no obvious reason for Spingarn's commitment to race reform (abolitionism was not part of his patrimony), once outside the academy, he began to devote most of his energy to the cause. Spingarn believed that a

life well-lived balanced intellectual with practical pursuits, and throughout his days, one biographer writes, he was animated by "the concept of
the scholar as man of action." In Spingarn's words, "Virtue is never solitary, it takes part in the conflicts of the world."[15] The notion that one
must combine the contemplative and the active life was hardly unique to
Spingarn, and like many reformers early in the century, he believed that
the existence of injustice required a commitment to social and political
reform. To the race activists, no problem was more worthy of attention
than the condition of the African-American population; and among the
reformers, none was more certain than Spingarn that the need for race
reform demanded close and unceasing attention. He poured heart and
soul into the cause from 1910 until the eve of the Second World War,
giving speeches, providing financial assistance, and working to keep the
NAACP operating smoothly. In 1914, Spingarn became chairman of the
board, and in 1930 he succeeded Moorfield Storey as the organization's
second president.[16]

Of the leading figures in the NAACP's early days, none was more significant than William Edward Burghardt Du Bois, the association's foremost African American and the preeminent figure in the battle for racial
justice in America in the first half of the twentieth century. Born in western
Massachusetts in 1868, Du Bois was educated at Fisk, the University of
Berlin, and Harvard, where he earned his Ph.D. in 1895, the first black
to do so. Blessed with a prodigious intellect, remarkable literary gifts, and
an enormous capacity for productive work, Du Bois was active in the
liberation struggle at home and abroad from late in the nineteenth century
until the presidency of John F. Kennedy. He grappled with the ideas of
Booker T. Washington, investigated the treatment of blacks in France after
the Great War, filed a petition on behalf of African Americans at an infant
United Nations, and worked with Ghanaian president Kwame Nkrumah
after Ghana gained its independence. The life of Du Bois is a palimpsest
for the black experience in the twentieth-century world.[17]

Du Bois joined the NAACP in 1910, one year after its founding, and
until his resignation in 1934, he stood at the center of its activities, serving
on the board of directors and as director of publicity and research. Beginning in 1910, his position as the editor of the organization's monthly
organ, *The Crisis*, gave him a highly visible platform from which to articulate his views on race relations in the United States and throughout the
world. Under Du Bois's guidance, *The Crisis* became America's premier
journal of opinion on the race question and was read in black households
throughout the country. As one scholar has observed, Du Bois believed
The Crisis was no mere mouthpiece for the NAACP, but the organization's
"pre-eminent division," which could serve as "the mentor of the race."[18]
And indeed, Du Bois's publication had a significant impact on black

Scholar, race leader, and the first African American to earn a Harvard Ph.D., W.E.B. Du Bois established the NAACP's monthly organ, *The Crisis*, in 1910. He would edit the journal until 1934, when he left the organization.

America. Every month it testified to the fact that racial injustice flourished in the United States, its forceful and energetic prose serving notice that a forum existed that aimed to abolish race hatred from the life of the nation. The journal was often passed by hand among those who could not afford a subscription, and its potent message surely provided readers psychological sustenance and uplift. As a former colleague wrote to Du Bois, although there had been black periodicals before *The Crisis*,

> never before in the history of our country have we had a single strong voice to speak to the Negro *legions* all the way from Maine to California and from Canada to Mexico, and never before, a single ear sensitive to their moanings or mutterings, to their cries of exaltation or of execration. When a soul was strangled in some southern hamlet, or when ambitions were frozen in the north . . . there was none to hear the story but the dejected and trembling neighbor; but *now*, touch one humble Negro in Texas, Georgia, Maine, or Oregon, and the whole gigantic body of ten million Negroes strain forward in sympathy to hear. . . . [We] are not yet wide awake, but, thank God! [we] are waking. Thank God, too, that there is a Du Bois keen to feel, swift to speak, and master in the art of expression.[19]

Despite or perhaps because Du Bois had enormous influence on the movement, his tenure with the association was at times stormy. Not infrequently, controversy arose in his relations with NAACP colleagues, due in part to his prickly temperament, but also, as Du Bois suspected, because the organization's white officials were unaccustomed to treating as an equal a brilliant, talented, and highly opinionated black man. Nevertheless, most of the association's leading figures recognized his profound contribution to the NAACP, and strong bonds of respect developed between Du Bois and two colleagues in particular, Joel Spingarn and Mary White Ovington. Indeed, the friendship between Spingarn and Du Bois remains one of the more uplifting chapters in the story of race reform in the first part of the past century.[20]

These are but some of the key figures in the NAACP's early days, and as the organization gradually achieved preeminence in the campaign for racial justice, its leadership focused on a few aims, the most important of which was the fight against lynching. During the next several decades, the association apportioned a significant part of its scarce resources to gaining passage of federal legislation against the barbaric practice.[21] If the anti-lynching effort was the most dramatic initiative the NAACP pursued, its leaders recognized that improving the lives of black Americans would demand a broad attack in several spheres, which led them to grapple with unfair treatment in housing, education, commerce, and voting.[22] Notwithstanding this ambitious agenda, the swirl of international events would cause the reformers to review their priorities, as developments across the Atlantic would draw peoples and nations into the greatest cataclysm the world had ever known.

As one of George Orwell's characters observed, "If the war didn't happen to kill you it was bound to start you thinking."[23] And with the start of the European war in the summer of 1914, the race activists' thoughts did indeed turn to overseas questions. But in thinking about the war, few activists initially perceived a clear link between the conflict and their domestic aims. Instead, they considered the question of American intervention and believed Woodrow Wilson would be grievously mistaken if he decided to enter the fray. While most race reformers favored American neutrality in the international struggle, they would ultimately come to support the notion that the United States had a special role to play in world politics and would link America's overseas mission to the cause of race reform.[24]

In April 1915, Oswald Garrison Villard, a leading proponent of American neutrality, suggested that the president should create a new cabinet seat, the secretary of peace, who would devote a portion of the resources allocated to the navy to the maintenance of peace. Villard contended that the militarists were "traitors to the nation and to the teachings of mankind,"[25] and he praised the president's early neutrality policy and would condemn what came later. According to Villard, Wilson's "first steps after the war clouds broke were all good," though eventually the president would violate "his own precepts for American neutrality." Villard would excoriate Wilson for his decision to go to war in 1917, writing that "the champion of democracy, struck it one of the deadliest blows" it had ever received, leaving prostrate every reform Wilson had ever worked for.[26] This descendant of William Lloyd Garrison expressed well why many race reformers opposed American intervention in the war. Worried about the conflict's potentially destructive impact on the domestic reform program that Wilson had promised, most reformers shared Villard's support for American neutrality.[27] But as we shall see, even Villard would come to believe that American belligerency might aid the cause of race reform.

Like Villard, Mary White Ovington strongly opposed the war, and in later years, she would argue that there had been "little to choose between English and German imperialism."[28] Eventually she joined the pacifists, and even after America went to war, she claimed there was little difference between the belligerents.[29] The sources of Ovington's view of war, one biographer writes, combined the "moral values derived from unitarianism, . . . a naive socialist faith in the working classes of the world and a personality that predisposed her to being a reconciler and a pacifier." War was barbaric, a destroyer of human life, economic prosperity, and idealism.[30] Nevertheless, once America decided to go to war, Ovington recognized, as did Villard, that belligerency would enable "the Negro [to] become a part of the country as he had not been before."[31] And after the war, she would acknowledge the conflict's impact on the condition of black Americans, observing that when the Europeans "pointed their guns at each other they did more for the advancement and emancipation of [the Negro] race than they did for any other people in the world."[32]

Several other NAACP officials, including Moorfield Storey, John Haynes Holmes, Jane Addams, and Lillian Wald, strongly opposed the war on moral grounds and feared American intervention would harm life in the United States. Moreover, during the two and a half years of American neutrality, they thought little about the opportunities the world crisis might provide for race reform at home. Shortly after the start of the conflict, Storey said it was the "greatest calamity that has visited the world in any time" and shuddered when he contemplated "the losses which the contending powers" are inflicting upon each other. Just before the United States entered the war, the Reverend John Haynes Holmes, a member of the NAACP's board, spoke from the pulpit of his New York church. "[W]ar is never justifiable at any time under any circumstances," he asserted. "If war is right, Christianity is wrong, false, a lie."[33]

Born three days before Lincoln's assassination, Mary White Ovington was one of the founders of the NAACP and would serve on the association's board from 1919 to 1931. For some thirty years, Ovington was at the center of the organization's activities.

Although most race activists opposed the war and were slow to recognize its potential impact on the movement, two figures perceived early on that the conflict might alter the character of American race relations. While their perspectives on the war's origins diverged, Joel Spingarn and W.E.B. Du Bois believed the struggle abroad and the one at home were organically connected, and both men consistently incorporated the conflict into the message they offered to their supporters and the nation. From early in the war, Spingarn articulated opinions that would have resonated well with Theodore Roosevelt and his circle of vigorous militarists, rather than with those working on behalf of black America.[34] Criticizing German aggressiveness and believing American intervention to be unavoidable and just, Spingarn advocated a policy of preparedness for the United States. He was convinced that German militarism had caused the war and assigned responsibility to the Central Powers for the conflagration. Spingarn's devotion to the Allied cause distinguished him from his NAACP colleagues, most of whom were far less certain about Germany's singular responsibility for the war, perceiving instead a fundamental similarity between the motives and morality of the European states. But Spingarn believed it was essential to stamp out German militarism, and he argued forcefully that to do so, one had to serve one's country.

Spingarn's reflections on the war, race reform, and, ultimately, the idea that the United States had a leadership role to play in combating aggression point to the reformers' distinctive internationalism. Linking lawlessness abroad and at home, Spingarn asserted in 1915 that "the real cause of the present war in Europe was a contempt for weaker people," which manifested itself in a desire for colonization. Significantly, he followed these thoughts on the war by examining black oppression in the South, which Spingarn argued had been spearheaded by racist southerners in Congress. As early as 1915, then, Joel Spingarn had begun to link the war to the plight of black America, a view he would express with growing frequency in the days ahead.[35]

Du Bois established an even stronger connection between the conflict and the race question, evaluating its origins in an explicitly racial context. In a 1915 essay, "The African Roots of the War," Du Bois explored the cause of the world crisis, mixing history with political economy, and scholarly analysis with polemical brilliance. The essay set the plight of black America in a global historical context in which oppression at home was organically connected to oppression throughout the world. Du Bois published the piece in the *Atlantic Monthly*, thus allowing him to present his ideas to a mainly white audience, which, unlike his regular *Crisis* readership, was not primarily concerned with racial questions. Du Bois began by asserting that in a "very real sense Africa is a prime cause of this terrible overturning of civilization," and contended that the roots of future wars also lay in the "Dark Continent." The Europeans' violation of Africa, which was "contemptible and dishonest beyond expression," had been achieved by "lying treaties, rivers of rum, murder, assassination, mutilation, rape, and torture," all of which had occurred because the rest of the world looked the other way. Although the war had exploded in the Balkans, Du Bois insisted that region was not the source of Europe's travails; instead, "the ownership of materials and men in the darker world" is the "real prize that is setting the nations of Europe at each other's throats today."[36]

While Du Bois inveighed against the imperial depredations of the European powers, his essay also expressed an underlying optimism, a view founded on the conviction that a new world might emerge from the crisis, one based on justice for all peoples. To be sure, the future of world politics was fraught with peril, but an alternative to interstate conflict was possible. It was unnecessary to sit by helplessly, waiting for the "awful prospect" of a "War of the Color Line" that would surpass "in savage inhumanity any war" the world had known before. Those committed to peace could do more than rail against the cost of war or recite humanitarian "platitudes"; they could look, instead, to the fundamental cause of war—the oppression of peoples of color—and decide the time had come to "extend the democratic ideal to the yellow, brown, and black peoples." Du Bois left no doubt as to who would help humanity realize this vision: the leaders of "the awakened Japanese and the awakening leaders of New China," the men in India and Egypt, and the twenty-five million grandchildren of the European slave trade, especially "the ten million of the United States, now a problem, then a world salvation." Oppressed peoples of color throughout the world could help move mankind toward "a new peace and new democracy of all races: a great humanity of equal men." To the well-educated white readership of a liberal monthly, Du Bois advanced the idea of a global community of the oppressed, which was working to break free from its historic bondage. Toward the end of the piece he seemed to ask his readers to support the crusade: "Our duty is clear. Racial slander must go. Racial prejudice will follow. Steadfast faith in humanity must come. The domination of one people by another . . ., be the subject people black or white, must stop."[37]

Of course, Du Bois was not alone in believing the war possessed transformative powers, which, if properly directed, could improve the lives of peoples in America and throughout the world. As philosopher John Dewey would argue, the conflict represented a "plastic juncture" that might allow enlightened leaders to reshape the nation, create "instrumentalities for enforcing the public interest," and ultimately rein in the excesses of America's "individualistic tradition."[38] And the president, whom Dewey and other Progressives believed embodied such enlightened leadership, would frame the war as an opportunity to reconstruct international politics, which, with America's guiding hand, could be made less unstable. Thus, if others came to see the war as providing the opportunity to sweep obstacles from the path to progress, Du Bois's understanding of the world crisis was not altogether novel. But in emphasizing the war's racial origins and suggesting that a more just world might emerge in its train, Du Bois propounded an idea of considerable significance. Although he may not have made the connection absolutely clear—one is somewhat uncertain precisely *how* the war would transform international and intersocietal relations—Du Bois did suggest that it could contribute to the abolition of oppression that had characterized the prewar era. It was but a sideways step to the notion that the war might benefit black America, and with increasing frequency in the months to come, many in the race reform community would articulate this idea.[39]

The pages of *The Crisis* reflected Du Bois's determined effort to join the war to the cause at home, and as early as November 1914, a lengthy editorial identified an interconnection between the world conflict and the plight of black Americans. Disputing the notion that the war was irrelevant to blacks, Du Bois claimed the European crisis was "one of the great disasters due to race and color prejudice," which served to foreshadow "greater disasters in the future." Just as Du Bois would argue some six months later in his *Atlantic* essay, the origins of the war were linked to race, specifically to the European exploitation of "darker peoples." In the "centers of modern culture," where theories of racial inferiority had become universal, states were battling over the spoils of empire, he wrote, "fighting like mad dogs to own and exploit" colonial peoples. Pointing to a common bond between the African-American population and the "black, brown, and yellow peoples" of the tropics, Du Bois identified a transnational solidarity among the oppressed.[40]

The editorial suggests how color-conscious internationalism informed the manner in which Du Bois interpreted the overseas struggle for his readers, who heard time and again of the great stake they had in its outcome. The editor declared black interests would be best served by an Allied victory, a surprising outlook from a man who had asserted continually that the morality and motives of all European states were the same. But according to Du Bois, the potential advancement of peoples of color made it imperative that England and France win the war. An excerpt suggests the potency of his perspective:

> [T]he triumph of the allies would at least leave the plight of the colored races no worse than now. Indeed, considering the fact that black Africans and brown Indians and yellow Japanese are fighting for France and England it may be that they will come out of this frightful welter of blood with new ideas about the essential equality of all men.
>
> [T]he triumph of Germany means the triumph of every force calculated to subordinate darker peoples. It would mean triumphant militarism, autocratic and centralized government and a . . . contempt for everything except Germany. . . . [T]his idea would mean a crucifixion of darker peoples unparalleled in history. . . .
>
> As colored Americans . . . and as Americans who fear race prejudice as the greatest of War-makers, our sympathies . . . should be with France and England; not that they have conquered race prejudice, but they have at least begun to realize its cost and evil, while Germany exalts it.

The editor rarely viewed the imperial powers in this light, and it was this notion that would later sustain the belief, endorsed by many race reformers, that it was necessary to support the United States when it went to war in 1917. Despite the apparent moral deficiencies of France, England, and (later) the United States, these nations possessed sufficient virtue to command the allegiance of those working on behalf of black Americans. And this view, which implied a distinctive role in world politics for the United States and its allies, would emerge with considerable regularity at critical moments in the twentieth century, especially when race reform leaders believed democracy was imperiled.

Also embedded in the editorial was the idea that the war had the potential to transform the outlook of peoples of color throughout the world. While Du Bois was at times elusive about the benefits the oppressed might gain from an allied victory, he was convinced the "colored races" fighting against Germany might emerge from the struggle imbued with a heightened sense of human equality. The idea that participation in the war might catalyze a new spirit and determination was one Du Bois would explore throughout these years, and as the crisis unfolded, he spoke often about the war's power to energize black Americans, deepening their commitment to obtain their rights as citizens. Moreover, Du Bois believed this sense of racial uplift might extend to peoples outside the United States. This realization led him to suggest the conflict could create a sense of interconnectedness between "black and brown and yellow" peoples throughout the world, causing them to stand "shoulder to shoulder," and collectively to demand "recognition as men."[41]

The pages of *The Crisis* provide a remarkable window onto Du Bois's thinking about the war, as month after month, the editor discussed the conflict with his readers. Even with America still at peace, he joined global to local matters in an effort to aid the cause of reform. In "Murder," a December 1914 piece, Du Bois used the war as a springboard from which to comment on race relations in the United States and castigated those Americans who were congratulating themselves for remaining at peace while the rest of the world was at war. The "wars of peace are often quite as horrible as the murder of war," he declared, noting that the United States had "the unenviable and shameful notoriety of being the country where murder is more prevalent than in any civilized land." He attributed white violence against blacks as well as black violence against whites to the "atmosphere of . . . hatred" that had grown in the "miasma of race prejudice."[42] The slaughter unleashed by the war permitted Du Bois to speak with his readers about violence in the United States, which, he contended, was a product of the pathological character of American race relations. At a time when federal anti-lynching legislation was a principal aim of the movement, Du Bois's decision to establish an interconnection among the war, violence in America, and race prejudice suggests how the overseas conflict became part of the grammar of reform.

Nevertheless, it must be said that Du Bois's desire to relate the war to domestic concerns was at times strained, as in May 1915, when a German submarine sank the liner *Lusitania*, killing more than 1,000 people, including 128 Americans. Du Bois placed the outrage on the high seas, the most sensational episode of the neutrality period, in the context of worldwide racial oppression, writing that the sinking demonstrated the failure

of European civilization. The war had not caused that failure, he observed, but had made it manifest: "Whatever of brutality and inhumanity,
of murder, lust and theft" has happened since the war began was "but
counterpart of the same sort of happenings hidden in the wilderness and
done against dark and helpless people by white harbingers of human culture." Du Bois told his readers about the enslavement of Negroes, the
rape of natives in the Congo, the murder of islanders in the South Seas,
and the lynching of 2,732 American citizens. The thrust of the piece concerned the hypocrisy of European civilization, which he claimed had long
been barbaric. "[H]umanity and Christianity and human kindness" had
never reigned in the "White World." This was a "great lie" unveiled by
the war. He felt privileged, he wrote, to belong to a race that "could stand
before Heaven with clean hands and say we have not oppressed, we have
been oppressed; we are not thieves, we are victims; we are not murderers,
we are lynched!"[43]

If the editor was forcing the issue here, compelling his readers to confront the subject of racial oppression in circumstances in which the link
was elusive, it was not the last time he would do so.[44] But Du Bois did
not compose such *Crisis* pieces idly, for he believed his work in the
monthly journal was supremely important to the NAACP's success. In
1914, he wrote to Joel Spingarn:

> What I am working for with *The Crisis* is to make the NAACP *possible*. To-
> day it is *not* possible. We can piddle on, we can beat time, we can do a few
> small obvious things: but the great blow—the freeing of ten million—and of
> other millions whom they pull down—that means power and organization
> on a tremendous scale. The men who will fight in these ranks must be edu-
> cated and *The Crisis* can train them: not simply in its words, but in its man-
> ner, its pictures, its conception of life.[45]

Du Bois's *Crisis* writings were not mere ruminations on race and reform;
they were, instead, a call to arms, which could improve the condition of
the black population and transform America. Sounding the tocsin each
month on the editorial page of *The Crisis*, Du Bois sought nothing less
than the reconstruction of American society, and by joining the war to
the domestic campaign, he believed he could advance that aim.

Joel Spingarn approached the task of reform differently. Like Du Bois,
Spingarn believed the war could contribute to black advancement, which
led him to work energetically to establish a segregated training camp for
black officers. If Du Bois used the conflict to strike out rhetorically against
racial injustice, Spingarn took a more pragmatic approach, based on the
notion that the war could provide concrete opportunities for black progress. In early 1917, Spingarn learned that with two hundred black appli-
cants, the army was prepared to establish a four-week training camp to

Joel Spingarn was a key player in the struggle for racial justice. A former literature professor, Spingarn became chairman of the board of the NAACP in 1914 and president in 1930.

prepare blacks for army service. Supporting the plan, he believed a black officer corps that was capable of leading black troops in battle might serve as a wedge in the struggle against discrimination in the military and, ultimately, throughout society. In February 1917, Spingarn issued a public letter to the "Educated Colored Men of the United States," which noted it was critical that they "should be given opportunities for leadership." You can no longer "remain in the background," he wrote, insisting that it was time to "come forward to assume your right places as leaders of American life." Although Spingarn opposed segregation, he believed the world crisis allowed for no debate and told potential recruits that "there is only one thing for you to do . . . and that is to get the training to fit you to be officers."[46]

Spingarn believed a black officer corps would weaken the military's perennial justification for the absence of black leaders, namely, that there were insufficient numbers of qualified black personnel. Speaking at Howard University in March 1917, he admitted he was not completely comfortable with the plan, which he described as a temporary and potentially useful means of achieving reform under current conditions. Spingarn told the black student body that he would not advise them to throw their "children out of a window on the fourth floor; but if the house was on fire, and all other means of getting the children from the burning building were closed, I would advise you . . . to throw the children out of the window to save their lives." This was no surrender of principle, Spingarn insisted; the struggle for equal rights had to continue without cessation. He hoped the colored officers' camp would place black Americans "in a position where they [might] agitate and insist with greater effect and efficiency," and he declared the time had come to have "colored heroes who are lieutenants, captains, colonels, and generals."[47] Writing to Dean William Pickens of Morgan College (a black institution), who would shortly join the NAACP, Spingarn said he hoped that with "two or three hundred properly trained officers, we can make a fight for a wide-open army; we can fight against segregation itself if we only have the men to put forward."[48]

At first, the NAACP took no official position on the matter, but given its opposition to segregation, Spingarn's plan had little support inside the organization. Nor did the plan win much favor in the black press. "[T]he theory that half a loaf is better than no loaf at all has long since been exploded," the *Chicago Defender* asserted. "We have put up with the crumbs that have fallen from the white man's table . . . so long we are considered ungrateful if we even dare to hint it is about time we were eating at the first table." Baltimore's *Afro-American* also rejected the plan, while the Cleveland *Gazette* issued the following order to Spingarn: "Attention! Doctor; about face! in this segregation officer-school business."[49] Although stung by the criticism, Spingarn did not waver in his belief that the camp could aid the cause. The attacks he suffered were not unexpected, he wrote to Du Bois, and he was proud that black opinion had reached a point where forceful views could be found in the black press. Observing that "the Association and the *Crisis* ha[d] made it possible for colored opinion to speak in this bold and manly way," Spingarn hoped he had had "some share, however small, in bringing that about." His goal was black uplift, and he remained confident the camp would contribute to it:

> [W]hat I am after is to help my country, and ten millions of colored Americans no less than the rest. . . . I do not know whether I could ask a single black man to volunteer, in case of war, until some of their heaviest burdens are lifted. But . . . war [will lead to] conscription, and I could hardly forgive myself if I saw black millions serving in the ranks and felt that I had not lifted a finger to help them to a position of leadership.

Spingarn wondered whether Du Bois believed the camp could be of "real practical service" and asked if the editor might mention the project favorably in *The Crisis*. But whatever position the journal advocated, Spingarn wanted his friend to know his feelings would not be hurt and he hoped Du Bois realized his only motive was "to help black men no less than white men."[50]

Despite his profound opposition to segregation, Du Bois decided to support the segregated officers' facility. Recognizing that the war could do more than create a sense of spiritual uplift among the black population, he believed the world crisis could provide tangible benefits for black America. In "The Perpetual Dilemma," an April 1917 editorial, Du Bois argued that blacks had to choose "between the insult of a separate camp and the irreparable injury of strengthening the present custom of putting no black men in positions of authority." There was little room for doubt. "Our choice is as clear as noonday. Give us the camp. . . . We did not make the damnable dilemma. Our enemies made that. . . . It is a case of camp or no officers." Once war came, he observed, the choice would be between conscription and rebellion, and the only sensible position at the moment was "to organize the colored people for leadership and service."[51]

On May 19, 1917, the War Department issued its final approval for the camp, and the following month the first group of black officers assembled at Des Moines, Iowa. *The Crisis* was jubilant: "We have won! The camp is granted; we shall have 1,000 Negro officers in the United States Army."[52] (In May, after America had gone to war, the NAACP had officially decided to back the camp.)[53] The following October, the first recruits, more than six hundred strong, received their commissions as officers. Overjoyed, Spingarn wrote to Du Bois, "You know how much I have worked for this thing. . . . [Many thought it] a preposterous dream. . . . [T]he dream has come true. There will be many more officers, when these have proved that our faith was justified; and these men have the solemn duty of proving our faith to the whole world."[54]

Another voice heard from within the reform community during the neutrality period was that of black columnist James Weldon Johnson, who regularly explored how America's overseas involvement might influence domestic race relations. Johnson, whose widely read column, "Views and Reviews," appeared in *The New York Age*, a black paper, joined the NAACP in late 1916 (rising to acting secretary the next year) and would shortly become a key figure among race activists. Born in Florida in 1871 and educated at Atlanta University, Johnson possessed a remarkably eclectic background, having been a teacher, songwriter, diplomat, author, editor, and poet.[55] As early as June 1915, he considered the subject of race in his discussion of the war. Writing about German-American negotiations following the *Lusitania* sinking, Johnson wondered where black America should stand if the country decided to intervene. Blacks should support a potential American war effort as they always had—with "unquestioned loyalty." After all, the United States is "our country as much as it is the country of any other class of American citizens." Blacks owed the same duty to the nation as that owed by all loyal

Americans, Johnson asserted, telling his readers that by refusing to fight, blacks would surrender the rights they claimed were theirs. "So long as we fully perform our duties as citizens, and, if we forego [*sic*] certain rights, do so only over our protest, we are on the safe side; we still have a clean case in court. Either to fail in our duties or to yield our rights without protest, would be to defeat our own cause."[56]

In early 1917, Johnson articulated a theme that would recur with increasing frequency in the months ahead. After writing about the deaths of five innocent black men who were killed at the hands of a Georgia lynch mob, he set the savage episode against the backdrop of the world crisis, and declared that Americans and their president were hypocritical and morally bankrupt. While many were no doubt disturbed by the acts of inhumanity described on the international page of their daily newspapers, Johnson averred that one did not need to look overseas to find barbarism, for it occurred regularly in the United States. He asked his readers to reflect upon the country's hypocrisy, noting that Americans were holding up their "hands in horror at German 'atrocities,' at what is being done in Belgium . . . and on the high seas, while the wholesale murder of American citizens on American soil by bloodthirsty American mobs hardly brings forth a word of comment." Johnson castigated the high-flown rhetoric of Woodrow Wilson, who refused to condemn lynching, which civil rights leaders had long implored him to do. The president continued "to talk about . . . bringing peace and righteousness to all the nations of the earth, but . . . [had] yet to utter one word against this outraging of humanity" in the United States. It was incomprehensible. How could a president who sought to bring such blessings to the world's peoples remain oblivious to the inhumanities practiced in his own backyard? But Wilson's ideals were not the problem, for Johnson supported the president's internationalism. What was unacceptable was Wilson's failure to practice those ideals at home.[57]

At the same time, Johnson condemned the American people for their moral blindness and "smug hypocrisy" as they looked with distress "upon the Turks for their treatment of the Armenians . . . [while] . . . the American lynching record makes the Turkish treatment of Armenians" look almost merciful. However inexplicable, the "wholesale murder" committed by "bloodthirsty mobs" in the United States interested neither the American people nor their president, whose attention lay elsewhere.[58] By drawing an explicit parallel between the violation of human rights overseas and at home, Johnson aimed to grab the attention of his readers and deepen their commitment to the domestic struggle, a strategy that Johnson and others used repeatedly in order to garner support for the movement.[59] It is no exaggeration to suggest that in presenting their case to the American people in the months ahead, many race activists would come to define their domestic struggle almost entirely in terms of America's campaign abroad.

By early 1917, overseas events made it impossible for the president to maintain American neutrality, and on April 2, Wilson asked Congress for a declaration of war. The months of waiting were over. Perhaps no president before or since was less willing to lead the United States into war than was Wilson, but the former professor saw no alternative to German actions on the high seas. In January, Germany had decided to embark on a policy of unrestricted submarine warfare and would sink on sight all shipping, belligerent or neutral.[60] The country would go to war, the president declared,

> to vindicate the principles of peace and justice in the life of the world as against selfish and autocratic power and to set up amongst the really free and self-governed peoples such a concert of purpose and of action as will henceforth ensure the observance of those principles.... [I]t will be insisted that the same standards of conduct and responsibility for wrong done shall be observed among nations ... that are observed among ... individual[s]. ...
>
> [W]e shall fight for the things which we have always carried nearest our hearts—for democracy, for the right of those who submit to authority to have a voice in their own governments, for the rights and liberties of small nations, for a universal dominion of right by such a concert of free peoples as shall bring peace and safety to all nations and make the world itself at last free.[61]

Rarely has an American president framed a war message in such idealistic terms: America would fight in order to help construct a world that honored and adhered to democratic principles, a world in which the conduct of nations would rest on those precepts that guided individual behavior. In prosecuting the war, Wilson wanted the nation to act on principles he understood to be distinctively American, the most significant of which was a devotion to democracy and freedom. The United States would fight, Wilson asserted, for "the ultimate peace of the world and for the liberation of its peoples." And most memorably, the president said the "world must be made safe for democracy." Much has been written about the character of Wilson's war aims, with many likening the president to a crusader who would bring American force to bear upon a recalcitrant world. For the race reformers, the president's message and the nation's war aims—particularly the goal of building a more just and democratic world—came to have significance in ways Wilson did not intend.[62]

In the first issue of *The Crisis* published after the country went to war, Du Bois expressed guarded support for Wilson's decision and implied that

America had a crucial role to play in the war and, more broadly, in world politics; indeed, Du Bois seemed to suggest that the United States could help preserve freedom itself. While he called war "an awful thing," and said it was "the end of civilization," Du Bois contended it was better than slavery. However terrible the world conflict, "German dominion [was] worse," as was the "rape of Belgium and France." Sounding almost Wilsonian, Du Bois suggested that America's decision to fight rested on the belief that the country and its allies could create "a world where war shall be no more."[63] Thus, in his earliest comments on the decision to intervene, Du Bois articulated the idea that the United States had a special role to play in the world and could help create a more peaceful and humane international order.

In supporting American intervention, Du Bois placed the conflict at the center of his reflections on the domestic crusade. On the same page as the editorial quoted above, readers encountered a Du Bois piece that castigated the South for spreading stories about the alleged disloyalty of black Americans. (The United States government feared German agents were trying to turn blacks against the United States, and such fears, the editor claimed, would lead to martial law, which would foreclose black migration northward.) "Any tale . . . by which the Bourbon South can get the country to believe the Negro is a menace would play straight into the hands of the slaveholders. . . . [But] the Negro is far more loyal to this country and its ideals than the white southern American," he noted, and blacks had always upheld the country's values—despite having been "enslaved, raped, and despised."[64] By juxtaposing Germany's wartime atrocities on the same page as the atrocities white southerners committed against black Americans, Du Bois aimed to clarify the character of American race relations. Thus, if it was necessary to combat German tyranny abroad, it was essential to combat racial tyranny at home. Equally significant, in supporting America's decision to fight and asserting that blacks were more loyal to American ideals than were some people in the United States, Du Bois suggested that black patriotism could not be gainsaid—and that blacks deserved the same rights as anyone else.

The NAACP quickly recognized the war's potential value for its domestic campaign, and one week after Wilson's war message, its board voted unanimously to "oppose and take every feasible step to prevent any discrimination" against blacks in the military or anywhere else in the country. Although several board members, including Mary White Ovington and Oswald Garrison Villard, recorded their opposition to belligerency (particularly to conscription), the board's unanimous vote on the motion suggests that the association's leaders were willing to subordinate their concerns about the war to the organization's larger goal of combating discrimination. According to Ovington, every member and "every branch must fight against allowing the Negro to be put in any position less than that of a citizen."[65]

In mid-May, within weeks of America's decision to fight, the NAACP sponsored a two-day conference where its members met with delegates from other black organizations. Believing the war might serve as a catalyst for change, more than seven hundred race activists came to Washington to stake out their demands. The gathering concluded with the adoption of a set of resolutions that suggests how civil rights activists understood the war and its potential for advancing their cause. The resolutions stated that the conflict's origins lay in race hatred and European exploitation of the world's "darker and backward people," and declared that permanent peace could be established only by extending the principle of government by consent throughout the world, particularly to Asians, Africans, West Indians, and black Americans. The delegates urged American blacks to support the war effort, calling it a "fight for eventual world liberation," and reminded them that America belonged more to blacks than it did to those who "lynch, disfranchise, and segregate." The conferees sought for blacks the right to serve their country and to lead troops in battle, along with the usual catalogue of reform demands: an end to lynching, the right to vote (for men and women), the abolition of Jim Crow cars, the repeal of segregation ordinances, and equal civil rights in all public institutions. The resolutions concluded by linking the war effort to the creation of a more just and democratic society in the United States and declared that black Americans, by contributing their "unfaltering loyalty" to the national effort, hoped to aid the cause of "world peace and self-government. . . ."[66] Unquestionably, the conferees believed it was possible to support the war without weakening their call for justice.

In the conference resolutions, one sees evidence of two elements of color-conscious internationalism: the belief in a transnational community of reformers and the conviction that the United States had a distinctive role to play in the international arena. In asserting that peace depended upon extending democratic governance to peoples of color throughout the world (including the United States), the delegates joined the domestic freedom struggle to a larger, global campaign in which black Americans were part of a crusade animating oppressed peoples everywhere. In addition, the refrain that America had a meliorative role to play in world politics, which necessitated creating a genuine democracy within the United States, would be heard time and again during the twentieth century. The conferees were clear that "the greatest hope for ultimate democracy" lay with America and its allies, and they pointed critically to Germany's autocratic form of government and its "wretched record" on racial matters. But while the United States had decided to help the more virtuous side in the war, it was crucial for America to confront the problem of injustice at home.[67]

The NAACP's 1917 annual report, entitled "Freeing America," which was published shortly after America entered the war, also illustrates the reformers' understanding of the world crisis. Convinced that American belligerency could serve as an agent of change, the association's leadership expressed the hope that the "present horror of war" might lead to "a new birth of freedom," which could compensate for the current carnage. In an increasingly common formulation, the report asserted that America's mission to reform world politics, which the president had articulated consistently, would be hollow without a similar transformation at home. Noting that the United States had come "forward to help freedom in the world," the document declared that it was essential to do so "with pure hearts and high ideals," no simple task for a society that tortured the innocent and burned men alive. Despite America's self-proclaimed mission of spreading democracy throughout the world, the report contended that the United States had allowed democratic government to die in a third of the land, while it maintained a caste system that led one to ask the nation to "clear her conscience" so it could "fight for the world's good with clean hands." That the United States possessed a special mission in the world crisis was clear; the report emphasized, however, that the fulfillment of that mission would be stunted by a failure to enact domestic reforms.

But the report did more than wed America's foreign mission to the necessity for instituting change at home. Under a heading titled "The Seething," the document introduced an idea that would achieve considerable significance during these years. The association pointed to a new feeling—vitalized by the war—that was stirring in the souls of the black population. This "new spiritual whirling in the breasts of Negro-Americans" flowed from a variety of factors: the black migration to the North, the liberating experience that would result from European military service, and the great economic contribution blacks would make as they replaced white soldiers who were serving overseas. In arguing that the world struggle might create "a tremendous inner uplift" among twelve million black Americans, the report raised an idea to which race reform leaders and average black citizens would refer frequently in the days ahead. Both inside and outside the NAACP, many came to see the global struggle as an energizing force with the power to galvanize black Americans, thus increasing their determination to achieve freedom.[68]

Perhaps the most important idea the race activists explored during the war concerned the notion that Wilson's international quest for democracy was organically connected to the aspirations of black America. In speeches, articles, and personal correspondence, the reformers argued that it was not possible to secure democracy abroad until it had been established in the United States, and they believed they could direct the language of democracy and freedom, which the president had released into the stream of public discussion, into constructive channels. To be sure, this appropriation of Wilsonianism led to one of the more striking ironies of the period. In recognizing the potential utility of Wilsonian rhetoric, the reformers were acutely aware that Wilson himself had proved unwilling to support race reform in the United States. Indeed, the president, a southerner, had impeded the cause at home, and had shown little inclination to provide for black America the democracy he was determined to provide for the rest of the world. The reformers repeatedly noted the hypocrisy inherent in the cause of an oppressive nation—whose leader had tightened the shackles of Jim Crow in government offices by segregating toilets, eating facilities, and work areas—that was fighting abroad for the liberation of peoples.[69]

In the summer of 1917, Mary White Ovington considered the matter of American hypocrisy in the pages of *The Crisis*. Observing that the Allies were "fighting for Democracy against Autocracy and Militarism," she explored the meaning of democracy by raising several questions that flowed from the movement's demands. Is it democracy, she wondered, "to treat a part of the population as not entitled to advancement? Is it to deny it the right to vote . . . ? Is it to set it apart in a ghetto . . . ? Is it to deny it the right of trial, visiting upon its members torture and death?" This was not democracy, but despotism, Ovington asserted, and unless the United States government, which she sardonically described as "the champion of democracy," enforced the Fifteenth Amendment and allowed its "men of color [to] stand before the world as citizens," America would become "a laughing stock to its enemies."[70] To distinguish itself from its adversaries and to maintain its international credibility, the United States had to abolish racial tyranny at home. Throughout the war—indeed, throughout the twentieth century—countless race reformers would deploy precisely this rhetoric.

While Oswald Garrison Villard (like Ovington) was deeply distressed by the war, he wedded the conflict to his passion for reform, observing in 1918 that the war held the potential to improve the condition of black people in America and throughout the world. Villard did not question the validity of the American mission as articulated by the president, and despite his tendency toward pacifism, he supported the Wilsonian crusade, which he called a "great war for the extension of democracy." He told his listeners about the estimable aims of the United States, which was helping to defeat German autocracy, while "planning to make war impossible abroad." As was true of most committed race reformers, Villard asserted that it was critical to attack "our own [domestic] evils where they connote a failure or denial of democracy," which he argued would fortify the position of the United States in the world and make "more consistent the moral position the country [had] chosen to occupy." That a pacifist like Villard could point to the war's potential benefits suggests the powerful effect it came to have on the race activists' understanding of their campaign, and it became an article of faith in the reform community that the domestic cause was inseparable from the country's overseas mission.[71] For Villard and his fellow reformers, true patriotism was concerned not just with oppression overseas, but with oppression at home.

Writing in the black press, James Weldon Johnson compelled his audience to consider the interconnection between the American mission abroad and the movement's domestic agenda. A month after the United States went to war, Johnson asked if it would not be fitting, as the country entered the conflict "in the cause of democracy and humanity, to begin by clearing its own conscience," so that it could fight "in sincerity and not in hypocrisy? Cannot America, while she is preparing to fight for democracy abroad, do something to remove the stain from democracy within her own borders?"[72] Like many race activists, Johnson often wrote hopefully about the war, arguing that it had the potential to transform all manner of things, including American race relations. "Old traditions, old ideas, old conventions, old governments, old civilizations are . . . being broken up and melted down in the crucible of this great war," he asserted in May 1917. "And they are all to be shaped and moulded anew."[73] The following year, sounding an almost Wilsonian refrain, Johnson observed that "America's participation in the war is based solely upon the determination to secure for the peoples of the world a larger degree of democracy; so we feel that in pressing the claim for a larger degree of democracy for the black people [in America], we are not only not hindering the war, but acting in fullest harmony with its ultimate aims." Beyond emphasizing America's altruistic war aims, Johnson considered the war's transformative character, asserting that the black American had been "seized by the spirit that has taken hold of all the submerged classes of the world. He . . . believes that something new and better" is going to come from the war. Having penned this ringing proclamation, Johnson suggested that the NAACP provided the most effective way to convert the energy generated by the conflict into concrete achievements for black America.[74]

During the months of American belligerency, the pages of the NAACP's journal were filled with talk of the war, as Du Bois persistently set the race reform agenda against the backdrop of the world conflict. With his distinctive and assertive style, Du Bois hammered away relentlessly at the idea that the war contained the seeds of social transformation.[75] The tone of Du Bois's editorials was mainly optimistic; in his view, the world stood on the threshold of enormous change, the principal beneficiaries of which would be peoples of color. As a result of the social and political forces unleashed by the war, black Americans were poised to make great strides. In the summer of 1917, he told *Crisis* readers:

> We are facing a new world. Never again are we going to cope with the . . . same social forces that we have faced in the last half-century. . . . [N]ew forces have been loosed and a new situation has arisen. It is the business of the American Negro not to sit idly by and see this rearrangement of the world, hoping that something [good] will come out of it. . . . [Instead, he must] put himself into the turmoil and work effectively for a new democracy that shall know no color.[76]

The following year, Du Bois propounded the idea that the war would transform the lives of peoples of color in America and throughout the world. "Never again will darker people of the world occupy just the place they have before." Having considered the salutary impact the war would have on the oppressed in China, India, Egypt, and Africa, he described the gains black Americans would derive from the conflict. "Out of this war will rise . . . an American Negro with the right to vote and the right to work and the right to live without insult." The editor was supremely confident, proclaiming that while such changes would not be achieved immediately, with the help of the allied armies, they were inevitable; indeed, they were "written in the stars."[77]

Assessing the war in Wilsonian language, Du Bois wrote of America's war for liberty and democracy, albeit with the caveat that such a conflict imposed special obligations upon the United States. In September 1917, he declared that the country ought to "enter this war for Liberty with clean hands. May no blood-smeared garments bind our feet when we rise to make the world safe for democracy." Highlighting recent episodes of racial violence in East St. Louis, Illinois; Waco, Texas; and Memphis, Du Bois demanded justice in the courts and sought an end to lynching, mobbism, disfranchisement, and Jim Crow. In short, he set forth the race reform demands of the early twentieth century, which he linked unambiguously to American war aims. Concluding his plea for justice, the editor embraced Wilsonianism—but with a difference: "We Americans, black and white, are the servants of all mankind and ministering to a greater, fairer heaven. Let us be true to our mission. No land that loves to lynch 'niggers' can lead the hosts of Almighty God."[78] It would not be possible to transform the world while leaving life unchanged at home.

Not limiting the pages of *The Crisis* to his own views, Du Bois permitted others, both well-known and obscure, to share their reflections on overseas developments. Poems, letters, and essays graced the journal's pages, allowing readers to encounter a continuous stream of writings on the conflict. An August 1917 letter from "An Asiatic Gentleman" touched on many of the ideas that regularly appeared in the magazine's pages.

The letter, prominently displayed on the first page of the editorial section, discussed recent race riots in the Midwest and other examples of "blind race and color prejudice. . . ." "[S]hocked beyond description" at the treatment endured by the black population, the writer observed that white Americans were "intoxicated with power, brute force in their eyes stands for manliness." The correspondent then turned to overseas matters and highlighted the notion of a community of the downtrodden, as well as the hypocrisy of Wilson's war for democracy: "There can be no democracy and peace in the world so long as . . . color and race prejudice reign supreme. . . . Yet the colored men of Asia, Africa, and America, . . . engaged in fighting for the allies and the United States in making the world safe for democracy! Oh! the hypocrisy of the whole thing! It burns my very soul." The writer concluded by offering a contribution to the NAACP, along with his assurance to *Crisis* readers that he was "one with you in your struggle for your rights as members of the human race."[79]

Occasionally, war poetry made its way into the journal, and even if not of the highest quality, it likely inspired *Crisis* readers. Appearing in June 1918, "A Sonnet to Negro Soldiers" (dedicated to the all-black 92nd Division) conjoined Christian imagery, the courage of the black warrior, and the emergence of a world without prejudice. Together, such themes might have led readers to experience a surge of patriotism and a renewed commitment to the domestic struggle.

> They shall go down unto Life's Borderland,
> Walk unafraid within that living Hell,
> Nor heed the driving rain of shot and shell
> That round them falls. . . .
> . . . And from their trembling
> lips shall swell
> A song of hope the world can understand.
> All this to them shall be a glorious sign,
> A glimmer of that Resurrection Morn,
> When age-long Faith, crowned with a grace benign,
> Shall rise and from their blows cast down the thorn
> Of Prejudice. E'en though through blood it be,
> There breaks this day their dawn of liberty.[80]

The notion that the war would usher in a new day for black peoples, when the "thorn of Prejudice" had been cast down, had captured the hearts of reformers and poets alike, and the *Crisis* editor, utilizing his words and those of others, labored to bring that day closer. He continually exposed readers to his deeply held conviction that the war possessed transformative powers, which, if deployed with wisdom and energy, could improve the plight of black America. In April 1918, as he planned a lecture tour focusing on "The Negro in the War," Du Bois wrote that "because of this war the colored races in the world, and particularly the Negro race in the United States, have gained more than at any time since emancipation." And while the "forces of race hatred" persisted, he believed that "strong organization and careful thought will keep for us the advantages which we have won and insure further steps toward freedom."[81]

Despite the pacifism of some key officials, the NAACP's leadership supported the American war effort. The association's annual report for 1918 observed that the "colored people of the nation, stirred as they have never been before by the idealism of an appeal to 'make the world safe for democracy,' have responded to the nation's call . . . in such a high spirit of devotion . . . as to have earned" the tributes of the American people and the Allies. A section entitled "Stirred by War for Democracy" quoted President Wilson's reasons for fighting, "for democracy, for the right of those who submit to authority to have a voice in their own government," while it asserted that the nation's international mission was consistent with the NAACP's purpose: to make "democracy—at home and abroad . . . the rule of American life and the aim of American statesmanship."[82]

Beyond the organization's official pronouncements, NAACP leaders, whatever their individual views of the conflict, perceived the war as integral to the African-American cause.[83] In July 1918, Archibald Grimké, head of the association's Washington, D.C., branch, took his case directly to the president, asking him to condemn lynching, a request long ignored. Enclosed with his letter to Wilson, Grimké included clippings from the *Washington Post*, which documented lynchings throughout the country during the preceding six months. He asked the president to repudiate the barbaric practice, telling him that these figures on lynching, occurring at a time when young black men were about to help stem the blow of the fury of the German army, would not make happy reading for thousands of black Americans. If they were less loyal, the black population would raise many questions when reading such figures and would ask why they were sending

> their sons and brothers to make the world safe for democracy when America . . . is not safe for them; if the lynching of women is a fair sample of the treatment they may expect. . . ; if this great government really includes them in its laudable program for world betterment. Finally, they would want to know if the President, speaking the demands of this country for freedom of the oppressed peoples of distant lands . . . cared whether his words were being compared by the civilized world with the attached record of unpunished . . . lawlessness.[84]

Grimké framed his request for a public condemnation of lynching by referring to the war's character, which the president had discussed repeatedly with the nation and the world. The reform leader compelled Wilson to confront his own language so as to persuade him to act. Grimké suggested, moreover, that international public opinion was at stake and that Wilson's failure to consider it would cause the "civilized world" to view America and its leader as hypocritical.

While the NAACP stood at the forefront of the reform campaign, reflections on the interconnection between the war and race reform were not confined to the association or its leaders. Indeed, the idea pervaded the discourse of reform, appearing in the black press, magazines, speeches, and sermons.[85] One of the most celebrated public declarations joining the war to the domestic struggle was issued in August 1917 in the wake of two brutal episodes of racial violence. In July, thirty-nine blacks had been killed in a riot in East St. Louis, Illinois, and the same month saw the premeditated incineration of a black prisoner, who had been dragged from a Memphis jail by a hate-filled southern mob. In response, Howard University sociologist Kelly Miller, a leading black intellectual, wrote an open letter to Woodrow Wilson, which he titled "Disgrace of Democracy." Asserting that blacks did not feel part of the American democracy, Miller compared their plight to that of the oppressed nationalities of Europe and Africa. He implicitly accepted the president's conception of America's role in the war and described Wilson as "the voice of the American people in the great world conflict" and the "spokesman of world democracy." But Miller reminded the president that "a chain is no stronger than its weakest link," declaring that a "doctrine that breaks down at home is not fit to be propagated abroad." Miller was relentless:

> If democracy cannot control lawlessness, then democracy must be pronounced a failure. The . . . world [had] a right to demand of us the workings of the institutions at home before they are promulgated abroad. . . . Every high-minded American must be touched with a tinge of shame when he contemplates that his rallying cry for the liberation of humanity is made a delusion and a snare by these racial barbarities.

Miller asked the president to bring federal power to bear against those who committed violent acts against black citizens and concluded by referring to a new spirit that was in the air: "Negroes all over the nation are aroused as they have never been before. . . . [They now possess] a determined purpose that this country should be made a safe place for American citizens to live and work. . . ." Miller's open letter, which the U.S. military banned from army posts, sold a quarter of a million copies throughout the country.[86]

Although Miller did not question the notion of a distinctive American mission overseas, he did reconfigure the president's ideas about the oppression of ethnic minorities and the superiority of democratic institutions, ideas Wilson had used to inspire the nation in war. Miller did so to rally the oppressed black minority at home and to legitimize the domestic reform campaign in the eyes of all Americans. If the president could use the rhetoric of right and justice to convince the nation it was worth dying to guarantee freedom to those who were imperiled in foreign lands, Miller argued it was critical to end racial persecution and to provide a full measure of democracy for every person in the United States. Throughout the war, he would return to these themes.[87]

Black religious leaders like the Reverend Francis Grimké (Archibald's brother), the outspoken activist who was the pastor of Washington's Fifteenth Street Presbyterian Church, also joined the war to the question of racial justice. From the pulpit of a Baptist church, the reverend delivered the eulogy for a black soldier who had become ill and perished as a result of his military service. Though Grimké discussed the fighting man's commitment to his country, his eulogy focused mainly on the plight of black America and the link between the war and black advancement. The minister wondered what black Americans would receive in return for their wartime sacrifice, and asked whether his people, once the struggle ended, would still be denied their rights. Could America fight, "as we profess to be, to safeguard democracy throughout the world, and yet be indifferent towards safeguarding it at home?" Could America "afford to be put in that light before the civilized world?" Once the war was over, Grimké asserted,

> colored citizens . . . expect to be treated just as other citizens are treated. . . .
> If they are good enough to die for the country, they are good enough to enjoy
> all the rights and privileges it has to confer. . . . Men who are willing to die
> in the defence of the rights of others, are not likely to quietly submit to the
> deprivation of their own rights.

Finally, Grimké asked his listeners, who were probably exclusively black, to have faith "in the ultimate triumph of true democracy even here in these United States."[88] As was true of Kelly Miller's words, Grimké's pronouncements on the domestic struggle were informed by Wilsonianism. His reference to the country's democratic mission abroad, which he seemed to embrace, and his suggestion that American soldiers were risking their lives to defend the rights of others, were consistent with ideas the president had articulated throughout the war. But as Grimké reminded his listeners, and as the reformers asserted repeatedly, democracy had to begin in the United States.[89]

As we have seen, William Monroe Trotter, who would cross the Atlantic in 1919 to set the reformers' case before the world, made the war the centerpiece of his message for change. In September 1917, the tenth annual convention of the National Equal Rights League (NERL), which Trotter headed, met in New York and resolved that America's entry into history's "most terrible war" could be "justified only by vouchsafing freedom and equality of rights to all [our] citizens." While one hundred committed delegates pledged their loyalty to the American cause, they also insisted that the "nation should enter the lists with clean hands."[90] The following year, Trotter's reform efforts reached the halls of Congress in the form of a petition on behalf of the National Liberty Congress, which the NERL had organized in the nation's capital. The 1918 petition set out a detailed catalogue of grievances and demands, including an end to Jim Crow and disfranchisement, and a call for federal protection against mob violence. The petitioners pointed to the substantial black contribution to the war effort and, foreshadowing arguments that would appear decades later, asserted that America risked weakening its "moral position, prestige, and power" throughout the world so long as its domestic racial policies continued to violate Woodrow Wilson's "noble pronouncements." The war's moral purpose—the democratization of the world, spearheaded by the United States—would fail if America itself was not made safe for democracy. In accepting America's exceptional role, the National Liberty Congress sought civil rights legislation "as an act of justice [and] of moral consistency," and in conclusion, the petition asked for Woodrow Wilson's words to "be applied to all at home."[91]

Devoid of any cheerleading for Wilsonianism or the American war effort was New York's *Messenger* magazine, a puissant voice on world affairs, which propounded a brand of internationalism markedly different from what has been considered to this point. Founded in 1917 by A. Philip Randolph and Chandler Owen, *The Messenger*, which was the successor to a union publication the men had edited, called itself "The Only Radical Negro Magazine in America." Propounding a socialist perspective on global developments, *The Messenger* was hard-edged, uncompromising, and iconoclastic, and sought, quite self-consciously, to stand at the forefront of what would shortly be called the "New Negro" movement. Randolph, who was born in Florida in 1889, was destined to become one of the towering figures in the history of the civil rights movement, and after graduating from Jacksonville's Cookman Institute, he headed to New York at the age of twenty-two in search of opportunity. Born the same year in North Carolina, Chandler Owen was educated at Virginia Union University and also trekked north, reaching New York at about the same time. The two men met in City College discussion groups, which had formed to debate socialism, and here, writes one scholar, they "dug into economics, politics, and sociology with zeal and earnestness."[92] Beyond their commitment to socialism, both men had no use for the current black leadership, a view their magazine asserted without a trace of reluctance.

In a lengthy piece published in January 1918, Owen discussed the failure of traditional black leaders. He was especially hard on Du Bois, whom he criticized for his insufficiently radical understanding of labor issues and his support for the segregated officers' camp, a position Owen thought was "indefensible." Mocking Kelly Miller, William Pickens, and Du Bois (again) for believing the war would help abolish race prejudice, Owen wondered when wars had ever benefited the "subject race." The notion that this war would be different was a "spurious promise," which the young Owen derided as "sheer claptrap." Given their education, black leaders ought to know better than to traffic in such "offensive and repulsive" ideas, he claimed, insisting that a new group was needed to help elevate the race with "a more thorough grasp of scientific education, and a calm but uncompromising courage." Concluding relentlessly, Owen described traditional black leaders as "mental manikins and intellectual lilliputians."[93]

Although the two men melded overseas matters to their discussion of domestic issues and shared Du Bois's analysis of the war's origins, their unalloyed belief that blacks should oppose the conflict was unusual. Quite simply, Randolph and Owen believed the war would provide few benefits for black America, and their unyielding antiwar posture made them targets of the federal government, which hounded the two activists so as to stop them from fomenting trouble among the black population. After speaking to a Cleveland crowd in August 1918, they were arrested and charged with violating the Espionage Act, which gave the government a variety of instruments for suppressing domestic opposition to the war. Although they escaped conviction because the judge could not believe these two "boys" were capable of writing such antiwar literature, the government kept both men and *The Messenger* under surveillance throughout the war. In the eyes of the U.S. government, A. Philip Randolph was the "most dangerous Negro in America."[94]

Consistent with a socialist worldview, Randolph and Owen believed the war had originated in the competition for control of the developing world's natural and human resources. Chinese oil and coal; African diamonds, rubber, copper, and cocoa; Indian agricultural products; along with the abundant labor provided by peoples of color and the control of trade routes to the fields of great wealth: these were the objects of the western powers, whose greed had caused the world war.[95] Analyzing the conflict in stark materialist terms, Randolph and Owen saw the struggle as an international catastrophe that devalued laborers throughout the world. "Men are dying on the battlefield. Women are in poverty at home. Children are starving. Their music is the bitter cry of the children, the wailing of women, the groaning of wounded men." But the world's governments continued to make war because that was what governments did. Peace could have been attained, they lamented. If "only one-half of the billions which have been expended in this war had been expended on real education [then] men would not now be killing one another because they were born on a different strip of land."[96]

To a considerable degree, *The Messenger*'s class-based analysis of the war was not tailored to appeal to an oppressed black minority. Nevertheless, while *The Messenger* viewed world politics through a socialistic lens and claimed that socialist governments would reduce or even abolish war, the perspective of Randolph and Owen was broader than what one might have expected from these two committed socialists. And in assessing the war, they melded class- and race-based analyses, sounding at times like the traditional race reformers we have heard earlier.[97] Finding the president's views useful for illustrating the hypocrisy of American war aims, the editors referred frequently to Wilsonian ideals. A 1917 piece, "Making the World Safe for Democracy," observed that Wilson's official reasons for American belligerency left blacks ready to do their bit for the cause, though they favored making "a clean job of it." The editorial noted the emergence of a "new Negro" who had jettisoned the "gospel of obey and trust" and replaced it with one of "rebel and demand." These "new Negroes" are convinced that "this world must be made safe for them," the editors contended, because until then "it is not safe for democracy." Randolph and Owen were persuaded the war would be instrumental in creating a more assertive black citizen, an unexpected perspective from two figures who maintained such a critical posture toward American efforts overseas. Even *The Messenger*, it seemed, could not escape the conclusion that the war had the potential to transform the character of American race relations. And its white-hot language often had more than a little in common with the rhetoric articulated by Kelly Miller or Archibald Grimké.[98]

As the war entered its final days in late 1918, the reformers pondered its significance for their cause and reflected on the coming peace settlement and its potential for advancing their agenda. Awash in optimism, they approached the postwar period with a sense of possibility, and just as Wilsonians believed in the pliability of the international system, many race activists looked at the domestic order in much the same way. Talk of reconstruction was in the air—for world politics and for the American democracy. In November 1918, John H. Hawkins, a black educator, former college president, and official in the A.M.E. Church, spoke at a large church gathering in New York. In answer to the question, "What does the Negro want?" Hawkins presented what he called his "14 Articles for Home Democracy," which the black press published throughout the country. Modeled on the "Fourteen Points" Woodrow Wilson had set out the preceding January in a celebrated address describing the shape of the postwar world, Reverend Hawkins's "fourteen points" detailed the full range of reform demands: suffrage; improvements in education, housing, employment, and penal conditions; and an end to segregation. Echoing Wilson's call for "open covenants of peace, openly arrived at," the churchman asserted that the "time is ripe for a free and open conference between the races. Let us get together and settle our differences."[99]

That same month, *The Crisis* rhapsodized on the changes wrought by the war. In "Patriotism," a remarkable, if at times perplexing, editorial that Du Bois published just before the war ended, the editor spoke of "the transformation in the souls of most Americans" that had occurred during the course of the conflict. Before the war, "nobody loved America," he observed; instead, Americans loved "Justice and Freedom," and sought "reform and uplift" in politics, in "health protection," or perhaps in the elimination of class tensions and race hatred. But beneath it all, he insisted, Americans did love their country, for what it might be if not for what it was. In language imbued with a Wilsonian sensibility, Du Bois advanced the idea that Americans believed their country was capable of realizing their "dreams and inspiring the greater world." The country's foremost race activist noted that black Americans, despite their suffering, thought it was possible to realize "their highest hopes and aspirations," and among those who had "toiled for higher and better things," there existed a passionate love for "what America might be—the Real America." Continuing this paean to the country's potential greatness, he claimed that men will only work and fight for a dream if they believe it is possible. Was the dream "less possible now that we fight for common decency in international affairs," rather than before when we aimed only for the "highest things" at home? According to the editor, the call of duty that the war demanded was even greater now that the struggle was waged not merely to improve life, but for life itself. "On some such foundation," he concluded, "is building the new Patriotism in America and in the World."[100]

Even as Du Bois's reflections on "inspiring the world" and fighting for "common decency" in global affairs might have come from the mouth of the American president, the sense that the war could bring to fruition the goals of those seeking "reform and uplift" was harmonious with the tone of most race activists. The reformers looked to the postwar period with optimism, hoping the Wilsonian vision would mean as much at home as it did abroad. In due course, they would learn whether the president's prescription for global comity could also help remedy the moral health of the nation.

Two

"THE MORNING COMETH"
The Significance of the Peace

AT 5:00 a.m. on November 11, 1918, the armistice was signed at Com-piègne, and six hours later, the world war—the bloodiest in history to that point—was over. The world's peoples, especially the victors, experi-enced a mixture of joy, relief, and hope. Eight and a half million combat-ants lay dead, more than twenty-one million had been wounded, and civilian casualties added several million more to this grim accounting. The great states of Europe lay prostrate; some would disappear. The peace was hard-won; the peace settlement would be bitter. Nevertheless, the vision of a brighter world helped lift some of the shadows from the inter-national stage, and as before, Woodrow Wilson sought to illuminate a path the world might follow, believing that with his leadership a new international order could be constructed on the rubble of the old.

In his first public statement on November 11, the president captured the significance of the event: "A supreme moment of history has come. The eyes of the people have been opened and they see. The hand of God is laid upon the nations. He will show them favour . . . if only they rise to the clear heights of His own justice and mercy." Later that day, he addressed Congress, referring to "these anxious times of rapid and stupendous change." After outlining the terms of the armistice, Wilson spoke of the war's meaning and shared with his fellow citizens his vision of the peace. He claimed the great nations that had banded together to destroy imperialism and militarism were now united to "set up such a peace as will satisfy the longing of the whole world for disinterested jus-tice." Their great purpose now was to "satisfy and protect the weak as well as to accord their just rights to the strong." Seeking nothing less than the transformation of world politics, the president would soon sail for Europe in order to make real his vision. Whether Wilsonianism was any-thing more than a string of mellifluous phrases would, in time, be known. On the day of the armistice, adviser Edward House cabled the president from Paris: "Autocracy is dead. Long live democracy and its immortal leader." As we have seen, it was a tribute with which Europeans would concur, and while millions had perished on the continent's battlefields, Wilson's reception upon reaching France suggested that hope had not been a casualty of the war.[1]

But Wilson's rhetoric would reverberate far beyond the shores of Europe, raising the hopes of America's race reformers, who believed the time was ripe for domestic change. More than three hundred and fifty thousand black Americans had seen military service in the conflict, and the president himself had repeatedly described the struggle as a noble crusade for democracy. With the start of the conference in Paris, which aimed, in part, to address the issue of oppressed peoples, it was difficult to imagine a more propitious moment for the amelioration of America's race problem. Was it not reasonable to believe that a government and nation that had long rejected the entreaties of the race reformers would now decide to make good its claim for world leadership by spreading the blessings of democracy at home?

During the peace conference and in the months that followed, those committed to domestic race reform aimed to internationalize America's race question. They argued that the nascent League of Nations had the capacity to enlarge the sphere of justice for the oppressed—throughout the world and in the United States. Democratization overseas, a central element in America's distinctive wartime mission, must be wedded to democratization in the United States, the reformers asserted. And after the war they articulated this view in a variety of forums in order to invigorate their supporters and to convince American policymakers, the American people, and even the international community that the time had come to provide a full measure of justice for peoples everywhere. In his first postwar column, James Weldon Johnson reminded his black readership of the Wilsonian ideals for which America had fought, declaring that the time was ripe for black America to "proclaim and insist" that the nation live up to those values at home. The sense of possibility was captured, too, in *Half Century Magazine*, a black monthly, which declared in a piece entitled "Dawn of a New Day," that the "hour is ripe for the Colored man and woman of affairs. . . . The old order is dying its needful death. The entire world is beginning a rehabilitation. . . . The triumphant note of jubilee is being sounded. . . . The bugle call is rich music to the happy ears of the . . . Negro race." While rejoicing was in order, *The New York Age* observed that America had to make good its wartime promises, claiming that "[d]emocracy must be made more than a mere catchword."[2]

In addition to strengthening the race reformers' determination to advance their goals, the war generated other more measurable effects, the most significant of which was the migration of thousands of black Americans from the rural South to the urban North. Between 1910 and 1920, the black population in cities like Chicago, Cleveland, Detroit, Philadelphia, Pittsburgh, and New York increased enormously, and of the more than three hundred thousand African Americans who headed north in these years, nearly all settled in urban centers.[3] Although the "great migration" had begun two decades earlier, for a number of reasons the war accelerated the phenomenon, which would continue in the years ahead. The war's increased demand for labor, particularly after 1916, pulled workers northward, while federal restrictions on immigration, imposed in 1917, decreased the available labor supply, which benefited those seeking jobs in northern industry.[4] Nature also played a role, as the boll weevil ravaged the southern cotton crop in 1915 and 1916. Along with severe floods in 1915, the insect wreaked havoc on southern agriculture, making the condition of rural blacks more perilous than usual. Moreover, white oppression of southern blacks undoubtedly contributed to the migration during the first two decades of the century. Convinced that the North offered the prospect of better treatment, many black southerners chose to leave home, hoping to escape segregation, disfranchisement, and mob violence. In the words of New York's Adam Clayton Powell, blacks were "tired of being kept out of public parks and libraries, of being deprived of equal educational opportunities . . ., of disfranchisement, . . . and [they were] sick of seeing mobs mutilate and burn unconvicted negro men."[5] This transformation of rural southerners into urban northerners, caused in part by the war, would have profound implications for the civil rights movement during the next several decades.

With the war over, reform leaders and those committed to change looked forward to a period of "reconstruction," a moment when the diplomats' efforts in Paris to build a new world order might produce the energy or even provide a model for the reconfiguration of American race relations. This sense of possibility even contributed to the establishment of a new organization, the Commission on Interracial Cooperation, which sought to improve black-white relations in the South.[6] Optimism about the postwar world is apparent in the writings of Kelly Miller, William Pickens, and Mary White Ovington, and even advertisements aimed at blacks referred to the potential for salutary change. The Allied Industrial Finance Corporation of New York tried to attract black investors, who, it said, had been ignored in the past, referring to the "NEW IDEA, which in economics spells FINANCIAL DEMOCRACY." Noting that blacks had long been prohibited from participating in such ventures, the ad claimed that from now on they would take "part in those interests of upbuilding which are so necessary in a developing and rehabilitating period" unlike any the world had ever seen. The corporation's ad claimed that "Colored People" ought to take their place among the "builders of the age" and in this "process of reconstruction . . . the world [had to] . . . be rebuilt financially, . . . physically and spiritually."[7]

Kelly Miller's pamphlet, "The Negro in the New Reconstruction," expressed splendidly the hopefulness that marked the views of many reformers just after the war. Observing that liberty was born out of travail, Miller asserted that "[h]istory abounds in convulsive epochs when the acute evils of society are eradicated." The Great War was yet "another act in the drama of human liberation," which would transform the world. Along with Jews and Asians, Miller claimed, blacks in Africa and America would benefit from the titanic struggle, which he called the "greatest epoch in the history of social evolution." He described the war as a battle between "power and principle" and averred that it had made sacred the "inviolability" of human rights. With sections on moral revolution, self-determination, and the reconstruction of thought, the pamphlet asserted that the "gallant part" played by the black American in the quest for liberty would help "liberalize the feeling and sentiment" toward him. Miller predicted the "whole fabric" of the United States would be transformed by "the new democratic spirit," and he declared that the heat of the war's ideals would dissolve the glacier of legalized discrimination.[8]

Reflecting on the potentialities of postwar reconstruction, the dean of Morgan College, William Pickens, observed that after the war would come "the greatest reconstruction period the nations have ever known," a time "pregnant with both opportunity and danger." War was like a great fire, he declared, for "it destroy[ed] old buildings that ought to have been destroyed long ago . . . and it [gave] us the privilege of building new ideas into new structures." With the conflict at an end, Pickens noted, the black American would expect "to be nothing less than an American citizen with equal rights before the laws."[9] Adding her voice to this hopeful chorus, Mary White Ovington penned an essay for the February 1919 *Crisis*, entitled "Reconstruction and the Negro," which argued that six months earlier everyone had thought only of war, whereas now the idea of reconstruction was paramount. She wondered what advance would be made "toward justice and humanity" and emphasized the plight of workingmen, women, small nationalities, and the so-called inferior races, who were all "engaged in a separate struggle to secure something of value" for themselves in the postwar chaos, a time when the world remained pliable. Before systems solidified once more, these groups all sought "to win the reality of democracy," with the black American, especially, demanding his citizenship rights. In examining the nature of the emerging postwar reconstruction for blacks, Ovington also drew an analogy between Woodrow Wilson's Fourteen Points and African-American aspirations, which included an end to lynching and segregation.[10]

As the preceding words suggest, the reformers approached the war's aftermath optimistically, and as the world emerged from years of death and destruction, it was unusual to encounter a race activist who did not incorporate such hopeful language into his or her meditations on the movement. In discussing "reconstruction" as they assessed the postwar world, race reform leaders referred to an idea possessed of considerable historical resonance for those interested in the American race question. While the word appeared frequently in reform discourse after the war, it is likely that the notion of "reconstruction" had the potential to vitalize black Americans who would have understood the period after the Civil War as one of unlimited possibility. Those heading the race reform movement thus addressed their listeners in language derived from the broader community of American reformers, while they established a link to an earlier moment of great historical significance for black America.[11]

The key figure who would explicate the postwar moment to black Americans was Du Bois. Throughout his trip to Paris, which was touched on earlier, Du Bois kept one hundred thousand *Crisis* readers abreast of his overseas activities with a stream of letters, stories, and opinion pieces, which he sent regularly to the New York office for publication. While he was away from February to April, and in several issues after his return, the monthly published a fascinating collection of material, which provided its readers with insights and reflections on developments in France. Exposed monthly to the idea that the activities of the peacemakers were related to the aspirations of the reformers, readers would likely have perceived the inextricable link between the outside world and the domestic crusade. And Du Bois made the connection explicit, asserting in the May issue that a "League of Nations is absolutely necessary" for Negro salvation.[12] The NAACP was equally clear in recognizing the relationship between the activities of the peacemakers and the quest for racial justice, stating that it had sent its most prominent black figure to France in order to bring "to bear all pressure possible on the delegates at the Peace Table in the interest of the colored peoples" at home and abroad.[13]

Some of the most striking pieces ever to appear in *The Crisis* described conditions in France in the wake of the world war, as Americans looked through the editor's eyes at the destruction caused by a distant conflict from which many in the United States had felt disconnected. Du Bois wrote of postwar Paris, all chaos and confusion, "its soul cut to the core, feverish, crowded, nervous . . ."; and of Toul, now dispossessed, whose "towers gloom dusky towards the murk of heaven." Of the battlefields, he described "the entrails of Rheims and the guts of Verdun, with their bare bones thrown naked to the insulting skies." Du Bois painted pictures of French villages, which "in dust and ashes . . . lay so low that they left no mark beneath the snow-swept landscape." Readers saw the countryside, "the trees, the land, the people [all] . . . scarred and broken." And everywhere were the graves, evoking "a certain breathless horror," broken only by "plodding soldiers and fugitive peasants." Into the homes of subscribers across America, *The Crisis* brought pictures of foreign desolation and despair, and transported its readers to the wider world.[14]

But there was another side to life in France, which suggested that all was not hopeless in the Old World, and Du Bois shared the story of events that might transform human affairs. Tears filled his eyes as he witnessed a ceremony in the Trocadero, where a mighty crowd gathered to show its respect and appreciation for the contribution made by French colonial troops in the war. He wrote of a black man, "lithe, tall, and straight," receiving the Legion of Honor in the name of the president of the republic, and he praised the French government for honoring the "black and yellow men" who had given so much. Once again, Du Bois observed, France was "leading the world," which caused him to wonder if such a celebration would have been possible in America.[15]

Du Bois had little time for such speculation, though, for in Paris sat "four unobtrusive gentlemen," who possessed the power to settle the problems of the world's peoples. Convinced the "world-fight for black rights [was] on," he believed it was necessary to place the difficulties confronting peoples of color into an international context, and he argued it would be impossible to "agitate the Negro problem in any particular country."[16] This perspective led Du Bois to devote considerable energy to the Pan-African Congress, and if his activities on behalf of Pan-Africanism do not bear directly on the American struggle, they are worth considering because they evince his conviction that the domestic race question was enmeshed in the broader, global challenge of racial oppression. Du Bois had ruminated on the Pan-African idea for some time, his efforts on behalf of the nascent movement dating back some two decades. Having attended the first Pan-African Conference in London in 1900, he would remain deeply devoted to Pan-Africanism for the rest of his life.[17] Just as Du Bois and other reform figures were certain the peace conference presented an opportunity to advance their campaign in the United States, Du Bois was persuaded that Paris was the ideal setting in which to pursue his commitment to Pan-Africanism, especially since one of the key challenges for statesmen concerned the disposition of Germany's African colonies. Moreover, Du Bois had argued for several years that the origins of the war lay in the struggle over African labor and resources, a perspective that suggested the conflict's end might provide an auspicious moment to focus on the aspirations of Africans and those of African descent.[18]

With these bold aims swirling about in the Parisian air, the first Pan-African Congress convened in mid-February, as fifty-seven delegates gathered in the Grand-Hôtel (although as one scholar writes, they had been delegated by no one, having come to Paris of their own accord). Sixteen came from the United States, thirteen from the French West Indies, seven each from Haiti and France, three from Liberia, and several others from various colonial possessions.[19] Blaise Diagne, deputy of Senegal, was elected as president of the congress, and Du Bois was chosen as secretary.

Meeting for three days, the congress issued a series of resolutions, which sought to secure a variety of rights in several spheres for Africa and its peoples, including land, capital, labor, education, medicine, hygiene, and culture. It asked the League of Nations to guarantee these rights in the event that any state failed to provide just treatment for the continent's native population. In its tone, the document would sound familiar to those acquainted with the declarations of contemporary transnational organizations whose mission is to safeguard the welfare of peoples in the developing world.[20]

Beyond sponsoring Du Bois's trip to Paris and providing financial support for the Pan-African Congress, the NAACP was represented at the congress by several high-ranking members, including Joel Spingarn, Charles Edward Russell, and William English Walling. Both Walling and Russell addressed the gathering, with Walling making the claim that the United States was moving forward in its quest for racial justice and alluding to a central tenet of Wilsonianism (the power of world public opinion), which he asserted had the potential to compel the United States to provide black Americans with "full justice and equality." For his part, Russell discussed the war's impact on race relations throughout the world and electrified the group by declaring that the conflict had helped slay the notion that one race was superior to another. Pointing to the possibility for change that the war had provided for Africa, Russell stated that the time had come for the continent to press its claims: "It is a great opportunity and yours is the duty to fulfill it." In globalizing the struggle for liberation, Russell told the Pan-African delegates it was crucial to "insist" upon their rights, and he reminded them of their "duty for Africa and for world democracy, for black and white."[21]

Along with the NAACP's overseas support for the Pan-African Congress, back in the United States, *The Crisis* covered the gathering, compelling its readers to consider the notion that the worldwide freedom struggle was inseparable from their reform project at home. As the journal observed in January 1919, the congress would "serve, perhaps better than any other means that could be taken, to focus the attention of the peace delegates and the civilized world on the just claims of the Negro everywhere." That same month at the association's annual meeting in New York, a rally was held at Carnegie Hall, the theme of which, "Africa in the World Democracy," testified powerfully to the idea that the organization imagined itself an integral part of a global community of reformers, which sought the liberation of the oppressed in the colonial world and in the United States.[22] After introductory remarks by NAACP Secretary John R. Shillady, Professor Horace M. Kallen of Harvard spoke on "The Future of Africa and a League of Nations," documenting the history of Europe's exploitation of Africa and evaluating the way the League of Nations could help relieve the injustices Europeans had inflicted on the continent.

The professor was followed by NAACP Field Secretary James Weldon Johnson, whose speech, "Africa at the Peace Table and the Descendants of Africans in Our American Democracy," considered the organization's interest in African developments, while examining the relationship between Du Bois's activities in Paris and the domestic plight of black America. Johnson addressed the concerns of some members who believed the association's interest in Africa would divert attention from its domestic aims and presented a detailed explanation justifying the NAACP's position, which catalogued the practical and philosophical reasons the organization was interested in the colonial world. Johnson's remarks indicate that the movement's leaders saw their struggle as part of a worldwide effort, the notion supported by his assertion that it would be "lamentable" if black Americans grew "so narrow and self-centered" in the wrongs they had endured that they felt "no sympathy for the wrongs and sufferings of others." While Johnson noted that the NAACP's main focus was on domestic reform, he observed that if black Americans maintained no interest in the condition of others, they would forfeit the right to demand that others take an interest in them. As Johnson concluded, he spoke about the war's positive impact on the African-American struggle, asserting that the most important thing blacks had gained from the war was "not the chance to fight in France, but the right to fight more effectively here at home for the things in the name of which this war was waged." Sharing his firsthand experience of watching New York's black regiment ("the Buffaloes") marching down Fifth Avenue as they headed to Europe, the field secretary asked how many New Yorkers must have looked with wonder at those men who strode off to war "so bravely to die to gain for others a thing which they themselves were yet denied."[23]

Johnson's reflections on the black fighting man remind us that one of Du Bois's key aims in France was to collect material for a history of the black soldier in the war, a project to which he would attend for some time, but never complete. While overseas, Du Bois gathered a considerable quantity of data for the study, some of which he published in the first half of 1919 in *The Crisis*, during and after his trip. In a tale both distressing and inspiring, *Crisis* readers had the chance to confront the wartime experience of the black soldier, and they likely understood the black fighter's ordeal in the context of America's international crusade.[24] In May, readers learned that American military authorities had circulated a document the previous August, which had informed the French military that it would be unwise to treat black Americans as equals. The Americans reminded the French that in the United States the black man was seen as "an inferior being with whom relations of business or service only are possible." Black vices were a constant danger. The alleged black propensity for rape, in particular, demanded that the race be handled with great prudence while on French soil. The document cautioned against any intimacy between French and black officers—courtesy was acceptable, though eating and shaking hands with black officers was not—and the French were warned to guard against excessive praise for black military performance, which might upset the white American enlisted man. The prospect of romantic relationships between French women and black soldiers also troubled the American military, which cautioned that everything possible should be done to discourage such dangerous behavior. In sum, the document sought to replicate in France American racial practices and betrayed no concern that this might clash with the war aims of the Allied Powers. In publishing the material in May 1919, *The Crisis* made clear that the French government had rejected it outright and ordered it destroyed. Nevertheless, the American military's issuance of such material to its allies in a war fought to "make the world safe for democracy" doubtless revealed to one hundred thousand *Crisis* readers no small measure of hypocrisy.[25]

This was not the only disturbing material that *Crisis* subscribers encountered in their monthly reading. They learned of a black chaplain, a lieutenant, unable to get a meal at the officers' mess in Bordeaux because of his color. After trying unsuccessfully to eat in the noncommissioned officers' mess, in his room, and with the privates (regulations forbade his being served in all these locations), the chaplain, hungry and insulted, was served alone at a side table in the officers' mess. Readers also learned that less than one-third of white soldiers saluted black officers in combat units and that wounded black officers, though entitled to a spot in the officers' ward, were often placed with privates in military hospitals.[26] Du Bois informed his subscribers of the "wholesale dismissal" of black officers, regardless of merit; of the widespread distribution of racist propaganda by American military authorities; of repeated and unfounded charges of black cowardice in the front lines; of the overwork and virtual enslavement of black stevedores; and of the dismissal and demotion of white officers who "refused to join the anti-Negro campaign."[27] In short, the editor uncovered a wealth of information that surely disturbed those who had hoped America's international crusade might exempt black Americans from the treatment inflicted upon them at home. That the American war effort had been framed in terms of Woodrow Wilson's meliorative overseas mission likely made such material even more painful to *Crisis* readers.

But there was more to the black experience overseas than humiliation and degradation. If white Americans and the military could not overcome age-old racial attitudes while waging the "crusade for democracy," the citizens of France were quite capable of treating the black soldier with dignity. African-American readers would have perceived the stark contrast between French and American racial attitudes, and the monthly journal made certain they learned that in at least one country black persons could enjoy the respect denied them at home. Appreciative of the black contribution to the war effort, the French rejected the suggestions and warnings proffered by the United States Army and welcomed the black soldier into their midst. With Du Bois supplying the narrative, *Crisis* readers learned how, after some initial uncertainty, residents of a small French town came to admire the "forms, handsome, vigorous, and athletic," of the black American warriors, these "Children of the Sun," whose faultless manners and bearing endeared them to the community. Upon their departure, tears fell, promises to write were exchanged, and a townswoman declared, "[Y]ou will always live in our hearts."[28] *Crisis* readers heard the story of a group of black soldiers who joined in song with the mayor of Domfront in the village inn high on a hill in Normandy, their "vibrant voices" swelling as they sang "La Marseillaise." Never before had black folk been "so uplifted at the vision of real democracy dawning on them in France." Despite the race hatred that lingered nearby among the American officers, the black soldiers reveled in a "purling sea of French sympathy and kindliness."[29] Du Bois described the much-admired efforts of black fighting men, of stevedores who did the arduous and essential work of unloading the matériel that helped make the world safe for democracy. He made certain readers knew of their "efficient and remarkable service" to the American cause, observing that as much as anyone, they had helped win the war.[30]

Having learned of race prejudice in the American ranks, *Crisis* subscribers also read about the kindness of the French, who showed an "utter lack of prejudice." Indeed, Du Bois contended, French decency and fairness largely explained the black man's devotion to the Allied cause. And significantly, he pointed out that the discrepancy between the American and French treatment of black soldiers would leave its mark, for blacks would come home "at once bitter and exalted!" These fighters would no longer "submit to American caste."[31] Those committed to the movement's goals who read the material Du Bois published in this period undoubtedly experienced a range of emotions. While surely outraged by the treatment meted out by the American military, they were likely warmed by the respect and affection the French had shown the black fighting man. Black Americans might have felt considerable pride in the heroic service rendered by the black soldier who had performed with vigor and loyalty under trying conditions. Outrage, pride, and affection: these emotions—and there were surely others—were effective tools for the task of reform, and by summoning such feelings, Du Bois sought to use his journey for maximum effect. While one cannot assess with certainty how one hundred thousand subscribers responded to the material he presented, it is reasonable to assume that they perceived a connection between events abroad and the plight of black America. More than this, by exploring the black experience overseas, Du Bois sought to enhance his readers' understanding of African-American domestic life and to familiarize blacks with the notion that they were members of a global community that was toiling for justice.

Du Bois returned to America on April 1, 1919, and while some in the NAACP had questioned the effectiveness (particularly the cost-effectiveness) of his mission, Mary White Ovington expressed her strong support for his efforts. What "you needed to do was to get something over in Paris. That you have done magnificently," she wrote.[32] For his part, the editor conveyed to his readers the idea that he was part of a community of activists engaged in an international struggle for justice, observing that he had gone to Paris because all the great nations, the little nations, "the little groups who want to be nations," and the races—Jews, Indians, and Arabs—were there. Indeed, "not a single great, serious movement or idea in Government, Politics, [or] Philanthropy . . . in the civilized world" had failed to send its "Eyes and Ears and Fingers" to Paris. Not to have gone would have been indefensible. Du Bois spoke of the global campaign waged by peoples of color, declaring, "I went to help represent the Negro world in Africa and America and the Islands of the Sea." And upon his return to the United States, the race leader displayed a resolute belief in the importance of his overseas mission.[33]

Du Bois was not the only race reform leader to travel to France after the war. I have also discussed William Monroe Trotter's visit, outlined the contributions of Charles Edward Russell and William English Walling, and noted that Du Bois's shipmate, Robert Russa Moton of Tuskegee Institute, crossed the Atlantic at the invitation of the U.S. government.[34] The journey of another veteran reform figure who ventured to Europe just after the war suggests how internationalist ideas resonated with those working to improve race relations in the United States. Mary Church Terrell, the Memphis-born educator, activist, and first president of the National Association of Colored Women, went to Europe after the war to participate in a gathering organized by the International Committee of Women for Permanent Peace, which had been established in 1915 to further the goals of world peace and the emancipation of women. In 1919, the organization, now known as the Women's International League for Peace and Freedom, convened in Zurich to consider the shape of the postwar world.[35] In describing her experience in Zurich, Terrell, a graduate of Oberlin College, would later recall the distinctive position she occupied at the gathering, where some of the western world's most accomplished women had come to address questions of war, peace, and justice. In an

Educator, activist, and author Mary Church Terrell appears here in a portrait from the 1920s. A graduate of Oberlin College, Terrell was the first president of the National Association of Colored Women.

article published a few months after the conference, she noted that women from all over the world were present, though as she pointed out, it was more accurate to say that women from all over the "white world" were there, since not a single delegate attended from Japan, China, India, or any country where the inhabitants were nonwhite. As Terrell observed, because "I was the only woman present who had a single drop of African blood in her vein, it was my duty and privilege to represent not only the colored women from the United States but the whole continent of Africa." In fact, Terrell claimed, she was the only one who "gave any color to the occasion at all."[36]

Terrell's public remarks to the delegates, delivered in faultless German (she had studied foreign languages in Europe after college), illustrate the convergence between a more traditional internationalism and the distinctive worldview held by American race leaders and suggest the extent to which this perspective shaped her understanding of the black freedom struggle. Her very presence at the conference points to Terrell's conviction that transnational institutions were capable of enhancing the well-being of the world's peoples, and she spoke enthusiastically about the organization's "earnest [and] conscientious efforts to solve the problems of reconstruction" and readjustment after the war.[37] Beyond embracing this tenet of traditional internationalism, Terrell made certain to tell her listeners about the worldwide struggle against racial oppression, which suggested a global community of race reformers was working to liberate peoples of color. In highly race-conscious language, Terrell, who claimed to speak on behalf of "the dark races of the world," wedded traditional to color-conscious internationalism, intertwining the goals of both ideas. As she would write later, she appealed to the delegates "for justice and fair play for all the dark races of the earth," telling them, "You may talk about permanent peace until doomsday, but the world will never have it till the dark races are given a square deal."[38] Significantly, Terrell spoke to the Europeans about American race relations and made clear that the postwar moment was propitious for alerting the world to the plight of black Americans. As she would observe later, it was important to have the chance to speak before an international audience because it might "enlighten" Europe about the challenges faced by black America. In addition, the resolution Terrell presented to the international body, which passed unanimously, was testament to the view that internationalist ideals could be harmonized with the aspirations of peoples of color: "We believe no human being should be deprived of an education, prevented from earning a living, [or] debarred from any legitimate pursuit . . . on account of race, color, or creed."[39]

Back on American soil in the months after the war, numerous race activists related overseas events to their domestic program so as to energize the foot soldiers of reform.[40] At the NAACP's annual conference in June 1919, speaker after speaker referred to the war and the peace settlement, determined to galvanize support for the cause. Thousands of activists went to Cleveland to attend the "mighty meeting," Du Bois reported, and its very theme, "To Make America Safe for Americans" (a reworking of the famous Wilsonian phrase), aimed to infuse the gathering with the idea of America's idealistic war aims. Those in attendance encountered the language of leaders like William Pickens, who joined the Wilsonian commitment to democratization abroad to the imperative for democratization at home.[41] Pickens delivered an inspirational address, replete with wartime references, the most vivid of which was his declaration that when "the black man went to France it was with a desire to better conditions at home. When a black American shot a German in France he hoped he saw a lyncher die a spiritual death in the United States. It is true that the Negro thrust his bayonet harder in Europe when he thought of conditions in Georgia." Reflecting on the war's significance, Pickens claimed it had taught Americans that our destinies were bound together and that the black man's "weakness is our weakness and his strength our strength." Pickens then expanded on the notion of domestic unity that might emerge in the period of postwar "reconstruction," stating that "the French are for France, the Belgians for Belgium, Japanese for Japan, and the American Negro and the white man must stand for America."[42]

Other speakers at the Cleveland conference also tied the question of war and peace to the domestic campaign. In a wide-ranging address on the African-American military experience, Emmett Scott (a special assistant to Secretary of War Newton D. Baker) noted that blacks fought first for the right to fight, and then had gone forth with courage, loyalty, and fortitude "to make the world safe for democracy." Black soldiers had "fought, bled and died for the stars and stripes on foreign battlefields" and thus had earned the right to demand that democracy "shall also be made safe for the world." Scott concluded by wedding the domestic reform impulse to an idea he believed was sweeping the world. At this moment of postwar readjustment, black Americans, like all other peoples, "stand with hearts and minds attuned to the melodies of liberty and freedom," and demand their due. They would insist that every program of international reconstruction would include the "black men and black women of America," and "of Europe and Asia." The hopefulness of the Cleveland gathering was captured by the Reverend John Gregg, bishop of the A.M.E. Church, who pointed to the changed conditions and fresh outlook of black Americans in the wake of the war. Gregg spoke of "this new adjustment and reconstruction," in which a new "Negro will never again fit into the old place he once occupied," and he described a "new vision" that had come to [the Negro] "amid bursting shells in No Man's Land." Rejecting discouragement, Gregg proclaimed that "God Himself [had] put into the mouth of our chief executive the slogan of world democracy, and that ultimately the tenets of this mighty nation shall no longer be mere sweet sounding words, but a full reality." Gregg concluded poetically: "Sometimes the darkness of despair seems almost impenetrable, but when I, standing on guard cry out, 'Watchman, what of the night,' I get this reassuring answer. 'The Morning cometh.'"[43]

There was no little tragedy in the fact that the optimism of the NAACP conference would shortly collide with the reality of violence, destruction, and death. The summer of 1919, a time James Weldon Johnson called the "Red Summer," caused the hopeful words of the movement's leading figures to ring hollow. From late spring until the end of the year, race riots erupted throughout the country. North, south, east, and west, in cities and towns, the spasms were not confined to any one section, but struck where blacks and whites had been thrown together: in rural Texas, Charleston, Chicago, Knoxville, Omaha, Washington, D.C., and in Elaine, Arkansas, blacks and whites clashed. There were more than twenty-five episodes in all, killing scores, injuring thousands, and destroying millions of dollars worth of property. In scope, severity, and depravity, the violence remains startling even today.[44]

While the origins of the riots were as varied as the distinctive conditions and local circumstances out of which each incident erupted, scholars agree the war was an important factor in unleashing the nationwide phenomenon. The collision between heightened black expectations for justice, a result of the war, and white determination to stifle those aspirations, undoubtedly contributed to the violence.[45] But the war influenced the Red Summer in a more tangible way, profoundly affecting the black reaction to the brutal attacks that white Americans inflicted upon black communities. As John Hope Franklin has written, having imbibed "freely of the [war's] democratic doctrine," black Americans met their would-be oppressors with a new-found spirit of resistance.[46] Given the continual refrain that the Great War had been fought to defend freedom and democracy, black citizens came to believe it was imperative to defend themselves, and as a result, they fought back against the white onslaught, turning some of the clashes into veritable race wars. In the wake of the world war, armed blacks defended their neighborhoods as they rarely had before and stood ready to die in defense of life, home, and community.

In the vanguard of this response to oppression stood *The Messenger*, which linked the world conflict to the more militant postwar ethos, declaring that this "new spirit is but a reflex of the Great War." The editors reminded their readers, moreover, that such change was not confined to the United States, but was a worldwide phenomenon, "simmering beneath the surface in every country" where justice was denied peoples of color.[47] At the height of the "Red Summer," the magazine responded to domestic events as had race activists throughout these years, by linking developments at home to the Wilsonian ideals that had animated the American war effort. In horrific detail, a July editorial described vicious acts whites had perpetrated against black citizens in "CIVILIZED AMERICA." Deriding the president's empty phrases, the editors noted that Woodrow Wilson's America was not yet "safe for the Negro." The nation that had crushed the Hun in Germany should take care of the "HUNS of Georgia," and the flag for which the black soldier had fought only "mocks and deserts him," while his life and property were lost. But a new day was coming, *The Messenger* averred, for a "new Negro is rising who will not compromise, surrender or retreat a single step." The country that had victimized its black population would regret its malevolence, and the new black citizen would possess "an iron will and an inflexible determination" to quash the Hun in America. There was an ominous ring to the magazine's assertion that the rule of the lynch mob would be crushed, "Law or no law, blood or no blood."[48]

Perhaps the most celebrated expression of this new spirit was Claude McKay's poem, published in *The Messenger* in September 1919:

> If we must die, let it not be like hogs
>   Hunted and penned in an inglorious spot,
> While round us bark the mad and hungry dogs,
>   Making their mock at our accursed lot.
> If we must die, O let us nobly die,
>   So that our precious blood may not be shed
> In vain; . . .
>
> .   .   .   .
>
> Oh Kinsmen! We must meet the common foe;
>
> .   .   .   .
>
> Like men we'll face the murderous, cowardly pack,
>   Pressed to the wall, dying but—fighting back!

In language consistent with the end of a bloody war abroad and the start of a bloody summer at home, McKay captured the spirit and resolution of many black Americans who were prepared to sacrifice their lives in the fight for democracy in the United States. It seemed an appropriate posture for a people, hundreds of thousands of whom had risked their lives to defend democracy overseas, and as *The Messenger* made clear, the war had "stiffened [the] back bone" of the "New Negro," giving him a "steady hand" and a "defiant eye." McKay's poem was typical of the fare that filled *The Messenger*'s pages after the war, as Randolph and Owen unambiguously (and often sardonically) linked the global conflict and the new spirit among black Americans. In September 1919, they observed that those who sought to achieve a desirable outcome in a just cause could do no better than to follow the "splendid example" of the American president, who had summoned his nation to employ "force, unstinted force" to win the war. The lesson had "penetrate[d] the minds of Negroes" and changed their "demeanor and tactics," providing them with a new war-bred spirit, which they would use to exact a toll on the oppressor. The editors' point was stark: black Americans were "determined to make their dying a costly investment for all concerned."[49]

But *The Messenger* leavened its defiance with a modicum of optimism, and while claiming the war had prepared blacks to resort to force if necessary, Randolph and Owen also pointed to the possibility that a new epoch might emerge in the history of race relations. A lengthy supplement to the March 1919 issue, titled "The Negro and the New Social Order," described how blacks might benefit from the postwar "reconstruction." In class-based language, the publication said it was necessary to establish a new order in America based on human rights rather than property rights and proposed a detailed program for improving black life in the United States. The piece concluded with some reflections on the "new Negro" and claimed *The Messenger*'s plan would introduce "a new era in the

Negro's life," one "fraught with bigness and consequence." Here readers saw *The Messenger* look to the postwar world with a cautious optimism, for it seemed the great crusade had made the prospect for racial progress brighter than before.[50]

Indeed, the notion that the war had given birth to a new spirit among black Americans extended beyond the pages of the reform journals. Although the main focus here is on the outlook of reform leaders, it is worth pausing to listen to other voices as they pondered the matter of postwar race relations, for the wartime experience touched the lives of average blacks, who recognized the connection between the international crusade and their domestic condition. As John Hope Franklin has observed, during these years black Americans came to perceive "the discrepancies between the promise of freedom and the reality of their experience," the war having left the black population "defiant, bitter, and impatient."[51] In 1919, Stanley B. Norvell, a black Chicagoan, described the world war's significance for black America, writing to the editor of the *Chicago Daily News* shortly after the bloody riot that had wracked the city: "[T]oday we have with us a . . . brand new Negro. . . . [S]ince the war the Negro has been jolted into thinking by circumstances. . . . [A]ny average Negro . . . of some education will tell you that he finally . . . counts as a part of his government. . . . It took a world war to get that idea into general Negro acceptance, but it is there now." A few months later, Harry Jones, a black teacher at Lincoln High School in Wheeling, West Virginia, expressed a similar view, writing that the black man, "having given his best . . . 'to make the world safe for democracy,' having had sounded repeatedly into his ears that all mankind is entitled to self-determination, has formed the opinion that Democracy ought to begin at home, and that he ought to share in the fruits of victory." According to Jones, "Negroes of all classes, from the radical to the conservative . . . [believe] that America must change its treatment toward their race. They differ only as to means."[52]

In letters to Du Bois, black soldiers also described how the wartime experience had generated a new inner spirit. They discussed the war's impact on their thinking about race in America, conveying the notion that upon their return they would no longer accept their prewar status. In a letter from Le Havre written in the summer of 1919, William Hewlett regretted his impending return and claimed the United States was not democratic but "autocratic" in dealing with its black population, a realization that led him to ask why America had fought at all. "Was it to make democracy safe for white people in America—with the black race left out; if we have fought to make safe democracy for the white races, we will soon fight to make it safe for ourselves and our posterity."[53] A black infantrymen in France, Charles A. Shaw, asked if the black soldier, having shed his blood so freely, would now be "given the same considerations and opportunities to live a life of happiness and contentment as other citizens." Shaw concluded forcefully: "I am braced to face the future in the belief that someday Right and Truth will triumph over all Injustice."[54]

It will be recalled that William Monroe Trotter had journeyed to Paris in the spring of 1919 to tell the world about the plight of black Americans. Several months later, in August 1919, Trotter headed to Washington to testify before Senator Henry Cabot Lodge's Foreign Relations Committee, which had convened to consider amendments to the peace treaty that had been negotiated in the French capital.[55] Trotter, the secretary of the National Equal Rights League, and several other race activists offered amendments to the treaty on the subject of racial equality, their testimony demonstrating the degree to which civil rights leaders linked the issue of international reconstruction to the improvement of African-American life.[56] The testimony and amendments Trotter and his colleagues placed before the committee indicate how completely they embraced the idea that an international association of nations could rectify the character of race relations in America. If their faith in the potential power of an organized group of sovereign states to work toward humanitarian ends was consistent with the views of many internationalists in this period, the race reformers' conviction that such an organization could help overturn decades of domestic racial oppression was unusual.[57]

In its original form, the treaty negotiated at Paris had addressed the issue of colonial injustice, stating that the members of the league would "undertake to secure just treatment of the native inhabitants of territories under their control." To this Trotter and his colleagues appended the following significant clause: "and agree to vouchsafe to their own citizens the possession of full liberty, rights of democracy, and protection of life, without restriction or distinction based on race, color, creed, or previous condition." Trotter made certain there was no ambiguity about his aims and implored the senators to understand that he was speaking on behalf of black America and representing the cause to which the National Equal Rights League was devoted. He was "pleading," he said, "for the life, liberty, and labor of 14,000,000 colored Americans." In the event this proposed clause was rejected, Trotter offered a stronger, lengthier amendment to the treaty, which reflected the reformers' conviction that an association of nations had the power to improve the lives of black Americans. The amendment sought to make "the reign of peace universal and lasting, and to make the fruits of the war effective in the permanent establishment of true democracy everywhere." It implored the allied and associated powers to

William Monroe Trotter, secretary of the National Equal Rights League and editor of the *Boston Guardian*, in a 1920 photo taken at his twenty-fifth Harvard reunion. The previous year, Trotter had gone to Paris to attend the peace conference, where he had spoken out boldly on behalf of African-American rights.

> undertake, each in its own country, to assure full . . . protection of life and liberty to all their inhabitants, without distinction of birth, nationality, language, race, or religion, and agree that all their citizens, respectively, shall be equal before the law and shall enjoy the same civil and political rights without distinction as to race, language, or religion, and all citizens of the members of the league who belong to racial or religious minorities differing . . . from the majority . . . shall enjoy the same treatment and same security in law and in fact as all persons of the majority race or religion.[58]

In advancing the twin ideals of universal peace and global democratization—and melding both to the goal of domestic racial, ethnic, and religious equality—the reformers offered the committee a splendid example of their distinctive internationalism, which suggested that an association of nations could assist the cause of race reform in the United States.

Beyond the amendments Trotter read into the record, his testimony was tinged with the rhetoric of internationalist uplift, which he linked to his domestic goals. According to Trotter, the world struggle had been fought "for a great human principle," which American officials had said was "to procure universal security of life and the protection of the weak from the strong." It was essential, he asserted, to amend the treaty so those soldiers "of every race and color" who had sacrificed their lives in battle had not died in vain, and so "we may truly have . . . the reign of world democracy and . . . universal liberty." Trotter spoke of the protections afforded other racial minorities at the peace conference and emphasized that no others "suffered the denials of democracy and the insecurity of life and liberty" to the same degree that black Americans did. He hoped the committee would adopt his amendments so as to ameliorate "the deplorable condition" blacks endured, and asserted that he had testified before the committee so "colored Americans . . . with all other nations on the earth, shall come into the enjoyment of full democracy, of full equality of rights, [and] of full liberty." As his testimony made clear, Trotter invested the League with the power and authority to transform American social relations, and he wedded Woodrow Wilson's global aspirations to the domestic goals of the race reform movement. Deploying language consonant with the dominant tone of internationalism, Trotter referred freely to "world democracy, universal liberty, [and] universal humanity," which suggests the degree to which the race reformers' worldview was consistent with the outlook of others who were working to achieve global cooperation.[59]

From his perch as *Crisis* editor, Du Bois also wrote about the distinctive power of the League of Nations, which he believed was essential for constructing a more just society abroad and at home. Claiming the League was "absolutely necessary to the salvation of the Negro race," Du Bois observed that without a "supernational power to curb the anti-Negro policy of the United States . . . we are doomed eventually to *fight* for our rights." According to the editor, the League would oppose the doctrines of "race antagonism and inferiority" and be open to "the larger influences of civilization and culture," which southern barbarism made ineffective in the United States. He concluded his paean to the League in language, which, in its emphasis on the power of international public opinion, was positively Wilsonian—though his words were not without a Du Boisian twist:

> What we cannot accomplish before the choked conscience of America, we have an infinitely better chance to accomplish before the Organized Public Opinion of the World. Peace for us is not simply Peace from Wars like the past, but relief from the spectre of the Great War of Races which . . . [could only be prevented] by a Great World Congress in which black and white and yellow sit and speak and act.

And this, Du Bois wrote, would mark "the Beginning of a mighty End."[60]

But what impact did such eloquent language have on the race reform movement and, more generally, on the state of American race relations? To be sure, one cannot argue that after 1919 the millennium had arrived in the struggle for racial equality; the "Red Summer" made that painfully clear. Nevertheless, the years between 1914 and 1919 provide a striking illustration of the way the race reformers used events overseas to advance their agenda for change. By appropriating the crusading internationalist rhetoric of Woodrow Wilson and incorporating it into their reform program, the race activists constructed a message, which, at its core, was dependent on the war and the peace. World affairs and America's role on the international stage thus determined the content of the reformers' message and the style with which they presented it to the American people.

And the significance of the war does not end there, for the reformers' purposive incorporation of overseas matters into their message had additional implications for the movement. In May 1919, in one of his most celebrated *Crisis* editorials, "Returning Soldiers," Du Bois discussed the relationship between the war and the domestic crusade against oppression:

> We *return*.
> We *return from fighting*.
> We *return fighting*.
> Make way for Democracy! We saved it in France, and by the
> Great Jehovah, we will save it in the United States of
> America, or know the reason why.[61]

His readership in *The Crisis*, the preeminent publication of its time devoted to the race question, was one hundred thousand. Five years earlier it had stood at just over thirty-one thousand.[62] And the NAACP itself saw an astonishing increase in its membership during these years. In April 1918, the NAACP had 9,869 members in 85 branches, while by the end of 1919, it had 91,203 members (90 percent of whom were black) in 310 branches, the majority living in the South.[63] By 1920, the NAACP had become a truly national organization and the undisputed leader in the struggle for racial equality, developments that would have been unimaginable without the war.

But the huge increase in the number of those committed to reform and the NAACP's emergence as the nation's preeminent race reform organization were not the only developments catalyzed by the war. The editor of *The Crisis* gave verbal form to the sometimes intangible effect the war and the peace had on black America, writing in July 1919 that "we helped to crush the most serious obstacle to the modern democratic movement since Napoleon . . . and . . . [more] important, we gained a new self-respect and a new consciousness of power."[64] And Du Bois was not alone in this view: more radical leaders, like A. Philip Randolph and Chandler Owen, and ordinary people like Harry Jones and Stanley Norvell, were all in agreement, convinced the war had instilled a new spirit in black America. A half dozen years after the peace conference was over, the writer Alain Locke began *The New Negro*, which would become the seminal text of the Harlem Renaissance, by observing that in "the last decade something beyond the watch and guard of statistics ha[d] happened in the life of the American Negro." Exploring this "metamorphosis," Locke spoke of a "new psychology" and a "new spirit" that was awake in the masses.[65] If the outlook of black America differed in 1925 from what it had been a decade before, the war had played a critical part in that transformation, for the conflict had profoundly influenced the sensibilities of countless black citizens.

In an effort to provide traction to advance the movement's agenda, the race activists reconfigured the meaning of Wilsonianism and placed the idea of color-conscious internationalism at the very center of the language of domestic reform. In so doing, they did more than increase the number of those committed to their cause. In their barrage of war-related activities—the speeches and editorials, the news stories and weekly columns, the sermons and meetings, the congressional testimony and overseas voyages—the reformers contributed to the spirit of a new age. In 1921, Joel Spingarn reflected on this transformation, observing that a "great change [had] come over the men and women of Negro descent. . . . [A] new sense of their power and destiny is in the very soul of black men and women." Ultimately, he wrote, "[I]t will force both races to seek and find some form of compromise or adjustment."[66] By interpreting the war in the distinctive way that they did, and by placing Wilsonianism and the world conflict at the heart of their message, the race reformers were critically important in the appearance of the "New Negro." No less significant was the notion that reform leaders and many average black Americans would emerge invigorated from the war and more determined than ever to erase the stain of racial persecution from the national landscape. At the start of the new decade, it was too soon to know how receptive the country would be to this heightened sense of commitment.

PART II

Between the Wars

Three

"FROM DEEP IN THE HEART OF RUSSIA"
The Reformers Look Abroad in the 1920s

SIX YEARS after the end of the Great War, in the spring of 1924, NAACP Secretary James Weldon Johnson appeared before the Women's International League for Peace and Freedom, which had been established to advance the twin causes of world peace and the liberation of women.[1] In joining the campaign for international peace and cooperation (a key theme of world affairs during the 1920s) to the subject of racial oppression, Johnson declared that greed, gain, and money were the fundamental causes of war, and he observed that with the world "conditioned" as it was, wars for gain and exploitation were "based on the idea of racial inferiority." According to Johnson, the cause of the Great War lay in the crimes Europeans had visited upon black Africa, which had stemmed from the conviction that Africans were "innately inferior." Johnson also discussed race relations in the United States, telling the gathering of female internationalists that the oppression of the weak by the strong could have implications that were not at first apparent. Indeed, he suggested, the oppressor did even greater damage to himself than to the oppressed. Just as Europe's exploitation of Africa had led to the world war and the destruction of the Old World, white America's oppression of the "defenseless" black man might similarly destroy the United States. Johnson contended that "the spiritual damage done to the dominant majority" exceeded any harm "that could possibly come to the Negro" and wondered what impact racial oppression might have on a small community that made sport and spectacle of a lynching. When "thousands of men, women, and children, women holding their babes up to witness the sight, gather around to see a human being baptized with gasoline and then set afire," he asked, "What must be the moral effect upon that community . . . ?" Surely the damage exceeded "the momentary suffering of the wretched victim."

Johnson concluded by considering the global effort to abolish war, joining a central tenet of internationalist thought in the postwar decade—the widespread desire to construct a more stable and peaceful world order—to the struggle for racial justice. While admitting he did not know if it would be possible to set up the "machinery" to achieve world peace, Johnson insisted the "surest safeguard against future wars [was] the abolishment of the idea of innate race inferiority."[2] Upon hearing such words,

Enormously gifted, James Weldon Johnson was one of the NAACP's leading figures. A poet, musician, diplomat, and writer, Johnson joined the NAACP in 1916
and became secretary in 1920.

Johnson's listeners would have grasped the notion that the quest for world
peace and cooperation was related to the effort to achieve racial justice
in the United States, and in linking peace and security to the domestic
campaign, Johnson was sounding an important theme of color-conscious
internationalism in the postwar decade. More broadly, Johnson's interest
in the problem of international cooperation and security suggests that
after the world war, overseas developments remained important to race
reform leaders.

    As an examination of three of the leading race reform journals of the
period—*The Crisis, The Messenger,* and the National Urban League's
Opportunity—makes clear, foreign developments continued to occupy a
prominent place in the reform discourse of the 1920s.[3] During the postwar
decade, the three monthlies together published hundreds of international
stories on a dizzying range of subjects, considering everything from health
education in the Panama Canal Zone to French colonial policy in Africa,
from Liberian rubber production to political developments in the
Transvaal. In examining an array of political, social, and cultural matters,
the journals focused on the activities of the colonized and the colonizer, on
European diplomats and native musicians. And in exposing tens of thousands of readers to subjects from around the world, the monthlies' international pieces sounded a distinctive tone, which rang out with the editors'
commitment to racial justice. Moreover, the magazines linked their con-

cerns about America's race problem to events abroad, which helped to highlight the odious character of racial oppression in the United States.

Beyond considering key international developments, the reform journals linked global to domestic matters by publishing numerous pieces chronicling the travel experiences of reformers and other important African-American figures. Such stories in the race journals and in the black press had the potential to affect deeply those who read about the adventures of Du Bois or William Pickens, or literary figures like Alain Locke or Claude McKay, all of whom traveled widely during the period and displayed an interest in foreign cultures and political systems. No mere tourists taking in the sights of other lands, they were keen observers, projecting their concerns about American race relations onto the mores of the world's peoples. In assessing new places, these reformer-travelers disclosed as much about their understanding of life at home as they did about life overseas.[4] When Du Bois left Harlem to see the world, he carried with him more than his suitcase and some good books; also tucked away were lifelong anxieties about American racial persecution, which not surprisingly shaped his view of life in France, England, or Russia. While no global crisis captured the attention of the reformers during the 1920s, they continued to look abroad, and as before, color-conscious internationalism shaped their perception of developments in distant lands like Russia and India or nearby locales like Haiti and Washington, D.C.[5]

In the fall of 1921, James Weldon Johnson offered the editors of dozens of black newspapers a forthcoming series of articles by the NAACP's publicity director, Herbert J. Seligmann, which would consider the international disarmament conference that was set to begin in Washington. Despite the expense, the NAACP had decided to send Seligmann to the meeting, for as Johnson observed, the gathering would undoubtedly consider questions about the "future peace of the civilized world" and the rights of the "increasingly self-conscious colored peoples of the globe." Moreover, Johnson noted, Seligmann would focus on those subjects that were especially important to "colored Americans."[6]

Attending the Washington Naval Conference, which sought to limit the international arms race at sea, Herbert Seligmann wrote nine articles on the meeting and fielded requests from more than thirty black papers that wished to publish his series. The NAACP shared its interest in global disarmament (a central concern of internationalists during the 1920s) with thousands of black readers,[7] and while detailing the conference proceedings, Seligmann's articles linked the quest for disarmament to the crusade to end worldwide racial oppression. Armaments did not prevent war, Seligmann claimed, but encouraged it. He also insisted that the armies and navies of the imperial powers had "held in subjection" countless "millions of the colored races of the world" and observed that the participants in the Washington Conference had all committed crimes against peoples of color in China, India, Africa, Indochina, or Haiti. The quest for profit, which had led the imperial powers to plunder the developing world, had to stop; it was time for the West to "change its methods in dealing with the colored races." In his final piece, Seligmann looked toward a nobler destiny for the world, when the values of artists, painters, sculptors, musicians, and poets of all races and every land would triumph. Articulating a distinctive conception of internationalism, he left his readers to ponder the rule of those individuals who would "override race prejudice" as they worked to "create" rather than "possess."[8]

As the great powers met in Washington, Du Bois wrote arrestingly in *The Crisis* about the gathering, observing that peace and security were particularly important to society's less fortunate. Advancing an argument that would appear decades later, Du Bois contended that America's massive defense expenditures precluded spending on other more worthy items and claimed the tax burden for such spending had become "intolerable," particularly for "the poor and the black." According to Du Bois, racial oppression had created global insecurity, which, in turn, had fueled the arms race. As he had often argued, Du Bois attributed international instability to the policies of a few white imperial nations, Britain especially, which continued to plunder and oppress colonial peoples. If the western powers would but forgo their imperial aspirations, world peace would be far easier to achieve.[9]

In responding to the widespread impulse for disarmament and the idea that humanity should work toward achieving global cooperation, race reform leaders also looked to the League of Nations for inspiration and assistance after the war. To *Crisis* readers, Du Bois left little doubt that the League, which the United States had refused to join, was supremely important in the worldwide struggle against racial oppression. In 1921, he called the League's inception "the most forward-looking event of the century," and considered the infant organization's potential for improving the lives of the oppressed. The first aim of the international body, Du Bois asserted, should be to wrest control from the "imperial, military, and industrial dictators of the world" in order to attain true self-determination for all people, "black, brown, yellow, and white." Given his optimistic tone, the editor apparently believed the League could ultimately attain this goal, and throughout the twenties, *The Crisis* spoke positively about the institution.[10] In 1923, the monthly observed that it was "the most hopeful international movement today in the world," mainly because it had "decisively risen above the hateful color bar" by admitting Ethiopia, which had taken its place alongside two other black nations, Liberia and Haiti. Looking to the League with optimism, *The Crisis* hoped it would continue to "live and grow."[11]

But the race reformers' internationalism would not be confined to the issue of constructing a more pacific world order, no matter how significant a question that was in the postwar years. In the summer of 1924, a young black man sent a letter to Du Bois at *The Crisis*, in which he related his experiences in the Soviet Union. James Jackson had written "from a village deep in the heart of Russia," telling Du Bois he was "an American-Negro, a native of the south . . . making a study of social conditions. The [village of Oodelnarya] is the seat of the summer colony of the University for Eastern Peoples, located at Moscow." Noting that he had been invited to the colony as a guest, Jackson observed that "[o]ne must visit Russia to understand and appreciate the many beautiful social developments that are taking place in this strange land!" Each night students from all countries produced plays in open-air theaters in the forests. "[H]ere life is poetry itself!" Jackson wrote. "It is the Bolshevik idea of social relation, and a miniature of the world of tomorrow." Before the Revolution, he pointed out, "Russia was burdened with many race problems, but today under the Soviet system there are no race problems."[12] That young Jackson assumed America's leading race reformer would be interested in such observations suggests that the Soviet Union had begun to attract the race activists' gaze in the 1920s.

From the time of the Bolshevik Revolution, Russian (and later Soviet) developments had captured the attention of a diverse group of internationally minded Americans. While intellectuals and reformers who sought to reshape American political and social institutions were drawn to Soviet affairs, businessmen, labor leaders, government officials, and ordinary people also found Russian matters intriguing. In tracing American perceptions of the "Soviet experiment" (the metaphor was quite common), one is struck, as Peter Filene has observed, by the extent to which those perceptions illuminated the way Americans understood democracy, capitalism, and their own society.[13] This was particularly true in the race reform community. Several reformers visited the Soviet Union, and the reform periodicals published numerous articles and opinion pieces on Soviet developments and the meaning of the revolutionary enterprise, which, not surprisingly, focused squarely on the race question. As the reformers' thoughts on Soviet matters are explored, it will be worth reflecting on the way readers might have responded to such observations, which were deployed to inspire and edify those committed to the domestic movement.

Throughout the decade, *The Crisis* published articles, travel pieces, and editorials on Soviet developments. In 1922, Du Bois described Russia as the "most amazing" and "most hopeful phenomenon," noting that "[s]he has been murdered, bullied, lied about and starved and yet she maintains her government, possesses her soul and is simply compelling the world to recognize her right to freedom even if that freedom involves the industrial reconstruction of her society."[14] Despite his hortatory prose, the editor pondered the significance of the Soviet Union, uncertain about its relevance for the cause of American race reform. Indeed, less than a year before writing the above tribute, Du Bois had been more circumspect in assessing the Soviet situation, observing that "Russia is incredibly vast, and the happenings there in the last five years have been intricate to a degree that must make any student pause." He spoke of "seeing some splendid results . . . and hearing of other things which frighten us." And yet, Du Bois contended, "the immediate work for the American Negro lies in America and not in Russia," a curious observation from one who regularly globalized matters of democracy, freedom, tyranny, and oppression. Moreover, while he recognized the Soviet system's achievements (and called himself a socialist), Du Bois did not believe "German State Socialism or the dictatorship of the proletariat" were "perfect panaceas," a skepticism rooted in his uncertainty about whether peoples of color, especially black Americans, could trust the working class.[15] Although he believed the ends sought by the Communists and socialists were estimable, Du Bois opposed the violent overthrow of the existing system, asserting in 1921 that he did not favor the adoption of their aims if "war or force or murder" were the means of achieving them. Nor did he believe that the "sudden attempt to impose a new industrial system and new ideas of industrial life" could succeed "without the long training of human beings." Socialism must be evolutionary; it was not possible "immediately [to] change the world."[16]

His reservations about the Soviet Union notwithstanding, Du Bois did not hesitate to publish material that reflected well on conditions there. In two *Crisis* pieces that appeared in 1923 and 1924, the black writer Claude McKay memorably described his utopian experiences in Russia. Not a race reformer (though his work was associated with 1920s race activism), McKay was one of the most original and influential writers of the period and a leading figure in the artistic and literary movement known as the Harlem Renaissance.[17] Having traveled widely, the writer described a land whose peoples were unique and whose tolerance for other races and ethnic groups made them unlike any he had encountered. Russia was a place where "all the races of Europe and of Asia met and mix." McKay observed that the English

> cannot think of a black man being anything other than an entertainer, boxer, a Baptist preacher, or a menial. The Germans are just a little worse. Any healthy looking black coon of an adventurous streak can have a wonderful time palming himself off as . . . a buck dancer. . . . An American student tells his middle class [German] landlady that he is having a black friend to lunch: "But are you sure that he is not a cannibal?" she asks without a flicker of a humorous smile!

But the Soviet Union was different:

> [I]n Petrograd and Moscow, I could not detect a hint of this ignorant snob-
> bishness among the educated classes, and the attitude of the common work-
> ers, the soldiers and sailors was still more remarkable. It was so beautifully
> naive; for them I was only a black member of the world of humanity.

Thus did tens of thousands of *Crisis* readers encounter the Soviet Union,
a place where a black man was treated not as a novelty but as an equal—
one whose art could stand on its own. Describing his experiences at artistic gatherings, McKay wrote that the Russians were courteous and consid-
erate, and noted there was "no overdoing of the correct thing, no vulgar
wonderment and bounderish superiority of a Negro's being a poet. I was
a poet, that was all." His listeners were far more interested in his work
and views on modern literary movements than they were in his color.
Claude McKay was a writer who happened to be black.

One wonders what *Crisis* readers thought of a society in which both
intellectuals and workers welcomed as an equal a talented black artist.
And how did subscribers perceive McKay's tale, which suggested he was
"in demand everywhere—at the lectures of poets and journalists, the
meetings of soldiers and factory workers"? The contrast between
McKay's Soviet world and his readers' American world was striking. In
the United States, after all, the president had segregated government
offices a few years earlier, contending he had done so to benefit black
citizens. If today one recognizes the chimerical quality of the Russia
Claude McKay presented to his American readers, in 1924 it was undoubtedly received quite differently—as an accurate and provocative depiction of life in the young Soviet state. By declaring Russia to be "prepared . . . to receive couriers and heralds of good will and interracial
understanding from the Negro race," McKay shared the story of a new
society that was markedly different from America, a land *Crisis* readers
knew all too well.[18]

The writer sought to compel his readers to confront the stark contrast
between the Soviet Union and the United States. Looking at the matter
through Russian eyes, McKay claimed the Russian people read "the terrible history of their own recent past in the tragic position of the American
Negro to-day." He employed class-based language to compare the revolution that had overturned Czarist Russia with one that might someday
overturn the American South, arguing that if "the exploited poor whites
of the south could ever transform themselves into making common cause
with the persecuted and plundered Negroes, overcome the oppressive oli-
garchy . . . and deprive it of all political privileges, the situation would be
very similar to that of Soviet Russia today."[19] McKay believed Russian
developments were instructive, implying that the destiny of the long-oppressed Russian was related to that of the black American who remained

under the yoke. Referring to the plight of the black population, which the poet placed in the context of a reformed Russia, McKay highlighted the persistence of racial oppression in the United States and suggested that the character of American race relations was not immutable.

At the end of 1926, Du Bois visited the Soviet Union as part of a remarkable journey that took him to some of Europe's fabled cities—Antwerp, Cologne, Berlin, Athens, Naples, and Constantinople—though he noted the "center of all this was Russia." Publishing his reflections on the trip in *The Crisis*, Du Bois provided the journal's subscribers with an evocative description of Soviet life. Before departing, he confessed his ignorance about the Russian Revolution, stating that he wished to gain a firsthand understanding of Soviet developments. While he did not know if the trip would provide him with any information useful for the domestic struggle, if there was anything to learn, he noted, he was eager to do so. Du Bois asserted that he would reach his own conclusions about life in the Soviet Union and would not "see the facts with any other eyes except my own."[20]

It was, by any measure, an extraordinary trip. After traveling up the Rhine, he crossed the Baltic from Stettin and arrived in Leningrad, where loomed the "dark red mass of the Winter Palace." He roamed the lovely park now called the Children's Village and strolled down the street known as Nevsky Prospekt. After a few days, it was on to Moscow for a month, where he walked through Red Square, visited Lenin's tomb, and "wandered into all the nooks and crannies of the city unattended." On his own or with the help of a single Russian speaker, Du Bois reported that he "met few officials and did not join the excursions arranged for foreigners." In fact, the editor described an unmediated encounter with Russia. "Alone and unaccompanied I have walked the miles of streets in Leningrad, Moscow, Nijni Novgorod and Kiev at morning, noon and night. . . . I have watched crowds. . . . I have . . . plied officials and teachers with questions and sat still and gazed at this Russia, that the spirit of its life and people might enter my veins." He saw palaces, museums, day nurseries, and factories and "looked into the faces of [Russia's] races—Jews, Tartars, Gypsies, Armenians, Caucasians, and Chinese." He spoke with peasants and laborers, commissars, teachers, and children. Amazed by it all, and admitting he had seen "only a very small part" of the country and "nothing of political prisoners, secret police and underground propaganda," this seasoned traveler stood "in astonishment and wonder at the revelation of Russia that has come to me. I may be partially deceived and informed. But if what I have seen with my eyes and heard with my ears in Russia is Bolshevism, I am a Bolshevik."[21] Thus did the most influential black reformer of the era describe the Russian experiment to tens of thousands of readers. The vast and exotic Russian canvas had moved him, and while

Du Bois was not yet a Bolshevik (a conversion that would occur later), what he observed in Russia was unlike anything he had ever seen.

Although Du Bois did not mention racial matters in his *Crisis* pieces on Russia, upon returning, he discussed race relations in the Soviet Union at the NAACP's annual conference. Noting that the country was composed of a great mixture of races, he considered the revolutionary government's approach to the race question. "Russia stands for absolute equality of races—political, social, and civil," he asserted, and "does not force racial segregation." The country's external race policy was similarly enlightened, Du Bois observed. "Russia has taken a firm stand for racial equality. She has demanded decent treatment for Africans and persons of African descent throughout the world and has gone out of her way to treat Negro visitors with courtesy."[22] One can only speculate as to the impact such language had on Du Bois's listeners. A government that stood for "political, social, and civil equality"? The mere advocacy of social equality between the races in 1920s America was a heroic act that exposed one to the prospect of physical violence. But according to Du Bois, the Soviet government supported just such a policy. Surely, those gathered at the NAACP conference in Indianapolis were stunned by such revelations and marveled at the enlightened character of the Soviet regime and the Russian people. A few months later, on the tenth anniversary of the Russian Revolution, Du Bois erased any doubts about his stance on the Soviet Union, sharing with *Crisis* readers his admiration for the Bolshevik achievement. Noting that the czar's oppressive regime had been supplanted by the revolutionary aspirations of the Russian people, he declared, "[H]ere's hoping that this is but the first decade toward its hundred years."[23]

NAACP Field Secretary William Pickens, introduced in part 1, would also travel to the Soviet Union during the 1920s. The son of former slaves, Pickens was born in South Carolina in 1881, the sixth of ten children. While still a small boy, Pickens and his family left the South for Arkansas, where it was hoped economic opportunities would be more plentiful. Education was enormously important to the family, and young William, a superb student, won a spot in Little Rock's all-black high school. Selected to give the valedictory address in 1899, Pickens was so impressive that one listener encouraged him to apply to Alabama's all-black Talladega College, which indeed admitted him into the sophomore class the following autumn. Three years later, having compiled an outstanding record at Talladega, Pickens enrolled as a junior at Yale, one of a handful of blacks to attend the university. A prize-winning student, he performed brilliantly in his major field, foreign languages, and was admitted into Yale's chapter of Phi Beta Kappa. With an Ivy League diploma in hand, Pickens decided to pursue a career in education, and for more than a decade he taught at black colleges throughout the South. In 1915, he headed to Baltimore's

Morgan College to become dean of the all-black institution. Five years later, Pickens, now a leading educator and a powerful public speaker, accepted an offer to join the NAACP, where he would quickly become one of the organization's most effective recruiters.[24]

At the end of 1926, Pickens traveled to Europe as the NAACP's representative to the Brussels International Conference of Oppressed Nations, a meeting organized by the Anti-Imperialism League. After delivering a series of speeches in England, Pickens crossed to Belgium for the conference, and upon its postponement, made his way to Moscow in early 1927 to visit a land that had piqued his curiosity for some time.[25] According to his biographer, Pickens was "not unsympathetic" to the program of the Communists and was drawn to their apparent willingness to accept blacks as equals. Moreover, Pickens's past writings suggested a tendency to view racial oppression and violence in class terms, which made him a target for Communist recruiters. A trip to the Soviet Union was part of their conversion effort.[26] Intrigued, Pickens wrote in the Party organ, *The Daily Worker*, that "[s]eeing Russia will doubtless get American Negroes . . . much nearer to the truth about that country than reading American newspapers about [it]" and added that the American press did not want blacks to see Moscow because they might decide "it is a darn sight better civilization than what they see" in this country. In early 1927, Pickens had the chance to find out for himself if this were true.[27]

Pickens told of being treated "with almost embarrassing courtesy" from the moment he entered the Soviet Union until his departure two weeks later.[28] His stay in Moscow was busy: Lenin's tomb, the churches, workers' clubs, science schools, the boulevards and squares. He even managed to arrange an audience with Leon Trotsky, a meeting Pickens left somewhat abruptly so that he could attend the film *Potemkin*. In an amusing postscript to his audience with the revolutionary, Pickens spoke to his cinema companions of the aborted visit, one of whom noted that most Russians "would crawl five miles on their hands and knees to get three minutes with Trotsky." But a woman later praised Pickens, telling him, "Well, Trotsky is so conceited that I am glad somebody did that to him."[29] In Pickens's accounts of his Soviet trip, which were published in the black press, he noted that there was "less color prejudice in New York than in Mississippi; less in England than in New York; less in France than in England; and not a god's bit in Russia."[30] Pickens called the existence of the Soviet experiment "an amazing fact," and observed that the notion of "peasants and workers guiding their own destiny, even if to God-knows-where, instead of being ridden by Czars and Grand Dukes, is a stupefying idea. Small wonder that thinkers want to see Russia."[31] But Pickens was not entirely uncritical of the Soviet Union, though his critique was well-tempered. Russia was not a violent society, he observed, and even if "your pockets may be picked, not a hair of your head will be hurt," something which could not be said of Chicago, where rich thugs might "crack your skull or shoot you through the back." Russia was no

> seventh heaven; it has poverty, inefficiency, demagoguery and some rob-bery—more poverty than New York but less robbery. But if one has an open heart of goodwill for his fellowman, he feels a thrill when he sees these plain people, who have come up like the bowels of a volcano from the nether regions, now standing there in the sunlight and attempting to achieve their own destiny.[32]

Again, it is worth imagining how black Americans might have responded to Pickens's observations about social relations in the new Russia. His portrait of a land in which there was "no kow-towing to superiors" was surely appealing, and his description of Russian equality must also have been attractive. "Nobody takes off his hat to anybody else in Russia; one removes his hat or keeps it on his head, as suits best his own comfort." His observation that the humblest worker kept his "head up" when in the presence of his superintendent must have intrigued black readers, who were accustomed to a society in which the slightest breach in accepted patterns of deference could have tragic consequences. Indeed, in this new society, Pickens wrote, "[d]eference and servility are resented by those to whom they are offered." For black Americans, Pickens's claim that there was a "cordiality of comradeship everywhere" in Russia suggested that at least one place existed where equality and justice were not mere words. One of the country's most prominent race reformers thus left Russia convinced that Americans had a mistaken image of a changing land. Having seen the Bolsheviks "in their own lair," he realized it was impossible to get a fair picture of the Russian people through the eyes of those not in sympathy with them. After looking at the Russians with his own eyes, Pickens could reject the "hysterical" ideas of those in the American press who depicted Soviet life as something other than it was. The journey fortified his interest in Soviet developments, and to those who saw Russia as a "dangerous experiment," he noted that all experiments were dangerous, a fact demonstrated by "advances in the knowledge of radio-active substances" and airplane technology.[33] The trip left him feeling respect and awe for the way Russia's oppressed had transformed their society, and Pickens believed he had encountered a people who were liberating themselves from economic slavery and achieving "mastery of their own fate."[34]

From the time of the Russian Revolution to the mid-1920s, Randolph's and Owen's *Messenger* offered its subscribers (approximately 18,000 individuals) a great deal of discussion on Soviet developments, which were depicted in acclamatory terms. Typical of *The Messenger*'s coverage of

Russian matters was a July 1918 piece that described Bolshevism as the "foreword of a true world democracy . . . [which had given the Russian] peoples a new hope, a new promise, a new ideal—economic and political freedom!" According to the editors, the "Soviets represent the needs and aims of the masses."[35] The invasion of Russia by foreign troops at the end of the world war led *The Messenger* to demand that the invaders "Get Out of Russia!"[36] It would be "the blackest of all international crimes in the history of mankind if the world condones any 'black hand' movement to blackjack the Russian revolution by military occupation." Continuing in this vein, the socialist publication pointed to the worldwide spirit of reaction and claimed it was washing over the victorious countries. But dangers lay ahead, for western diplomats were walking upon the "crater of an international social volcano, whose molten lava of class passions threaten [*sic*] to drench the land in blood" and wash away the "dikes of our false civilization." In its place would arise a "new civilization, a new social order, a true international people's republic." Concluding this white-hot analysis, the editors claimed the Soviet Union was "the most significant experiment in the international laboratory of world politics . . . and economics. If allowed to pursue its natural course unhindered, the science of government will be immeasurably enriched by the legislative and administrative invention which shall emerge out of the process."[37]

The Messenger often placed Soviet developments in an explicitly racial context, as suggested by a 1919 essay, "Did Bolshevism Stop Race Riots in Russia?" by W. A. Domingo, a West Indian businessman, committed socialist, and frequent contributor to the magazine. According to Domingo, although it seemed a long way from "Alabama to Turkestan," the link between the two places was not as "nebulous" as it appeared. Indeed, Domingo wrote, there was "a great connection between the future of the Negro race . . . and the success of the theories—now under trial in Russia—which are collectively known as Bolshevism." Domingo compared the plight of black peoples in the United States, England, France, and elsewhere—all of whom were victims of economic, social, and political oppression—to that of the subject races of Czarist Russia, which had been "disfranchised, oppressed, and murdered." But the Czar's overthrow and the establishment of Bolshevism meant that Russia could now enjoy the "absolute equality of all the races." Domingo concluded with an unambiguous answer to his opening question: Soviet Russia is "a country from which the lynch rope is banished and in which racial tolerance and peace now exist." In Domingo's judgment, developments in Russia were meaningful to black America because Bolshevism might produce racial equality in the United States. One can easily imagine that Domingo's article (published during a summer of American racial violence), which asserted that Bolshevism could prevent "disgraceful occurrences" like the riots in

Washington and Chicago, would have resonated with many thousands of readers.[38]

Throughout this period, *The Messenger* painted a bright picture of Soviet life, claiming the nascent state had realized social equality and an end to racial oppression, which of course made Soviet society enormously appealing. But the Soviet Union was not merely an object of fascination; more significantly, *The Messenger* asserted that the Bolshevik achievement could serve as a guide to action for those determined to achieve political and social change.[39] Thus, from the magazine's founding until the mid-1920s, when it became more popular and less overtly political, the editors used the Soviet experience to advance their domestic economic and social agenda.[40] Moreover, the editors looked enthusiastically to the worldwide influence of Bolshevism, declaring in an editorial typical of many *The Messenger* published, that the Soviet government "bids fair to sweep over the whole world. The sooner the better. On with the dance!"[41]

While figures like Du Bois, Randolph, and Pickens were not prepared to embrace Bolshevism completely, each was drawn to Soviet affairs and published reports and firsthand accounts chronicling Russian life, which provided thousands of readers with a distinctive understanding of Soviet developments.[42] But what made Russia so intriguing? Why did Du Bois expose his audience to such material, and why was William Pickens determined to share his Soviet experience with his readers? *The Messenger*'s coverage raises similar questions. The race activists who traveled to the Soviet Union in the 1920s and the periodicals that covered Soviet affairs described the transformation of a land and its people. Among the many developments the reformers observed, the most impressive was the character of Russian social relations. Both the travelers and the reform monthlies contended that Russia had overcome the oppression of the downtrodden and supplanted it with complete social equality. As Pickens observed, there was no "kow-towing" to superiors in Soviet Russia; the Russians scorned such deference. To the race reformers, unlike other Americans who pondered the Soviet experiment in the 1920s, the character of Soviet race relations was enormously important. While some intellectuals were concerned with Soviet political and social life, and labor leaders considered the plight of Soviet workers, American race leaders made racial equality the central element in their developing perception of the Soviet state. The experiences of Pickens, Du Bois, and McKay, along with other material published in the reform monthlies, hammered home the notion that racial practices in the Soviet Union were fundamentally different from those in the United States. Blacks were treated with unfailing courtesy, and their opinions and talents were recognized—as was their humanity. The chasm separating the reformers' descriptions of Soviet racial practices from racial practices in 1920s America is as striking today as it must have seemed at the time, and the thousands who learned of this new society surely noted the difference. No lynch ropes dangled from the trees in Soviet Russia.

For race leaders, the Soviet Union demonstrated the possibility of creating a society in which social relations rested not on oppression, but on justice and equality. To build a land without racism no longer seemed a utopian dream; Russia proved it was possible. What the reformers were seeking in America, a society based on social and political equality, had been realized in the Soviet Union—or so they imagined. And they held it aloft, believing it to be a society that had attained the goals they so ardently desired. In considering developments in the Soviet Union, the reformers were reacting less to conditions in Russia than to conditions in the United States. Their perceptions of this emergent society vitalized the dreams they harbored for America, and their desire to realize such dreams explains their keen interest in Russian affairs.[43] In their glowing accounts of Soviet life—the essays, editorials, columns, and speeches—American race reform leaders sought to inspire their supporters and perhaps to enlist new ones.

Before considering other overseas matters, I shall touch briefly on some key domestic developments in the 1920s. The postwar decade was not one in which the reform impulse thrived in America; indeed, as one historian writes, reform was "a low-priority item" at this time.[44] The slow rate of progress notwithstanding, the 1920s saw African Americans continue their historic move northward and into the nation's cities. Between seven hundred and fifty thousand and one million blacks left the South during the decade, and while the southern black population increased by a mere 5 percent in these years, the northern population increased by 63 percent. In 1910, just over a quarter of the black population had resided in cities; by 1920, the proportion was a third; and by decade's end, more than 40 percent of blacks were urbanized, while in the North, nearly 90 percent of blacks lived in cities.[45]

On a different plane, the 1920s witnessed a remarkable cultural flowering, the Harlem Renaissance, in which literary, artistic, and musical life blossomed in ways that would have been impossible to imagine ten or fifteen years before. As Arnold Rampersad has observed, the Harlem Renaissance was significant partly because it "succeeded in laying the foundations for all subsequent depictions in poetry, fiction, and drama of the modern African-American experience." The center of this glorious explosion was Harlem, which James Weldon Johnson described as the "great Mecca for the sight-seer, the pleasure-seeker, the curious, the adventurous, the enterprising, the ambitious and the talented of the whole Negro world." Calling the northern part of Manhattan a "large scale laboratory experiment in the race problem," Johnson suggested that developments there might allow black Americans to build a better life throughout the country. Indeed, several important race reformers, including Johnson, were integral to the Harlem Renaissance and the New Negro movement with which it was entwined. By contributing to a developing sense of black identity, the renaissance was a critical part of the struggle for racial justice between the wars.[46]

A few miles south of Harlem, at 70 Fifth Avenue, stood the offices of the NAACP, which emerged from the war as the leading race reform organization in the country and continued to work for improvements in housing, education, and employment. Most significantly, the association labored tirelessly for passage of federal anti-lynching legislation, which remained its primary aim. While this legislative initiative would not succeed, the number of lynchings did decline markedly over the course of the decade, a fact that was partly attributable to the NAACP's lobbying efforts on behalf of the anti-lynching bill.[47] With greater success, the NAACP also pursued its objectives in the nation's courts, and the 1920s saw some notable legal victories. The first was the 1923 decision in *Moore v. Dempsey*, in which the Supreme Court ruled against mob influence in an Arkansas courtroom. In a sham trial, an Arkansas jury had sentenced six black farmers to die and sixty-seven others to long prison terms, charging them with violence that in 1919 had led to the deaths of several white men. (In essence, a white mob had determined the verdict, declaring that without convictions, lynchings would ensue.) With the NAACP's assistance, all the black defendants were eventually freed. And in one of the decade's most celebrated legal battles, the association became involved in the trial of black physician Dr. Ossian Sweet of Detroit. In 1925, Sweet, along with several family members and friends, was unjustly charged with murder after white mobs had violently tried to prevent him and his family from living in the house he had purchased. The NAACP enlisted the services of Clarence Darrow, the nation's most famous trial lawyer, to represent Sweet. The first trial ended in a deadlocked jury, and in 1926, Darrow won the acquittal of Sweet's brother, Henry, in the lone retrial that occurred.[48]

Yet even as they focused on such critical activities, a number of global developments continued to engage the reformers, who were especially drawn to reflect on the plight of the oppressed in the colonial world. India generated considerable interest among race activists during the twenties, and Du Bois's *Crisis* pondered Mohandas Gandhi's struggle against British rule. It is impossible to read the journal from these years without recognizing the editor's profound respect for Gandhi and his efforts on the subcontinent.[49] Consistent with the tenets of color-conscious internationalism, Du Bois discussed the parallels between the Indian and African-American freedom struggles, and joined the fates of Indians and black

Americans, identifying an "imagined community" between the two peoples. Conveying to his readers the interconnectedness between the respective crusades—and setting the quest for racial justice in the United States in the context of a worldwide struggle—Du Bois hoped to vitalize those committed to American race reform.[50] Indeed, Du Bois was not alone in forging a link that would achieve considerable significance for the movement in later years, and as early as the 1920s, leading reformers had begun to consider whether Gandhian principles were applicable in America.[51]

Responding to a fellow editor overseas who had asked him to contribute to his Hindi publication, Du Bois penned a revealing message to the Indian people in 1925. While directed at an Indian audience, the words were quintessentially Du Boisian in evoking the brotherhood of the oppressed:

> Twelve million Americans of Negro descent, grandchildren and great grandchildren of Africans, forcibly stolen and brought to America, are fighting here in the United States a spiritual battle for freedom, citizenship and the right to be themselves both in color of skin and manner of thought. This is the same terrible battle of the color bar which our brothers in India are fighting. We stretch out . . . hands of fellowship and understanding across the world and ask for your sympathy in our difficulties just as you in your strife for a new country and a new freedom have the good wishes of every Negro in America.[52]

Determined to inform his American readers about Indian developments, Du Bois published several issues of *The Crisis* in 1921 that included material on colonial oppression in India and Gandhi's efforts to liberate his people. Du Bois reprinted "An Open Letter from Gandhi," in which the Indian had spoken directly to the British people, detailing his plans and objectives. Because the English had made the Indians powerless to "wrest the sceptre" from British hands, Gandhi's goal was to evoke the "bravery of the soul" of his people.[53] The following year, *Crisis* subscribers encountered a lengthy biographical study of Gandhi, which claimed he was among "the great men of the world," who would achieve "a permanent niche in the repository of the benefactors of mankind." Readers were likely moved by the story of Gandhi's long-oppressed country, which depicted the virtuous Indian leading mankind toward the "promised land." Significantly, America's foremost race reform journal discussed the idea of passive resistance, claiming that it "kills without striking its adversary . . . and disarms its enemies." In encountering Gandhi, *Crisis* readers met a saintly figure, whose advocacy of peaceful resistance might help liberate the downtrodden.[54]

Although a later generation of reformers would ruminate on the suitability of Gandhi's methods for the African-American struggle, as early as 1924, the young sociologist E. Franklin Frazier considered the potential utility of "non-resistance" in America. A few might be able to love their oppressors, Frazier argued in the pages of *The Crisis*, but for most such an attitude would yield little. The vast majority would respond to their "enforced inferior status" with sentiments of accommodation or hatred. And for Frazier, hatred, not love, could serve as "a positive moral force" because it might forestall accommodation, which had stifled black progress. Love was "irrelevant" to the problem of racial oppression in the United States, Frazier claimed. The "Negro does not want love. He wants justice." Someday, love might be a useful principle upon which to base social relations, but in contemporary America, he contended, "we prefer to fight for the observance of the established principles of democratic political society."[55]

The young sociologist had not referred explicitly to Gandhi or his methods in the March 1924 article, but three months later, when the subject of "non-resistance" reemerged, the Indian's name appeared. According to Du Bois, one or two readers had written to protest the March piece, and he had decided to publish the sociologist's unambiguous rejoinder. In his rebuttal, Frazier noted that as a resident of the South, he had to "breathe in daily the stench of race prejudice." His primary goal was to save "the Negro's self-respect," and if this could be done without hatred—which he doubted—so much the better. But Frazier believed it would be preferable for "the Negro's soul to be seared with hate than dwarfed by self-abasement." What would occur if a Gandhi arose "to lead Negroes without hate in their hearts" to stop tilling the fields, to cease paying taxes that kept "their children in ignorance," and to ignore disfranchisement and Jim Crow? "[W]e would witness an unprecedented massacre of defenseless black men and women . . . and there would scarcely be enough Christian sentiment in America to stay the flow of blood."[56] In repudiating Gandhian precepts, Frazier's piece did not conform to the typical pattern of writings on Gandhi that Du Bois and others regularly published in this period. Here the notion of human brotherhood and shared struggle was rejected, and Gandhi's approach was described as ill-suited for America. Nevertheless, as early as the 1920s, such debates had entered the stream of discussion within the reform community. What is both intriguing and puzzling is the fact that Du Bois authored a supportive introductory paragraph to Frazier's effort, calling the young academic's perspective "eminently clear and sound." This was surely a peculiar opinion for the editor to express, given Frazier's rejection of the message of Gandhi, a figure whom Du Bois regularly sanctified.

Whatever his attitude toward Frazier's view, Du Bois clearly revered the Indian leader. Early in 1929, Du Bois wrote to the Mahatma, identifying himself as the editor of a small magazine that circulated among "educated

Negroes," and asked the Indian if he would send a message to "twelve million Negroes who are the grandchildren of slaves, and who [despite?] difficulties are forging forward in America." The editor was understanding, writing, "I know how busy you are with your own problems, but the race and color problems are world-wide, and we need your help here." Some two months later Gandhi responded: "I was delighted to receive your letter. . . . It is useless for me even to attempt to send you an article for your magazine. I therefore send you herewith a little love message." Gandhi's "little love message," which was boldly announced on the cover of the July 1929 issue, was published along with a biographical sketch (no doubt by Du Bois) that described the Indian as "the greatest colored man in the world, and perhaps the greatest man in the world." The message, "To the American Negro," read:

> Let not the twelve million Negroes be ashamed of the fact that they are the grandchildren of slaves. There is no dishonour in being slaves. There is dishonour in being slave-owners. But let us not think of honour or dishonour in connection with the past. Let us realise that the future is with those who would be truthful, pure, and loving. . . . Love alone binds and truth and love accrue only to the truly humble.[57]

However puzzling the contradiction between Du Bois's apparent support for Frazier's views and his triumphant publication of the Mahatma's words, the editor repeatedly told thousands of *Crisis* readers of Gandhi's greatness, wedding the freedom struggles waged in India and in the United States.

Nor was *The Crisis* the only place in which black America could learn about India in the 1920s. While *The Messenger* did not devote nearly as much attention to the subcontinent as did the NAACP's organ, it did print opinion pieces condemning British imperialism in India, one of which compared the Indian revolt to that waged by the Americans in 1776. The socialist monthly declared that Americans ought to encourage the Indian uprising. All "sincere, honest, liberty-loving people" should help create "a free and independent India."[58] Among a number of *Messenger* pieces on India, one examined Gandhi's tactic of nonviolent resistance, while another linked American race reform and the Indian struggle. The "keen-minded Negro recognize[d] his own exploiter in the exploiter of the Hindu," and could not watch the Indians' quest with indifference, but sought the chance to aid the Indian masses.[59]

Marcus Garvey, who attracted hundreds of thousands of black Americans to his organization, the Universal Negro Improvement Association, was another observer of Indian developments in the postwar decade. Preaching a message of black pride that rejected the notion that blackness was a badge of inferiority, Garvey, in John Hope Franklin's words, "exalted everything black" and "insisted that black stood for strength and beauty." Black Americans should take pride in their African heritage, asserted the Jamaica-born leader, and he questioned whether white America would ever allow blacks to attain equal status in the United States. Consequently, Garvey's program aimed to effect the return of the African-American population to its ancestral continent. While the plan was a practical impossibility, Garvey and his followers were significant, Franklin writes, because they represented the first mass movement among black Americans and highlighted black doubts about the prospect for achieving "first-class citizenship in the only homeland they knew." While Garvey represents a different aspect of the African-American protest tradition from others in this study—his declared aim was to abandon not to reform America—a look at his reaction to Indian affairs is worth a short detour.[60]

During the years of his popularity in the United States, Garvey spoke often about Indian developments and commented on Gandhi's activities, drawing analogies between the Indian struggle and that of his own people. Despite Garvey's ardent nationalism, he talked repeatedly about a worldwide movement in which millions were striving to liberate themselves from tyranny, whether in Ireland, Egypt, the West Indies, or America. As Sudarshan Kapur has observed, Garvey believed strongly in the "communality of the struggle of oppressed people everywhere," and the Indian example served as an important model that he set before his followers.[61] In letters to Gandhi and in speeches throughout the United States, the black nationalist leader expressed his support and that of his followers for the Indian's efforts. In 1921, Garvey asked Gandhi to accept the "best wishes of 400,000,000 Negroes through us their representatives, for the speedy emancipation of India from the thraldom of foreign oppression. You may depend on us for whatsoever help we can give." And later he urged the Mahatma to "[f]ight on for the freedom of your people and country," assuring him that "[w]e are with you."[62] Direct communication with Gandhi was of course less frequent than were Garvey's repeated public references to Indian affairs. Upon Gandhi's arrest early in 1922, Garvey spoke to a New York crowd about the Indian's greatness, identifying a bond between the cause of India and the cause of black peoples throughout the world. Gandhi was "one of the noblest characters of the day," Garvey said, and his arrest was not unexpected; it was "customary for [the British] to execute and imprison the leaders of the cause of liberty." Associating himself and his own cause with the Indian struggle, Garvey claimed he was "in deep sympathy with Gandhi and with the new movement in India" and pledged "the support of all Negroes of the world . . . to the cause of India's freedom." Indeed,

"400,000,000 Negroes . . . are prepared to stand behind 380,000,000 Indians to see that they get their freedom."[63]

Throughout the 1920s, the race reformers kept a watchful eye on Gandhi's heroic leadership. From their vantage point, the Indian example possessed both inspirational and instructive value—inspirational because the notion that hundreds of millions of Indians were battling against white rule suggested to black Americans that they were not alone in their crusade for change, and instructive because it was reasonable to imagine that Gandhi's method of passive resistance might illuminate the path to black liberation in the United States. Whether American reformers could (or should) replicate the Mahatma's methods for liberating his country was an intriguing question for race activists in these years, and in subsequent decades, it would become an important subject of debate among members of the reform community.[64]

The gaze of the reformers was not confined to India, Russia, or the notion of world peace, for a host of overseas developments captured the race activists' attention. As has been suggested, an examination of the reform periodicals demonstrates the reform community's capacious interest in the world throughout this period, which leads one to ponder why the editors thought it was worth exposing their readers to such a broad array of topics. In bringing the outside world home to their readers, the editors imagined themselves to be part of a global community of reform leaders and viewed the domestic movement as part of a worldwide phenomenon, a conviction they hoped to nurture among their subscribers. If those who picked up a copy of *The Crisis* in a friend's home in a southern town or flipped through *Opportunity* at a barbershop in black Chicago might never have the chance to venture much beyond their rural county or urban neighborhood, perhaps they would understand that in their commitment to the cause of racial justice and their hope for a better life, they were bound to a group of determined people across the globe. Or equally important, perhaps they would recognize that American-style racial oppression was not universal.

While *Opportunity* focused mainly on domestic matters and claimed to approach the race problem scientifically, its foreign coverage indicates that the journal's staff recognized that discussing overseas developments might help advance the reform agenda. A 1928 editorial on the black liberation struggle in South Africa identified the blood ties between black South Africans and black Americans and pointed to the fundamental similarity between the race problem in Africa and in the United States. In discussing the "courage and patience" of South African race activists, the editors contended that the status of black Americans differed "in degree rather than in kind" from that faced by black Africans. Significantly, the editors observed that advances in communication and transportation were drawing peoples "closer together," which would mean that the "world aspect of the Negro problem" would demand increasing attention. Finally, readers were asked to consider the idea that their aspirations were shared by peoples of color overseas with whom they had "much in common."[65]

Superbly exemplifying the internationalization of the race question was Alain Locke's "Black Watch on the Rhine," which *Opportunity* published in 1924. In graceful prose, Locke (who would shortly edit *The New Negro*, the seminal text of the Harlem Renaissance) described his overseas travels, drawing explicit and implicit comparisons between the treatment of blacks on both sides of the Atlantic. Considering the responsibilities of black French colonial troops stationed in Germany, Locke noted that they endured no discrimination in their assigned tasks as an occupying force. He examined their conduct, which had become the subject of scurrilous German charges of widespread transgressions, and insisted that their behavior belied such allegations. Their deportment had been exemplary. Beyond providing his readers with the reflections of a highly literate man on the intercultural contact created by the foreign occupation of Germany, Locke recounted his moving conversation with the black colonial troops. Deeply interested in America, the soldiers queried Locke and his party about race relations in the United States, inquiries Locke described as either "very naive or very profound." Confessing his shame, Locke noted their questions were "not answerable." "Why do you stand for it?" they wondered. Perhaps black Americans could become Frenchmen, a choice the soldiers suggested would mean fair treatment. Dismayed and "confounded," Locke could not respond satisfactorily to the questions posed by the colonial warriors.

One can only speculate as to how readers understood such an article and note that its character, if not its precise subject, was similar to many published in the reform journals during the period. The feelings of equality expressed by French colonial troops must have proved striking to *Opportunity*'s black readers, who would have recalled the oppressive experience of the African-American soldier in the recent world war. "Whoever is willing to die for France is no foreigner," the colonial soldiers told Locke, who wrote that they were part of France, "not only in arms but in all the basic human relationships." Locke's readers learned of fraternization between black and white soldiers: military service had taught them to be "naturally and humanly brothers in all the fundamental relations of life." *Opportunity*'s subscribers surely perceived the disjunction between the conditions endured by the black American soldier and those experienced by the dark-skinned colonial warrior, and, more generally, between race relations overseas and at home. When Locke questioned Frenchmen about the "unique spirit" of race relations in the

French military, he was met with puzzlement or a shrug. "Why shouldn't it be so?" Did not such sentiments sound profoundly enlightened to Locke's readers in Philadelphia or New York, to say nothing of Atlanta or Washington, D.C.? Locke's assertion that "prejudice must go at a sweep and not bit by bit," along with his observation that the "social logicality of the French mind ha[d] made a clean sweep of the whole field" served as a potent reminder that not all societies labored under the weight of American racial oppression. Locke's readers surely pondered the stark contrast between racial attitudes overseas and those at home. What Locke's experience demonstrated was that alternatives existed to the American system of institutionalized persecution.[66]

As had been true since the war, *The Messenger* devoted a significant amount of space to foreign affairs in the 1920s, and Randolph and Owen were particularly interested in the colonial world. Since its first wartime issues, the journal had propounded a view of international politics that divided the world into the exploiters and the exploited, and after the war, the magazine continued in this vein, analyzing global affairs according to a Leninist formulation.[67] Month after month, *The Messenger* exposed readers to the notion that Britain, France, the United States, Germany, and other western powers were systematically exploiting Asia, Africa, and parts of the western hemisphere, wringing from millions of unfortunate peoples every drop of profit they could. In addition to the stridently materialist tone of its international coverage, *The Messenger* also approached racial questions in a manner that went beyond a strict Leninist analysis of world politics.[68]

In the postwar decade, the magazine's editors were especially interested in Asian and African developments, their assessment of which referred consistently to a long history of western exploitation, a condition the editors believed was waning. At the same time, a racial message was sometimes embedded in *The Messenger*'s analysis, which undoubtedly resonated with black readers. Several 1927 pieces on Chinese independence, for example, demonstrate how the journal combined a materialist and a race-centered analysis of international politics, which highlighted the emerging racial self-awareness of the Chinese. The editors called China "an outstanding actress," in the global drama, which was fighting "the age-old obstacle of foreign oppression, western financial imperialism." As the Chinese chased out western imperial influence in order to build a new society, the editors identified the dawn of a new historical epoch, "the beginning of the end of the unchallenged control and supremacy of the white race over the darker races." Indeed, developments in China "sounded the death knell to the haughty, sinister and disastrous creed of Nordic supremacy" and signaled the "shifting of world control from the Atlantic to the Pacific, from the white to the darker peoples."[69] If this was a materialist analysis of world politics, it was idiosyncratic; nor was it an atypical example of *The Messenger*'s understanding of the world.[70]

In examining European matters, *The Messenger* often framed the subject in terms that would have resonated with black readers. Two travel pieces by J. A. Rogers recounted his recent experiences in England and France, which, not surprisingly, reflected poorly on American domestic life. In England, Rogers had never "met a single discourteous person," an experience so novel it made him uneasy. Accustomed to living among white Americans with their "coarse, crude, raw colonial manners," Rogers confessed it took him months to quiet his "combative instincts" and stop regarding Englishmen as his enemies because of their white skins. And across the Channel, he encountered French attitudes that surpassed those in England; indeed, the French treated blacks chivalrously. With no little irony, Rogers observed that because American democracy had made little headway in France, the black man was treated as an equal. And in assessing the stark difference between French and American racial attitudes, he shared a vision of a better life overseas—where enlightened Europeans treated blacks with dignity. By contrast, American racial attitudes seemed antediluvian, and Rogers advised his readers that distancing themselves from the United States was the only way to "realize what a horribly barbarous thing this American color prejudice is."[71]

One of the more interesting *Messenger* pieces to appear in this period was a 1927 editorial that evinced a key internationalist ideal—the notion that increased cultural exchange among educated people (whether intellectuals, artists, musicians, or students) could contribute to global cooperation. The editors contended, moreover, that contacts between black Americans and the world's peoples could ameliorate the race problem in the United States. Travel could expand one's outlook, they claimed, pointing to the delegations of social workers, students, educators, businessmen, and scientists that were journeying overseas to study a variety of subjects. Elaborating on this idea, *The Messenger* suggested that a black delegation animated by "the new economic, social, religious, educational and political viewpoints" could travel abroad to study all phases of international life, whether in Europe or Africa, in fascist Italy or Soviet Russia. The group would obtain a wealth of information about global developments and could also provide foreign peoples with "a true picture of . . . Negro [life, about which] Europeans and Asiatics are distressingly misinformed. . . . As the European intelligentsia come to tell us about Europe, let us go and tell them the truth about the Negro." By focusing world opinion on the race problem in America, *The Messenger* insisted, it would be possible to "successfully challenge our bigoted detractors."[72]

More than any reform publication, *The Crisis* overflowed with coverage of world affairs during the 1920s. By flipping through its pages, one
recognizes that Du Bois compelled his readers to fix their eyes upon a
world in which the campaign for racial justice at home was but one facet
of a global crusade against racial oppression.[73] And one did not have to
read about the determination of the Indian people or the dynamism of
Soviet society in order to perceive the international character of the
American struggle. Anyone thumbing through the journal might come
upon less grandiose but equally powerful prose describing the experiences of black men and women living abroad, which inevitably served to
highlight the nature of racial oppression in the United States. *Crisis* readers encountered the evocative language of poet Countee Cullen, whose
pieces conveyed the flavor of European life and the social acceptance a
gifted black artist experienced abroad. Who could not be touched by
the compelling ordinariness of Cullen's depiction of life overseas—a life
difficult to fathom in America?[74] One could also hear the voice of Idabelle
Yeiser, a young black woman who had journeyed to France to pursue
her studies, as she pondered French tolerance. With her student days in
Toulouse free of race prejudice, the young scholar told *Crisis* readers
there was no place where one could find "a greater democracy," for the
French nation was not ruled by the "petty question of color." And if it
became so, would that not be "a step backward in civilization rather
than a step forward?" she wondered.[75]

Of course, Africa was of profound importance to Du Bois, and
throughout the twenties, *The Crisis* reflected his determination to inform
readers about unfolding developments on that vast continent.[76] The
monthly covered the three Pan-African Congresses that convened during
the 1920s, gatherings at which Du Bois, an architect of the Pan-African
idea, played a key part. (As has been noted, the first Pan-African
Congress met in Paris in 1919 during the peace conference.)[77] Beyond
publishing the resolutions adopted at each conference, Du Bois regularly
conveyed the meaning and import of Pan-Africanism to *Crisis* readers.
He asserted that the challenges facing black America were inseparable
from the problems black peoples confronted throughout the world, a
notion he claimed was central to Pan-Africanism.[78] In 1923, he wondered
if a "local and personal problem [could] be settled without reference to
other folk and the rest of the world." While Du Bois acknowledged that
the Pan-African movement had accomplished nothing tangible, he would
not yield to pessimism. "[W]e have kept an idea alive . . . and some day
when unity and cooperation come, the importance of these early steps
will be recognized."[79]

Late in 1923, Du Bois visited his ancestral home, a journey he documented in the pages of the magazine with his customary brilliance. With

thousands of readers, he shared the story of his African journey, which the long-time traveler called his greatest adventure. His prose reaching heights worthy of the experience, Du Bois noted that his previous travels had been "painfully white," observing, "Today I am drifting toward darkness. . . . I set my face toward Africa—the Eternal World of Black Folk." But before reaching "this gate of the darkest world," Du Bois, like all great travel chroniclers, described the road leading to his long-awaited destination. And this allowed *Crisis* readers to hear not merely about the ancient glories of Europe, but about the way black men were treated in foreign lands. Floating down the Rhône with Du Bois, readers saw the "sweet and unseen beauty" of Provence; they viewed Carcassone "sitting like a tale that is told above the earth"; and they saw the "Pyrenees romp with heaven." The editor told his readers about an English conference on imperial matters where he saw "brown men" speak and white men listen to what they had to say. In Spain, his "brown face" attracted no attention. He was "simply a man." And this left him relieved, for he could forget himself and study others. Lisbon was kind. He conversed and offered a cigarette to a native gentleman, who commended its flavor. Their conversation over, the Portuguese raised his hat, bowed, and wished the American a good night. Du Bois reminded his readers that in New York the man "would have shouldered me warily and explained on the other side the ubiquity of 'damn niggers'!" But this was not America; here a black man was not the object of contempt.

Soon, Du Bois would set sail from Portugal, and when his feet "again touch[ed] earth—the earth will be Africa."[80]

I see Africa—Cape Mount in two low, pale semi-circles, so pale it looks a cloud. So my great great grandfather saw it two centuries ago. Clearer and clearer it rises . . . and melts dimly into the mist and sea and Cape Mount begins Liberia—what a citadel for the capital of Negrodom! When shall I forget the night I first set foot on African soil—I, the sixth generation in descent from my stolen forefathers.

Crisis readers followed him on his Liberian journey in December and January, reliving the diplomatic mission during which he met with Liberia's president as the American Envoy Extraordinary and Minister Plenipotentiary, the special representative of President Calvin Coolidge. Subscribers could ponder Du Bois's public statement linking the destinies of black Liberians and black Americans, in which he spoke of the "special and peculiar bonds" that drew together the two peoples. He pointed out that "eleven million persons of African descent" resided in America, all of whom were citizens, "legally invested with every right that inheres in American citizenship." Speaking on behalf of the American president, Du Bois observed that in "the great battle against color caste in America, the ability of Negroes to rule in Africa has been . . . a great and encouraging reinforcement." In parsing Du Bois's words to the Liberian president, *Crisis* readers might have recognized the subtle connection the editor made between the black experience in America and the achievements of the Liberian people. And Du Bois made sure to emphasize that in their quest for justice in the United States, black Americans drew sustenance from the continent of their ancestors.[81]

From Africa to Europe, from India to Russia, month after month, the reform journals exposed countless thousands to developments from around the world. It is hardly an exaggeration to suggest that there was no part of the globe that did not interest the reformers in the postwar decade. To their readers, they described noble efforts devoted to political and social reform—efforts that aimed to liberate Russians, Indians, and Africans from the historic forces that oppressed them. Even the strivings of the great powers to create a more pacific international order could be deployed by those laboring for racial justice in America. At the same time, the reformers exposed their supporters to a different sort of overseas story, which, if less grand, was no less meaningful: a young black woman's encounter with democracy in France; an African-American man of letters discussing the question of racial equality with French colonial troops. In the decade after the Great War, the race reformers presented such overseas tales and made them part of their campaign to build a better society. They explored a variety of subjects, from the heroic struggles of people seeking to overcome oppression to more intimate encounters with equality that blacks experienced in foreign lands. In so doing, reform leaders sought not only to inspire their followers to persist in their efforts, but also to demonstrate that racial oppression was not universal. At decade's end, none could claim the reformers had created the society they so ardently desired, and few could doubt that much work remained to be done. In the 1930s, as epochal developments erupted that would prove still more significant to their cause, the race activists would continue to look outside the United States to advance their program. In responding to the upheavals of the next ten years, the reformers would affect profoundly the movement's trajectory in ways impossible to foretell.

Four

"SOUNDS SUSPICIOUSLY LIKE MIAMI"
The Turbulent World of the 1930s

IN THE SUMMER OF 1931, W.E.B. Du Bois once again sought a word of encouragement from Mohandas Gandhi, which he hoped to publish on the twenty-first anniversary of the founding of *The Crisis*. "We are fighting a battle in some respects similar to that which the people of India are carrying on," he noted, and wondered if it would be possible "in the midst of [Gandhi's] strenuous labors" for him to send a short statement to the magazine. The editor assured Gandhi that it would "do much . . . to encourage the American Negro." Receiving no reply, Du Bois repeated his request, writing that black Americans were "tremendously interested at the effort of the Indian people to achieve independence and self-government."[1] As in the previous decade, the reformers maintained a strong interest in India's struggle against colonial rule, and they continued to look to developments on the subcontinent to inspire and instruct their followers. And in speeches, the black press, and other publications, race leaders continued to set Gandhi's struggle before their followers by comparing the persecution of Indians to the persecution of blacks in the United States. More broadly, as the international situation became increasingly unsettled during the 1930s, race reform leaders remained keenly interested in overseas affairs, relating developments in Ethiopia, Germany, and Spain to their domestic agenda.

The editors of *Opportunity* and *The Crisis*, in particular, brought the liberation struggles of colonial peoples into the homes of American readers, and throughout the thirties, the two journals served as windows onto developments in Africa, Asia, and India. As *Crisis* editor, Du Bois wrote not only to Gandhi, but also about him in the NAACP monthly and elsewhere. "[L]et the world sit and watch the most astonishing of the battles of peace which it has ever seen: The civil disobedience campaign in India, led by Gandhi and Nehru," Du Bois wrote in *The Crisis*.[2] The editor often wrote brief pieces comparing the plight of blacks and Indians, as in one offering that claimed the Indian revolution was "a mighty experiment" that the "black folk of America" ought to look upon with "reverence, hope, and applause."[3] Beyond his thousands of *Crisis* readers, many more encountered Du Bois's views on India in his column in New York's *Amsterdam News*. In 1931, Du Bois posed an obvious question, wondering

why one had to look "half-way round the world for problems" when
blacks faced "a winter of suffering and starvation" right here at home.
Articulating his deeply held view on the global character of the race problem, he observed that

> the plight of no colored people is unimportant for us. If we are going to make
> our way in this modern world, we must know what the world has been doing
> to other colored folk and how it has done it, and what they are doing to
> achieve freedom and manhood. In the long run, this comprehensive knowl-
> edge is of more importance than our own narrow, provincial problem . . .
> because our own problem depends upon the problems of the world for
> its solution.[4]

Among the many race activists who ruminated on Indian developments
in the 1930s, William Pickens compared the plight of the oppressed in
speeches and columns, telling a New York gathering in 1932 that black
America could do nothing "but sympathize with the people of India. The
Negro knows full well what it means to struggle for equal rights in opposition to entrenched snobbery and organized greed masquerading as superior culture and civilization." The following year, Pickens told a large
crowd in Carnegie Hall that the "imperialist exploitation of the people
of India and the domestic exploitation of the Negroes of Mississippi are
two evils of one breed." After highlighting the similarities between the
two situations, Pickens contended that all types of oppression—whether
of races, groups, or classes—were enough alike in their motives and consequences as to make it "imperative that the oppressed make common
cause" against their oppressors.[5]

As Sudarshan Kapur has shown, the black press played a key part in
conveying the importance of Gandhi's message to African Americans.[6]
Throughout the 1930s, millions of black readers encountered columns
and editorials in the press comparing the Indian and American campaigns,
which suggested that Gandhi's program of nonviolence could be effective
in the United States. In a Kelly Miller column, "Passive Resistance of
Gandhi," the distinguished scholar noted that the "position of the Hindu
under British dominion is much analogous to that of the Negro under
Anglo-Saxon dominion." Miller described both groups as "hopelessly
overpowered" and told his readers that Indian liberty was inevitable because there was "no human or heavenly sanction that will permit one race
or nation to hold another in perpetual subjugation on the bare difference
of race and color." Concluding, Miller wrote that the "American Negro
can learn valuable lessons from Mahatma Gandhi."[7] The reformers thus
emphasized both the educational and the inspirational value of Gandhi's
efforts and compelled black Americans to keep their eyes fixed on the
transformative events unfolding in the developing world.

While the Indian drama engaged the movement's leaders, a more explo-
sive overseas development at mid-decade would capture the attention of
the reformers and much of black America. In the autumn of 1935, the
forces of Italian dictator Benito Mussolini invaded the African state of
Ethiopia in pursuit of his grand program, which aimed to recapture the
glory of the Roman Empire. The fascist dictator hoped the decision for
war would redeem the humiliating defeat Italy had suffered there in 1896
and, more significantly, provide this unlikely Caesar with an African colony. The diplomatic wrangling that preceded and followed the invasion
and the factors that explain Italy's decision to wage war have been considered elsewhere.[8] More pertinent here is the response of America's race
reformers, who were distressed by the invasion of Ethiopia, one of the
few places in the world where black peoples governed themselves. Beyond
the reform community, average black citizens were also moved by Ethiopian developments, a point made by black journalist George Schuyler,
who observed that in "the most remote parts of rural Mississippi I have
found the colored people intensely interested in the present struggle and
burning to do their little bit to aid the largest remaining independent colored nation in the world."[9]

In the months before the Italian invasion and for some two years afterward, movement leaders made the subject central to their reflections on
world affairs, drawing parallels between the Italian military campaign
and the oppression of black Americans. Representing the NAACP, Secretary Walter White was especially drawn to the Ethiopian question, communicating not only with the movement's supporters, but also with U.S.
government officials and even Ethiopian Emperor Haile Selassie in a determined effort to assist the cause. By the time of the Ethiopian crisis,
White had been a key figure in the NAACP for more than fifteen years,
becoming its secretary in 1931. A light-skinned, blue-eyed person of color,
White, who was born in Atlanta in 1893, came from a comfortable family
in which achievement was encouraged and expected. In 1917, White, a
graduate of Atlanta University, began working for the NAACP's branch
in his hometown, and after an encounter with James Weldon Johnson, he
was invited to join the organization's national staff in New York. Putting
aside a touch of uncertainty about whether to devote his life to the cause,
White headed to New York in early 1918, where he quickly became an
important figure in the NAACP. In his early labors for the association, he
was adept at investigating white violence against black citizens, because
his appearance, which led people to assume he was white, allowed him
to work and travel freely in the Jim Crow South. As White's organizational power and influence expanded, he became one of the country's
leading spokespersons on behalf of race reform. And for some thirty-five
years—through the upheavals of the Depression decade, the global crisis

of World War II, and the uncertainties of the post-1945 era—White was a central figure in the struggle. Moreover, White, who was known as "Mr. NAACP," was profoundly interested in world affairs, which helped the association maintain its international orientation.[10]

In April and May 1935, with the Italian threat to Ethiopia increasing, White wrote to Secretary of State Cordell Hull, expressing the organization's concern about developments in Abyssinia (the name was used interchangeably with Ethiopia). White suggested that the United States government should do what it could to support the African country's continued existence, asserting that American action might help "avert a bloody and disastrous war." A few weeks later, in late May, White sent a letter to Haile Selassie, communicating the "profound interest" black and white Americans had in Ethiopia's resistance to Italian aggression and assuring the African leader that the NAACP would do everything it could "in defense of Ethiopia's sovereignty and freedom from invasion."[11] The next month, in resolutions passed at its annual conference, the association condemned Italy's behavior, along with the "imperialist selfishness of all nations," and urged the United States to oppose this sort of international aggression.[12]

Throughout 1935, before the autumn invasion, *The Crisis* published a wealth of material on Ethiopia. For the most part, these pieces, bearing titles like "Last Gobble of Africa" and "The Missionary Racket in Africa," sketched the historical background of Abyssinia and contended that developments there epitomized the machinations of European imperialism. *Crisis* readers learned that in stalking its African prey, Italy was behaving precisely as had those other perennial victimizers of the world's less-developed regions, Britain and France. A February 1935 editorial described "the grim chess game being played by the nations of Europe," in which Ethiopia might well be the victim of a cold-blooded sacrifice. No one knew what "the oily European diplomats really have up their sleeves," but "American Negroes [were] watching developments with deep interest." Another piece called for African Americans to aid the Ethiopian cause, claiming it was necessary to exert "concerted pressure on our government to use every effort to prevent an attack." Moreover, black America should help Ethiopia by providing trained economists, engineers, and educators, whose expert aid could be followed by machinery and technical help that would lend concrete assistance to the African kingdom.[13]

In October 1935, the month of the invasion, Du Bois published a lengthy essay in *Foreign Affairs*, the quarterly of the Council on Foreign Relations, which explored the global significance of the Ethiopian crisis. As he did so often, Du Bois interwove several analytical threads—historical, religious, sociological, and economic—which aimed to reveal what he described as the "inter-racial implications" of the crisis. More striking than his prediction that Italy would "subdue" Ethiopia (due to European complacency and Italian military superiority) was his emphasis on the impact the struggle would have on peoples of color. Du Bois contended that the unavoidable defeat of the African state would not lead the "whole colored world—India, China and Japan . . . Africa and America, and all the South Seas and Indian South America" to recognize its weakness; instead, it would "point the path to strength." The Italian aggression would fortify the conviction among peoples of color that their common plight demanded a unified effort to overcome the oppressive reign of the white world. Thus, in one of the country's most distinguished forums for the discussion of traditional internationalism, Du Bois propounded an internationalism of a different kind.[14]

Before the invasion, economist Charles H. Wesley considered the subject in *Opportunity*, telling readers it illustrated a well-worn historical phenomenon, "the conquest and exploitation of a submerged darker race" by the dominant white race, something "colored Americans" had seen before. Blending historical description with political and economic analysis, Wesley observed that Italy's conquest of Ethiopia, through direct military occupation or indirect economic exploitation, would adversely affect world peace and the progress of international race relations. A few months later, the journal's editors focused on Ethiopian leader Haile Selassie's fighting slogan, "Die Free," noting that Europe's imperial states feared that such a credo could spread throughout the continent, awakening "Africa's already restless millions." The editors claimed, moreover, that Ethiopia had become the "spiritual fatherland of Negroes throughout the world," including America, and suggested that an Italian invasion might create the "unity of colored races" that "the prophets of Nordic supremacy" had long dreaded.[15]

For peoples of color, the meaning of Ethiopia was perhaps best captured by poet Langston Hughes, whose "Call of Ethiopia" appeared in *Opportunity* just before the Italian invasion. In establishing the resonance of the Ethiopian struggle for all black peoples and contending that freedom was their foremost concern, the poem illustrates why Ethiopia mattered to black America. It was a cause, Hughes claimed, for which black peoples might risk their lives.

> ETHIOPIA,
> Lift your night-dark face,
> Abyssinian
> Son of Sheba's race!
> Your palm trees tall
> And your mountains high

> Are shade and shelter
> To men who die
> For freedom's sake—
> But in the wake of your sacrifice
> May all Africa arise
> With blazing eyes and night-dark face
> In answer to the call of Sheba's race:
>
>> Ethiopia's free!
>> Be like me,
>> All of Africa,
>> Arise and be free!
>> All you black peoples,
>> Be free! Be free![16]

On October 3, 1935, one hundred thousand Italian troops, bearing modern weapons and equipment, crossed the Mareb River and advanced into Ethiopian territory. Early reports of the attack, which were transmitted around the world, indicated that the Italians, though confronted by a determined if poorly armed Ethiopian defensive force, had established a foothold in the northern part of the country. All humanity was interested in the outcome, proclaimed the *Pittsburgh Courier,* for the conflict might signal "the beginning of the end of white world domination," while the *Chicago Defender* published a poem to Ethiopian leader Haile Selassie, which invoked the historical experience of American slavery in order to rally the gallant Africans:

> . . . O'er those who now seek to rule you,
>   And make of you their slaves,
> May you be triumphant,
> And victorious banners wave;
> Let it not be like our Southland,
>   Whose slaves were shackled and
>   chained,
> God made all men equal,
> Why take lives for greed and gain.[17]

Shortly after the invasion began, the Ethiopian leader appealed to the American people for assistance, declaring a need for doctors, male nurses, medical supplies, and equipment. According to one black paper, talk would not help the Ethiopians, nor would harassing Italian shopkeepers in black neighborhoods. Instead, funds for medical assistance raised by agencies like the Committee for Ethiopia could help the wounded and gassed black soldiers who were defending their native soil. With this in mind, William Pickens criticized black America for not doing enough, pointing to a mass rally in Harlem that demonstrated a willingness to talk but a reluctance to come up with the money needed for "powder and planes." After making his plea for black assistance to the Ethiopian cause, Pickens shifted gears and linked a commitment to overseas matters to affairs at home. Concerning the question of "fighting for our own cause," he remarked that black financial support for domestic reform initiatives like the anti-lynching bill was similarly deficient. In the reformer's words, when it came to domestic and overseas affairs, "a little DEED is worth a whole car-load of hot air."[18]

From October 1935 until the following May, when the Ethiopian military position became untenable, forcing Haile Selassie to flee his country, the movement's leading journals examined the importance of developments in the African state.[19] In the face of a determined Italian aggressor, Opportunity and The Crisis emphasized the themes of imperial aggrandizement and the impotence and unwillingness of the League of Nations—an institution in which the reformers had once placed considerable faith—to respond effectively to the invasion. In the fall of 1935 (shortly before the invasion), Opportunity had doubted whether the League would have the "moral courage" to act, noting that if it failed to do so, it would forfeit the "confidence of the small nations of the world" and cause many to question its usefulness as a mechanism for protecting the weak.[20] Once the Italians had launched their attack, the condemnation of the League increased considerably, as the reform journals appeared to lose faith in the organization. Opportunity declared the League to be "practically useless" and contended that in the future it would likely become an "international debating society or a showy advisory body." Lamenting the earlier hopes of those who had believed in the power of such organizations, the editors noted that the peace lovers would have to seek "new methods to attain their goal of a warless world." The Crisis was similarly disillusioned by the failure of an organization in which it had once reposed enormous trust. A lengthy essay published in the fall of 1936 observed that the need for "some legal means to settle international disputes" had become clear. In an impressive theoretical and historical treatment of the subject, the author suggested that by creating an effective league—one "properly organized with adequate means to enforce its decisions"—it would be possible to build a more stable international order. But until that was achieved, the world would have to face "the shame and humiliation of allowing the strong to browbeat the weak." In the estimation of at least one analyst, therefore, the ideal and the potential efficacy of collective security was not at issue; what was needed was the creation of a more effective mechanism for preserving the rights and safety of the world's weaker states.[21] The race reform community's commitment to transnational institutions, while shaken by the Ethiopian disaster, would not dissipate completely, though it would not reappear for some ten years.

In light of the League's failure to act, *Opportunity* and *The Crisis* both noted the helplessness of black Ethiopia in its clash with the white imperial oppressor, a notion that surely resonated with countless readers. A January 1936 article in *Opportunity*, titled "R.I.P. Ethiopia," observed that events there were "nothing new under the African sun," but represented the "same old game of carving up a helpless continent." Readers learned of a weak, nonwhite land "in a world of strong white nations" that would pay the price in the ongoing campaign, which aimed to reduce Africa to servitude. Concluding sardonically, the article noted that, one way or another, "Ethiopia is to be civilized."[22] *The Crisis* echoed this idea in an editorial on the civilizing mission of the Italians, whose huge bombers rained "destruction from the skies," while armored tanks spit "death from machine guns." American readers confronted the image of the "Great White Fathers" laying waste the land of the "civilian heathen," with the "civilized plagues of gas bombs and chemicals" that could burn "the bare feet of the natives."[23] Beyond numerous pieces on the League's fecklessness and Italy's imperial rapacity, one especially affecting *Crisis* offering characterized Haile Selassie as a "modern King Arthur" and noted that in ancient times the "great lords from Rome" had strode into the medieval king's banquet, and, like today, demanded tribute. Their request refused, "those great lords / Drew back in wrath, and Arthur strove with Rome." Shifting to biblical imagery, the writer refused to believe that God would allow the enemy to succeed, but contended that if He did, everyone would recognize that He had sacrificed the liberty of ten million Ethiopians so that "hundreds of millions of His dark sons" might "nourish a common sympathy" that would "burst the bonds of race prejudice" and so take their "rightful . . . places in the sun."[24]

Throughout the war, the NAACP worked to advance the Ethiopian cause, speaking vigorously against Italy's actions and organizing demonstrations on behalf of the African state. An association press release issued shortly after the invasion expressed concern about the possibility of a world war, declaring that Italy had "brazenly set fire under the powder keg of white arrogance and greed which seems destined to become an act of suicide for the so-called white world."[25] The organization was also active in the heated debate over neutrality legislation in the United States, which could affect Italy's ability to obtain war matériel.[26] With the Italian conquest of Ethiopia, the NAACP worked energetically to prevent American recognition of Italy's sovereignty over the vanquished country, a position sustained by Franklin Roosevelt, who withheld formal recognition of foreign rule over the once-independent land.[27]

Throughout black America—whether among reform leaders or average black citizens, in the black press or the reform journals—countless thousands were drawn to Ethiopian affairs and stood determined to help the African nation against the kind of international violence many believed the Europeans had long visited on people of color. Moreover, for those who pondered the Italo-Ethiopian conflict, the persecution of Ethiopians and the persecution of black Americans were intertwined. As Walter White told a huge crowd a few days before the invasion, the Italian threat had compelled the world's people of color to realize that the "arrogance of white nations and their conscienceless exploitation of colored races" had to be stopped. Few white people realized how deeply this was "imbedded in the consciousness . . . of American Negroes," he contended. With the conquest of Ethiopia at an end, the *Pittsburgh Courier* declared, "There is nothing we can do about fascism in Italy, but there is a great deal we can do about Fascism in America," and as the race activists constructed their reform message in this dramatic period, they made the two stories practically indistinguishable.[28]

A discussion of race reform in the 1930s cannot neglect a brief consideration of domestic matters, for in the age of Franklin Roosevelt, the movement witnessed developments of great significance. The economic depression of the 1930s hit black America harder than any other group, and blacks in the rural South, who represented more than half the country's African-American population, were hit worst of all. With the price of cotton dropping dramatically, millions of black farmers were ruined, and lacking relief programs, many headed to the South's growing cities, where life was but marginally better. Stiff competition from an economically beleaguered white population, along with unyielding discrimination, dampened employment opportunities for these transplanted black farmers, and what meager urban relief programs there were in the South discriminated unhesitatingly against blacks.[29] Outside the South, where more than two million blacks lived in 1930, the employment situation was poor. Close to 50 percent were out of work in Harlem; black unemployment exceeded 55 percent in Philadelphia; and in Chicago and Detroit, more than 40 percent of black men and 55 percent of black women were without jobs.[30]

Notwithstanding the uncertainty of conditions outside the South, blacks continued their historic move northward, and over the course of the decade, the search for economic opportunity and social equality propelled more than four hundred thousand to leave the South. The vast majority headed to the urban northeast, a smaller number moved to the north-central cities, and a still lesser number went west. While only one northern city had a black population of more than one hundred thousand in 1930, within five years, that number had risen to eleven.[31] Although northern relief programs were superior to those in the South, there was little to be had, and without federal assistance, cities and states could not provide adequate help on their own.[32] Many came to believe that it was essential for the federal government to shoulder some of the burden, and when the Roosevelt administration decided to utilize federal power to aid those in distress, it would transform the social, political, and economic landscape of twentieth-century America.[33]

Despite FDR's reluctance to lend clear support to the race reformers' aims, including equality in employment, voting, housing, and education, New Deal programs did benefit the black population by providing a measure of relief from the harshness of the Depression. While Roosevelt was ambivalent in responding to the race question, his administration did show a new concern for black America, which, given the long history of presidential neglect, helped blacks feel that someone in Washington cared about their well-being. Several New Deal agencies helped black citizens cope with the grave economic conditions they confronted, although discrimination persisted in the provision of government assistance.[34] Beyond such aid, less tangible factors contributed to the notion that FDR cared about blacks. The president's wife, Eleanor, who behaved unlike any national figure the country had ever seen, played a key role in conveying this concern.[35] Her willingness to interact socially with black Americans, a bold act in 1930s America, sent a powerful message to those who had experienced indifference or worse at the hands of the nation's leaders. Blacks noted that Mrs. Roosevelt visited black schools and was on friendly terms with the black educator Mary McLeod Bethune and with Walter White.[36] For this reason and others, a key political development, the movement of blacks into the Democratic Party, occurred in these years. While the decision to leave their historic home among the Republicans has no simple explanation, a significant number of blacks decided to vote for Franklin Roosevelt during the 1930s. (As early as 1928, blacks had shown a willingness to vote for non-Republican candidates, but not until the 1936 presidential election did the trickle became a flood.) And in the electoral landslide of 1936, blacks voted in record numbers for FDR, making the election a transformative event in twentieth-century political history.[37]

On the world stage, the preeminent development in the 1930s was the emergence in Germany of the National Socialist leader Adolf Hitler, who gained control of the German government in early 1933. If Hitler's impact on twentieth-century world politics would be profound, Nazism would have a significant impact on the tone and the momentum of the struggle for racial justice in the United States. Beginning in the early 1930s, American civil rights leaders demonstrated an acute awareness of Hitler and Hitlerism and repeatedly incorporated their unique understanding of developments in Nazi Germany into their message. Although not a perfect expression of the reformers' distinctive internationalism, this interest exemplifies yet again how the reform community skillfully deployed a critical overseas development in these years in an effort to advance the cause. Indeed, the reformers' focus on European fascism indicates that their concern about the plight of persecuted peoples was not always confined to those of color.

Before tracing the reform community's response to Nazism in the thirties, it is interesting to note that some ten years earlier, *The Messenger* had begun to look warily at fascism (first in Italy) and worried that it might spread to America with dire consequences for blacks. In 1923, several articles claimed that the fascist threat already existed in the United States, though it had assumed the form of the Ku Klux Klan. In the "Fascisti in America," the editors asserted that fascism "like Ku Kluxism is the white guard of plutocracy," and they urged readers to make sure that it did not succeed.[38] A few months later, in October 1923, the journal took note of the acute political and social distress in postwar Germany, which it attributed to the scourge of "world imperialism." *Messenger* readers learned about the dangers posed by the "Bavarian leader of reaction," who had raised the "banner of fascism. . . . His name was Adolf Hittler [*sic*]." And in December, the editors linked European instability to a "hurricane of anti-Semitism." In Germany, Poland, and southeastern Europe, Jews had been "hunted down like rats, spat upon like dogs and massacred like vermin."[39] Thus, one publication had begun to take seriously the fascist menace some ten years before it became central to the language of reform.

On a September evening in 1936, listeners tuned to radio station WMCA in New York heard Walter White discuss the relationship between Nazism and race prejudice in the United States. In examining the dangers Hitlerism posed to the American people, White looked most closely at the threat to the nation's ethnic minorities, particularly the black population. White noted that black Americans were amused by those who were wondering whether fascism might come to their country, and observed that for "three centuries the Negro has known little else." The "forces of bigotry" began by oppressing a nation's most vulnerable group, he contended, a development that over time caused people to become indifferent to the denial of human rights. According to White, this permitted the nation's undemocratic forces to extend their oppression to other groups, which ultimately prepared the ground for the emergence of a "ruthless dictatorship." Liberty was "not the exclusive right of any racial . . . group," White claimed, noting that the oppression of one minority inevitably harmed the "rights of other minorities," and ultimately the majority as well. Urging all groups in America to "join hands against the common enemy," White asserted that national unity could be achieved only by a "sincere devotion to the ideals of fair play" for all. Indeed, without such a commitment, the nation would be vulnerable to the sort of policies that had emerged in Nazi Germany.[40]

Whether Walter White's assessment of the origins of dictatorship conforms to the analyses of social scientists is less important than the fact that White believed and argued repeatedly that developments in Nazi Germany were crucial in the context of the American civil rights movement. The NAACP secretary appealed to the self-interest of the American people, warning them that their failure to extend tolerance to all racial and ethnic minorities might endanger the welfare of the entire country. In a world increasingly threatened by hostile foreign forces, the organization's leader sought to join the fates of all Americans, and throughout the 1930s, White used developments in Hitler's Germany to fortify his case that America ought to work to abolish racial oppression in the United States. And throughout the decade, the reformers made Hitler's policies and Hitlerism an important component of their language and pointed to the threat fascism posed to America, noting the similarities between the plight of German Jews and that of black Americans.

Late in 1933, NAACP Field Secretary William Pickens wrote to a female acquaintance who was working in Europe and expressed his concern that her heart would be "much burdened with the suffering and injustice which you shall observe." Pickens conveyed his distress about developments in Germany. "I never thought anything could happen so evil in the world today as the Fascist mischief in Germany," he wrote.[41] Throughout the period, Pickens grappled with the mistreatment of German citizens, particularly Jews, and did what he could to help those in need. His determined effort to assist some Jewish friends and his concern for their young daughter, all of whom had fled Berlin to live in Denmark, makes for melancholy reading.[42] But the reform leader's response to Nazism extended beyond helping German Jews, and Pickens, believing the persecution of the Jews could be linked to the plight of black America, repeatedly joined the fates of both peoples.[43] In speeches, articles, and radio broadcasts, Pickens used German developments to strengthen the language of reform and to garner support for the NAACP's goals. In a 1934 radio address entitled "Hitlerism's Challenge to Human Brotherhood," Pickens contended that the racism of Hitler was dangerous not just for the Jews of Germany, but for "the entire world, for civilization." He condemned Nazi racism because it signaled a return to "disproven and discarded theories of racial origins and racial values" and feared his own country was not immune from the disease. Pickens worried that Americans might embrace Hitlerism, and, inspired by "this monstrous thing in Germany, we can expect to hear of the revival . . . of ku-kluxism in Georgia, of vigilantism in California, and of lynching in Mississippi." While he acknowledged that the United States had not yet reached the crisis stage, Pickens warned against complacency, claiming that those who believed in human brotherhood had not been as active as those who had emulated the dictators. Finally, he urged everyone who believed in freedom, equality, and peace to work actively to combat the evil of Hitlerism.[44]

Listeners tuned to Pickens's 1934 broadcast heard him examine the danger Nazism posed to all peoples, and in relating the global threat to the American scene, the reformer asked those who valued freedom and equality to rise up before the infection weakened and destroyed the body politic. They heard the NAACP official speak of the Klan and lynching, deeply meaningful references to black Americans and those committed to reform. In establishing a parallel between the international threat of Nazism and the domestic threat of racial violence and persecution, the speech illustrates how race activists used the German ideology to cast a shadow on the American landscape and warn their countrymen that it was critical to remain vigilant against the perniciousness of racialist ideas.[45] Since it was hoped that every decent American rejected the values inherent in Nazism, it seemed reasonable to assume that by establishing a fundamental similarity between American racial practices and those in Hitler's Germany—which Pickens did by detailing the indignities of life in the Jim Crow South—average Americans might better comprehend the character of their own society.

In a 1936 speech focusing on lynching and the violation of black rights, Walter White noted that many Americans were distressed over what was "being done to racial and religious minorities in Germany" and were just "beginning to realize that a counterpart of Hitlerism ha[d] existed in the United States for many generations." Before documenting the numerous injustices blacks confronted in America and how increased access to voting could help blacks overcome them, White explicitly compared the development of foreign and domestic oppression. "Fascism and racial bigotry learn the technique of oppression of the most vulnerable" and over time extend their oppression to other weak groups.[46] But White did more than equate Nazism with Jim Crowism; he spoke, too, about the shared plight of German Jews and American blacks, and by identifying a fundamental similarity in their respective conditions, he sought to generate a fraternal feeling toward Jews in the Third Reich. In November 1938, in the wake of *Kristallnacht*, in which synagogues, shops, and offices of Jews were destroyed or damaged throughout Germany, White issued a statement to New York's leading black paper, the *Amsterdam News*: "We Negroes know what this means since it has happened to us. . . . We must join with all those condemning Nazi terror because what happens to one minority can happen to others—a lesson which Jews, Negroes, and all other minorities must learn. . ."[47]

Speaking to a Jewish audience in late November 1938, White told a gathering at The Free Synagogue in New York that he stood before them as "a member of a race which also has known suffering and felt the cruel lash of racial hatred. For three centuries . . . we Negroes have been taught what it means to feel the searing agony of the blowtorch, the faggot and the rope of the lynching mob." The NAACP leader claimed this experience enabled blacks to "understand better than some others the Golgotha into which [Hitler] was driving Jews, Catholics and all others in Germany . . . who [refuse] to bow down before . . . race hatred." Having established a fraternity of the persecuted, White turned to the question of domestic reform and declared it essential to secure human rights for all citizens, including those in the minority. The brutality of Hitlerism had done more than arouse American opposition to German developments, he asserted. The Nazi terror had forced "us to re-examine our concepts and principles of fair play in the United States." As White reminded his listeners, developments overseas compelled Americans to ponder the character of their own society, and if they found it to be deficient—and White claimed that it was—all Americans were obliged to repair it.[48]

Like others in the NAACP, Roy Wilkins frequently wove the story of Nazi racial practices into the language of reform. A key figure in the organization during the Depression and for decades thereafter, Wilkins was the association's assistant secretary. Born in St. Louis in 1901, Wilkins, whose mother was a teacher and father a college graduate, spent most of his childhood in St. Paul, Minnesota, where he and his siblings were raised by relatives after their mother's death. As a boy, Wilkins became acquainted with Du Bois and the NAACP's work through *The Crisis*, which the family eagerly awaited every month. Demonstrating an aptitude for writing, Wilkins was president of his high school literary society and salutatorian of his graduating class in 1919. He then headed to the University of Minnesota, where he was drawn to journalism, developed an interest in race relations, and became secretary of the St. Paul branch of the NAACP. In August 1923, he traveled to Kansas City, Missouri, to attend the association's Midwestern Race Relations Conference, where he had the chance to see Du Bois, Pickens, Walter White, and James Weldon Johnson in action. A little more than a month later, he left Minnesota for Kansas City to begin a $100-a-month job for the black paper, the *Kansas City Call*, where he would remain until 1931, when Walter White asked him to come to New York to work for the NAACP.[49]

During the 1930s, Wilkins wrote a regular column, "Watchtower," in the *Amsterdam News*, which reached a weekly audience numbering in the tens of thousands. In 1937, he told his readers that what Hitler had done to the Jews was "a pretty good indication of what the Nazi theory is for all 'non-Aryan' races." Although black Americans were willing to fight fascism, they could do so with more enthusiasm if the "'land of the free' had given us our just share of American democracy." In an especially compelling column, Wilkins recalled the story of a Berlin policeman who had stopped four Jewish Girl Scouts from walking together through a park, claiming it was illegal because they might be plotting against the government. Wilkins concluded the Berlin tale by alluding to an outbreak of racial violence against blacks in Florida: "Sounds suspiciously like Miami . . . and its treatment of Negroes, does it not?" The best way to stop this in America, he asserted, was to maintain democratic government and preserve the "rights of the individual and of minority racial and religious groups."[50]

Throughout the 1930s, *The Crisis* was replete with coverage of Nazism and the persecution of Jews. Although after 1934 control of the monthly would no longer rest with Du Bois (for reasons that will be discussed), the magazine continued to strike out boldly against oppression. Readers regularly encountered discussion and analysis of European fascism in editorials, essays, cartoons, letters to the editor, and in reprints of speeches and editorials from elsewhere. In the spring of 1934, *The Crisis* published a speech by Rabbi Stephen S. Wise, the leading Jewish religious figure in the country, which he had delivered the previous January at the NAACP's annual meeting. To those committed to race reform, the Jewish leader conveyed a message of fraternity and shared oppression. Hitlerism had been tried in America with "the most disastrous results," Wise claimed, and he asked when the day would arrive when Americans would accept the idea that the members of all races had "exactly the same right to be themselves" as had the members of any other race. As Wise told the largely black audience, his own people were not the only ones subject to persecution: "You, too, have been wronged . . . [and] deeply wounded— in . . . your own [home]." The rabbi spoke about the shared plight of blacks and Jews, declaring that both peoples would endure the persecution that threatened their existence. The Jews will survive Hitler, he insisted, and "you will survive the trials and the injustices and the abysmal wrongs of which you are the victims."[51]

Similar rhetoric could be heard at the proceedings of the NAACP's annual conferences, where the movement's leaders gathered to chart the course of domestic reform.[52] At the annual conference in 1935, association president Joel Spingarn delivered a hopeful message. After considering the movement's historic goals, Spingarn claimed a "terrible race" was emerging between democracy and fascism, and warned his listeners about the consequences that would follow should democracy lose. Blacks, especially, would suffer under a fascist regime, in education, employment, and in their social relations. It was essential, Spingarn argued, for whites and blacks jointly to oppose fascism, and the prospect of such cooperation led the aging activist to observe that he felt "hopeful for American democracy, and . . . for the future of the colored race." In predicting that a fraternal response to adversity could lead to constructive change, Spingarn was articulating a somewhat unusual response to the fascist menace.[53]

And how did Du Bois respond to developments in Nazi Germany? Part of the answer to this question is provided by the race leader's six-month round-the-world journey in 1936–37, which he would chronicle in his *Pittsburgh Courier* column.[54] Before his departure, Du Bois was contacted by anthropologist Franz Boas, who asked him to join a new organization, the American Committee for Anti-Nazi Literature, which sought to educate and enlighten Americans about the nature of Nazism. But Du Bois declined, noting that he had just received a commission to study in Germany from the Oberlaender Trust, a group devoted to promoting cultural understanding between the United States and German-speaking countries. Though he could say what he liked when he returned, Du Bois told Boas it would be unwise to join the committee before leaving, because doing so might jeopardize his trip.[55]

And on June 15, 1936, the SS *St. Louis*, with Du Bois aboard, docked in Southampton, England. The coming journey would take him through the heart of Europe, which he said represented "the center of modern human culture." Despite American "boasting," Du Bois observed that civilization was centered not in the United States but across the Atlantic. While he claimed that America's problems were similar to those faced by Europe, he believed the Europeans were doing a more systematic job of confronting the challenges of governance, labor, production, agriculture, and urban planning.[56] To investigate such questions, Du Bois spent some five months in Hitler's Germany in 1936, where he penned a number of columns. Noting the "overwhelming" support the German people were giving to their leader, he described a country that was generally "contented and prosperous," had low unemployment, good and pure food, and "perfect" public order. But all was not well in Germany, for according to Du Bois, the country was "silent, nervous, suppressed." Of the German people, he wrote that they spoke "in whispers."

Du Bois told his readers about German race prejudice, perpetrated "openly, continuously, and determinedly against all non-Nordic races, but specifically against the Jews." In its "vindictive cruelty and public insult," he wrote, it surpasses "anything I have ever seen; and I have seen much." Social scientist that he was, Du Bois sought to explain the phenomenon by recourse to recent German history, noting the tribulations the German people had endured since the Great War. This was no apology, but an attempt to understand how a nation that he knew so well (he had studied there years before and visited it since) had embarked on its current path. As many would learn, it was not easy to uncover a convincing explanation for the rise of Hitler, which Du Bois acknowledged, observing that when a "group or nation acts incomprehensively [sic], the answer lies in a background of fact, unknown or imperfectly comprehended by the onlooker."[57] In several columns, Du Bois devoted considerable attention to the subject of Nazi racism and ethnic persecution. Though he was critical of German anti-Semitism and described the Nazi state as a "tyranny," which those accustomed to freedom could not possibly endure, his condemnation of Hitler's creation was different from that offered by other race activists.[58] In his *Courier* columns, he did not link the plight of German Jews to that of black Americans, nor did he parallel German and American racial practices. Indeed, he explicitly distinguished German from American prejudice, writing that the German dislike of Jews was "not at all analogous" to the white dislike of American blacks. Du Bois claimed that the black American could not "readily understand" German religious prejudice, and with uncharacteristic murkiness he wrote that it was more instinctive than color prejudice, contending that the German variant had an economic explanation "built on a foundation of religion and clan solidarity." So while Du Bois declared that there was "no tragedy in modern times equal in its awful effects" to the Nazi persecution of the Jews—he likened it to the Spanish Inquisition and the African slave trade—his overseas columns did not overtly deploy Nazism to fortify the case for domestic reform. The closest he came to linking the two matters was in his assertion that Hitlerism had "set civilization back a hundred years" and had made "the settlement and understanding of race problems more difficult and more doubtful."[59]

Before leaving Germany for points east, however, Du Bois described an incident for his readers to ponder. A renowned professor, who, upon hearing that Du Bois was passing through his city, invited the American into his home and treated him to wine, dinner, and cigarettes. Du Bois was shown the workroom, library, and unfinished manuscript of this distinguished German academic, an experience that led Du Bois to write about the "surprise of being treated like a human being" and to wonder where in America this could have happened. "At Chicago? At Columbia? At Harvard?" Left to reflect on the significance of the event, countless thousands of readers surely puzzled over how a black man in the heart of Hitler's Germany could receive the respect denied him in America.[60]

In 1936, the Olympic Games were held in Berlin, and with Hitler a conspicuous presence, African Americans performed brilliantly—much to the chagrin of the Nazi leadership. For black America, the extraordinary feats of sprinter Jesse Owens and other black athletes were viewed as a victory over the ideology of Aryan supremacy, which buoyed the pride of the black population. Decades later, Roy Wilkins would describe his sense that black people were "making their way forward," and point to the inspiration provided by Owens's achievements.[61] Black periodicals and the black press covered the story closely, and *The Crisis* described how the Nazi dictator had purposefully snubbed Owens, the winner of the 100-meter race. The journal noted the significance of the event and claimed the meaning of fascism was "becoming clearer and clearer to millions of Negro Americans" who had given it little thought before. But Hitler had changed all that, for the "high priest of fascism . . . [had] ignored American Negro world and Olympic champions. Ergo, fascism is the last thing American Negroes want." The German system was "as bad as Mississippi."[62] Writing his column while overseas, Du Bois discussed the event's importance and pointed to the enormous popularity of Owens, who had performed before the "astonished eyes of the world." Nevertheless, Du Bois observed, "it must be followed by other things." Sport was not enough. "We must be represented . . . in science, in literature, and in art." Others shared Du Bois's view, with the *Pittsburgh Courier* claiming the Olympic episode could be a spur to change and insisting that the return of the victorious black Olympians demanded that black Americans devote themselves to reform. By providing a world stage on which to display black athletic ability in the face of overt Nazi hostility, the 1936 Olympics contributed to a sense of black accomplishment, which raised the spirits of black America during a dismal time.[63]

The reformers' response to European fascism extended beyond German and Italian malefactions, and while the Spanish Civil War did not engender the same intensity among reformers and black Americans as did Nazism or the Italo-Ethiopian War, Francisco Franco's effort to overthrow the legitimate government in Madrid did engage the reform community's attention.[64] And in Spain, unlike in Ethiopia, black Americans had the opportunity to serve as volunteers with the Abraham Lincoln Brigade in the fight against Franco's regime. As one study indicates, those ninety or so black volunteers fought not merely to defend democracy, but to extend black American "claims to equality and self-determination."[65] It is worth pausing to consider the actions of the volunteers who left America to participate in a cause brimming with international and domestic significance. Walter Garland, who went to Spain in 1937, where he would command a machine gun company, expressed well the view that the Spanish conflict was related to the one at home: "You know . . . we Negroes who have been in Spain are a great deal luckier than those in America. Here we have been able to strike back, in a way that hurts, at those who for years have pushed us from pillar to post. I mean this— actually strike back at the counterparts of those who have been grinding us down back home."[66]

While race reform leaders fired no machine guns and lobbed no grenades, their words conveyed this same belief, and numerous writings in *The Crisis* and the black press illustrate how the reformers linked the Spanish conflict to their cause. According to Roy Wilkins, the Spanish situation was important to black Americans because "we have been kicked around nearly all our lives." Wilkins observed that in any struggle blacks should find out "who is doing the kicking around and who is being kicked," and they should of course side with the latter because "[n]ine times out of ten he is just like we are." After establishing a distinctive black empathy for the victims of persecution, Wilkins pointed to a fundamental similarity between the oppressors, a group that included Hitler, Mussolini, and Franco, as well as notorious American racists such as Alabama's Senator Tom Heflin. Wilkins enthusiastically supported Spain's Republicans, the legitimate government that Franco's forces sought to topple: "We have got to help make a world where there will be less kicking around, where a man won't be lynched because he is black [or] beaten and spat upon because he is a Jew. . . . The job is not for one color, one race [or] one nation . . . [but] for all men . . . who want . . . a voice in shaping the kind of world in which we must live."[67]

In the summer of 1938, William Pickens traveled to Spain, and upon his return, he told a large crowd in New York about the efforts of the brave Americans—male and female, black and white—who had gone to Spain because they believed in liberty, a belief nurtured since childhood. He described the heroic exploits of a young black man, Luchelle McDaniels, wounded in the thigh after driving back an enemy company with a bundle of hand grenades, and he noted how inspiring it was to witness the youthful soldier's itch to return to the front. Pickens pointed out that in Spain one found many "colored boys, fighting and singing," and he wondered why a "Virginia Negro" went to fight for Spanish democracy. The race activist considered this question in a lengthy *Crisis* piece, in which he told his readers that the fight of the Spanish people, a battle for self-government, "is our fight." Spain had no color problem, he observed, for over there "people are just people." Pickens shared the words of Joe Taylor, a young black man who had crossed the ocean to help preserve democracy in Spain. Recovering from his wounds in an integrated hospital ward near Barcelona, Taylor said, "It's not like the states here, for here I get some breaks."[68]

The black press also exposed readers to images of the Spanish Civil War and compared the battle waged by Spain's Republican forces to the campaign against home-grown racial persecution. A *Chicago Defender* editorial, "Our Brothers in Spain," was typical, noting that aside from the Ethiopian conflict, blacks in America and throughout the world had more at stake in the Spanish struggle than they did in any other interna-

In 1938, the NAACP's William Pickens (*fourth from right*) told black Americans
that the Spanish Civil War was "our fight." That same year, he traveled to Spain,
where he encountered African-American soldiers who had taken up arms against
the fascists.

tional event. Fascism meant many things, but to blacks it "implie[d] a
cancellation of those rights and privileges for which we have shed our
blood. . . . The desperate struggle of a people who wish to rid themselves
of the yoke of serfdom [and] oppression . . . could not leave us indifferent
to their plight." In 1937, when the German air force, in support of Franco's troops, rained death and destruction on the Spanish city of Guernica,
The Crisis captured perfectly the reformers' response to fascism: "It matters not whether the Fascists are Italians or Germans and the victims
Basques or Ethiopians, Fascism means death to men and to freedom."
Concluding ominously, the monthly declared: "[Y]esterday Ethiopia,
today Spain, tomorrow ——?" To the movement's leadership, the fascist
contagion, whether it flourished in Germany, Italy, Spain, or Mississippi,
represented everything they were working to abolish.[69]
    The political and ideological struggles that roiled world politics in the
1930s, which the reformers incorporated into their message, overlapped
with an ideological conflict waged within the movement itself, and if this
domestic conflict caused no bloodshed and toppled no buildings, it did

alter the movement's trajectory in these years and later. The economic crisis of the 1930s led a group of younger figures, including political scientist Ralph Bunche, economist Abram Harris, and sociologist E. Franklin Frazier, to question the traditional path mainstream reform leaders had mapped out (especially in the NAACP), and these younger activists would ultimately embrace more economically based solutions to the problems confronting black America. In the words of Roy Wilkins, who was a target of the younger reformers, liberals and radicals believed the NAACP was weak because it lacked an economic program and an economic philosophy.[70] In response to this critique, the association called a conference in 1933 to discuss "the present situation of the American Negro and just what ought to be done."[71] Meeting for three days at Troutbeck, Joel Spingarn's estate in Amenia, New York, the delegates debated the future course of the movement, and in making their recommendations to the NAACP, they emphasized the need to focus on economic issues and to move toward creating an interracial labor movement. While most senior NAACP figures did not support the group's recommendations, the conference was significant, according to one scholar, because it emphasized the growing importance of economic questions and pointed toward the approach the NAACP would begin to implement in the near future.[72]

An unexpected result of the conference concerned the reaction of Du Bois, who, in his long tenure with the organization, had become embroiled in a number of internal controversies. None had proved insurmountable, but this time would be different. Reflecting on the Amenia proposals, Du Bois reformulated the delegates' criticisms into a broad attack on the association's goal of integration, a position he began to enunciate in *The Crisis* in 1934. His approach, which he described, not accidentally, as one of "voluntary segregation," set off a firestorm within the NAACP leadership, the black press, and among others committed to reform. While it is unnecessary here to explore the intricacies of Du Bois's program, the race leader urged blacks to pursue a policy of self-help and racial solidarity, and to create economic institutions and financial resources that would allow them to "prevail in the long struggle" for justice. As Du Bois declared, "I do not consider this compromise. I consider it common sense."[73] While leading figures in the association opposed Du Bois's program—the organization's fundamental aim was to abolish segregation—other factors fueled the conflict, which ended in the summer of 1934 with Du Bois's resignation.[74] After a quarter of a century in the organization, Du Bois would henceforth continue to work outside the NAACP, though he would return briefly in the 1940s. The race leader's departure meant the end of an era for the association; for a generation the presence of Du Bois had provided the NAACP not only with intellectual heft, but also with a profound devotion to effecting change.

As founder and editor of *The Crisis*, he had railed against injustice for decades and used the monthly to fortify the optimism, confidence, and assertiveness of black Americans, for whom the magazine provided a voice in a nation that wished to silence them. And of course, Du Bois had helped make world affairs a critical component of the association's approach to change. The new editor, Roy Wilkins, would face a daunting challenge indeed.[75]

Even as the NAACP was growing and attempting to address the dissatisfaction of younger activists who believed the old guard opposed a more radical approach,[76] a movement emerged at mid-decade that aimed to improve black life by charting a new course. Growing out of a 1935 conference held at Howard University under the direction of Ralph Bunche, who had earned his Ph.D. in political science from Harvard, and John P. Davis, a Harvard law school graduate and race reform advocate, the National Negro Congress first met in Chicago in February 1936.[77] According to A. Philip Randolph, who would serve as the organization's first president, it was needed because the "magnitude, complexity and danger of the Negro's present condition demands the mobilization of overwhelming mass pressure and force."[78] More than eight hundred delegates representing nearly six hundred organizations gathered in Chicago in 1936 for the first meeting of the National Negro Congress, the declared purpose of which was "to meet the increasingly difficult economic and social problems" confronting black America. The diversity of its membership suggested a new type of organization for black advancement, a fact noted by Roy Wilkins, who reported to the NAACP that "it enlisted great sections of young colored and white people . . . from the so-called working class and mass organizations" who were committed to a militant fight.[79]

At the organization's first two conferences in 1936 and in 1937, key figures gave centrality to world affairs in speeches, announcements, and in the passage of resolutions. It is clear that the emerging message of the NNC—especially as propounded by Randolph—embraced the idea that domestic matters could not be isolated from the gathering storm of international politics. Those leading the way in Chicago in 1936 and in Philadelphia one year later compelled hundreds of delegates to ponder the significance of Hitler, Mussolini, imperialism, and a world in which democracies and dictatorships were vying for supremacy. Moreover, a substantial number of the resolutions passed in these two years concerned foreign affairs or explicitly tied the spread of fascism to the aspirations of black Americans.[80] Randolph's 1937 keynote address, "The Crisis of the Negro and the Constitution," epitomized the internationalist character of the National Negro Congress and suggests how one reformer related the domestic goals of the new organization to a world in distress.

Labor leader and National Negro Congress President A. Philip Randolph delivers the presidential address on Constitution Night at the meeting of the Second National Negro Congress in 1937. To more than a thousand delegates, Randolph described an "hour of crisis" at home and abroad.

Discussing the "hour of crisis" at home and abroad, Randolph employed class-based language to reflect upon matters both contemporary and historical. Beyond detailing the movement's aims, which included a federal anti-lynching bill and equal employment and educational opportunities, Randolph expressed his concern about events on the Iberian peninsula. A Franco victory could mean that "a world flood of fascism [might] not be far behind," he worried, a development that might "imperil free peoples everywhere." In his stirring conclusion, Randolph—perhaps the country's best orator—spoke of worldwide oppression, panning the globe from Africa to China to Spain. Deftly shifting his focus to the plight of black Americans, he then intoned the names of Nat Turner, Harriet Tubman, Frederick Douglass, and others in the black pantheon, the heroes and heroines of the freedom struggle. With his closing reference to Lincoln's Emancipation Proclamation, Randolph sustained this eloquent juxtaposition of the local and the global, suggesting an intrinsic relationship between both spheres. More than a thousand delegates thus heard one of the country's foremost race leaders place worldwide developments at the core of his demand for domestic reform.[81]

Despite a hopeful start, the impact of the National Negro Congress faded swiftly, as a variety of factors, the most significant of which was the growing Communist influence within the organization, caused a rapid loss of prestige. By 1940, the Communist Party had assumed a leading role in the congress, a development that Randolph and Ralph Bunche both decried. When the third Congress convened that year, Bunche lamented that its followers would soon consist mainly of "devout party members" and "fellow travelers," and he observed that the organization had "dug its own grave." According to Randolph, who had dramatically quit the presidency of the organization, "until the stigma of Communist front is wiped from the Congress, it will never rally the masses of Negro people."[82] While there is disagreement over the impact that Communists had on the decline of the National Negro Congress, by the early 1940s, the organization had lost much of its luster, and its potential for improving the life of black America had dissipated. But Communist influence did more than enervate the potential of the National Negro Congress, for significant changes were apparent in the way race reform leaders responded to Communism and to developments in the Soviet Union.[83]

Although the reformers still reflected on Soviet affairs, their interest in Russia was notably different from what it had been ten years before. During the thirties, race activists were less concerned with Russian developments per se than with the question of Communism's potential for influencing black life in the United States. While the reform journals continued to provide some coverage of Soviet politics and culture, the type of pieces that had appeared earlier were replaced by discussion and debate on Communist efforts to influence American race reform, and tales of Soviet life had become less interesting to the reformers than the potential transplantation of the Soviet ideology in the United States.[84] NAACP president Joel Spingarn addressed the subject in 1932, contending that the Russian Communists' dream of a classless society should not be understood as a "society of equals." If Communism came to America, he insisted, it would be distinctively American, and "composed of Georgia crackers and labor leaders who hate Negroes, and who would say . . . you can have equality if you are like us—and like us would mean being white." According to Spingarn, the success of Communism in America meant that the NAACP would be more necessary than ever.[85]

The Communist Party's increased effort to garner African-American support during the 1930s caused some in the race reform community to worry that they would lose control of the movement. Particularly troubling to race leaders was the way the Party—to demonstrate its commitment to racial justice—responded to events involving blacks, which led many reformers to express strong reservations about the Communists' determination to win black support. Although the Communists' domestic activities lie outside the scope of this study, a few points are worth noting. After achieving dismal results during the 1920s in trying to gain African-American converts, the Communist Party revised its strategy in 1928 and began a determined move to broaden its influence among black Americans. That year, at the Sixth World Congress of the Communist International, the Party announced a new doctrine, "the right of self-determination of the Negroes in the Black Belt," which, in Harvard Sitkoff's words, transformed black Americans from a racial minority into an "oppressed separate nation seeking self-determination." The Party hoped that this new orientation toward blacks would demonstrate a deeper commitment to their plight and increase the number of black Party members, which stood at a few hundred in the late 1920s.[86]

Other Communist efforts to gain black support included involvement in two celebrated legal battles in which black southerners had been victimized by an oppressive judicial system. The Scottsboro case, which grew out of the alleged rape of two young white women by nine black youths on a freight train in Alabama, gave the Party an opportunity to demonstrate its newfound commitment to black America. The Party organized fund-raising drives, demonstrations, and legal appeals throughout the country on behalf of the "Scottsboro Boys," several of whom had been sentenced to die in the electric chair as a result of the legal charade that had masqueraded as a trial in the Jim Crow South.[87] In 1932, the Angelo Herndon case provided the Party with another opportunity to gain black support, as Herndon, a young Birmingham coal miner who had led a demonstration of the unemployed outside Atlanta's Fulton County Courthouse, was charged, tried, and convicted of inciting to insurrection, a crime for which he was sentenced to eighteen to twenty years on a chain gang. The Party worked zealously on Herndon's behalf, and according to his attorney, no white group more effectively set the "world of white supremacy and racial hatred against the forces of freedom and dignity."[88]

Black self-determination, the Scottsboro Boys, the Herndon case, and the critical question—could Communism improve the lives of black Americans?—generated febrile discussion and debate among the reformers throughout the thirties. In a 1934 volume, *Negro Americans, What Now?*, James Weldon Johnson, who had left the NAACP in late 1930 for a position at Fisk University, considered the plight of black America in a world he claimed was in "a state of semi-chaos." Johnson discounted the notion that Communism would solve the American race problem, and, while hoping the Soviet experiment would succeed, he saw no reason to place a "childlike trust" in any economic or social theory. Indeed, Johnson noted, American Communists would be composed of Americans—which allowed scant cause for optimism. Moreover, Johnson saw little chance that Communism would triumph in the United States and worried that support for the revolutionary cause would subject blacks to the hostility engendered by Communism, even as they continued to endure the age-old antagonism of race hatred. Such lack of faith in the Communist solution to the race question was not uncommon among traditional race activists.[89]

In an article published in *Harper's* magazine, Walter White used the response of the Communists to the Scottsboro case to question their commitment to black America. Depicting the Party as opportunistic, he decried its effort to characterize NAACP officials as "tools of the capitalists" and rejected the Party's charge that the association's officers were "in league with the lyncher-bosses of the South." He described Communist efforts to break up association meetings by sowing deceit and disorder, and in painting an unflattering picture of the movement, White went beyond criticizing the Party's unsavory tactics. As did James Weldon Johnson, White observed that black Communists would be "in doubled jeopardy" [*sic*] if they faced both anti-Communist and anti-black antagonism, and he demanded the enactment of the NAACP's program, reminding those who worried about black support for revolutionary doctrines that the antidote was "even-handed justice."[90] Writing about Scottsboro, Du Bois was similarly critical of the Communists. In a lengthy *Crisis* piece composed in 1931, he contended that the Communists' primary aim was not to save the accused boys, but to prove that "anything less than the radical Communist program" would not free them. As did White, Du Bois lambasted the Party for its critique of the NAACP and accused it of lying and deception, tactics he described as "old capitalistic, bourgeois weapons of which the Communists ought to be ashamed." Du Bois questioned the basis of the Communist appeal to blacks, claiming the idea of an alliance between black and white workers was absurd. He wondered who it was that had killed, harassed, and starved black men, disfranchised them, and discriminated against them in every walk of life. Who had formed the "backbone of the Ku Klux Klan" and provided the rope to lynch thousands of blacks? White labor was guilty of these acts, Du Bois asserted, and any talk that sought to convince the black man that his interests lay with those of white labor was like waving "a red flag before a bull." It was essential, he declared, for black Americans to continue to fight for their social and political rights "on the old battleground, led by the NAACP."[91]

On the whole, traditional race activists met the Communists' efforts to gain black support with antagonism. NAACP leaders were dismissive of the Party's program and questioned its tactics and sincerity, along with Communism's potential for effecting change. A letter from William Pickens to Claude Barnett, head of the Associated Negro Press, acknowledged that the Communists had done some good by publicizing the Scottsboro case. But Pickens also emphasized the "Evil" they had done. He noted their practice of "systematic lying" in discussions about the race problem and observed that this, along with "the sowing of dissension among colored groups," would achieve no "ultimate . . . or immediate good." Not surprisingly, Pickens defended the NAACP's program, claiming that only the Communists were more "radical" than were the association's leaders, who were continually attacked for their extremism. Despite such criticisms, the NAACP—unlike the Communists—did not resort to "purposeful lying" or to starting fights between other black groups that were devoted to overcoming the "great obstacle of race prejudice." In Pickens's view, and it is one with which many of his fellow reformers would have concurred, the Communists sought to "injure and destroy . . . every non-Communist thing," including the NAACP. Beyond that, Pickens doubted the efficacy of their approach and opposed such "foolish tactics," claiming their methods would "not advance the cause. . . . In fact, they are likely to do harm."[92]

In comparing such attitudes toward Communism in the 1930s with the views many reformers held a decade before, one sees a striking transformation: familiarity with what were seen as the Communists' unsavory tactics had bred contempt among many race activists.[93] As for the way the reformers perceived the Soviet Union, few would have disagreed with a 1935 *Crisis* editorial that claimed Russia's once-vaunted idealism was "in reality hard-boiled opportunism," which had proved as shameless as that of any other state. Rejecting the "pious flub-dub" of the Communists, the editors pointed to Moscow's purported "love for the . . . exploited black people" and its policy of "self-determination for the Black Belt," and they compared the Communists to the "southern ruling class," a view that would have been impossible to imagine ten years earlier.[94] In the twenties, when considering the revolutionary ideology and its achievements inside Russia, reformers like Pickens, Du Bois, and Randolph had been sanguine about Communism's potential for ameliorating the problems of black America. But in the 1930s, after confronting the Communists' efforts to gain black support and to influence the direction of race reform, the movement's leaders began to view Russia and Communism in an altogether different light. Convinced that Communism would prove inimical to black interests, the race reformers were determined to prevent the Communists from seizing control of their struggle.

More broadly, throughout the Depression decade, the race reformers continued to utilize world affairs to advance their campaign. In an address given at the NAACP's Thirtieth Annual Conference in 1939, Walter White noted that the organization had long sought to help America conquer the disease of race hatred. He observed that the NAACP had worked to sustain a "conception of democracy" that was "fighting for its life" all over the world. Americans of all colors and creeds now realized that "only a strong democracy at home" would allow their country to preserve freedom from the forces threatening it from abroad. Indeed, he declared, the self-interest of all American citizens made it imperative that blacks be granted a full measure of democracy. Observing that his country had paid little attention to the black struggle, White claimed that Americans were now "witnessing the harvest of race hatred that is being reaped on a world front." He pointed to Italy's "rape" of Ethiopia, Japan's "dismemberment" of China, Germany's "absorption" of Austria and Czechoslovakia, and the fascist threat to democracy in Spain. White spoke, too, of the Nazis' treatment of the Jews, which he described as "the virtual wiping out of the Jewish people in Germany and Italy by the most violent racial persecution of modern times." The world picture "dramatize[d] our stake in democracy at home," White said, and using language not heard since the Wilson era, he asserted that if America wished to stand as a "beacon light for the world," she had to provide "her Negro citizens . . . [with] full citizenship." In White's estimation, international events made clear that the NAACP's thirty-year struggle was no "isolated fight of a single disadvantaged group" of Americans, but was part of something larger; in fact, "America's rise or fall" depended upon its capacity to make democracy work in the United States.[95]

As such language suggests, when the reformers scanned the world in these years, they saw an unfolding story of religious, racial, and political persecution. Believing that liberty and equality were under siege, they constructed a message that emphasized the parallels between oppression abroad and oppression at home. If the forces of fascism and imperialism denied justice and liberty to those in Ethiopia, Germany, Spain, and India, the reformers were convinced the domestic equivalent denied freedom and equality to black citizens in the Jim Crow South. Before the decade was over, the start of a global war would provide race leaders with a still more effective opportunity to look overseas in an effort to advance their quest.

PART III

From World War II to Vietnam

Five

"DEMOCRACY SHOULD BEGIN AT HOME"
The Struggle for Equality and the Second World War

ONE WEEK AFTER Germany invaded Poland in September 1939, an act that would plunge Europe and ultimately much of the world into war, the *Pittsburgh Courier* declared that the European conflict "need not detain us because it will make no difference to us who wins." The immediate concern of black Americans, the paper insisted, should be the perennial battle at home against racial oppression, which was not a contest between "dictatorship and democracy," but between "survival and destruction." Notwithstanding the perspective of this leading black newspaper, World War II would prove supremely important in the quest for racial justice both in the United States and overseas, a realization that would animate race reform leaders from the war's earliest days. Indeed, even before America went to war in 1941, the reformers identified an organic connection between the global crisis and their domestic goals, and the centrality of race in the world struggle meant it would not be difficult for reform leaders to relate overseas developments to their agenda for change.[1]

While the war would mark the point at which debate on civil rights could no longer be shunted to one side of the national agenda, it must be said that in some respects, continuity rather than change characterized the reformers' response to global developments in these years. As they studied the world, race leaders continued to propound their distinctive internationalism and consistently returned to their decades-old strategy of utilizing overseas matters to assist their cause. The race activists understood the war as a global struggle against tyranny and oppression, and in linking it to their domestic campaign, they came to support the idea that the United States had a key role to play in vanquishing the dictators. But to do so, they asserted, America had to abolish the system of institutionalized racial oppression. As was true during World War I, many race reformers would embrace the idea of American activism abroad and would argue that such engagement could not be undertaken effectively by a country that maintained legal racial discrimination at home. In addition, the reformers' understanding of colonial developments was less a grand departure than a continued expression of their longstanding belief that the Asian, African, and Indian struggles were of special moment to black America. Throughout the war, the reformers compared the international battle against totalitarianism and colonialism to the domestic battle for racial equality. And toward the war's end (as the next chapter will show), the reformers' conviction that transnational organizations could help solve international and domestic problems would surface once more.

In at least one respect the race reformers' response to developments during the period of American neutrality differed from the way many had viewed the neutrality period of a generation before.[2] Between 1914 and 1917, few race activists had given much thought to the war's potential for advancing the cause of racial justice, and many feared the conflict would destroy the broader program of Progressive reforms. But during the period of American neutrality in World War II (from 1939 to 1941), most race reformers energetically linked the international and the domestic struggles. Though they did not support American belligerency before the attack on Pearl Harbor, most race leaders made the war central to the language of reform.[3] And unlike the period from 1914 to 1917, they consciously wove global events into their message and embraced the idea that the world conflagration could advance their cause. The reformers responded differently to the outbreak of war in 1939 primarily because the conflict's racial dimension fortified the notion that the war bore directly on the plight of black America, and unlike their predecessors in 1914, the race activists did not fear that war might weaken America's will to pursue a broader reform agenda.

In its first issue after the war began in 1939, *The Crisis* looked optimistically at America's concern over the threat to freedom and the country's willingness to defend democracy from the forces that menaced it around the world. The talk about fighting for the "rights of oppressed minorities" and for "equality, justice, and freedom" reminded the editors of World War I, as did the rhetoric about defending for all people the privilege to "determine their destiny." Readers were told about the movement's historic aspirations—suffrage, anti-lynching legislation, an end to residential segregation, abolition of the Jim Crow car, and equality in education and employment—and the journal declared it would have more confidence in the nation's distress over the threat to democracy abroad when America manifested a greater willingness to fight for democracy in the United States. To demonstrate this "new affection for democracy," America would have to sweep aside the legal oppression of its black citizens.[4]

From the war's earliest days, black America heard commentators suggest that the conflict possessed significance for the domestic campaign. Just after Germany invaded Poland, a cartoon in Baltimore's *Afro-American* pictured a black man, head bowed in prayer, with the caption: "Dear God, Keep us out of war, but when we have to fight, please make us strong to give race prejudice hell." According to an editorial in the *Afro-American*, while war was savage and barbaric, it was unnecessary to fear

American intervention because a fight against intolerance anywhere would aid tolerance at home. Kelly Miller, who for years had linked world affairs to domestic matters, described a country, which, though neutral in conduct, could never be "neutral at heart." Illustrating the distinction the reformers made between the outbreak of hostilities in 1914 and in 1939, Miller wrote that unlike last time, this war was deeply significant to black America. "The Negro's provocation against Hitler is immeasurably greater than against Wilhelm," for the Nazis' "hatred and slaughter against the Jews and all other weaker breeds" had shocked the conscience of mankind. Whenever the country decided to fight, the black American would again serve loyally. Unlike before, he would not be robbed of the fruits of victory, but would "participate in the benefits of that victory which he helped to win."[5]

Those attending the NAACP's annual conference in Philadelphia in June 1940 heard speaker after speaker link the global struggle against tyranny to the historic battle against racial persecution. While America was not yet ready to shed its discomfort with European embroilments, the nation's most important meeting of race activists attached great significance to war-related matters as the reformers set out their agenda. The preamble to the resolutions the delegates adopted highlighted the disappearance of democracy throughout the world and the grave threat it faced in America—from within and without. Beyond favoring sufficient defense to protect the country from attack, the association claimed it was equally important to strengthen the democratic process at home so that all citizens, irrespective of race, creed, or color, could feel they had a "vital stake in democracy." The first resolution, headed "National Defense," committed the organization to fighting against "the spirit of Hitlerism" and rejected the Nazi leader's assertion that the Germans were a master race. It denounced Hitler's description of black people as "half-apes" and his plan to deny blacks the opportunity for higher education. The delegates were determined to prevent this same "spirit of Hitlerism" from making gains at home, and they declared they would work for equal opportunities for all United States citizens. The resolution concluded with a set of specific demands and called on the president to end segregation and discrimination in the armed forces and in industry. As this "national defense" statement made clear, the problem of racial persecution in the United States was a key to the country's defense effort.[6]

On the convention floor, delegates heard some of the movement's leading figures describe the war's significance to the cause. NAACP President Arthur Spingarn considered Hitler's disparagement of black people, observing that the German leader aimed to "take away each and every right . . . from the Negro" and return him to the place he occupied before emancipation. Noting the loyalty of blacks throughout American history,

Spingarn pointed to their longstanding suffering, which was "contrary to the letter and spirit of democracy." And he even recalled the language of an earlier crisis: "We cannot make the world safe for democracy until we first make democracy safe in America."[7] Numerous reformers eloquently linked the war to the domestic cause, their words indicating that even before America had decided to fight, many believed the conflict could serve as a wedge for change.[8] Skillfully capturing the spirit of the proceedings, Walter White claimed that blacks would work as hard as any group to preserve American democracy, though they would settle for nothing less than "true democracy." Tragic events had befallen Europe, he said, and a meeting devoted to preserving democracy in such a world seemed "almost academic and unreal." Offering the concluding words of the conference, White boldly addressed the entire nation: "Build your planes and battleships and we will help you," though he insisted his country should "stop being hypocrites and give us the opportunity to earn a decent living . . . [and] give us protection from the howling mob. . . . Give us reason to love America."[9]

Throughout the neutrality period, *The Crisis* (now under Roy Wilkins's editorship) emphatically linked the war and the domestic cause. In "Lynching and Liberty," a July 1940 editorial, he wrote of America's near hysteria over the threat to democracy posed by Hitler's marching legions. But he contended, in a common formulation, that unchecked mobs in America were still likely to "hunt down, shoot, hang, or burn alive a Negro" because they knew nothing would be done. Criticizing the Senate for its failure to pass anti-lynching legislation, Wilkins contrasted American constitutional guarantees with the absence of such guarantees in Nazi Germany and implied that little distinguished the two systems in practice. While the journal regretted the brutality and death Europeans were enduring, it demanded democracy in Alabama, Mississippi, and the United States Senate. On the same page, a piece titled "Out in the Cold" argued that the government's defense buildup had done little for blacks, noting the elusiveness of economic gains and the persistence of racial discrimination in the military. The journal told its readers that "the strongest defense of democracy lies in giving all the people a stake in it," which should be measured not in comparison with Hitlerism, but "by the professions of democracy itself."[10]

Beginning in mid-1940, a striking change would mark the way a number of reform leaders came to speak about Hitler and Hitlerism. Some began to propound the view that American democracy—no matter how flawed—was preferable to the suffering German totalitarianism would bring to black America. This change, which emerged at about the time the French Army was disintegrating in the face of the German onslaught, is attributable not only to a growing understanding of the nature of Nazism, but also to the realization that war might come to America. As a result, many reformers began to argue that the war's outcome was critical for achieving progress at home, and their assertions that black America had a stake in foreign developments began to assume a degree of urgency that had been lacking before. From this point on, they would make the case, which they had been somewhat reluctant to advance earlier, that America had an increasingly important role to play in the world, and that to do so effectively, it was crucial to overcome the challenge of racial oppression in the United States.

Howard University political scientist and race activist Ralph Bunche captured the drama of the moment in a letter written on June 12, 1940, two days before the Germans marched into Paris. To the Committee to Defend America by Aiding the Allies, an organization that sought to convince American policymakers to deepen the country's commitment toward potential allies in Europe, Bunche asserted that American democracy, while flawed, was worth saving:

> I am a Negro. But above all I am an American. . . . American Negroes have more at stake in this moment of supreme world crisis than any other group of Americans . . . [and] have more cause to fight to the death for the perpetuation of the democratic ideal . . . than any group. . . . We suffer many disabilities here. . . . But every thinking Negro knows that our . . . aspirations . . . are inseparably bound to the destiny of this great country. . . . The ominous shadow of the racially-minded dictators . . . threatens to eclipse our hopes for the future. . . . We need no vivid imagination to visualize what might happen to minority groups here under Fascist domination.

Writing to the British scholar Harold Laski six months later, Bunche deemed it "racially suicidal" to claim that little distinguished the admittedly imperfect American or English democracies from the Nazi ideology. Black advancement was in fact predicated on continuing the struggle for equality "only within the democratic framework," and the defeat of the democracies would imperil that progress.[11] Bunche would express such views in more public settings during this period, arguing at Howard University in July 1940 that European events were critical to black Americans in their quest for change. He derided as "soap-box logic" the view that the war was nothing but a struggle between imperialist powers, all of whom were the same, and contended that the "vital war question" for blacks was simple: "who will win it?" Bunche highlighted the differences between life under the Nazis and life in the colonies of France and England, and while he was partly seeking to critique Communist attempts to gain support among black Americans, he insisted a German victory in Europe would imperil the nation's black population. After painting a gloomy picture of the way a fascist America would appear to blacks,

Bunche said he did not wish to incite nightmares. "American democracy is bad enough. But in the mad world of today I love it, and I will fight to preserve it."[12] It is difficult to imagine a more vivid expression of the race reformers' distinctive internationalism in these years.

The Urban League's *Opportunity* advanced a similar view, which, while not suggesting immediate support for American belligerency, led the journal to highlight how different life in America would be from life under Hitler. The monthly's readers would become well-acquainted with the idea that a German victory in Europe would have disastrous consequences for black America, a position that represented a significant departure from the notion that racial practices in the United States differed little from those in Nazi Germany. A July 1940 editorial claimed that some blacks saw little to distinguish "whether the Negro [was] exploited by Germans or Italians or Belgians" and believed a Nazi victory in Europe was unimportant to black Americans. Was Germany really more "rapacious" than Britain or France? Was Hitler's racial philosophy not similar to the ideas and practices seen in the British Empire? The editorial also noted that some blacks wondered why European events concerned them at all; surely, what truly mattered was equality in the United States. But the editor contended that this argument, which was heard among some blacks in urban America, was fallacious and short-sighted.

The journal observed that Hitler's ideas and policies were qualitatively different from those practiced by British and French imperialists, and (by implication) from those in the United States. The Nazi ideology made no effort to recognize the "dignity of the Negro as a man," and would relegate blacks to "perpetual serfdom," denying them "every semblance of legal status." A German victory in Europe would make the United States "the last great stronghold of the democratic principle of government," the editorial asserted, which would encourage the purveyors of racial oppression in America and give sustenance to "the Negro haters" and "the Jew baiters." As a result, black Americans would find themselves in a far worse position than the one they currently occupied, causing them to "begin the most bitter struggle" of their existence. *Opportunity* contended that critical distinctions separated Nazi from American racial persecution, a notable claim given the repeated assertions of the 1930s that insisted that little separated Senator Theodore Bilbo's South from Adolf Hitler's Germany.[13]

The expression of such sentiments became rather widespread among leading reformers, particularly after Germany's triumphant march across Europe. It was not that the reformers had come to see America as a bastion of democracy and equality; instead, they had concluded that the survival of the United States represented the best way to continue to enlarge the sphere of justice for black Americans. As William Pickens wrote to a minister who had commended him for a column claiming Germany's conquest of Britain would be calamitous to blacks, the "only thing for the American Negro to do is to stand by his own country. . . . His destiny is inseparably bound to that of the United States. . . . We have no perfect democracy here and no perfect dispensations of justice. But we want the privilege to continue to fight and to make what we have better."[14] As did others, Pickens often expressed such views in the months before America went to war. In one column from this period, "Colored People Have a Stake in the War," Pickens asserted that a fascist victory would destroy a variety of freedoms and be especially dangerous for black peoples. While black life in England and America did not measure up to the democratic ideal, life in a Hitlerian world would be far worse. And so blacks should support American aid to Britain in its struggle against the dictators. Such clear support of the Allies during this period stands in marked contrast to earlier critiques of the imperial powers, which the race activists had frequently offered. Pickens's assertion that the Union Jack now stood for "the salvation of Europe and the security of America," and that Britain's defeat would leave the world in chains, illustrates the extent to which earlier claims equating Nazi Germany with the American South had become untenable as Hitler's legions blasted their way through Europe.[15]

Late in the neutrality period, the black educator Mary McLeod Bethune would give powerful expression to the idea that blacks had a stake in the war's outcome. Bethune, the daughter of former slaves, had worked her way through Chicago's Moody Bible Institute and then returned to her native South Carolina to begin her teaching career. Deeply committed to the work of racial uplift, in the 1920s, she established and became president of Florida's Bethune-Cookman College, a coeducational institution for African Americans, and in 1932, she founded the National Council of Negro Women. Before the end of Franklin Roosevelt's first term, Bethune had established a link to Eleanor Roosevelt through the National Youth Administration, a position that allowed her to monitor and help shape the New Deal's impact on black America. She articulated her opinions throughout the country—in the black press and in frequent speeches—and her views were heeded in Washington and across America. Discussing the war in October 1941, Bethune contended that the "Negro stands on the threshold of tomorrow." Today's actions, she asserted, would determine whether blacks would enter "the lighted halls of full freedom" or return to "yesterday's darkness of oppression, discrimination, even slavery." Despite the indignities of domestic racial persecution, Bethune called the battle against Hitler "our fight," declaring, "We have the dual task of defeating Hitler abroad and Hitlerism at home." She reminded her listeners that while much progress had already been achieved, a long road lay ahead; but under Hitler, such progress would be impossible. It was crucial

to give "our voices, our strength, our skills, yes even our lives to defend
. . . the sovereignty of the United States against Hitler . . . not so much for
what America is, but for what America can be."[16]

A. Philip Randolph also argued forcefully in this period that the outcome of the war was critical to black advancement, publishing numerous
strongly worded articles on this theme in the *Black Worker*, the official
organ of the Brotherhood of Sleeping Car Porters. In a fall 1940 editorial,
written during the uncertain days of the Battle of Britain, he asked if it
mattered to America—and to black Americans—whether Britain or Germany won. A German victory meant the defeat of democracy and liberty,
he wrote, and the triumph of "a new slavery and barbarism, terrorism and
darkness." It meant tyranny, despotism, and mass murder. Under Hitler,
Randolph asserted, "Negroes would be re-enslaved" and returned to their
former status as chattel. While Britain was no paragon of racial equality,
it did regard blacks as human, permitted them to receive a higher education, and was gradually granting blacks equal status. Early in 1941, Randolph argued that black Americans should support "all-out aid" to Britain, whose cause was democracy, the "only hope and salvation of
minority groups." Giving a dramatic twist to the analogies of the past,
he contended that democratic England is "as different from totalitarian
Germany . . . as New York is from Georgia." Randolph was convinced,
moreover, that black Americans would suffer like no other people under
the "dreadful darkness and tragic terrorism" of totalitarianism, and he
declared that "the Battle of Britain is the Battle of America and the Battle
of America is the Battle of the Negro."[17]

While the reformers were not unanimous in arguing that it was essential
to aid the Allies, this position represented a significant departure from
earlier reactions to overseas developments.[18] Previously, the race activists
had spoken of the unsavory practices of foreign regimes so as to highlight
the unjust treatment blacks endured in the United States. But by the early
1940s, as they came to understand the true character of Nazism, witnessed Germany's brutal military victories in Europe, and recognized the
threat posed to Britain and perhaps America, the reformers began to interpret German developments quite differently. Pointing to the threat Nazism posed to western democracy, they now argued that it was imperative
for America to end racial oppression in order to build the most effective
fighting machine possible. This made it essential for the country to overturn Jim Crow in its hour of need. Consequently, the reformers linked the
German threat to western democracy to the need for equality in the armed
forces and in the country's expanding defense industries—and these twin
goals would become the movement's key objectives during the war.

Spearheading these efforts during 1940 and 1941 was A. Philip Randolph, who would assume the lead role in the March on Washington

Movement (MOWM), a new organization that sought equal opportunities for blacks in defense production and in the military.[19] On September 27, 1940, Randolph, Walter White, and T. Arnold Hill of the Urban League met with Franklin Roosevelt to discuss racial discrimination in the nation's armed forces and defense industries. According to White, the president listened attentively to the three leaders, assuring them he would try to weaken or eliminate such practices. He promised to report back to them after conferring with aides, and on October 9, White House press secretary Stephen Early issued an official statement, which, in Walter White's words, "fell like a bomb on public opinion."[20] Early's statement made clear that the government's military segregation policy would remain essentially unchanged and implied that this course had been agreed upon by the three black leaders at their meeting with Roosevelt. They had done no such thing, of course, and after a vigorous denial from White, Early issued a retraction stating that they had urged ending segregation in the armed forces. At the end of this unpleasant episode (before the retraction, the black press had pilloried the three leaders), one point was clear: the government was not prepared to budge from its original position and remained unwilling to integrate the military or the defense industries.[21]

In light of this experience, Randolph became convinced that traditional avenues of protest like White House meetings and telegrams to Washington were fruitless; a new approach—based on mass action—would be necessary.[22] On January 15, 1941, Randolph issued a press release stating that he intended to lead a march on Washington to protest racial discrimination in the country's defense industries and armed forces. The powerfully worded statement claimed the nation's defense policy "reeks and stinks with race prejudice, hatred, and discrimination." Randolph demanded justice for blacks in the factories, mills, mines, and offices that were part of America's defense preparations, as well as in the army, navy, and the air corps. It was a call for mass action, which proclaimed that power resided not in the few, but in the masses, and more specifically, in the "organized masses" that were "united for a definite purpose." The method would be simple: "TEN THOUSAND Negroes [would] march on Washington, D.C. with the slogan: 'WE LOYAL NEGRO AMERICAN CITIZENS DEMAND THE RIGHT TO WORK AND FIGHT FOR OUR COUNTRY.'" The goal was not to hamper the nation's defense efforts; on the contrary, the statement declared, "[W]e seek the right to play our part in advancing the cause of national defense and national unity." The march aimed to "wake up and shock Official Washington" as never before. Thus was born one of the earliest national efforts at mass action in the history of American race reform.[23]

The detailed story of the March on Washington Movement, which worked with the NAACP to secure fair treatment for blacks in defense industries and the armed forces, has been told elsewhere.[24] After confronting the threat of a huge July 1 gathering of black Americans in the nation's capital (the number had grown from ten thousand to one hundred thousand), on June 25, 1941, Franklin Roosevelt issued Executive Order 8802, which established the President's Committee on Fair Employment Practices (FEPC) and banned discrimination based on race, creed, color, or national origin in industries holding government contracts. In response, Randolph called off the proposed march. While the president's directive provided less than black leaders had originally demanded (it did not address the issue of segregation in the military), many viewed it as a great victory.[25] Significantly, Randolph, the MOWM's key figure, had placed overseas developments at the core of his message, and more broadly, defense jobs and equality in the military became the movement's two concrete demands before America went to war. As is suggested by the reformers' writings in the black press and the reform journals, along with the addresses they delivered at conferences and rallies, the movement's leaders believed the world crisis had given them the opportunity to extract tangible gains from American policymakers.[26]

But it was not merely the prospect of employment opportunities or equality in the military that motivated the reformers at this time, for their willingness to relate external to internal matters extended beyond their wish to achieve such concrete goals. As the sociologist Charles S. Johnson wrote in the summer of 1941, the struggle against the racist philosophy of Nazi Germany had particular "importance for the Negro . . . [and] it may well be that the nation, if it has to fight or sacrifice to defend a principle may eventually come to believe in it and practice it."[27] Whether American belligerency would give life to Professor Johnson's optimistic ruminations remained unclear. What is certain is that many reform leaders were convinced that the United States had a role to play in the international crisis, and they believed, as did an increasing number of Americans in the months ahead, that engagement overseas would bring the nation closer to realizing its historic promise.

On the morning of December 7, 1941, at five minutes before eight o'clock, a wave of 190 Japanese planes struck the American fleet and military installations in and around Pearl Harbor, Hawaii. One hour later, a second wave of 170 planes followed. When the attack was over, more than twenty-four hundred Americans lay dead and over eleven hundred had been wounded. In addition to the bloodshed, the loss of war matériel was severe: the Japanese had destroyed or put out of commission 8 battleships, 3 light cruisers, 4 miscellaneous vessels, and 188 airplanes.[28] The next day, Franklin Roosevelt went before Congress to ask for a declaration of war, and having asserted that December 7, 1941, was "a date which will live in infamy," he told the nation, "No matter how long it may take us to overcome this premeditated invasion, the American people in their righteous might will win through to absolute victory." Within thirty-three minutes, both houses of Congress had passed the war resolution, with but one dissenting vote.[29]

Throughout the country, there was great support for American belligerency, as the nation's reluctance to become involved in the war evaporated almost overnight. A man in line at a Norfolk, Virginia, recruiting station declared, "I want to beat them Japs with my own bare hands," while a steelworker of similar temperament remarked, "We'll stamp their front teeth in."[30] And in fighting with all its enormous power, the United States would embark on a policy of direct and energetic involvement in world affairs, which, over the next four decades, would alter the fabric of twentieth-century American life and of world politics as well. Of more immediate concern was the fact that four days after the Japanese attack on Pearl Harbor, Germany and Italy declared war on the United States. America was again involved in a world war, which in the magnitude of its scope, carnage, destructiveness, and sheer depravity would exceed anything humanity had ever known. At the same time, World War II would provide an unprecedented opportunity for the race reformers to deploy their distinctive internationalism so as to advance their cause. And not surprisingly, they wasted little time in doing so.

On December 8, at its regular meeting, the NAACP's board issued a statement declaring that black Americans would give "unqualified support to the protection of their country," even as they continued to struggle for "full citizenship rights" in a land that denied them democracy. As they had in every war, blacks would fight loyally, but would insist on the right to do so as equals. That same day, Walter White submitted a proposal to the board calling for a conference as soon as possible, where representative black leaders would draft a statement that would include the terms upon which "Negroes [could] be satisfied to support" the country's foreign and domestic policy. According to White, such a statement would cause the government and the people to recognize that "the Negro [would] fight as an equal but not as a vassal." White observed that by drafting a "sober, intelligent, and convincing document," this proposed committee could help the cause of reform not just during the war, but at the peace table afterward. Clearly, the head of the association believed American belligerency presented race activists with an extraordinary opportunity to articulate their aims during the coming struggle.[31]

The reaction to American belligerency by other race reform organizations, in black newspapers, and in the reform journals suggests widespread recognition that involvement in the war could aid the movement.[32] Just after Pearl Harbor, A. Philip Randolph published a number of pieces that contended black Americans had a great stake in the war and that compared the American democracy favorably with Nazi Germany and Japan. "We must fight to preserve democracy and liberty such as we now have . . . so that we may make it sounder and better," Randolph wrote, urging blacks to demand the right to work and fight alongside "white Americans as full and equal citizens." He asserted that the fight to destroy totalitarianism overseas meant that black people were obligated to fight for their "constitutional, democratic rights and freedoms here in America." And in an intriguing reformulation of a common wartime idea, Randolph alleged that if black men, while fighting to defeat Japan and Germany, did not fight to strengthen democracy in America, they would be traitors to democracy and to "the liberation of the Negro people."[33] With great conviction, Randolph wrote directly to Roosevelt, asking the president to "strike down" the "hydra-headed monster" of discrimination, which he claimed would benefit not just blacks, but the unity of the country and its potential for victory. Only Roosevelt, the "champion of democracy and liberty," could effect such change, which was necessary to combat the "most dangerous, bloodthirsty and conscienceless militarists the world has ever known."[34]

The reform journals were no less determined to relate America's overseas aims to their domestic aspirations, and while pledging black America's fullest support in the war effort, *The Crisis* asserted that this was no time to remain silent about the breaches of democracy at home. An especially powerful editorial published just after America went to war contended that the "highest expressions of patriotism" during the conflict would come from refusing to ignore "those evils among us which are blood brothers of the evils against which we are now warring." The blood of America's fighters and the sweat of its workers would be sacrificed to help construct "a new world" from which both Hitler and Hitlerism had been extirpated. To thirteen million "American Negroes that means a fight for a world in which lynching, brutality, terror, humiliation, and degradation through segregation and discrimination, shall have no place—*either here or there.*" It was imperative to reject injustice wherever it existed, *The Crisis* declared. "[W]e must speak, even as we fight and die."[35]

In the wake of Pearl Harbor, the black press also bound the country's international duty to vanquish tyranny to its domestic obligation to abolish racial persecution. Several weeks before the *Pittsburgh Courier* proclaimed its historic "Double-V" campaign, the paper published a page-one editorial, "We Are Americans, Too," which described a "dastardly, cunning, and deceptive" Japanese attack, and contended that America had not asked for war. Providing an overview of the contribution (military and otherwise) that blacks had made throughout the nation's history, the paper assured America of the "unswerving loyalty of . . . 13,000,000 Negroes." But the editors said more, calling on the president and Congress to declare war not just on Japan, but on domestic race prejudice.[36] Advancing a similar argument, the *Chicago Defender* referred to the "dastardly attack" unleashed by "the mad dogs of the Empire of the Rising Sun" and proclaimed that the heart of America's black citizens beat as one with the heart of all other Americans. Despite black allegiance to the nation's international cause, the editors warned that the black population wanted to serve as equals and would reject the abbreviation of their rights. Echoing the sentiments heard in *The Crisis*, the *Defender* claimed it was just as important for blacks to insist upon strengthening "the weak spots in [America's] armor of democracy" as it was to fight on the fields of battle. A bold headline, splashed across the *Defender*'s front page in one-quarter inch type, captured the sentiments of committed race reformers in these early days of American belligerency: "AWAKE WHITE AMERICA, THE HOUR IS AT HAND!"[37]

A notable aspect of the reformers' reaction to the war was the frequency with which they considered the black experience during World War I. Before and after Pearl Harbor, race activists reflected on the unfulfilled aspirations of the earlier crusade and averred that this time they would not allow America to deny blacks the fruits of victory. While black Americans would support the American war effort, they would not enter the conflict with a blind faith in the country's willingness to grant them democracy, and throughout the war, the reformers would press the government to end racial persecution. Unlike in the last war, when Du Bois issued his call for blacks to "Close Ranks," race activists would now work relentlessly to realize their aims, and none would counsel their followers to forget their grievances; instead, they would work tirelessly to overcome them.[38] At the NAACP's annual conference in June 1940, Walter White pointed to the events of 1917–19 and contended that blacks, made wiser by the experience, would not be duped again. In a speech filled with the standard list of reform demands, the secretary said that if called, blacks would fight with the same devotion and courage as in the past. After the war "to make the world safe for democracy . . . the Negro soldier returned confident that he would be given at least a small portion of that democracy for whose preservation he had fought," White recalled. Instead, he was lynched and burned at the stake. The black man found "the same doors shut as sharply in his face when he sought employment, education and a decent place" to live as "he had encountered before he went to Flanders Fields to fight for freedom." The nation had to understand that black men, if called to serve, would ask, "What point is there in fighting and perhaps dying to save democracy if there is no democracy to save?"[39]

In the summer of 1943, the *Journal of Negro Education*, a Howard University quarterly, published a powerful document comparing the black experience at home and abroad during the world wars. According to the editor's introduction, the volume sought to provide a "timely perspective" that might contribute to improving the status of black Americans during and after the war. Several distinguished contributors explored everything from life in the military to the role of blacks in war industries and government agencies. Essays on black religious and cultural life, the role of pressure groups and educational agencies, and the "Negro [role] in Post-War Reconstruction," all were included in the journal's pages. Though a brief overview cannot do justice to the volume's richness, some excerpts suggest its range.[40] Roscoe Lewis, a Hampton Institute professor, considered how pressure groups helped maintain black morale during the world wars and observed that the earlier conflict had consolidated the NAACP's position as the country's leading race reform organization. Lewis also noted that in the current struggle such organizations sustained the sense among blacks that the "American way of life [was] being pushed steadily . . . along a path that some day [might] lead to democracy." NAACP attorney Charles Houston summarized the black role in the nation's armed forces during the world wars, writing that blacks had been denied a fair opportunity to serve their country in both instances. According to Houston, America could not fight effectively or assume a world leadership role until it integrated the black population into the armed forces more seriously than it had yet done. Together the essays serve as an extraordinary window onto black assessments of the unfolding war and on the earlier conflict. As the volume made clear, many believed World War I contained lessons applicable to World War II, and they agreed with Ira De A. Reid's observation that it was essential for justice to prevail in the current crisis. Reform leaders, it seemed, were determined to do whatever they could to prevent history from repeating itself.[41]

If a retrospective assessment of the Great War represented a novel approach for aiding black America, the reformers' response to events in the colonial world between 1939 and 1945 was consistent with the way they had previously integrated such questions into their domestic program. Despite the war in Asia and Europe, the race activists remained interested in Africa and India and continued to use developments in both areas to inspire their supporters with the notion that theirs was a shared crusade. Indeed, the democratizing rhetoric that was central to the wartime experience served to magnify the reformers' conviction that peoples of color throughout the world harbored dreams and aspirations similar to those embraced by black America. Before and after December 1941, *The Crisis* regularly examined African developments, with George Padmore, the distinguished commentator and activist on colonial issues, contributing several pieces to the journal. In October 1939, Padmore documented the exploitation, labor unrest, and developing political consciousness of oppressed peoples in British West Africa. He assayed Britain's response to the economic and political strivings of indigenous peoples, called British actions "fascist," and noted that black America had a "moral obligation" to support the African workers and peasants who were struggling to escape "the democratic imperialist yoke." Exhorting *Crisis* readers to get their organizations to speak out against the oppression of black Africa, Padmore reminded them that they had a "splendid opportunity to show solidarity" with their African brothers.[42] Throughout the war, in documenting the liberation struggles of black Africans against European oppression, the editors nurtured the idea that shared aspirations bound together the black populations of the United States and Africa.[43]

But the attention paid to the developing world extended beyond Africa. In early 1944, Roy Wilkins wrote on the NAACP's behalf to Anup Singh of the India League of America (which represented the Indian National Congress in the United States) on the occasion of the league's India Independence Day meeting. "Our people understand . . . the conditions forced upon India. They resemble in many respects the proscription suffered by colored Americans." Having observed that the arguments justifying Britain's continued oppression of the Indian people resembled those that kept blacks from becoming full-fledged American citizens, Wilkins insisted the association believed that granting independence to India would demonstrate more than any other act that "the United Nations are sincere in their crusade for a better world."[44] Wilkins's message to this leading Indian freedom organization illustrates the reformers' irrepressible interest in Indian affairs during the war, and Britain's continuing exploitation of peoples of color during a conflict in which the race question was vital intensified the reformers' scrutiny of developments on the subcontinent.

As before, the race activists continued to discuss Indian developments with their supporters in the hope that this might inspire those who learned about the heroism of Gandhi and his people. Moreover, the Gandhian philosophy of nonviolent disobedience began to seep into the rhetoric of American race reform and would contribute to the emergence of a new organization. In the black press, Roy Wilkins linked the Indian freedom struggle to domestic race reform, even as he acknowledged that the two situations were not precisely the same. Writing in March 1942 about the Indian contribution to the Allied war effort, Wilkins noted that if India were to fight in the war, "she wants to fight for herself and her people." Beyond this, once the Indians returned from the world's battlefields, they did not want to find their system unchanged, and they would no longer work to produce the wealth, while their British masters drank scotch and sodas. There was "something for American Negroes in this steadfast Indian attitude," Wilkins claimed, and both situations, while somewhat different, were characterized by "exploitation based upon race and color." Britain told India the time was not yet ripe for change, and blacks heard the same in the United States, but neither the Indian nor the black American should believe it. Asserting that "India has shown us the way," Wilkins predicted that hundreds of millions would live differently after the war.[45]

The Crisis also included numerous wartime pieces focusing on Indian affairs, which compared the circumstances of Indians and black Americans.[46] In a fascinating article, an Indian student described a personal encounter with Gandhi, who, in a wide-ranging discussion, considered the meaning of American democracy. When the student assured the Mahatma that America had solved its race problem after the Civil War and was now free and democratic, Gandhi smiled and suggested that the young man ought to supplement his textbook knowledge with a trip to the American South—without his turban or his Indian clothes. Travel as a black man in the South, the Indian leader recommended. "Be calm and never protest. Take all the humiliations, insults and pin pricks. Then write to me how it feels . . . to be a Negro in America." The young writer confessed a certain confusion, unsure what was "passing thru Gandhi's mind." But the youthful Indian ultimately comprehended what Gandhi had wanted him to experience, and *Crisis* subscribers surely had no difficulty understanding the point of the older man's advice, which revealed an appreciation of the true character of American democracy.[47]

In a still more significant development, Gandhian ideas began to inform race reform discourse during the war, influencing the perspective of leaders like A. Philip Randolph and the March on Washington Movement. Writing in the *Chicago Defender* in September 1942 about the two-front war black Americans were waging at home and abroad, Randolph rebuked the British government for its indifference to the Indian cry for freedom. He asserted that the British imperial mindset was paranoid and delusional, and suggested that this pathological mentality, which rejected "equality, freedom, and independence [for] the darker races," might cause the Allies to lose the war. After observing that the "patterns of oppression and exploitation" were similar throughout the world, Randolph asked what distinguished the plight of black Americans from that of the Indians. Nothing, he asserted, for both countries were influenced by racist doctrine, and blacks and Indians were subject groups that lacked the "constitutional, civil and political rights" of free peoples. Indian efforts to secure justice and equality had led to a program of civil disobedience, Randolph observed, while black America's desire for full citizenship had led to the March on Washington Movement. Ascribing universal significance to each struggle, he noted that both peoples sought to achieve not just their own freedom, but the "moral and spiritual salvation" of their respective countries and of all western civilization.[48]

In 1943, Randolph began to reflect closely on the relationship between Indian methods for overcoming oppression and on tactics that might prove effective in America. In public remarks and in the black press, he explicitly linked the MOWM's approach to the race problem with Gandhi's tactics in India. While the Indian's ideas and techniques could not be applied to the American scene without modification, it was "the principle, the spirit, [and] the discipline" of Gandhi's approach that he was advocating. Randolph contended that to achieve their aims, blacks did not have to march to the sea for salt or weave cloth for their own garments, as Gandhi had done. Nevertheless, the principles of nonviolence and civil disobedience were valid in America, and the "promise of victory" was no less certain. Blacks had to pursue the "negative approach" and refuse to accept second-class accommodations, ride in Jim Crow buses, or attend Jim Crow theaters or segregated schools. Randolph insisted that the spectacle of a "sincere and organized protest" could provide the protestors with strength and confidence, and he wedded this new approach to the reformers' foremost wartime goal, the abolition of segregation in the military.[49]

A wide-ranging series of articles that appeared in the *Defender* in mid-1943 provides further insight into the labor leader's conception of nonviolent civil disobedience and its potential benefits in the United States. According to Randolph, blacks were at a crossroads and faced new challenges, made more complex by the war. To solve such problems, it was necessary to reorient the race reform program; the old strategies and techniques no longer sufficed. The goal of the March on Washington Movement was complete equality: economic, political, social, and racial. Calling for a conference in Chicago centering on the theme, "We Are Americans, Too," Randolph again proclaimed that the MOWM would explore a new strategy based on Gandhi's idea of nonviolent civil disobedience and noncooperation, an approach he labeled "Constitutional Obedience or Non-Violent Goodwill Direct Action." Randolph swept aside the doubts of those who insisted it was inappropriate for America and pointed to the universality of certain principles of human behavior, including the deeply rooted desire for freedom and happiness. Unlike the Indians who sought to abolish British imperial rule, the MOWM did not wish to overthrow the government. It aimed, instead, to maintain and improve American civil law, particularly where it no longer functioned or where mob law reigned. Black Americans were not seeking independence as a "separate racial unit," he declared, but genuine inclusion in the American democracy. "Non-violent goodwill direct action" was based upon "the theory of the common unity of all peoples," and while differences existed between the means and aims of Indian and American reformers, the MOWM program owed much to the tactics that the Indians were employing against imperial Britain.[50]

If Randolph's speeches, articles, and rallies did not lead to a massive wartime campaign of civil disobedience, his activities sowed tactical seeds that would prove significant in the postwar era.[51] Beyond this, Randolph and the MOWM helped inspire a group of younger figures who established the Congress of Racial Equality (CORE) in 1942, an interracial organization based on Gandhian principles. Clearly, the Indian leader's ideas had begun to influence the actions of numerous race reformers, who for some time had identified a connection between the goals of colonial peoples and those of black Americans.[52] Although the impact of Gandhian thought would not be felt until later, Randolph (and CORE) helped to nurture and sustain a commitment to such ideas, which would be critical in the years ahead.

While concerned with India and colonial oppression, Randolph was of course engaged with the war. With the world ablaze, Randolph, described by one biographer as black America's "most popular and sought-after . . . political figure," continued to place the conflict at the center of his message, and in his writings and speeches, he gave voice to the reformers' distinctive internationalism.[53] Although Executive Order 8802 led Randolph and others to cancel the march on Washington, the labor leader was determined to maintain the March on Washington Movement, and for the next few years, it remained central to the struggle. Tirelessly, Randolph organized mass rallies around the country, which employed the slogan "Winning Democracy for the Negro Is Winning the War for Democracy," and he called on the government to allow blacks to take their place as full citizens in the American polity.[54] A 1942 piece in the *Black Worker* illustrates how Randolph wedded America's international struggle—which he enthusiastically supported—to the movement's aims at home. The black American was obligated "to vigorously fight for all of the democratic privileges and rights enjoyed by other American citizens," he noted, emphasizing that the wartime quest for racial justice was "wholly comparable" to the nation's campaign "to preserve this democratic system and . . . [its] ideals . . . in this world struggle."[55] Interestingly, Randolph did not believe the source of international oppression was singular, and he did not attribute it solely to the policies of Nazi Germany or other fascist regimes. While it was essential to defeat fascism wherever it occurred, he insisted it was also necessary to abolish European imperial rule, which plagued the world's "darker races." Randolph's wartime language focused, therefore, on the battle against Nazi oppression and on the antidemocratic policies practiced by countries (including the United States) that were allied against the Axis powers. Black Americans and peoples in the developing world thus had a common stake in the multifaceted battles against oppression.

In September 1942, Randolph set his views before the policy conference of the March on Washington Movement. He called for the triumph of the Allies against Hitler, Hirohito, and Mussolini, and observed that the fate of black America was "tied up with the democratic way of life." While the defeat of Nazism, militarism, and fascism was crucial, it was not enough. Equally important was the destruction of the Anglo-American empire, the story of which, Randolph contended, was "one of exploitation for the profit and power of a monopoly capitalist economy." Sounding like the young socialist who had edited *The Messenger* some two decades before, Randolph declared that once the war was over, people would desire more than the "dispersal of equality and power among individual citizens" in a liberal democracy; they would also insist upon the "dispersal of equality and power among the citizen-workers in an economic democracy that will make certain the assurance of the good life . . . in a warless world."[56] The address, typical of many Randolph gave during the war, placed the movement's domestic goals against the backdrop of what he perceived to be a complex global struggle for justice and equality.[57] He harnessed the democratic energies released by the war, which American leaders spoke of in their wartime pronouncements, to inspire his followers and deepen their commitment to achieving racial justice. "We are fighting for big stakes," he told his supporters, for "liberty, justice, and democracy. Every Negro should hang his head in shame who fails to do his part now for freedom. This is the hour of the Negro."[58] But Randolph had a larger audience in mind. And in framing the message as he did—particularly by speaking repeatedly about the worldwide struggle against oppression—it seems clear that he hoped all Americans would reflect on the hypocrisy inherent in fighting for freedom abroad while tolerating oppression at home.[59]

After December 1941, at the three NAACP conferences held in wartime (none was held in 1945), the association's leaders continued to embed the domestic reform enterprise in the international struggle. And *Crisis* readers also confronted an enormous amount of coverage of the world conflict, as essays, editorials, and poetry demonstrate how completely the war permeated the discourse of reform. Still more dramatically, NAACP chief Walter White journeyed to the war's European and Pacific theaters to highlight the interrelationship between the campaigns against tyranny abroad and at home. In Los Angeles, in July 1942, the NAACP held its annual conference, guided by the theme, "Victory Is Vital to Minorities." Assistant Secretary Roy Wilkins, the keynote speaker, told the crowd that the stakes had never before been so great, the issues so clear, or the pressures so crushing. With the world in a state of upheaval that would shatter and then remold the destinies of nations, peoples, and races, Wilkins claimed it was a "time for action," not silence. Pointing to a recent lynching in Missouri and the battle for the right to vote, Wilkins told his listeners that the status quo was unacceptable and that democracy—if it meant anything—meant "equality of opportunity extended to all peoples, to all races, [and] to all creeds." Wilkins powerfully linked the world conflict to black aspirations and American race reform, asserting that the war was "one with our people's plight." Indeed, the movement's goals and the very conference itself were inseparable from the overseas struggle. Wilkins reminded the delegates that what they were doing "with the greatest spiritual dedication . . . is in essence the war effort. That's what the war is all about. These things that we feel in our hearts . . . [that] we are determined to fight to have." Both the war and the movement were about "man's striving onward and upward for equality, for a better place in the sun." Exhorting his listeners to continue to pursue the goal of racial justice at this critical moment, Wilkins thundered, "We cannot sit supinely by so that generations from now they will say we did not meet the issue at the hour when it was to be met."[60] Thus did Wilkins identify a unity of purpose between American war aims and the movement's goals.

Not surprisingly, the war remained the central issue at the NAACP's annual conferences in 1943 and 1944, with the former labeled an "Emergency Conference on the Status of the Negro in the War for Freedom." The 1943 conference convened in Detroit in early June, just two weeks before the city erupted in a spate of racial violence, which would plague several cities that summer.[61] The NAACP declared itself appalled by the discrepancy between America's "professed war aims of democracy and freedom and the treatment meted out to the Negroes" at home. The delegates hailed Franklin Roosevelt's Four Freedoms (freedom of speech, of religion, from want, and from fear), declaring that "American Negroes and colored people all over the world" would regard them as "hypocrisy unless the President act[ed] to end discrimination" in the American military. Just as they had done during World War I, the reformers referred to the words of an American president to highlight the notion that democracy ought to begin at home. And as the words of Langston Hughes suggest, poets did the same:

> The President's Four Freedoms
> Appeal to me.
> I would like to see those Freedoms
> Come to be.
> If you believe
> In the Four Freedoms, too,
> Then share 'em with me—
> Don't keep 'em all for you.[62]

The following summer, more than thirty thousand people gathered in Chicago's Washington Park for the closing session of the association's annual conference. Publisher Marshall Field told the throng that the war had brought into "focus the need to give practical meaning to our professions of democracy," and he observed that enlightened groups throughout the country, which could not reconcile the disjunction between the "slogans of freedom and equality" with prejudice and discrimination, were working to change American race relations.[63] Walter White, in his address, covered a range of international issues, including the trip he had taken earlier that year, a three-month journey, during which he had visited the European theater of operations, Italy, North Africa, and the Middle East. Distressed by what he had seen, White said he wished it were possible to report that "fighting to destroy Nazism had transformed the racial behavior" of the American soldier. But sadly, he said, "We have merely transplanted to other lands the American pattern."[64] Devoting the last several minutes of his keynote address to his trip, the internationally minded NAACP chief discussed the memorable experience (one of his two great wartime expeditions) with several thousand activists at the most important gathering on the reform calendar.[65]

The previous September, White had written to Assistant Secretary of War John McCloy, expressing a desire to visit the war theaters (Europe first and later the Pacific) to observe the condition of black soldiers abroad, and, if possible, to buoy their morale. If the government wished, he would report his findings to the War Department, and he noted that while abroad, he intended to write about the trip for a variety of periodicals. White told McCloy he hoped the journey might allay the fears of black soldiers "regarding the experiences Negro troops are undergoing" in the war theaters. He penned a similar letter to Franklin Roosevelt a few weeks later, telling him about his plans.[66] His request granted, White left for the European theater on January 2, 1944, an accredited war correspondent in the employ of the *New York Post* and *Life* magazine. Assuming an internationalist stance from the outset, White wrote in the *Chicago Defender* that he wanted to focus the attention of "white America upon the tremendous role" black soldiers were playing in helping to win the war, and he sought to convince the country that the "color problem" was "no longer a national issue but a global one." He recorded his overseas observations in detail, describing the trip in his journalistic pieces, and the following year in a small volume, *A Rising Wind*.

Upon his return, White would tell thousands of NAACP members in Chicago about the journey and would also speak to a national radio audience about the experience. Clearly, the NAACP head was determined to share his observations on racial conditions in the United States military with as many Americans as he could.[67] Speaking on the CBS radio network in April 1944, White described a situation eerily reminiscent of World War I, telling listeners about an aggressive but vocal minority of white soldiers who were spreading vicious stories about black fighting men so as to poison Europeans against them. Blacks had tails; they barked to communicate; they were illiterate; they were diseased: this is what the Europeans heard from white American soldiers fighting against Hitler's racial tyranny. Such behavior puzzled the Europeans, White observed, for they did not understand why some Americans could bear such enmity toward their fellow countrymen, especially as they battled for a common cause. American segregation also surprised the Europeans, who wondered why a country "fighting a war for freedom, should send abroad two armies—one white and one Negro." A few months later, standing before the NAACP delegates in Chicago, White spoke of the galling military practice of designating certain towns and areas "off limits" to black fighters, which made it difficult to find diversions while on leave. He noted the unfair use of courts-martial against blacks, a practice that aimed to intimidate them. In all, White painted a grim picture of the conditions the black warrior endured overseas—conditions White hoped to remedy by bringing them to light. White also submitted an extensive list of recommendations to the War Department, in an effort to abolish the discriminatory practices he had witnessed during his fourteen weeks abroad.[68]

Though White undoubtedly believed his trip had given him the opportunity to help the black soldier, the objectives of his journey were more expansive. The head of America's leading race reform organization had not spent months traveling in perilous battle zones, nor devoted additional time to speaking and writing about the experience, merely to aid the black soldier, no matter how worthy a task that was.[69] White's highly visible activities during and after the trip, which included publishing articles in black and white periodicals, giving speeches before the NAACP in Chicago and on the radio, and writing a book on his adventure, suggest that the NAACP chief believed his travels would allow him to convey a far larger message—one related to the very significance of the war. As the nation battled against tyranny, Walter White journeyed far from home in order to remind anyone who would listen about the importance the war held for American democracy. Toward the end of *A Rising Wind*, he wondered whether America would permit racial discrimination to persist after the war and asked if the country would allow "itself to be led by the nose by demagogues and professional race-hate mongers," or if it would, instead, "slough off" prejudice and "chart a new course."[70] It is clear that White had traversed much of the globe in order to remind all Americans about institutionalized racial oppression, which persisted in the United States even as the country was grappling with antidemocratic, racist regimes.

Walter White, a leader in the black freedom struggle for more than thirty-five years, joined the NAACP's Atlanta branch in 1917 and moved to the New York office the following year. In 1931, White, who became known as "Mr. NAACP," was chosen to head the organization, which he led until his death in 1955.

In helping to "chart a new course," the organization White headed expanded enormously during the war. The association's membership climbed from 50,000 in 1940 to 205,000 in 1943 to 325,000 in 1944 to over 400,000 in 1945. With its growing numbers, the NAACP aimed to end discrimination in the military and the armaments industry and continued to work on the domestic front for many of the same goals it had fought for in the past, particularly equality in education and the right to vote.[71] Beyond its dramatic wartime growth, the association experienced some key personnel changes in these years, including the resignation in 1942 of William Pickens, who had spent more than twenty years in the organization.[72] If Pickens's departure severed a link to the association's early days, that connection was partially restored two years later with Du Bois's return to the NAACP. At the annual conference in 1944, Walter White announced to resounding applause that the legendary activist would again serve the organization, now as director of special research. According to White, Du Bois would focus on postwar issues and help prepare material that pertained to "the Negro's cause" at the postwar peace gatherings. These were key questions, White asserted, for if the peace treaty rested on "white overlordship over the peoples of the earth, another war [was] inevitable." Black peoples at home and abroad were determined to have their voices heard, he observed, and the association wanted Du Bois to play an active part in this critical postwar mission.[73]

As did so many race activists who pondered the potential impact of the war, Du Bois believed the conflict could aid the movement, and throughout these years (before and after his return to the NAACP), he considered the gains black Americans and colonial peoples might expect. Writing to the editor of *Fortune* magazine in 1942, Du Bois described the world war as a campaign, albeit not a conscious one, "for racial equality." While acknowledging the war might end before racial equality was achieved, he contended it would serve as "the first phase of this inevitable struggle." Having gone to war to fight the dictators, America now wanted to "make it a war for democracy," by which "we meant democracy in Europe and North America." In Du Bois's estimation, it had become clear that the real issues of the war could not be settled without extending democracy to Asia and Africa, a theme he regularly set before thousands of readers in the black press.[74] "This is a war for freedom," he wrote in the spring of 1942, and if he was not certain for whose freedom it was being waged— Asiatics, Africans, southern blacks?—he asserted that if it was a war for those peoples, "my gun is on my shoulder." Du Bois also considered the progress black Americans had made in these years, though he admitted he had once doubted any gains were possible. But now it seemed the "American Negro was on the way to gain[ing] a great deal" from the conflict, particularly as "his war becomes a determined fight for entrance into industry." While not completely successful, this had "succeeded to an extraordinary degree," Du Bois claimed, for the war had "broken down bar after bar held up by employers." Later, it would only be "necessary to hold the ground thus gained." In Du Bois's view, the global conflict had provided concrete gains for black America.[75]

And Du Bois was not alone in embracing such sentiments. In the words of Roy Wilkins, the war had encouraged discussion of the "Negro problem," making it more "heated and constant" than it had ever been. It had stimulated black Americans, for it was "*not* like other wars. . . . The villains talked of 'master races' . . . [and] of the necessity of conquest and slavery."[76] Alain Locke also reflected on the world struggle, observing with a mixture of prescience and optimism in 1942 that not since the Civil War had any event been of greater significance for the "Negro's cause." In looking to the future, Locke, like many others, hoped the country's commitment to democracy abroad would help clear the United States of its "present undemocratic inconsistencies."[77]

Like a boldly colored thread, the world war ran through the writings, speeches, and correspondence of countless individuals who were committed to racial justice. It is impossible to study the words and actions of those who worked or thought seriously about race reform in these years without concluding that the global conflict was vital to the way they articulated their message and set forth their agenda. Convinced that America's worldwide struggle against tyranny and their campaign against racial oppression were intertwined, the reformers believed the war could galvanize support among their followers and among potential activists. And this belief was borne out by the NAACP's spectacular growth in this period. Reform leaders were persuaded, in short, that the war could transform American race relations, a notion Langston Hughes captured in verse:

> DECEMBER 7, 1941,
> From Harlem to India to Africa's land,
> Jim Crow started his last stand.
> Our battle yet is far from won,
> But when it is, Jim Crow'll be done![78]

Just as the war shaped the contours of American life, it shaped the campaign for racial justice and, in a fundamental sense, informed the actions of reform leaders, along with the tone and composition of their message. The movement's supporters heard speeches, gathered at meetings, and convened at conferences, all of which were defined by American actions overseas. The March on Washington Movement was a product of the war; subscribers to the reform journals read unceasingly about the significance of the war; and readers of the black press confronted countless articles and columns about the war's centrality. With the triumphant conclusion of the world conflict in August 1945, there was in America a sense that racial matters had reached a new juncture. A study published that year observed that the war had "changed the entire course of race relations and brought America face to face with the contradictions in our culture . . . to an extent which made it impossible for either Negroes or whites" to continue to evade them.[79] If this assertion was true—and there is no reason to doubt that it was—the transformation would have been impossible to imagine without the unwavering efforts of the reformers. In the days ahead, they would remain committed to highlighting the "contradictions" in American culture. With the country's victory overseas, the race activists would persist in seizing upon global developments and continue to place the momentous events of the postwar era at the center of their crusade.

Six

"TO HELP SAVE THE WORLD"
Seeking Race Reform, 1945–1950

IN MID-APRIL 1945, just weeks before the war in Europe ended, W.E.B. Du Bois was invited to a party at the home of a New York friend who had long been devoted to the cause of race reform. The race leader declined politely, noting that on the date in question, April 19, other matters would occupy his attention. On the nineteenth, Du Bois observed, "I shall leave for San Francisco to help save the world."[1] When the nineteenth arrived, the NAACP's Walter White spoke to the press before boarding a train for San Francisco, where he and Du Bois would serve as consultants to the American delegation at the founding meeting of the United Nations. White reflected on the significance of the conference for peoples of color throughout the world and for blacks in America. "It is our hope to induce the San Francisco conference to face what is one of the most serious problems of the twentieth century—the question of race and color." The association's leader noted his concern about the disposition of the colonial empires and the well-being of their people and stated that the plight of the exploited had "direct bearing on the future of Negroes in the United States." With that, White and Du Bois left for California, where they hoped to contribute to the reconstruction of world politics, a mission that might, in turn, aid the domestic struggle to which they had devoted their lives.[2]

There was no shortage of merriment aboard the special train the State Department had arranged to carry diplomats and correspondents to the gathering in San Francisco. Upon hearing that White and Du Bois were aboard, the black staff made certain the two travelers did not lack for cigarettes or Scotch. No less copious were the questions the two men fielded concerning the problem of race relations in the postwar world. According to White, he and Du Bois talked "morning, noon, and night" to foreign journalists and writers, who wondered how a land blessed with vast resources, famed for its generosity, and addicted to making statements about "democratic and Christian principles" could continue to maintain racial policies "based on hate and prejudice."[3] As the two men headed west, Roy Wilkins wrote a letter of encouragement and support to White, in which he considered the NAACP's upcoming mission in San Francisco. The letter, which White received upon arriving in California, noted that the "spotlight in Negro America will be on us so that . . . [we must] advance with skill and vigor the aspirations of colored people in this world crisis." Wilkins advised White to work "fearlessly and honestly," a course consistent with the NAACP's traditions, and told his fellow re-former that the conference gave the world's peoples the opportunity to "impress their yearnings upon those who will frame the peace."[4]

It is difficult not to view in symbolic terms the long journey to San Francisco undertaken by some of the country's leading race activists. During the next several years—in the wake of the war—the movement for race reform in America gathered increasing momentum as the community of reformers inside and outside the NAACP placed their domestic struggle at the center of the quest for justice that peoples of color were waging across the world.[5] After 1945, the race reformers persisted in melding domestic and world affairs as they set their program before their supporters, the nation, and the international community. And more powerfully than ever, color-conscious internationalism shaped their approach to reform. In these years, the emergence of the United Nations as a force for international comity and domestic justice, and America's emerging competition with the Soviet Union, which came to dominate the nation's political and cultural life, would both have a profound impact on the race reform campaign.

Not surprisingly, four years of American involvement in the war and the country's emergence from the conflict as the most powerful nation on earth had made global affairs a critical domestic preoccupation, ending whatever inclination persisted in the United States for remaining aloof from international politics. The country's swift transformation from the circumspection that had defined American diplomacy in the months and years before December 1941 to the crusading activism that would become a hallmark of the post-1945 era was altogether remarkable, and the struggle for racial justice would not remain untouched by this dramatic change.[6] The realization that American involvement in the world war had further globalized the cause of race reform was clear at the time, a development Walter White discussed in early 1946. The war had made the race issue at home and abroad one of the major challenges to be met if peace was to last, White said. World War II had destroyed forever the "illusion of white omniscience and omnipotence," and in its wake, "[c]olored peoples throughout the world . . . [were] determined once and for all time to end white exploitation and imperialism." This attitude, he noted, was particularly true among black Americans, and because the race question at home was now "part and parcel of the problems of . . . colored peoples" everywhere, the NAACP would work on "international as well as national phases of the question." In this new era, then, color-conscious internationalism and postwar American globalism would be interrelated.[7]

As had been true at the end of World War I, those committed to race reform saw the postwar moment as one of unlimited possibility, and some were persuaded that the United States could play a key part in shaping a more just international order. In fact, this optimistic view began to emerge well before the war was over, as reform leaders started to reflect on the shape the world might assume once peace arrived. An *Opportunity* editorial, "The Post War World," published just six months after the attack on Pearl Harbor, described the magnificent opportunity the war afforded the United States, which, if it were prepared to abolish domestic discrimination, would be able to marshal the active wartime support of colonial peoples. If the American president would accept this challenge, he could wield "the mightiest weapon ever fashioned," the power of which would crush the Allies' enemies from without and within. Sounding a Wilsonian tone, the editors warned that history would judge whether America was prepared to fulfill its manifest destiny and discharge "its duty to mankind."[8] Writing incisively a few months later, Charles S. Johnson identified a series of developments that would emerge after the war, the most significant of which would be the changed status of the world's oppressed peoples. The day of imperialism had been swept aside by a "wave of nationalism and freedom," he wrote, and the war had destroyed the "association of color with inferior status." Significantly, Johnson linked these epochal developments in the colonial world to the condition of blacks in postwar America, which he argued could not remain as it was before the war. Though the status of black Americans would not change overnight, Johnson saw the conflict as the seminal event in a transformative process that would improve the lives of peoples of color everywhere, the United States included.[9] Less than a year after America had gone to war, therefore, some in the reform community had begun to ponder the conflict's potential for helping to create a more just world.

In the spring of 1944, *Crisis* subscribers read "The Task for the Future," the text of a speech given a few months earlier by Saville Davis, a white journalist who spoke optimistically about the postwar era. The war was "liberalizing the world," and a "great tide of social and economic ferment" was sweeping the globe. In these revolutionary times, millions were demanding that "democracy make good on its pledge." This was true abroad and at home, where after the war, "the problem of the colored man . . . [would] be on the front line of democracy." For black America, it would be a moment to "press for action," while for white America, it would be a time to recognize that repression was no longer an adequate response to the race problem.[10] Even Du Bois, who was not given to excessive optimism about the prospects for racial progress, seemed to believe a better world might emerge after the war, a world the United States might help shape. He offered Rachel Davis Du Bois (no relation) some thoughts on a scholarly work she was writing, suggesting that she should focus on the idea that the future peace and progress of the world would rest not on biology or economics, but on the "meeting and cooperation and mutual exchange of experiences ... between an infinite number of cultural groups." While every area of the globe, whether Europe, Asia, or Africa, had something distinctive to contribute to the commonweal, he said, the United States, because of its diversity of peoples and its pledge to democratic policies, might serve as an example to the world, if only Americans could "learn to ... live together in peace and harmony ... and increase their mutual respect for each other." Du Bois was not certain his country could serve as an avatar (it might revert to race hatred and discrimination), but his letter reveals a cautious optimism, buoyed by the belief that the postwar period might be characterized by progress in the quest for human cooperation.[11]

The sense that a better world might emerge after the war was not confined to the reformers, for statesmen also recognized the potential for expanding global cooperation once peace came. To this end, a plan to establish an international organization that could calm the turbulent waters of international politics began to take definite shape in the summer and fall of 1944 at a lovely mansion in the Georgetown section of the American capital. At Dumbarton Oaks, thirty-nine delegates from America, Russia, Britain, and China laid out the structure of what would become the United Nations and agreed, among other things, to meet the following spring in San Francisco for the formal establishment of the organization.[12]

Recognizing the potential power and authority the institution might possess for assisting the oppressed in the colonial world and blacks in the United States, race reform leaders closely observed the 1944 gathering. While some believed the organization could help overcome the age-old problem of racial oppression, others (Du Bois especially) expressed reservations about the United Nations and were critical of the proposals the delegates had drawn up, claiming they virtually ignored the fate of colonial peoples. In the wake of the Dumbarton Oaks Conference, Du Bois, who was representing the NAACP, spoke to the Americans United for World Organization, a meeting held at the State Department in October 1944. The race leader argued that, in effect, the Dumbarton Oaks proposals had told colonial peoples that "the only way to human equality is [through] the philanthropy of masters who have historic and strong interest in preserving their present power." Du Bois was particularly distressed by what he perceived to be the state-centered provisions of the new organization, which made it impossible for races, groups, or colonial peoples to seek redress through the international body. "[D]epressed" by this realization, he declared it a "union of nations," rather than a union of races or groups not recognized as nations. Shortly after the end of the State

Department meeting, in an effort to forge his concerns about the Dumbarton Oaks proposals into constructive action, Du Bois wrote to a number of international religious and philanthropic groups, seeking their views on the question of colonies in the postwar world and hoping that such organizations would work with him to achieve a more equitable adjustment of colonial problems after the war.[13]

As the San Francisco conference neared, the race reformers presented their vision for the world. In various settings, they spoke and wrote about their hopes for the meeting and demonstrated their determination to influence the gathering. On March 12, 1945, the NAACP board passed a resolution written by Du Bois and forwarded to American Secretary of State Edward R. Stettinius, which contained several "demands" meant for the diplomats who would shortly arrive in California. In an effort to make war less likely and less profitable, the first demand called for the conference to establish in international law the racial equality of "the great groups of mankind." Concerning colonial authority, the association demanded that the ruling countries move to provide their subjects with "a voice in their own government," and eventually declare their willingness to liberate or integrate them into the "mother country with full rights of citizenship." America's leading race reform organization was thus demanding that the San Francisco delegates vanquish the idea of racial inequality and end the exploitation of peoples of color. The NAACP did this, it asserted, in order to help achieve "social progress and democracy" and to rescue mankind from continued war.[14]

In a similar spirit, on April 6, 1945, three weeks before the opening of the San Francisco conference, Du Bois and the NAACP helped organize a meeting in New York attended by forty-nine representatives from both the colonial world and black America, the purpose of which was to assemble "the essential facts concerning colonies and their demands." Meeting at the 135th Street branch of the New York Public Library, delegates from the Caribbean, India, southeast Asia, Africa, and the United States discussed the best way to address the poor conditions in the colonial world and drafted a statement intended for presentation at San Francisco, which declared that the future of colonial peoples and their territories was a global problem. The representatives agreed that holding colonies was a cause of war, oppression, poverty, famine, and disease. As a consequence, they proposed the creation of an international colonial commission, composed partly of colonized peoples, which would facilitate a rapid move toward independence. Significantly, the conferees also resolved that nations practicing discrimination at home, whether based on race, creed, or color, would be barred from the supervision of colonial areas. International security, they asserted, depended upon moving toward the liberation of colonial peoples, whose self-determination was the responsibility of the entire world.[15] The recommendations drawn up in New York in early April would help guide the activities of the NAACP's representatives a few weeks later when they reached San Francisco.[16]

Among those joining White and Du Bois, whom the U.S. government had invited to attend the San Francisco conference, was Mary McLeod Bethune (also representing the NAACP), along with leaders from more than forty national organizations, who would serve as observers at the gathering.[17] After some controversy over the selection of Bethune,[18] the three settled down at the conference and energetically presented the NAACP's perspective and goals to the American delegates and those from abroad. Throughout the meeting and after it had ended, White, Du Bois, and Bethune sought to influence American policymakers, claiming it was necessary for the nation to address the subject of colonial exploitation and to take the lead in framing a plan to liberate the oppressed. If the United States and the other victorious powers failed to do so, the reformers contended, World War II—the most destructive event in history—would have been fought in vain.

Du Bois was remarkably busy during his five weeks in San Francisco, meeting statesmen, preparing petitions, writing articles, and attending the plenary sessions of the conference. He delivered lectures, met with John Foster Dulles (an adviser to the American delegation and the future secretary of state), and had interviews with members of the Liberian, Haitian, and Ethiopian delegations. On May 2, Du Bois, with White and Bethune, presented a formal statement to the American delegation, which, brimming with internationalist fervor, declared that the "main groups of mankind, commonly called races, are essentially equal in capability . . . and deserve equality of treatment." Drafted by Du Bois, the statement affirmed the brotherhood of all peoples and proclaimed their right to freedom of thought, expression, and movement, as well as their right to justice in the courts and equality in the civil, economic, social, and political spheres. The declaration claimed, moreover, that it was the duty of the United Nations to abolish the colonial system, which was undemocratic, socially dangerous, and a cause of war. The NAACP's statement also asserted that no group should be "deprived of effective voice in its own government." On the same day that the NAACP issued its declaration, the entire body of American consultants presented a statement to the American delegation, which contained the portentous phrase: "the nations are to assure justice to peoples of their lands." After the representative of the Federal Council of Churches had read the statement, Walter White rose immediately and declared that the NAACP wished to emphasize that the phrase applied not only to colonial peoples, but also to "citizens within the home countries." Without question, the NAACP's representatives had undertaken a dual task in San Francisco: they would speak on behalf of oppressed peoples everywhere—whether they lived in distant lands or in America.[19]

While in San Francisco, Mary McLeod Bethune discussed the plight of colonial peoples, along with the need to improve the lives of black Americans, especially women. Upon receiving her invitation to attend the conference, she observed that "Negro women like all other women must take part in building this world, and must therefore keep informed on all world-shaping events."[20] Bethune also took note of the "common cause" that linked America's aspirations to the goals of black Americans and the world's "little people," suggesting that the lofty aims of the conference might have a salutary effect upon the United States. She was "jealous for the best possible America," and looked toward a time when such aims would find "fullest expressions [sic] among all Americans in all parts of the country."[21]

Bethune's internationalism would be no less apparent once the United Nations Conference had ended. Before leaving California, she issued an invitation for a June 23 meeting in Washington, D.C., where black leaders would gather "to chart a broad course of action to lay before our people and the country." The invitation made clear that the San Francisco gathering had provided the American race reform community with the energy that could propel the movement into the postwar period. In requesting the presence of black leaders at the June 23 meeting, Bethune considered the impact the United Nations Conference had had on those committed to domestic race reform, observing that those in attendance had realized that unity of action could help overcome the "problems of our people, our nation, and the world." Beyond suggesting that black America's problems were linked to a larger set of domestic and global challenges, Bethune spoke optimistically about the postwar period. Since blacks had achieved "many gains" they could not afford to lose, unity was especially important in a time "rich with possibilities of an ever growing future" for blacks and for America. Bethune, like many reformers, was optimistic about the postwar years and was determined to use the San Francisco conference as a springboard into the coming era.[22]

During the United Nations Conference, the NAACP's representatives exerted continual pressure on the American delegation, repeatedly bringing their concerns and aspirations to the attention of Secretary of State Stettinius and his associates. While Du Bois, White, and Bethune focused primarily on colonial issues in their contacts with the American delegation, they did not neglect to consider the plight of black America, believing the international organization might improve black life at home. While such domestic initiatives were not yet central to the association's orientation toward the United Nations, it is clear that from the birth of the global organization, the reformers regarded it as a forum for addressing their particular aims. As Walter White wrote to the secretary of state in a May 15 memorandum on the subject of United Nations jurisdiction on domestic matters: "I think we, as Americans, should be willing to have some of our own practices examined"; it was not enough to "advocate examination of the practices, colonialism and otherwise, of other nations."[23]

Throughout the conference, White and Du Bois kept readers abreast of developments in San Francisco, and leading black newspapers devoted an enormous amount of attention to the meeting. A close reading of the black press suggests the major papers shared the perspective of White and Du Bois, namely, that the gathering might rectify racial injustice on a global scale, while also helping to address the race problem at home. White told his readers that what emerged at San Francisco would be of "paramount importance to the Negroes of America" and to all peoples of color, and he described "the ferment of freedom" that was sweeping the world "like a prairie fire among brown, yellow, and black peoples." On the same page of the *Chicago Defender*, Du Bois noted that whatever the delegates decided, the "situation of the Negro race in Africa, in the West Indies, and in America cannot and will not be neglected."[24]

Once the conference had ended, its reverberations continued to influence the activities of White, Bethune, and Du Bois. Invited to meet with Harry Truman at the White House to discuss a variety of matters, Walter White told the new president (he had been in office just over a month) about his strong disagreement over American reluctance in San Francisco to support "eventual independence" for the colonial world. It was essential, White insisted, for the United States to amend its position, and as he recalled later, Truman seemed quite interested in developments in San Francisco and appeared genuinely distressed over the pessimistic report White set before him.[25] For her part, Mary McLeod Bethune chaired the June 23 meeting that she had planned while in San Francisco. The focus of the gathering, held at the Washington, D.C., headquarters of the National Council of Negro Women, suggests the extent to which the concerns of the international meeting influenced those working for domestic change. Addressing more than fifty representatives from some thirty organizations, Bethune situated the black struggle in a global context, drawing on ideas she had encountered in San Francisco a few weeks before. Although she noted that black Americans had made progress in several areas, to a large extent they remained "a subject people—men and women with little more than colonial status in a democracy." She then advanced an idea that would become increasingly common among the reformers in the near future: that America's unwillingness to provide freedom and equality to all its citizens, "regardless of race, color, or religion," would prove a liability on the world stage. In Bethune's estimation, until the United States established conditions of social, political, and economic freedom at home, the nation would be unable to "fulfill her role as a world power."[26]

Later that summer, Du Bois testified before the Senate Foreign Relations Committee, which was conducting hearings on the UN Charter. While he expressed support for the document and called it a "step for peace and justice," he also shared his concerns about its failure to address adequately the colonial question. Employing distinctively American rhetoric, Du Bois spoke of the greed, oppression, and exploitation of the colonial system and declared that Americans had long rejected the tyranny of a system of "taxation without representation." The peace of the world demanded that the charter should make clear that all races were equal; it was also critical, he contended, for the document to stand for the "universal application of the democratic way of life." Recalling Lincoln's words, Du Bois observed that what was once true of the United States, was now true of the world: "we cannot exist half slave and half free."[27] Clearly, Du Bois and other leading reformers saw the establishment of the United Nations as a critical development for oppressed peoples, and they believed it could serve as a forum for debating and perhaps vanquishing the problem of racial exploitation and oppression. As shall be seen, American race leaders would ultimately invoke the authority of the United Nations to resolve the problems of black America, convinced the international institution could legitimately address such national concerns.

But the most significant development in the summer of 1945 did not concern the United Nations. A few weeks after Du Bois told the Foreign Relations Committee that the failure of the UN Charter to address the problem of racial oppression might lead to humanity's demise, America dropped two atomic bombs on Japan, thus ending World War II. Despite the significance of the war's end and the dawn of the atomic age, New York's *Amsterdam News* reminded its readers that the battle for justice would continue: "For the Negro, peace has only limited the battlefield."[28] Almost a million black Americans had served in the war, nearly half of whom had seen action overseas. In Europe, they had worked in port battalions, as engineers, as ordnance men, and in the transportation corps. More than twenty black combat units had fought in the European theater. The 761st Tank Battalion had waged war in six countries and fought in the Battle of the Bulge, and throughout the Mediterranean and Pacific theaters, blacks had served gallantly. More than eighty black pilots, who had escorted bombers and carried out strafing missions, were awarded the Distinguished Flying Cross, and black personnel were among the first to go ashore at Okinawa. The African-American contribution to the war effort was substantial: black soldiers and sailors had helped win the war.[29] And when peace came, black Americans—soldiers especially—were determined to become full partners in the nation's democracy. In the words of one enlisted man, Private Herbert Seward, the black fighter was not prepared to come home and take up where he had left off: "We are going to have the things that are rightfully due us or else. . . . The old southerner was through, just as Germany and Japan are through." Seward wanted all America to know of the "new spirit" that had taken hold among all of America's fighting men; military service, he asserted, had created a new belief in egalitarianism.[30]

African-American wartime economic gains were significant. More than one million blacks had entered civilian jobs, and almost two hundred thousand had joined the public employment sector between 1940 and 1944; in addition, millions more went to work in the defense industries.[31] By 1945, the continuing black migration into the urban South and into northern and western cities had dramatically altered the residential patterns of black America. Between December 1941 and March 1945, seven hundred thousand blacks left southern farms to look for work, four hundred thousand of whom headed to the West Coast, the Midwest, and the East. The wartime quest for employment, which profoundly influenced the urbanization of blacks across the country, contributed to a process that would have enormous social and political implications long after the war's end. The growing number of northern black voters would provide black Americans with increasing political power, and the rising concentration of urban blacks in the South would enable race leaders to mobilize large numbers of supporters who would play a crucial part in the civil rights movement.[32]

While such developments helped pave the way for advances in the domestic battle, race reform leaders persisted in working to build a just society. The NAACP experienced an extraordinary increase in membership during the war years—from fifty thousand in 1940 to four hundred fifty thousand in 1946—and remained at the forefront of the movement to sweep aside Jim Crow. Equality of opportunity in higher education, a permanent Fair Employment Practices Committee, and abolition of the poll tax were three postwar goals, as was anti-lynching legislation, a decades-long aim that remained high on the organization's agenda, especially in light of an outbreak of postwar violence against southern blacks.[33] Inside and outside the NAACP, many reformers were encouraged by the support President Truman provided for their cause. No twentieth-century American president, not even Truman's beloved predecessor, had spoken out so forcefully against racial injustice as did the former Missouri senator.[34] On several occasions, particularly at the closing session of the NAACP's highly publicized annual convention in June 1947, Truman told the American people that the quest for racial justice was one of his administration's priorities. His appearance at the conference, the first by an American president, was of historic significance, and according to *The Crisis*,

Truman's speech (which is considered later) was "the most . . . forthright statement on the rights of minorities in a democracy" that an American president had ever delivered.[35]

But Truman's efforts did not end there. Later in 1947, with the release of "To Secure These Rights," a report issued by the President's Committee on Civil Rights (PCCR), Truman sought to make good his commitment to reform. He had decided to establish the committee a year earlier, after a September 19, 1946, meeting at which Walter White and several others painted a gloomy picture of the state of American race relations and the treatment of minorities. White told Truman about lynchings in Georgia and Louisiana and about the spate of anti-Semitic, anti-Catholic, anti-labor, and anti-immigrant literature that dozens of hate groups were spreading throughout the country. The president was shocked by the description: "My God! I had no idea it was as terrible as that! We've got to do something!" Consequently, Truman appointed the PCCR, which, one scholar writes, "transformed the civil rights drive of the late 1940s," bringing the president into the movement in a wholly new way.[36] Truman's 1947 address and the PCCR will be examined below in the context of unfolding international developments, but for now it can be said that the movement appeared to have someone in the White House who was determined to help the cause.

In the spring of 1945, as has been discussed, the reformers had participated in the meeting establishing the United Nations, and devoted considerable attention to the organization's colonial policies. The next year, in looking again to the young institution, they sought to apply its authority to consider issues closer to home. Du Bois was at the center of the NAACP's effort to place racial matters on the UN's agenda, and in August 1946, he wrote to Walter White, suggesting that the association should prepare a petition to submit to the United Nations General Assembly that would document African-American domestic grievances, along with recommendations on how the UN might address them. One hundred to two hundred pages long, the petition would be distributed to the entire General Assembly and to major libraries and distinguished leaders around the world. Noting that other oppressed groups were preparing such documents, Du Bois claimed it would be difficult to explain the NAACP's failure to do the same.[37] Over the next several months, Du Bois organized a group of scholars to write the proposed document,[38] and five men (Earl B. Dickerson of the NAACP's board and the Illinois assistant attorney general, Milton Konvitz of Cornell University, Leslie Perry of the NAACP's Washington, D.C., branch, William Ming of the University of Chicago, and Howard University's Rayford Logan) would ultimately participate in the project, a draft of which would be completed in January 1947. Du Bois then submitted a version to Walter White, and after several

months of revisions, the petition was completed, circulated among leading diplomats and statesmen (including Truman and Secretary of State
George Marshall), and ready for formal submission to the United Nations
on October 23, 1947.

On that day, Du Bois and White presented the petition to the Division
on Human Rights of the United Nations, with Du Bois calling the document "a frank and earnest appeal to all the world for elemental Justice
against the treatment which the United States has visited upon us for three
centuries." He noted the care that had gone into its preparation, observing that its composition had been entrusted to "scholars trained in the
highest universities." Their work, Du Bois declared, was a blend of historical, legal, social, and scientific data, which sought to "induce the nations
of the world to persuade this nation to be just to its own people." In
conclusion, the aging race activist highlighted the universal significance
of the American race problem, claiming that the NAACP firmly believed
"the situation pictured here is as much your concern as ours."[39] For his
part, White wedded the fate of black Americans to that of other oppressed
peoples, declaring that "injustice against black men in America ha[d] re-
percussions upon the status and future" of peoples in India, China, and
Africa. Significantly, White stated that war would continue to plague humanity until racial oppression had been abolished at home and abroad.[40]

In White's public remarks, he argued that freedom was indivisible and
claimed its denial to peoples anywhere abridged the liberty of all mankind. Moreover, as White and Du Bois both asserted, the oppression of
black Americans was but one aspect of a global problem in which peoples
of color were the object of state-sanctioned racial oppression. The petition
itself sought to persuade United Nations officials that the organization
possessed the authority to address the race problem in the United States
and the power to help black Americans obtain equal treatment under the
law. The document thus reflected an assumption long embraced by leading reformers, namely, that the global nature of racial oppression made it
both essential and appropriate for transnational institutions to confront
racial injustice—even in the domestic sphere. Significantly, in the petition's conclusion, Du Bois wrote that the treatment of black Americans
was not merely an internal question for the United States, but "a basic
problem of humanity" and democracy, which demanded the world's "attention and action." No nation was so great, he claimed, that the world
could afford to permit it to "continue to be deliberately unjust, cruel and
unfair toward its citizens."[41]

The NAACP petition received widespread publicity throughout the
country and the world, and served to amplify the association's call for
change. According to the *De. Moines Register*, the document had "accomplished its purpose of arousing interest in discrimination," while a *New*

York Post columnist noted that the petition might provide the country with a chance to face the race problem squarely and "see how it looks in the bright light of world opinion, and . . . prove our declaration of democracy by boldly moving to correct a glaring injustice." In *P.M.* magazine, the political writer Saul Padover observed that by setting the American race problem before the world, the petition might advance the cause of domestic reform. Padover insisted, moreover, that the "disease of racism" had to be tackled, or it would "continue to plague us abroad and . . . undermine the whole democratic structure at home." In Washington, Senator Arthur Capper of Kansas introduced a summary of the petition into the *Congressional Record*, while in the academy, historian Arthur Schlesinger, Jr., said the NAACP had done "a superb job." Writing to Walter White, Schlesinger said he hoped the document had "the effect it should have in rousing the conscience of the world and in stimulating our own government into more effective action." Schlesinger was hopeful that with the assistance of the United Nations, the world might be moved to register its collective repudiation of American racial oppression.[42]

The United Nations undoubtedly did not possess the authority to effect race reform in the United States, a problem that had not eluded Du Bois. Indeed, he and Rayford Logan had pondered the question of the organization's legal authority to reach into the polity so as to address the domestic race problem, and Logan, who was responsible for examining the subject in his chapter of the petition, doubted that such authority could be found in the UN Charter.[43] Notwithstanding the apparent limitations of the United Nations, the NAACP's petition was not a failure. By setting the document before the international institution, America's oldest race reform organization had focused national and international attention on racial oppression in the United States. More broadly, the decision to submit the petition to the United Nations was one part of the larger process by which the reformers worked to globalize America's domestic dilemma—in this instance, by appealing to an organization whose very birth reflected the internationalist impulse of the immediate postwar period.[44] As Du Bois wrote to Warren Austin, America's chief delegate to the United Nations, it would be an act of enlightened statesmanship for the country to set its race problem before the world organization and admit, even if American democracy was not perfect, that we were willing to "acknowledge our faults and to bring the matter before the world . . . with the hope that this unfortunate condition [would] be corrected within the near future."[45]

The NAACP's distinctive internationalism emerged in other ways in the period after the war. At conferences, in the activities of its key figures, and in the pages of *The Crisis*, the organization continued to manifest a profound concern for developments in the colonial world. In a particularly fine expression of the internationalist mindset, the Reverend Archibald J. Carey told thousands of members in his 1946 keynote address at the association's annual gathering, "We must all be citizens of the world. . . . Negroes must lift their eyes from their own problems to see the world around them. . . . They must articulate the hopes . . . of other little people as well as of themselves."[46] Year after year, thousands of delegates at the NAACP's conferences supported resolutions that expressed concern for the plight of colonial peoples and tied the aspirations of the colonized to the African-American freedom campaign. And throughout the postwar years, developments in distant lands captured the attention of NAACP leaders and members, who wove such issues into their program. As a declaration adopted at the 1948 annual conference stated: "In this common struggle we are not alone," for beyond the democratic elements present among all races and nations, our allies include "the vast and unnumbered colored peoples of the world."[47]

Beyond the passage of resolutions and the declarations of principles, the organization's leading figures advanced the idea that conditions in the developing world were the province of those seeking racial justice in America. At the 1949 annual conference, after discussing the NAACP's history and achievements, Acting Secretary Roy Wilkins turned to overseas matters, telling those who had gathered to hear his keynote address that it was now

> apparent that the so-called race problem is no longer a national one. The majority of the [world's] people . . . belong to colored races. They have . . . suffered the . . . humiliations and cruelties of the color line. But now there is a surge toward freedom among them. They seek to control their own destinies and to wipe out the colonial system. . . . We offer to them every assistance within our power. The race problem is bigger than a few states in the Deep South. . . . It has assumed world-wide proportions and the American Negro is prepared to take his place in the world-wide struggle.[48]

Reflecting the association's internationalism, one of the speakers that summer was Vijaya Pandit, India's ambassador to the United States, who presented Dr. Ralph Bunche, the acting UN mediator on Palestine, with the NAACP's Spingarn Medal. The appearance of Pandit, a leading figure in Indian politics (and Nehru's sister), suggests the organization's global perspective, along with its continuing interest in developments on the subcontinent. The words of the ambassador likely possessed added power because they were articulated by the representative of a free India, the country having gained its independence from Britain two years before.[49] Pandit told the delegates that her country's civilization rested on the belief that freedom was indivisible and that the failure to grant it to all races meant there could be no "lasting freedom for any one nation." India had

India's ambassador to the United States, Vijaya Pandit, presents the NAACP's Spingarn Medal to United Nations official Ralph Bunche at the association's annual conference in July 1949.

made "common cause" with the world's oppressed during its own liberation struggle, she said, declaring that all people, "regardless of race or religion must have the opportunity to contribute . . . to the design of the new world we seek to build." To those who heard Pandit on that summer afternoon, the global character of the NAACP's struggle against racial oppression would have been undeniable.[50]

The notion that the association's work had assumed global proportions emerged not only from the rostrum of its annual conferences, but also from the public writings and activities of figures like Walter White and Du Bois. More than any reformer, Du Bois had long rejected the notion that the reform crusade could be confined within the boundaries of a single country, and in the postwar years, he continued to internationalize the movement.[51] The global sweep of Du Bois's postwar concerns is apparent in his journalistic output, and through 1948, the year he left the NAACP, his weekly column in the *Chicago Defender* exposed thousands to the idea that racial oppression could only be understood in the context of unfolding international developments. Even in considering the implications of the atomic bomb, he wondered what "the Colored and Colonial world" had to say and whether it would be possible to keep the secret of atomic energy "as a monopoly of white folk." Surely the "intelligence of India and the rising intelligence of Pan-Africa" would someday "master this language of force," a development that Du Bois cleverly suggested would benefit those with "nothing to lose but their chains." As had been true for decades, Du Bois would compel thousands of African-American readers to confront the idea that their struggle extended far beyond the American frontier.[52]

The internationalism of Walter White was equally clear. The persistent external focus of his *Chicago Defender* column, along with his speeches and overseas peregrinations, testify to his conviction that racial progress could be realized only by globalizing the struggle. In the fall of 1948, White journeyed to Paris to attend the meeting of the United Nations General Assembly. Chosen by the Truman administration to attend the gathering as a consultant to the United States delegation, White represented the NAACP and served as the eyes and ears of the American race reform community. On the General Assembly's agenda were matters of considerable importance to the reformers, including a human rights declaration, a genocide treaty, and the omnipresent issue of colonial trusteeship. In print and on the radio, White discussed the meaning of the conference, making clear to his varied audiences that overcoming oppression was a global challenge.[53] Before leaving for France, White told his mainly black readers about the stake they had in the outcome of the Paris gathering, writing that developments there had "a direct bearing" on the welfare of black Americans and "colored peoples throughout the world."[54] While he acknowledged that the goal of human equality would not be achieved in Paris, he urged *Defender* readers to follow developments in France and to convey their opinions to American officials, especially if the United States delegation pursued a policy founded on expediency rather than principle. Let your voices be heard, he exhorted; insist that America's spokesmen "fight with honesty instead of compromise."[55]

In Paris, White shared his observations on the proceedings with *Defender* readers and did not shrink from directing strong criticism at the American delegation. On several issues, he asserted that America had failed to stand up to the imperial schemes of the colonial powers (mainly Britain), a position he thought would leave America vulnerable to the charge that it favored the continued "exploitation of black, brown and yellow" peoples. America's stance on the future status of colonial peoples, which White called "inexplicable and distressing," led him to call for the dismissal of General George Marshall as secretary of state and head of the American delegation. A nonmilitary person was needed, he declared— someone who would provide unselfish support for international policies that were "consistent with the pledges of justice, opportunity and equality" that were central to the UN Charter.[56] In an intriguing column, a frustrated White criticized black America for its parochialism, noting the "abysmal failure" of blacks to take advantage of the forum offered by the United Nations to present their case to the world. If "one millionth of the sum spent annually by Negroes on liquor and automobiles and parties" had been spent on presenting and publicizing their case to the world organization, he acidly noted, "the Negro's cause could have been advanced immeasurably" at home and abroad. Experts on human rights, genocide, economics, and the colonial system should all have been sent to Paris to articulate black America's needs to the world, and black newspapers should have provided "intelligent coverage" of the meeting, where decisions were made that would affect the future of humanity. White excoriated the black press, claiming that events in Paris were as important as who was sleeping with whom or the election of a sheriff in "Chitling Switch, Mississippi." The "sights of American Negroes" must be raised; it was essential for blacks to help their cause by taking advantage of "the ready-made instruments of world opinion and action."[57]

The following year, White was again active overseas. In the summer of 1949, he participated in a world tour undertaken by America's *Town Meeting of the Air*, which had brought regular citizens and leading Americans together since 1935 to discuss current affairs before a radio audience numbering in the millions. In 1949, when the program's originator, George V. Denny, Jr., decided to produce the weekly program from a number of far-flung locales, White joined a group of distinguished men and women who traveled to London, Paris, Berlin, Ankara, Cairo, Karachi, New Delhi, Tokyo, and other major cities. In radio broadcasts and meetings with local journalists, politicians, and regular citizens, the participants debated the international questions of the day, while millions of Americans gathered around their radios to hear what the rest of the world thought about the grave issues confronting humanity.[58]

As White noted in his column and later in his memoirs, American race relations were of great interest to everyone the group encountered. Wherever they went—from Europe to the developing world, from the Middle East to the Far East—people questioned him about racial persecution in the United States. "We love America but are bewildered by the contradiction of her professed ideals of human freedom and of her treatment of the Negro," an Italian told the group in Rome.[59] In Ankara, a questioner pointedly asked what American educators were doing to implement the UN Declaration of Human Rights. In India, the group was greeted by two front-page stories in the Delhi *Statesman*: one noted the tour's wish to promote "tolerance, reason, and justice," while the other described in horrific detail the bombing of black homes in Birmingham, Alabama.[60] White told his readers that people throughout the world, especially in places where many were "dark-skinned" (he mentioned Turkey, Egypt, Lebanon, Syria, Pakistan, and India), were deeply interested in the plight of black America. The NAACP head shared the story of an intelligent Pakistani woman, a diplomat's wife, who could not conceal her surprise that White and Edith Sampson of the National Council of Negro Women (with White, she was the only other black American on the trip) were permitted to travel on an equal footing with and share the same accommodations as the others in the *Town Meeting* party. She wondered, too, how Mr. White and Mrs. Sampson had obtained an education equal to that earned by the rest of the group. White explained that black Americans had graduated from some of the country's finest academic institutions—from Harvard, Yale, Smith, and Swarthmore. Blacks were making progress, he told his Pakistani acquaintance; their "relentless campaign against racial segregation" was breaking down barriers, even in the South.[61]

What did the head of America's preeminent race reform organization hope to achieve by meeting foreign notables, participating in international broadcasts and seminars, and discussing his trip with black readers in his newspaper column? And what does White's expedition suggest about his understanding of and approach to the race problem in America? Clearly, White had long believed the effort to end racial persecution in the United States was part of a greater enterprise, and he was convinced that a defining characteristic of the post-1945 period was the freedom campaign peoples of color were waging throughout the world. For White, nothing illustrated this more clearly than his round-the-world tour, even if his American traveling companions did not share his perspective. As he wrote from Karachi in early September, it had become clear after the war that "it was as short-sighted and futile to think of the race question in an exclusively American framework as it would be to believe that what happened to Negroes in Mississippi had no bearing on what happened to Negroes in Massachusetts." As White told his black readers, the tour had demonstrated "the pressing need for us to lift our sights and see the world problem of race and color in its overall significance," and he insisted that black Americans were "better prepared" and "organized" than any group in the world to work for change. The "responsibility and opportunity" thus rested on their shoulders.[62] In this new era, White believed, American blacks could help other peoples of color achieve their freedom, and he repeatedly sought to convey this notion to his followers in the United States.

More than this, White's speeches and writings during and after his international journey brim with an irrepressible optimism. To his mainly black readership, to his larger audience of radio listeners, and to the foreigners he encountered, White spoke hopefully about the prospect for black advancement overseas and at home. He perceived a world in flux, where transformative forces were reconfiguring international politics and social relations. Technology, in particular, was creating a smaller world, causing the fate of all peoples to become increasingly interconnected. As he observed in a broadcast from Karachi, "Whatever happens in America directly affects Southeast Asia. Whatever occurs here has instantaneous effect on the United States." This realization led him to conclude that international comity would not be attained until "every man, wherever he lives, whatever the color of his skin, is free and equal."[63] While White understood that great challenges lay ahead, he returned home energized by what he had seen, convinced that millions of people throughout the world were watching and supporting the movement for racial justice in the United States. He was persuaded that his trip had enabled him to enlighten the world's peoples about the strides black America was making, and when the occasion allowed, White did not miss the opportunity to tell those he encountered about the improving status of the country's black citizens.

But the overseas public was not the only group that could gain important insights from the tour.[64] In White's estimation, those traveling with him had been compelled to confront the idea that in the eyes of the world, American race prejudice mattered—and that realization was of considerable moment in these years. Many who had started the tour thinking that American "racial practices were of minor importance are now convinced that it is one of the most important problems which we must solve," he observed.[65] In city after city, White's tourmates would grapple with a stark reality: American racial oppression was tarnishing the nation's reputation on the international stage. And this suggests a critical dimension of White's journey, which occurred at a moment when the East-West competition had assumed primacy in world politics. As we shall see, the race reformers viewed the worldwide struggle as a grand opportunity, for they were convinced the Cold War might aid their cause.[66] If, as will be argued, the conflict between Washington and Moscow would come to occupy an important place in the story of American race relations, Walter White's 1949 tour is testament to the idea that American domestic life could not be divorced from the challenges of world politics in the postwar era. The response of foreign peoples to American race relations, a blend of puzzlement, distress, and hostility— which White conveyed to his readers—forced his influential companions to consider the risks Jim Crow posed to the United States in its newly acquired, self-proclaimed role as the leader of the free world. Throughout the postwar years, the race reformers hammered away at this theme, reminding American policymakers that it would be costly if the United States, while working to protect democracy abroad, failed to construct a genuine democracy at home.[67]

With the end of World War II, tensions between the United States and the Soviet Union had quickly become the most salient feature of international politics, as the wartime alliance between Moscow and Washington crumbled owing to a complex blend of strategic and ideological divisions that neither side proved able or willing to overcome.[68] Given the nature of the struggle between the two countries, which most Americans (poli-cymakers and regular citizens alike) believed pitted democracy and free-dom against tyranny and oppression, it is no surprise that the race reform-ers were deeply interested in the Cold War. As the conflict came to dominate the international and the domestic landscape, members of the reform community made it central to the message that they set before America and the world, and they used the East-West contest to prod the nation into building a more just society.[69]

While the Cold War's impact on the civil rights campaign is a highly contested subject, which the next chapter will consider, it is suggested here that the global competition between the United States and the Soviet Union fortified the movement over the next several years. The race activ-ists quickly incorporated East-West tensions into their program for change, and as early as December 1945 they began to argue that a funda-mental inconsistency marked the public policy of the United States, which, while clamoring for democracy in Europe, had not yet established a democracy within its own borders. Responding to Secretary of State James Byrnes's call for "free democratic elections" in the Balkans, *The Crisis* claimed the South Carolinian had exhibited no such concern about the franchise in his own state, where the poll tax, the "white" Democratic primary, and other discriminatory laws kept thousands of blacks from voting. The journal pointed to the "unenviable position" of the United States, which appeared as a "hypocrite in international affairs," a circum-stance surely appreciated by the Soviet government, which was the target of Byrnes's remarks.[70] Du Bois was similarly critical of Byrnes, who was in no position to "represent democracy before the world." In one column, he quoted Byrnes's statement to a Bulgarian representative at a 1946 meeting in which the secretary of state had spoken of America's commit-ment to maintaining "civil rights for all the population." Asserting that Byrnes had no right to "point the finger of criticism at Russia," Du Bois highlighted a recent lynching in Georgia, which he said was in the same "cultural orbit" as Byrnes's native South Carolina. Such columns, which Du Bois wrote for the *Chicago Defender* throughout this period, demon-strated his conviction that emerging East-West tensions were germane to the race reform movement.[71] One is struck, moreover, by the directness with which Du Bois expressed support for Moscow at this time, especially in light of the rapid change that saw the Soviets slip from wartime ally to postwar adversary. More than any leading figure in the movement, Du Bois made no effort to hide his positive preachments on Russia's foreign and domestic policies, and to his varied audiences he conveyed the idea that America had a great deal to learn from the Soviet Union.

In 1947, while Americans were listening to their government describe the grave threat Moscow posed to freedom and democracy throughout the world, Du Bois was using language redolent of the 1920s. Russia had much to teach America and the world about "what can be done for the real progress of workers and the real implementation of democracy."[72] Indeed, the previous year, Du Bois had suggested that the origin of the tensions between America and Russia lay with the former not the latter and declared there was but "one reason why we cannot live together in peace" and that was because "America especially has harked back to that pre-war feud" over Russian economic organization. Pleading with his fellow citizens to let the Russians try to abolish poverty and institute "real democracy," Du Bois concluded, "[i]n God's name then let us have peace," a prayer directed not at the Kremlin but at Washington.[73] In his newspaper pieces, Du Bois frequently criticized the United States and its allies, and whether writing about Moscow's international actions or Soviet ideals, he compared East to West and highlighted the injustice that he believed inhered in the American and British systems. In one Du Boisian flight of fancy, Truman, Stalin, and British Prime Minister Attlee gathered to discuss democracy: the American leader considered the Senate's failure to pass legislation banning racial discrimination in employment; Attlee spoke of British oppression in India; and Stalin, a man who talked straight, reflected on Soviet economic and educational achievements.[74] Winston Churchill's "iron curtain" speech of 1946, which considered the Communist threat to Europe, also aroused Du Bois's ire. The race reformer excoriated Churchill, calling him a man who had been on the wrong side of "every great social question" of the day, who spoke for a government, which, despite its claim to represent the interests of free peoples, oppressed 400 million "colored" souls. Burgeoning East-West tensions thus gave Du Bois the opportunity to target the West vis-à-vis the Soviets and to emphasize western hypocrisy and the malignancy of western oppression.[75]

Within the reform community, America's self-proclaimed commitment to democracy in western Europe and its persistent condemnation of Soviet actions in the eastern part of the continent engendered much comment. Walter White, who wrote and spoke extensively about the East-West struggle and repeatedly linked it to the subject of domestic persecution, captured the spirit of such commentary in an April 1946 column in which he supported Russian statements suggesting that the United States should clean up its own house before it presumed to "criticize the housekeeping of other nations."[76] And with the start of the Cold War, the reformers' rhetorical broadsides on the subject were central to the movement's message, and time and again, the reformers wondered how America could commit itself to the preservation of democracy and freedom around the world, while so many Americans remained equally committed to the preservation of an undemocratic system in the United States. In addition, foreign nations and the world press referred continually to the hypocrisy of the United States, which claimed to support freedom and democratic rule everywhere—except within its own borders. Thus, the reformers' persistent rhetoric and the recurrent message from abroad made it extraordinarily difficult for American policymakers and the general public to avoid confronting the glaring incompatibility between the country's overseas commitments and its domestic practices.[77]

American initiatives in Europe in 1947 and 1948 became an object of discussion and criticism among reform leaders, who reacted vigorously to the Truman Doctrine and the Marshall Plan, which aimed to combat what American policymakers identified as the Soviet threat to Greece, Turkey, and western Europe. At public gatherings, in the press, and in the reform journals, they propounded the idea that American actions overseas could not be disentangled from the movement's domestic aims. In March 1947, President Truman asked Congress for $400 million in military and economic aid to help Greece and Turkey counter an alleged Soviet threat, which, he claimed, was one piece in a global struggle that was forcing peoples to "choose between alternative ways of life."[78] The reformers' response to the Truman Doctrine differed dramatically from that of many engaged Americans, with Du Bois, especially, hurling scathing indictments at the president's plan, which he called "stupid and dangerous." Du Bois declared himself willing to pay taxes to feed Europe's starving masses, but refused to prop up the British Empire or American oil profits. The race leader also spoke well of Russian Communism, the target of the president's initiative, claiming it sought nothing more than an end to poverty, illiteracy, and unemployment.[79] The following week, Du Bois's *Chicago Defender* readers confronted a piece juxtaposing America's determination to spend $400 million to save democracy in Greece and Turkey with its unwillingness to work for similar ends in Mississippi and Georgia. Sardonically, Du Bois asked, "Didn't the dirty Russians wipe out illiteracy in thirty years? . . . We've been pretending to educate Negroes for seventy-five years and a third still can't read and write."[80] Considering aid to Greece, he wondered why the United States boasted so about democracy, which we claimed "insure[d] the triumph of justice through the right to vote." Was it possible to "export democracy to Greece and not practice it in Mississippi?" Had we "achieved enough democracy in America to teach Turkey or Poland?"[81] Walter White likewise considered the American initiative to help Greece and Turkey and reminded his readers that nearly everyone had forgotten that generations of "white Anglo-Saxon crimes of colonialism and ruthless imperialism" had prepared the ground for totalitarian rule. Repeating the reformers' ubiquitous refrain in these years, White pointed to the hypocrisy inherent in America's global crusade for democracy, which was conducted while racial oppression flourished in the United States. This country had no business spending "dollars and lives" to demand democratic governments throughout the world, he wrote, when it had failed "completely to provide democracy in Mississippi."[82]

The reformers also evaluated a second, larger American assistance program in these years, the Marshall Plan, which would provide economic help to Europe as it struggled to rebuild after the war. In Melvyn Leffler's words, the plan, which Secretary of State George Marshall outlined in a June 1947 address at Harvard, was "one of the great initiatives in postwar international relations." By helping Europe, the United States hoped to keep it from succumbing to the appeal of political forces that might prepare the ground for the continent's full-fledged support for Soviet-inspired factions. The European Recovery Program (the plan's formal name) was linked closely to Truman's decision to aid Greece and Turkey; indeed, the president himself had noted that they were "two halves of the same walnut," both halves of which intrigued the reformers.[83]

In testimony before the Senate Foreign Relations Committee in January 1948, Walter White expressed support for the plan to assist western Europe. Claiming to speak for 1,627 NAACP branches across the nation and over half a million members, White presented a message centering on racial oppression. While American policymakers undoubtedly saw little connection between the Marshall Plan and the race question, White suggested the program, which was concerned with geopolitics and economics, was intrinsically related to racial matters abroad and at home. In fact, White used the hearings to highlight several race-related issues as he considered the aims of the Marshall Plan, which he claimed was rooted in the "traditional generosity" of the American people. Having insisted that the United States ought to provide assistance "without political or other strings," the NAACP secretary told the committee that it was critical to extend American aid not just to Europe, but to the "needy in Asia, Africa, and the Caribbean." It was necessary, he said, "to remind the United States Senate that hunger is as painful to brown, yellow, and black stomachs as it is to white ones." White also observed that many potential recipients of American aid derived their economic strength from colonies, which they were unwilling to liberate, and he contended that in helping the European colonial powers, the United States had a "moral obligation" to demand that they rapidly provide self-determination and freedom to their subject peoples. It would be "utter folly" for America to do otherwise since the persistence of the reign of "white supremacy" over "hundreds of millions of brown, yellow, and black people" would inevitably lead to a third world war.

White joined the country's overseas activities to the existence of racial persecution and pointed to the "necessity of assuring equitable treatment" of minorities here at home, which, he argued, was closely linked to the international questions he had just discussed. The NAACP chief claimed a dozen Marshall Plans could not "overcome the danger to the good name of the United States which is daily being done by the continuation of discrimination based on race, creed, [or] color." He pointed specifically to discrimination in the army, noting that such prejudice diminished America's international prestige and "cast doubt upon the integrity of [the nation's] intentions." In concluding, White asked the country to help those in need, irrespective of race, creed, or belief, for only this could make the free society of which Americans boasted "a reality," which would prove "its superiority above all others."[84]

At the NAACP's annual conferences throughout this period, leading reformers highlighted the interconnection between America's competition with the Soviet Union and the movement's aims. In presenting their program for change and vision for the future, they described a conflict in which the forces of freedom were arrayed against the forces of tyranny and set their movement against the backdrop of the global struggle. Central to their language was the conviction that the United States had a leading part to play in world politics, though the reformers insisted that such a role demanded an end to racial persecution in America. Speaking at the 1947 annual convention, held in Washington, NAACP chairman Louis T. Wright told the delegates about the organization's work during this "crucial time of adjustment" in the affairs of the nation and the world. Toward the end of his address, Wright placed the association's domestic goals into the context of America's global aims, superbly expressing the NAACP's internationalist vision:

> In pursuing our objectives we also aid our country in the task of world leadership it has assumed following the war. If America is to convert the people of the world to democracy, we must demonstrate that it works in our own land. Our diplomats must not be embarrassed in Moscow, Berlin, Paris, and London by questions [about] undemocratic practices against minorities within our borders. In working to eliminate these inequalities we are in reality working for the peace, freedom and security of all mankind.[85]

A. Philip Randolph likewise looked to international developments in articulating his message after 1945. Dividing his energies, Randolph continued his union activities as head of the Brotherhood of Sleeping Car Porters, labored on behalf of a permanent Fair Employment Practices Committee (FEPC), and fought to end segregation in the military.[86] His voice stood out among the chorus of reformers in the immediate postwar period, and the labor leader consistently exposed listeners and readers to the idea that America's global effort to preserve democracy against the alleged threat of Soviet totalitarianism would be undermined by a failure

to create a true democracy in the United States. With considerable eloquence, Randolph carried this theme all over the country, from the halls
of Congress to the campuses of the nation's black universities, and compelled thousands to recognize that the race reform struggle was not merely
a domestic matter. Speaking in favor of S-984 (the bill that sought to make
the FEPC permanent) before the subcommittee of the Senate Education
and Public Welfare Committee in June 1947, Randolph argued that the
measure would have profound international implications. Its enactment
would "strengthen democracy within and without. We need to prove our
faith by our daily works and thereby to make it a shining example that
will enlist the allegiance of other peoples confronted with the choice between democracy and totalitarianism in the great showdown that now
seems to be rushing upon the world." Randolph cited the words of diplomats George Marshall and Dean Acheson to fortify his argument that the
United States, to realize its global aspirations, needed to establish a genuine democracy at home for all American citizens.[87]

Randolph repeatedly spoke out against Soviet Communism, contending that Russia had nothing of value to offer black America. In a
commencement address at Tuskegee Institute, he acknowledged that capitalism was "bankrupt and hopeless," but declared Communism could not
"save the world from crisis, chaos, confusion, and slavery." He claimed
the Communists made "a fetish of lying, deceit, misrepresentation, [and]
falsehood," but said it was not enough for America to combat Communist
expansion by supporting Europe's "reactionary governments" with
"money, munitions, and men." The country would not win the global
competition merely by preaching democracy abroad, especially when the
United States failed in its practice at home. Conditions the Tuskegee grad-
uates knew firsthand—Jim Crow, the white primary, and the poll tax—
had diminished the nation's prestige in Europe and throughout the developing world. "Democracy is as democracy does," Randolph declared.
If America was "sincere in its democratic professions" and could send
countless millions across the seas to carry democracy to Berlin and Tokyo,
it should be willing to carry a "little democracy below the Potomac."[88]

While Randolph integrated Cold War concerns into his reform language, he also discussed the worldwide liberation efforts of peoples of
color. Toward the end of the war, he had argued that the issue of race and
color had become one of the central questions of the time, observing that
"a casual glimpse . . . will reveal that the darker races are in motion."[89]
Two years later, in 1947, Randolph deployed the reformers' internationalism in the union paper, the *Black Worker*, asserting that the global battle
against racial oppression was of a piece with the movement for domestic
reform. The "revolt of the world of color against white world supremacy"
was the foremost development of the past year, he claimed. Colonial peo-

ples were challenging the oppressive rule of the imperial states in a "struggle to the death for independence." Expanding on the internationalist
idea, Randolph observed that numerous peoples of color—whether Indians, Chinese, West Indians, Africans, or black Americans—were "thirst-
ing for the fresh waters of freedom."[90]

As was noted earlier, in 1947, President Truman became the first American president to address the NAACP's annual conference in person. In
speaking before the country's leading race reform organization and a national radio audience, the president joined the nation's overseas objectives
to the aspirations of the reformers, identifying an overlap between the
international and domestic spheres. From the steps of the Lincoln Memorial, Truman told a crowd of ten thousand that the country had reached a
"turning point" and that he wished to speak about civil rights and human
freedom. "Recent events in the United States and abroad have made us
realize that it is more important today than ever before to insure that all
Americans have these rights." After he declared, "When I say all Americans—I mean all Americans," Truman went on to assert that the "extension of civil rights today means not protection of the people against the
Government, but protection of the people by the Government."

Having decried discrimination based on race, religion, and color, the
president looked beyond the shores of the United States, and his words—
which explicitly wedded the nation's international objectives to its domestic challenges—are worth quoting at length:

> The support of desperate populations of battle-ravaged countries must be
> won. . . . We must have them as allies in our continuing struggle for the
> peaceful solution of the world's problems. Freedom is not an easy lesson to
> teach . . . to people beset by every kind of privation. They may surrender to
> the false security offered so temptingly by totalitarian regimes unless we can
> prove the superiority of democracy.
>
> Our case for democracy should be as strong as we can make it. It should
> rest on practical evidence that we have been able to put our own house in
> order. For these compelling reasons, we can no longer afford the luxury of
> a leisurely attack upon prejudice and discrimination. . . . Our National Gov-
> ernment must show the way.

Truman concluded by declaring that the hope of America, guided by a
belief in the principles of freedom and justice, might serve as "a symbol
of hope for all men, and a rock of security in a troubled world."[91] After
proclaiming his determination to remove the "barriers which stand between millions of our citizens and their birthright," Truman turned from
the crowd and told Walter White, "I mean every word of it—and I am
going to prove that I do mean it."[92] Though it is difficult to identify transformative moments in the history of unfolding long-term developments,

Truman's address at the NAACP convention in 1947 was such an instance. On that June afternoon, Americans heard the president assert that the national interest of the United States demanded the eradication of institutionalized racial oppression and that postponing action on this grave issue could prove a liability in the perilous international conflict in which the nation was engaged. Truman had compelled all Americans, not just reform leaders and movement supporters, to ponder the idea that developments at home were organically connected to developments overseas. The essence of the race reformers' message, which they had articulated repeatedly in these years—indeed, over many years—had begun to hit home. In the era of the Cold War, policymakers had come to echo the words and embrace the perspective of civil rights leaders.[93]

A few months later, in October 1947, the President's Committee on Civil Rights (established in 1946 after a meeting between Truman, Walter White, and others had convinced the president domestic circumstances warranted an examination of racial and ethnic relations) issued its report, "To Secure These Rights." Based on the testimony of dozens of witnesses; extensive correspondence with individuals and private organizations; and information provided by national, state, and local government agencies, the report exposed the pervasiveness of discrimination in the United States and highlighted the gap separating American ideals from the reality of American life for blacks and other minorities. Asserting that the federal government needed to assume responsibility for protecting the civil rights of all Americans, the report presented a "program for action," which delineated ways the government could help construct a more just and democratic society. Upon receiving the document, Truman called it an "American charter of human freedom," while Walter White said it was the "most courageous . . . document of its kind in American history." Comprehensive, candid, and startling, "To Secure These Rights" reminded the nation of the goals the race reformers were battling to achieve, while it demonstrated how much remained to be done.[94]

As was the case in Truman's 1947 NAACP speech, the international dimension of the report was clear. World affairs had become consequential in the domestic policymaking process, and those in a position to shape the government's response to the race question had begun to heed the message the reformers had advanced so persistently throughout the postwar period. As Mary Dudziak has noted, the president's committee looked seriously at the impact racial discrimination would have on the nation's foreign policy goals and worried that a failure to address the problem would weaken the position of the United States on the world stage. The report stated, "Our foreign policy is designed to make the United States an enormous, positive influence for peace and progress throughout the world. . . . But our domestic civil rights shortcomings are a serious obstacle." It went on to assert that none could deny America's civil rights record had become "an issue in world politics"; moreover, those countries with philosophies in competition with the United States had sought to "prove our democracy an empty fraud." With some trepidation, the report looked to the future, declaring that "the United States is not so strong, the final triumph of the democratic ideal is not so inevitable that we can ignore what the world thinks of us or our record."[95]

One of the core elements of color-conscious internationalism—the contention that American leadership in the world demanded a commitment to domestic race reform—had thus become part of the discourse of the nation's policymakers during the Cold War era. Indeed, the president advanced this idea yet again in a February 1948 message to Congress on civil rights, stating that America's position "in the world today" made the subject of civil rights "especially urgent." While he acknowledged that American democracy was not perfect, Truman observed that it was surely preferable to totalitarianism and claimed that if the United States hoped to "inspire the peoples of the world whose freedom is in jeopardy . . . [and] restore hope to those who have already lost their civil liberties, . . . [then] we must correct the remaining imperfections in our practice of democracy."[96] The following summer, in July 1948, Truman sought to give teeth to his declared commitment to civil rights by signing Executive Orders 9980 and 9981. The first mandated the integration of the federal government's workforce and began the process of dismantling the institutionalized segregation that had reigned in official Washington throughout the twentieth century. And Executive Order 9981 would order the American military to begin to integrate the armed forces of the United States. To be sure, segregation in the military would not disappear immediately, but the attainment of one of the movement's central goals, which Joel Spingarn, Du Bois, White, Randolph and others had toiled for decades to realize, was closer than ever before. In the words of one scholar, Truman's decision to sign Executive Order 9981 was significant because it "marked a move by the federal government to support integration rather than segregation."[97]

In one sense, the postwar years resembled earlier periods in which race leaders gazed beyond the United States to advance the movement at home. But of course the immediate postwar period was distinctive, for the geopolitical tensions between Washington and Moscow differed from anything that had come before. Central to the East-West conflict was the new international posture assumed by the United States after 1945, which led American policymakers to deem much of the world to be of vital importance. The zeal with which the United States shouldered the burden of leadership in the Cold War provided the race reformers superb rhetorical possibilities, which they seized by demanding to know how America could claim to be the world's defender of democracy while it had failed to construct a genuine democracy at home. By the late 1940s, this aspect of the reformers' rhetorical attack on Jim Crow, which led some race leaders to support America's global mission while demanding an end to institutionalized racial oppression, had begun to weaken the edifice of state-sanctioned racial discrimination—or at least to make it difficult for policymakers to circumvent the charge that it was hypocritical to ask Americans to aid "free peoples" everywhere while some in the United States remained unfree. As Ralph Bunche told a crowd of NAACP activists in 1949, America's "position of world leadership" was made "morally undefensible by the harsh rattling of the race-relations skeletons in our closet." According to Bunche, neither this nation nor the world could afford to have America made "ineffective by the taunt 'Your undemocratic deeds speak so loudly that your democratic professions cannot be heard.' " The defenders of democracy had nothing to fear "if democracy [could be] made to work."[98] Beyond East-West concerns and the possibilities presented by the United Nations, when the reformers looked at the postwar world, they identified, more clearly than ever, the globalization of the race reform struggle, and insisted that the battle against colonial oppression had become indistinguishable from their own campaign. They were optimistic, moreover, that the quest for liberation in the colonial world might do more than loosen the shackles binding peoples of color in foreign lands, and they hoped the anti-imperial crusade could inspire black Americans and contribute to their eventual liberation.

The global developments that unfolded between 1945 and 1950 mark these years as an epochal time in the history of the twentieth century. The period that began in the summer of 1945 with the end of a world war in Japan would conclude five years later with the start of a limited war in Korea.[99] Between the conclusion of one conflict and the beginning of the next, the East-West competition emerged, and the liberation efforts of millions of peoples of color intensified. While the outbreak of war on a distant peninsula in June 1950 was not an auspicious way to start the new decade, the next several years would witness a variety of events, in Washington courtrooms and southern streets, that would transform the character of the race reform campaign and lend it the momentum and support the movement's leaders had long sought.

Seven

"STRUGGLING TO SAVE AMERICA"
The Reformers and the World of the 1950s

IN THE SPRING OF 1950, *America's Town Meeting of the Air*, the national radio program, traveled to Pittsburgh to debate the question, "What Effect Do Our Race Relations Have on Our Foreign Policy?" Moderator George V. Denny began the broadcast by observing that American foreign policy was a "paramount concern to our own country and to the rest of the world." According to Denny, "the eyes of the free people of the world have turned upon us with increased concentration," which explained why he had chosen the evening's question. Toward the end of the lively half-hour broadcast, a man in the audience rose to query Congressman Brooks Hays of Arkansas, who shared that evening's platform with Fisk University president Charles S. Johnson. He asked the congressman whether the country was "building a foreign policy on issues which it does not intend to tolerate here in America," to which the Arkansas politician responded, "I hope not. We could certainly not sustain such a policy."[1]

Throughout the decade, American race reformers raised this very question in a variety of settings, and in looking outside the country, they were persuaded that no issue was of greater moment. By articulating a concern they had raised throughout the twentieth century—how the United States could expend blood and treasure to defend democracy abroad while it was unwilling to establish a just society at home—race reform leaders would again challenge the nation to reflect not merely on its international mission, but also on its domestic purpose. Moreover, during an era in which the East-West conflict came to dominate life in the United States, the reformers hoped their persistent allusions to the Cold War would give added resonance to their message for change. And despite its corrosive effect on countless individuals and institutions in the United States, Washington's global competition with Moscow did have significant positive implications for the race reform struggle, as the reformers effectively articulated their distinctive understanding of the Cold War, which they made part of their unique brand of internationalism.[2]

Beyond their interest in America's self-proclaimed role as the world's guarantor of democracy, race reform leaders continued to track colonial developments throughout the decade, and as had long been true, they linked the struggles waged by Africans and Asians to their domestic efforts. What distinguished the reformers' reflections on anticolonial matters in this period from their earlier response to this question was that now they typically related anticolonialism to the geostrategic concerns of the United States. The reformers contended that by failing to establish an authentic democracy at home, America risked alienating colonial peoples around the world. And this, they warned, might prove costly in the East-West conflict, an argument that provided color-conscious internationalism with greater saliency than it had ever known. The reformers thus fused the two grand themes of world politics in the postwar era, the Cold War and the strivings of the oppressed in the developing world, so as to strengthen their case that it was essential to end domestic racial oppression. Unless the United States constructed a just society, they asserted, the nation's international position—and perhaps its very existence—might be imperiled.

On June 25, 1950, the North Korean Army poured across the thirty-eighth parallel into South Korea. Although the Korean peninsula was thousands of miles from the American mainland, the United States responded militarily to the North's aggression, believing a failure to do so would send the wrong signal to the Communist governments in Beijing and Moscow, which were thought responsible for the invasion. Unwilling to repeat the mistakes of the 1930s, when the West had failed to respond strongly to Nazi aggression, President Truman decided to go to war to protect South Korea from the dangers of what was seen as a monolithic Communist threat. Returning to Washington from his Missouri home, Truman reflected on the past: "In my generation, this was not the first occasion when the strong had attacked the weak. . . . Communism was acting in Korea just as Hitler, Mussolini, and the Japanese had acted." If the North Korean invasion went unchallenged, "it would mean a third world war, just as similar incidents had brought on a second world war."[3] Emboldened by a novel conception of national security in the postwar era and convinced that it was defending the cause of freedom, the United States would fight in Korea. And in embracing a policy of overweening globalism, America would embark on a course that in time would make nearly every corner of the world vital to the security interests of the United States.

It was hardly surprising that the race reformers were interested in Truman's decision, and from early on they advanced a distinctive view of the war. In its first meeting after the start of hostilities, the NAACP board "condemned unreservedly" the North's invasion, claiming it was "aided and abetted by the Soviet Union." Significantly, the board resolved that "guns alone" would not provide an American victory over the world's "sinister Communist forces," and stated that to win the support of Asia and Africa, America would have to "demonstrate that democracy is a living reality which knows no limitation of race, color or nationality." Hoping for an early victory, the association's governing body called for an end to racial discrimination and segregation in all walks of American life.[4] *The Crisis* not only condemned the Communist invasion, but also advanced a critique of American foreign policy in Asia, while commenting on the racial dimension of the Korean conflict. America would surely win the "hot war" in Korea, but it was less certain whether the country was prepared to win the peace. The monthly contended that it was essential for American policymakers to understand the Asian people, to work with them, and to design a program that would meet their needs. *Crisis* subscribers encountered the words of India's Prime Minister Nehru, who complained that western decisions affected "vast areas of Asia" without understanding the "minds of the people." Even as old forms of empire had been abolished, the Indian leader observed, "new types of colonialism" were emerging, which led him to worry that the fate of Asia was still being determined by western statesmen. Anticipating a charge that many would hurl at the United States in later years, *Crisis* editors declared that America could not win the struggle in Asia by supporting "reactionaries" like Bao Dai in Indochina, Chiang Kai-shek in Formosa, and Syngman Rhee in South Korea. Moreover, victory in Asia would elude the United States so long as American servicemen saw Koreans and Asiatics as "gooks." America had a grand opportunity in Korea (and throughout Asia), where countless peoples of color were fighting to achieve nationhood. Declaring that "Asia [was] in revolution," the editors wondered whether the United States would live up to its own revolutionary past by helping the continent's "struggling masses" achieve economic security and political independence.[5]

In the *Chicago Defender*, Walter White considered the American decision to fight on the Korean peninsula, and more broadly, the meaning of the war itself. Placing the conflict's racial dimension at the center of his analysis, White asserted that Korea had "brought the United States face to face with the global race question" much sooner than many had expected. While his reasoning was at times elusive—White argued in one column that the parents of those Americans who would die in Korea would realize their deaths were caused mainly by "the flaming resentment of non-white peoples all over the world against racial bigotry" in America, Asia, and Africa—his readers would likely have pondered the notion that the Asian conflict was a consequence of global racial oppression. In linking the war to the race problem at home and abroad, White aimed to convince his readers that it was essential to construct a just domestic and international order, if only to lessen the dangers confronting the West. As he observed in August 1950, "racism and colonialism" had put the "United States and the white world" in as perilous a position as any they had faced for three hundred years. The implication of such a formulation was clear: the West might lose the larger struggle against totalitarianism if it did not work to establish an equitable world order.[6]

In their response to the war, the activists fused their interest in the yearnings of colonial peoples to their concern about America's competition with the Soviet Union, and linked both to the domestic quest for racial justice. In the summer of 1951, Ralph Bunche captured superbly how race activists joined these themes, telling those attending the NAACP's annual conference about the rank hypocrisy to be found in the United States Senate, where politicians indulged in "breast-beating oratory" about American democracy and embarked on "rhetorical flights about the free world and free peoples." Was there any "greater mockery of democracy" than the Senate's refusal to pass civil rights legislation, even the "mild" program proposed by the president? There is "aggression on the [Senate's] own threshold which urgently demands [its] attention—a . . . shameful aggression against the Constitutional rights of 15,000,000 . . . loyal American citizens," who were shedding blood for their country. Bunche asked if there was any "greater devotion to flag and country than American Negroes fighting in Korea to protect rights and privileges for the Koreans which the Negroes who fight and die have never enjoyed at home?" In words reformers had uttered throughout the twentieth century, Bunche claimed it was necessary to remind the Senate that "freedom and justice must begin at home." Moreover, America's reputation and security were at risk; the country's "moral position and prestige in the world" suffered deeply from its domestic defects, Bunche observed, reminding the delegates and the nation that the attitudes of the world's peoples would decide the outcome of the current global struggle. Furthermore, these were largely nonwhite peoples, and the "vast millions of Asia, Africa, the Middle East . . . and Latin America" were highly sensitive to America's "undemocratic racial practices." It was essential to reform American democracy so that it could be applied to peoples of all colors.[7]

On the day the North Korean Army invaded South Korea in June 1950, Walter White spoke to the NAACP's delegates meeting in Boston's Mechanics Hall at the closing session of the annual conference. The past three years had made clear that the world's survival depended upon finding answers to two questions, White argued: the first concerned whether democracy and Communism could coexist, while the second concerned "the problem of race and colonialism." Because the world war had smashed "the myth of white superiority," the race leader claimed that the colonial world was "aflame with revolt against white arrogance and greed." He asserted that the persistence of domestic race prejudice had caused widespread distrust of the United States and contributed to the loss of those allies in the developing world that were needed to win the

Cold War. White said it was "imperative" to relate world affairs to "the titanic struggle" the association had been waging for forty years, and he reminded the delegates of Du Bois's celebrated observation that "the problem of the twentieth century is the problem of the color line." In knitting together the Cold War and colonial affairs, White declared that "if Asia as a whole goes over to Russia's side," democracy's chances of survival will have ended. He concluded by reminding his fellow activists that it was necessary to "push back our horizons and understand that this problem of race relations on which we work is intertwined into every other question facing the world today."[8]

Throughout these years, numerous NAACP officials and other race activists spoke similarly. In 1952, the Reverend James Robinson, a Presbyterian minister from New York, addressed the association's annual conference in Oklahoma City. Having recently concluded a six-month overseas journey, in which he claimed to have met several hundred thousand students in twenty-one countries, Robinson noted that the organization's work extended well beyond the geographic boundaries of America and was, in fact, "part of the survival of the free world." Intoning the persistent themes of these years, Robinson observed that American race relations undermined the nation's influence, particularly in the Middle and Far East. He had encountered a deep awareness of American race prejudice in remote villages that lacked telephones, radios, newspapers, and electricity, and he claimed the world's peoples—especially those of color—knew about American racial oppression. The Communists were hardly the sole carriers of such news, Robinson said; instead, the color-conscious population of the developing world was concerned with the "fact and the deed" of American democracy. Despite the fact that during his travels Robinson's identity was occasionally misconstrued—Indian students thought he was the boxer Sugar Ray Robinson, and some Japanese believed he played second base for the Brooklyn Dodgers—it was clear that wherever he went, he was challenged on the incompatibility between America's rhetorical support for freedom and the persistence of American racial persecution.

With striking clarity, Robinson knitted together the colonial struggle and the East-West competition. A revolution was shaking the world, which was inspired not by the Communists, he claimed, but by the desire of people everywhere to achieve "freedom, security and self-respect." And despite the shortcomings of the United States, its progress and achievements had energized the world's peoples (Asians especially), who looked to American heroes like Jefferson, Lincoln, and the two Washingtons, George and Booker T. Joining the story of noble efforts against colonial oppression and the struggle against totalitarianism, Robinson declared that a little American imagination would make it possible to gain the support of colonial peoples and "win this great mass to our way and use their whole weight on the scales against Communism." The pastor concluded his address, titled "International Implications of the Association's Work," by leaving the delegates to reflect on the idea that those devoted to the domestic cause were fighting for the "future peace and security of men everywhere" and for the "survival of our democratic way of life."[9]

While *The Crisis* covered the international scene broadly throughout the 1950s, it most closely examined the struggles in the developing world and the conflict between Washington and Moscow. Tens of thousands of *Crisis* readers were regularly exposed to pieces on the incompatibility between America's self-proclaimed role as the defender of democratic values and racial oppression in the United States. Moreover, the publication asserted that the disjunction between rhetoric and reality was a liability for the United States in its competition with Moscow.[10] Offering a striking example of the way activists knitted the North-South struggle to the Cold War, a 1951 *Crisis* piece by Roy Wilkins emphasized the notion of a world rent by conflict in which the forces of freedom confronted the forces of oppression. Newspapers and radio told a tale of global turmoil, he observed, the prime cause of which was man's quest for a free and secure life. Asia saw "dark billions" seeking "liberty, stability, and national and personal dignity"; the Middle East was in a state of continual eruption; and in Europe, the forces of western democracy grappled with eastern totalitarianism, with armies on both sides growing apace. The United States, the world's most powerful force for democracy, confronted a "nation of godless communism," which sought not only to maintain a repressive system within its own borders, but also to spread its "evil conspiracies" abroad, toppling nations and peoples "beneath its slave banner." Wilkins wondered how the leader of the world's democratic forces could fight most effectively against such oppression. Neither armed force nor a "fantastically productive economy" was sufficient, he insisted. Instead, something less tangible was required—the employment of those "spiritual forces" that rested on America's democratic political ideal, which, Wilkins observed, was embodied in the Declaration of Independence, specifically in the phrase, "all men are created equal." Black Americans believed in the Declaration, he contended, and were convinced the survival of American democracy in the current crisis depended on the strength the nation could muster from "the minds, hearts, and spiritual convictions of all its people."[11]

Consistent with a long-standing tradition in the reform journals, in the 1950s, *The Crisis* considered European perceptions of the American race question. In previous decades, as has been shown, readers had encountered an enlightened European perspective on racial issues, which inevitably reflected poorly on American life. But unlike then, when the international cost of America's domestic failings was low, with the emergence of American globalism, the inconsistency that Europeans observed between America's ideals and its racial practices had become expensive, and this could imperil its standing in the world.[12] In a wide-ranging discussion of European views on American race relations, *The Crisis* examined how the Continental press treated the subject, sifting through forty newspapers and magazines, which represented a broad spectrum of opinion in nine western European countries and one (Romania) in the east. *Crisis* readers could contemplate the extraordinary interest Europeans had in the race question, which was clearly "a live issue" in the Old World. According to *The Crisis*, Europe's fascination with the subject resulted partly from America's use of a Jim Crow army to fight Nazi Germany and partly from the resentment European intellectuals felt toward the United States, which was "meddling in Continental affairs." (The journal noted that America's postwar efforts to aid Europe had aroused the continent's "deeply rooted" prejudices against the United States.) Whatever the origins of Europe's interest in the plight of black America, *Crisis* readers could not avoid the central theme of such foreign reporting, which highlighted the contrast between America's democratic preachments and American racial persecution. This notion—which was also common within the reform community—seems to have pervaded European press coverage of American race relations. *The Crisis* quoted Frenchman Georges Duhamel, who discussed America's delight at lecturing Europeans on the evils of colonialism, when the United States "is still troubled in body and soul by her Negroes"; and it cited the London *News Review*, which spoke of Washington's "hypocritical horror" over foreign persecution, while America "shut its eyes" to its own racial inequalities. A German newspaper contended that "Americans like to indulge in endless reproach of Europeans for their 'racism' and 'colonialism,'" even as they allowed lynchings to go unpunished in the American South.[13]

The editors of *The Crisis* reminded their readers that the European critique was not the product of Communist propaganda or distortion; instead, the Europeans were observing the "moral cancer of American racism" and contrasting it with America's age-old rhetoric about "individual freedom and the American way of life." *Crisis* readers were asked to reflect on the implications of European perceptions of American race relations, which the journal claimed had caused many to doubt whether the United States could provide the world with moral leadership. From a European perspective, the American race problem had become especially disturbing, the consequence of a historical moment when the United States had assumed the role of the defender of freedom throughout Europe and beyond.[14]

In the 1950s, A. Philip Randolph continued to speak out forcefully on global affairs, which he had done with great conviction for more than thirty years. He repeatedly discussed the competition between Communism and democracy and the liberation efforts animating millions in the colonial world. As had long been true, Randolph incorporated such issues into his demand for change at home, making it difficult to disentangle his civil rights message from his analysis of unfolding global developments.[15] What is striking about Randolph's public pronouncements during the 1950s is the virulent anti-Communism he brought to his assessment of overseas matters. His characterization of Soviet motives contained not a trace of ambiguity, as the labor leader regularly assailed Moscow with charges of duplicity, treachery, and a disregard for the aspirations of black America. Time and again, Randolph described the dangers that Soviet Communism posed to the free world, and derided the notion that black Americans were less imperiled by Russian expansionism than were other freedom-loving people. The totality of his ideological transformation was striking; the former radical who had once seen the future in the Soviet experiment had become one of Moscow's bitterest critics.

A June 1950 letter, penned just days before the start of the Korean War, illustrates Randolph's vision of what he believed was the crisis confronting America and the world. The labor leader noted that Communism at home and abroad posed a "great danger to liberty, justice and progress and the future of the Negro in the United States . . . and peoples of color throughout the world." Embracing the principles, if not the practice, of western-style democracy, Randolph noted that the hopes of those struggling against oppression, especially peoples of color, lay in the "reality and integrity and strength of democracy." Without the basic freedoms the democratic system provided, it would be impossible to move forward in the quest for "security and first-class citizenship."[16] Still more arresting was a 1952 letter, in which Randolph noted the importance of possessing the right to fight for one's rights, which he claimed gave the oppressed the opportunity to improve democracy. The race reformer harbored no illusions: "[O]ur American democracy is no lily of purity. . . . Its difficulties, shortcomings and limitations are all too obvious. . . . [The American system needs] much cleansing of its sins against minorities, especially Negroes." Despite this, he preferred it to the totalitarian alternative, where under the "Stalins and Hitlers," one lived in dread of "the knock upon the door in the dead of night." Under such regimes, he asserted, "the heart of liberty [would] wither and die."[17]

Outspoken in his support of America's decision to fight in Korea, Randolph linked the war to the quest for racial justice. Scoring Russia for secretly backing the invasion, Randolph likened Moscow's deceptive behavior to that of a thief who fingers an innocent bystander in order "to divert attention from the loot under his own arm." Russia's actions should serve to remind "smaller nationalities, Negroes and other minorities" that the Soviets were bent on world conquest, their protestations of peace notwithstanding. Concealed in Moscow's hand, Randolph claimed, was a "dagger aimed at the heart of democratic peoples everywhere."[18] At a Harlem rally in the summer of 1950, Randolph called on listeners to give their complete "moral and material" support to the democracies' fight against "the ruthless march of the Russian empire of totalitarian communism." He asked free peoples throughout the world for help, regardless of their race, color, religion, or national origin, and insisted the Soviet action heightened the insecurity of smaller nations, pointing specifically to Haiti, Liberia, and Ethiopia, as well as Israel and the countries of southern Asia. The response of the United Nations, which had shown its capacity to "arbitrate and adjust international conflicts," was the only insurance against the start of another world war. Significantly, in advancing a pro–United States perspective and contextualizing the Korean conflict in racial terms, Randolph told his largely black audience that without American intervention, the forces of the free world would serve as easy prey for Russian tyranny, which threatened to destroy the hope and opportunity for "peoples of color to become truly free." And closer to home, Randolph called on black Americans, who were marching shoulder to shoulder with their white brethren against totalitarianism, to continue fighting relentlessly for "civil rights and complete equality" in the United States. Claiming their struggle was right, Randolph told his Harlem audience that the fight for racial justice allowed blacks to render the country a great service, "for every concession of civil rights to Negroes" is the most powerful propaganda weapon America could wield in the Cold War.[19] The notion that American prestige was a potential victim in the struggle against totalitarianism was a centerpiece of Randolph's Cold War rhetoric.

Throughout the fifties, Randolph told thousands of Americans that the conflict between western democracy and Russian totalitarianism was one of the supreme challenges facing the world, and to audiences both at home and abroad, he said it would be impossible to exaggerate the significance of the struggle. Soviet Russia was determined to expand its power and authority to every corner of the globe. In a typical address, Randolph told a Boston audience that the Cold War was "the most important single subject before the world today" and declared a Russian victory meant the "extinction or the subjugation of American democracy." For black Americans and for peoples of color elsewhere, the stakes could not have been higher; indeed, he noted, "the greatest single enemy and menace to the Negro today is Russian Communism in the United States and the world." Without the right to fight for expanding their domestic freedoms—a right American democracy provided—black Americans could not move forward in their historic struggle. Randolph claimed deep familiarity with the meaning of Russian Communism for America, Europe, Asia, and Africa, and, having studied the subject for more than thirty years, he had concluded that the road to equality passed not through the Soviet Union but through the western democracies. It was imperative that blacks gained the right to organize and demonstrate in order to make Americans aware that discrimination in government, in education, and in the military should be abolished. Such rights simply did not exist under the Communist system, he told his Boston audience, and his task was to convey this truth to black America. Though the domestic quest was far from over, blacks had made significant gains in their struggle, and as long as democracy survived, he was convinced they could expect further achievements.[20]

Expanding on this theme, Randolph argued that the United States, by providing leadership to colonial peoples in their quest for liberation, would fortify its position in the international arena and strengthen the West in its battle against Soviet totalitarianism. No less important, America could enhance its status in the eyes of the colonial world by confronting the challenge of racial persecution. Reflecting on a visit to Asia in 1952, the labor leader knitted together the themes of American influence in the colonial world, the Cold War, and the need to overcome domestic oppression. While he acknowledged that military strength would play a key part in the East-West conflict, he observed that the United States needed to demonstrate to the Asian world that "an authentic morality of democracy has an existential reality, independent of the fight against the Soviet Union." We need not portray ourselves as the perfect society, he wrote, but we must emphasize the inherent strength of the democratic system, which, contrary to the Communist model, possessed the potential to achieve "progress, freedom, and justice." Randolph identified the most difficult question America faced in the colonial world: "How does the United States reconcile racial discrimination with democracy?" Widespread international awareness of American racism made it pointless to deny the problem; thus, Americans had to acknowledge the existence of racial persecution. "[F]rankness [and] honesty" were essential, along with a determination to point to America's resolute willingness to confront the nation's "sins of racialism." As long as the country faced the problem squarely and conveyed democracy's capacity to overcome discrimination, Randolph believed that Americans could enhance their status among the oppressed. In the United States, minorities could "struggle for the attainment of complete freedom," whereas the citizens of the "Communist Russian slave system [were] unfree to fight to become

free." He insisted that "Democracy [would] prevail if it be true to itself
... [and] fail if it be untrue to itself."[21]

While many race leaders linked their perception of the external Communist threat to the race reform movement's domestic goals, some were
also distressed about Communist influence inside the United States and
worried that Communist infiltration of the civil rights movement could
undermine their efforts. In the age of Joseph McCarthy, when America's
intolerance for dissent would reach pathological heights, such concerns
powerfully affected the outlook and message of many reformers. While
the Communist Party did not make significant inroads into the civil rights
movement during these years, worries about Communism led the NAACP
to decide in 1950 that Communists would be barred from membership.
The organization also empowered its executive board and national staff
to address the issue of Communist infiltration of those branches that
seemed vulnerable. Many American race leaders were determined not to
allow themselves to be described as "Communist sympathizers" at a historical moment when they believed such accusations would have harmful
consequences for the movement.[22]

But it was not just for tactical reasons that some in the reform community harbored concerns about Communism; among certain reform leaders, there was also a sense that the goals of the Communists and the reformers were not compatible. From his years as head of the National
Negro Congress in the late 1930s through the early 1940s, A. Philip Randolph had consistently taken an uncompromising stand against Communist influence on the reform struggle. And after 1945, he was determined
to prevent the Communists from exerting influence on either the civil
rights campaign or the labor movement. In the *Black Worker* and in
speeches around the country, Randolph argued that Communists were
inimical to race reform, claiming that their commitment to an "anti-dem-
ocratic program" and their employment of "ruthless and dictatorial tactics" meant they had to be monitored and isolated in order to prevent
their destroying democratic movements in the United States.[23] Walter
White also spoke out against the dangers of Communist infiltration, especially of the NAACP, though he claimed the Communists' past inability
to do so left him unconcerned about the association's vulnerability. In a
sweeping assessment, which was part of a 1953 book, White delineated
his thoughts on the subject. A chapter entitled "Why Has the Negro Rejected Communism?" considered a variety of historical, philosophical,
and sociological reasons, which, according to White, helped explain why
Communism had garnered so little support among the black population.
In addition to discussing the "opportunism" of the Communists, especially in the 1930s, he emphasized black opposition to the notion of "boss
rule" (a result of slavery), which made blacks wary about supporting a

system that placed "arbitrary power" in one man or a small clique. White also argued that blacks were convinced the current political system in the United States had enabled them to make "noticeable gains," which diminished Communism's appeal. The best way to confront the domestic Communist threat, in White's estimation, was to create a genuine democracy in the United States.[24]

Crisis readers also had ample opportunity to ponder the alleged threat Communism posed to the movement and the nation. A 1951 piece by NAACP Assistant Field Secretary Herbert Hill castigated the Communists, arguing that the goals of the race reform movement and those of the Party were at odds. Offering a historical overview of Communist efforts to garner black support for their program since the 1920s, Hill claimed it was essential to get behind the Party's "facade" to discover its true aims and methods. A key to these "realities," *Crisis* readers were told, was that the American Communist Party was nothing more than an "instrument" of Russian foreign policy, which undermined the idea that it was working to aid black America. According to Hill, when a conflict arose between black interests and Russian interests, the "Communists abandon[ed] Negroes like rats [abandoned] a sinking ship." Concluding with a scathing description of the American Communist Party, Hill called it "one of the Negro's implacable enemies in his fight for equality," an organization that stood for "more efficient segregation."[25]

Crisis subscribers also learned about the tribulations of two black artists of the period, the activist-performer Paul Robeson and the writer Langston Hughes. In 1950, Robeson, an outspoken and powerful critic of American foreign and domestic policies, had his passport revoked by the U.S. government, which prevented him from leaving the country. Illustrating the extraordinary fear that reigned in 1950s America, the State Department and the FBI were convinced that Robeson's activities abroad— namely, speaking openly about the persistence of domestic injustice—were unacceptable. Consequently, he was forced to remain in the United States, unable to share his views with peoples overseas. Tellingly, a 1951 *Crisis* piece described the singer's descent from his role as a champion of equal rights to his current status as one who had jettisoned his critical faculties in evaluating world politics. Quoting Walter White, whose profile on Robeson had recently appeared in the black periodical *Ebony*, Robert Alan told *Crisis* readers the legendary artist was now a "bewildered man who is more to be pitied than damned." More pertinent than the discussion of Robeson's alleged fall was the contention that the path to racial progress in America lay not with the Communists but with the traditional forces of reform. Writing that the Communists had achieved little for the black population, Alan doubted that they had ever truly cared about black interests and noted that black membership in the Communist

Party stood at a mere fourteen hundred. For *Crisis* readers, the point was unambiguous: organizations like the NAACP and the National Urban League provided the best means for pursuing black advancement; as for Paul Robeson, the article claimed he had become a "tragic figure."[26]

Two years after the Robeson piece appeared, the journal published excerpts from the testimony of Langston Hughes, who had been summoned to Washington to testify in March 1953 before Joseph McCarthy's Senate Permanent Sub-Committee on Investigations about his writings and some past associations the committee thought were suspect. The episode, in which McCarthy and Roy Cohn participated, is notable for this study because of the message the NAACP's journal was determined to convey by providing an excerpt from the poet's testimony.[27] Without commentary, the editors published Hughes's admission that he had once found appealing "some of the promises of communism," an attraction that had begun in the days of the Scottsboro case. The shocking signing of the Nazi-Soviet Pact in 1939 had caused the attraction to wane, though Hughes told the committee he had long been drawn to participate in social struggle, a consequence of his family's devotion to such things and his experiences as a poor black man in America. Nevertheless, Hughes insisted, "I am not now and have never been a member of the Communist Party." Hughes spoke, too, of his desire to preserve his "freedom of action" and his wish for full integration into the American body politic, which led him to harbor profound reservations about the Communist program. (He noted the Communists' regimentation of the artist and their earlier plan for a "Negro state for the Black Belt.") The poet also discussed his recent shock on hearing about the persecution of Soviet Jews and voiced his dismay at the lack of freedom of expression in the Soviet Union. The *Crisis* piece concluded with Hughes observing that blacks were making great strides in America, a place where people were free to vote and "work out their problems." Reading from his most recent work, he observed that in the United States, "all of us are part of democracy," and that America could become "the most wonderful country in the world." From the tone of the *Crisis* excerpt, readers would have likely concluded that Hughes believed Communism had little to offer black Americans and that it would deny them freedom of expression and preclude their integration into the larger culture. And this, of course, was precisely the view mainstream reformers held of Soviet Communism.[28]

In considering the ideological repression of the 1950s, one must look finally at Du Bois, who, after leaving the NAACP in 1948, continued his work, albeit outside the movement's organizational mainstream. While Du Bois's penchant for subscribing to iconoclastic ideas was not new, his left-of-center political activities and ties to "suspect" individuals and causes in the age of Joseph McCarthy were unacceptable to the United

States government. According to Gerald Horne, who has closely considered Du Bois's activities during these years, the government's scrutiny of the reformer's work in this period was a result of the link between those working to crush domestic Communism and those seeking to maintain Jim Crow. Consequently, Horne argues, for the government (and especially for the House Committee on Un-American Activities), Du Bois represented a double threat. For those trying to protect the country from what they saw as its ubiquitous internal and external foes, Du Bois was both a leftist and a race activist—an apparently lethal combination that would force the legendary reformer to endure much anguish.[29]

In February 1951, a few months after Du Bois had been defeated in a bid for a U.S. Senate seat in New York (he had polled 206,000 votes on the American Labor Party ticket), the U.S. government indicted the eighty-two-year-old reformer for allegedly serving as an unregistered agent of a foreign power.[30] Describing the incident in his autobiography, Du Bois writes of being "handcuffed, fingerprinted, bailed, and remanded for trial." The case, which attracted a great deal of domestic and international attention, came to trial the following November, and the reformer's memory of the ordeal serves as a testament to the baneful obsessions of the American government during this period. Poignantly noting that throughout his life he had confronted countless unpleasant and even dangerous experiences, Du Bois observed that

> nothing has so cowed me as that day . . . when I took my seat in a Washington courtroom as an indicted criminal. I was not a criminal. I had broken no law, consciously or unwittingly. Yet I sat with four American citizens of unblemished character, never before accused even of misdemeanor, in the seats often occupied by murderers, forgers and thieves; accused of a felony and liable to be sentenced before leaving this court to five years of imprisonment, a fine of $10,000 and loss of my civil and political rights as a citizen, representing five generations of Americans.[31]

Acquitted after a short trial, Du Bois claimed it was no mere personal victory, but "a triumph for free speech and the right to defend peace."[32] Despite his acquittal, he noted that the government continued to harass him in a variety of ways. He was watched; his mail was opened; his writing was not published; he was barred from speaking. And perhaps most disheartening of all, the NAACP—the organization he had helped build—fearful that associating with Du Bois would tarnish its reputation and weaken its program, refused to allow local branches to invite him to lecture. It was a bitter experience, he wrote, and he "bowed before the storm." But the reformer did not break. While he continued to speak and write when and where he was permitted to do so, Du Bois acknowledged that his profile in the reform crusade had been diminished. "I lost my leadership of my race. . . . The colored children ceased to hear my name." But as he would insist several years later, all was not hopeless, for the "color line was beginning to break. Negroes were getting recognition as never before."[33]

And surely the aging crusader was right. For despite the indignities visited on Du Bois, Robeson, and others, the trajectory described by the civil rights movement during the 1950s was that of a long upward arc, as the nation and the world would witness a series of memorable achievements and epochal events. Notwithstanding the malignancy of McCarthyism, the central theme in the story of race reform during the 1950s concerns neither America's extraordinary preoccupation with Communism nor its pathological muzzling of dissent. Instead, the decade saw a critical victory in the nation's highest court, the triumph of thousands of determined people in Montgomery, Alabama, and the emergence of new leaders, tactics, and appeals that would change the face of the movement and lend the crusade the sound and shape with which all Americans would soon become familiar. In addition, significant economic and demographic changes, though less apparent, would play a role in launching the movement into a new era.

In surveying the civil rights movement after 1945, Harvard Sitkoff has identified several key economic and demographic factors that abetted black progress in these years, including the spectacular growth of the American economy, the industrialization of the South (including the mechanization of the cotton industry), and urbanization.[34] While the gross national product nearly doubled between 1940 and 1955, the median income of the black population grew at almost the same rate, and this extraordinary economic expansion had both tangible and intangible effects on African-American life. The great demand for labor drew blacks into industries from which they had previously been barred, and the national economic expansion meant that black advancement did not have to come at the expense of white Americans, which had proved a source of racial tension in the past. The industrialization of the South contributed to the decline of the region's historically dominant cotton culture, which decreased the demand for rural, unskilled black labor. At the same time, power shifted from rural to urban areas, where an urban professional class, often employed by absentee-owned corporations, came to view segregation as an anachronistic economic liability. Industrialization also quickened the pace of southern urbanization, and the movement of a large group of white-collar employees and their families into the South increased the number of individuals who were not committed to maintaining a color-based caste system. The mechanization of southern cotton production also decreased the demand for labor and pushed rural blacks from the farm, while the increased demand for urban labor drew blacks to the cities of the South and beyond. More than a million blacks would leave the South during the 1940s, while 1.5 million more would depart in the following decade. As Sitkoff writes, the movement of blacks to the city "fundamentally altered the configuration of the race problem," making it national in scope. No longer constrained by a rural caste system, urban blacks could now gather in large numbers, which would help "foster group consciousness and solidarity." The urban setting allowed blacks to secure employment and educational opportunities that had scarcely existed before, and the city, unlike the countryside, made possible the mobilization of political power.[35]

As these changes were reshaping the postwar social and economic landscape, several events riveted the eyes of the nation on the civil rights crusade. On May 17, 1954, Chief Justice Earl Warren announced that a decision had been reached in the case of *Oliver Brown et al. v. Board of Education of Topeka*. Reading from the bench, he stated that education was the key to opportunity and advancement in America and was a right that "must be made available to all on equal terms." Warren then posed the central question of the case: "Does segregation of children in public schools solely on the basis of race, even though the physical facilities and other 'tangible' factors may be equal, deprive the children of the minority group of equal educational opportunities?" Pausing, Warren declared, "We believe that it does." According to the Chief Justice, "in the field of public education the doctrine of 'separate but equal' has no place. Separate educational facilities are inherently unequal."[36] For Roy Wilkins, May 17, 1954, was "one of life's sweetest days." For fifty-eight "miserable years," he wrote, since the Supreme Court had handed down the 1896 decision in *Plessy v. Ferguson*, which had ruled that segregation was not an infringement on the rights of blacks as long as they were provided with equal facilities, the black population had been helpless under the law. Through decades of mistreatment—in the classroom, on the job, at the polls, in peace and war—blacks had known that "moral justice and the country's political principles were on our side." At long last, wrote Wilkins, the law was "on our side, too."[37]

At the NAACP's annual conference, which met six weeks after the *Brown* ruling, several speakers discussed the case and joined the verdict to the question of America's international influence and prestige. In a striking inversion of the practice we have seen heretofore, NAACP reformers could at last point to a positive domestic development, link it to overseas affairs, and argue that the United States had taken a great step toward achieving justice and could not turn back without diminishing its international prestige. Claiming the ruling was as important as the Declaration of Independence, the Constitution, the Bill of Rights, and the Emancipation Proclamation, Channing Tobias, the head of the NAACP's board, contextualized the decision in terms of the East-West conflict: "The propaganda value of this ruling for America and the free world in the life and death struggle against communism is beyond measure." Moreover, Tobias warned, if the nation retreated from the implication of the decision, it would prove costly to the cause of domestic unity and America's world-wide prestige.[38] Attorney Thurgood Marshall, the man of the hour, who had argued the case before the high court, also pondered its effect on world politics, noting that it had been "beyond the expectation of anyone." With the exception of Russia and its eastern European satellite states, every nation had commented favorably on the case, which he claimed was heralded "as a new hope for democracy." Like Tobias, Marshall warned that the world was watching America—and waiting to see how southern school boards would implement the ruling.[39]

At the conference's final session, Walter White asserted that the court had dealt a "death blow" to segregation, telling the delegates that in light of the case, they had just attended the greatest convention in the NAACP's long history. White shared the comments of a southern journalist, who had observed that white southerners were in truth the ones liberated by the ruling for they now stood on the threshold of a process that would cure them of "the evil influence of racial arrogance and bigotry." Turning to the international sphere, White discussed the "world background" of the decision, noting that the verdict had positively influenced the global prestige of the United States. The free world had acclaimed the Supreme Court's decision as the "best news that had come out of America in the twentieth century," and he quoted an African educator who believed that *Brown* had "restored America to its rightful place as champion of democracy." Echoing the words of Tobias and Marshall, White spoke of America's obligation to uphold the letter and spirit of the ruling and declared the country could not allow bigots to weaken the world's emerging confidence in American democracy. There were southern politicians who would defy or denounce the Supreme Court, he said, but they were merely contributing to the Communist cause. As for the Soviet press, which had asserted that the decision was made purely for propaganda purposes, the association was determined to show the Communists and the entire world that *Brown* meant what it said and would be "implemented to the hilt."[40]

Even the American president, who was in no way a friend of the civil rights movement, was not immune from imparting global significance to the Supreme Court's decision. In a greeting to the annual conference, Dwight Eisenhower said the ruling represented "a milestone of social advance," and claimed that the nation's reception of the decision was enormously important to America and the "cause of freedom in the world." For the president, the *Brown* case and the country's response to it were significant because of America's global competition with Communism; as he told the association's members, "We must have continued social progress, calmly but persistently made, so that we may prove without doubt to all the world that our nation . . . [is] truly dedicated to liberty and justice for all."[41] Clearly, reform leaders were not alone in linking the court's decision to the East-West conflict, and just as White, Tobias, Marshall, and other reformers deployed *Brown* to convince the nation to remain committed to civil rights, American policymakers were persuaded that the case could enhance American credibility on the world stage. In the wake of *Brown*, it had become impossible to ignore the connection between America's global struggle against Communism and the domestic movement for racial justice, a link the reformers had worked energetically to establish since the end of World War II. It was apparent that the most significant Supreme Court decision in the twentieth century had become enmeshed in the country's overseas crusade, and more broadly, as Gary Gerstle has observed, that geopolitical concerns would "impel" American leaders "to advance the cause of racial equality" and enhance the movement's success.[42]

Just as the decision rendered in a Washington courtroom would in time influence the lives of black Americans, the momentous events in Montgomery, Alabama, in 1955 and 1956 would also have significant implications for the black population and the reform crusade. The story of Rosa Parks and her refusal to surrender her seat to a white passenger on a bus as local law required is rightly seen as one of the seminal episodes in the movement's history. In the words of Martin Luther King, Jr., the Atlanta-born minister whose star would rise as a result of the bus boycott, "She was anchored to that seat by the accumulated indignities of days gone by and the boundless aspirations of generations yet unborn." Mrs. Parks recalled the decision more simply: "I felt it was just something I had to do."[43] Beyond the emergence of King, who held a doctorate from Boston University and had graduated from Morehouse College and the Crozer Theological Seminary, the boycott helped shift the movement's orientation from the courtroom to the street and, according to Harvard Sitkoff, "proved the power of organized collective action as an effective agent of social change." The determination of the black citizens of Montgomery helped catalyze "an age of open confrontation" against Jim Crow and encouraged thousands of black Americans to heed King's call. More specifically, the boycott led to the formation of the Southern Christian Leadership Conference (SCLC) in January 1957, which provided an organizational framework for southern black clergymen who would become critically important as the movement gathered momentum. Offering the language of nonviolent resistance, the southern black church would, at the same time, provide a strong base of support for the reform campaign, financial assistance, and "a place to meet, to plan, to gain faith and courage." The church would lend the movement a unifying language with which to battle racial oppression—a powerful rhetoric "expressed in biblical oratory and hymns," which imbued the decades-old struggle with a Christian legitimacy it had never possessed.[44] The black and white elites that had spearheaded the efforts for legislative and judicial action for some fifty years would in time be supplanted by a group of southern black church leaders who sought to effect change through the mobilization of large numbers of regular black citizens.

A striking and little-noted aspect of the Montgomery episode were the global references the youthful King made during the boycott, in which he powerfully identified the aspirations of black Americans with the struggles of peoples of color throughout the developing world. In conjoining the domestic and global struggles, the young minister deployed an internationalist rhetoric similar to that used by other activists, who, in the 1950s and earlier, had infused their message with images of liberation crusades in the colonial world. What distinguished King's remarks from the efforts of his predecessors was the sheer eloquence of his oratory, which, to be sure, was no small difference. In June 1956, King discussed the bus boycott with more than a thousand association members at the NAACP's annual conference, including Rosa Parks, whom he called a "great symbol in our struggle." It was a sweeping speech that touched on the black experience in America during the time of slavery, which he said had been replaced by a form of "mental slavery." But one could see the emergence of something important, King contended, a "brand new Negro in the South," possessed of a "new sense of dignity and destiny." Montgomery was "the story of fifty thousand Negroes who are tired of oppression and injustice and are willing to substitute tired feet for tired souls, and walk and walk and walk until the sagging walls of injustice have been crushed by the battering rams of historical necessity."

Turning to global developments, King spoke of the historic oppression the world's "colored peoples" had endured and observed that those who had lived under the "yoke of colonialism" were at last gaining their freedom. In words not unlike those uttered by many other race reformers, King warned his country that if she did not "wake up, she will discover that the uncommitted peoples of the world are in the hands of a communist ideology." But he offered a distinctive argument for change—one based on neither pragmatism nor geostrategic necessity. America had to strive to give blacks freedom and justice, not just to compete with "godless communism" or because it was "diplomatically expedient," he insisted, but because it was "morally compelling" and was the right thing to do. Thus, while King offered a perspective similar to that of his predecessors, the young reformer had summoned the capacity of the clergyman to guide the argument into the ethical domain. Continued progress was the key, he asserted. "If you can't fly, run; if you can't run, walk; if you can't walk, crawl, but by all means keep moving!"

King went on to consider the philosophy of nonviolent resistance, which would define his approach to reform during the next ten years. Nonviolent resistance was not difficult to understand, he said, explaining that it meant "we will refuse on a nonviolent basis to cooperate with the evil of segregation." Violence would be both "impractical and immoral," he observed, noting that history was "replete with the bleached bones of nations who failed to hear these words of truth." The young clergyman discussed the overseas provenance of the philosophy, implicitly pointing to the global interconnectedness that had led him to choose this path to reform. Acknowledging that it was not new, he said it had been tried by a "little brown man in India" (he did not identify Gandhi by name) who had looked at the vast British Empire with its powerful military machinery and confronted it with soul force. The little man had employed this method to free his people from the political and economic exploitation, and the humiliation, that Britain had inflicted upon them. Like the Indians, King said, we in America must be willing to use this powerful force to attain racial justice.[45]

Several months later, from the pulpit of Montgomery's Holt Street Baptist Church, King spoke again about overseas developments, emphasizing world affairs to fortify the language of reform. His listeners were privileged to be alive in "one of the most momentous periods in human history," he said, a time when men stood between two worlds, "the dying old and the emerging new." The reformer spoke of discontent in Asia, uprisings in Africa, nationalistic longings in Egypt, and "racial tensions" in America that suggested to many the "deep and tragic midnight" of civilization. This was not a sign of decline, however, but a mark of progress, for such developments signaled the "necessary pains that accompany the birth of anything new." In the minister's estimation, a "new world order" was being born as the old was passing away. The old order was characterized by colonialism and imperialism, which were responsible for the political and economic exploitation of hundreds of millions of peoples of color who endured lives of segregation and humiliation. But 1.3 billion of these formerly oppressed peoples were now free to control their own governments, economies, and education, as the exploitative order was passing away. Nor was this transformation confined to the developing world, King asserted, for the United States was itself in the throes of change; a new order was emerging in America. The old order, marked by *Plessy*, segregation, slavery, and the Dred Scott decision, had caused black Americans to accept "insult, injustice, and exploitation." But transformative processes—urbanization, industrialization, and education—had caused "the Negro to take a new look at himself," and led him to feel "that he was somebody." Just as the old order was disappearing throughout the world, it was being supplanted here in America by "a new structure of freedom and justice."[46]

The emergence of Martin Luther King, Jr., along with the establishment of organizations like the SCLC and the widespread southern resistance to *Brown*, would affect the primacy of the NAACP's leadership position in the civil rights campaign. During the second part of the 1950s, forces throughout the South engaged in "massive resistance" to the high court's decision, organizing quasi-legal, illegal, and sometimes violent campaigns to harass the association so as to impede its efforts on behalf of school desegregation. By 1958, these campaigns had contributed to the loss of 246 NAACP branches in the region as the organization was forced to divert time, energy, and resources to combat southern intransigence.[47] Nevertheless, the association did not flag in its efforts. And the critical leadership change in April 1955, when Roy Wilkins was chosen to head the NAACP after the death of Walter White, did not dampen the organization's commitment to its decades-long mission. As we have seen, White, who had joined the organization in 1918 and headed it since 1931, had long displayed a profound interest in global developments. While it is difficult to gauge such matters with precision, the accession of Wilkins, a man seemingly less interested in overseas matters, appeared to cause the organization's global perspective to diminish somewhat. Despite this, world affairs still occupied a significant place in the association's post-1955 message, and colonial developments and the Cold War remained key elements in the NAACP's rhetoric of persuasion.[48]

In April 1955, representatives from twenty-nine African and Asian nations gathered in Bandung, Indonesia, for what that country's President Sukarno called a "new departure in the history of the world." The Afro-Asian (or Bandung) Conference brought together delegates representing 1.5 billion people peoples of color from the developing world who were united, in Sukarno's words, by "a common detestation of colonialism . . . and of racialism." Speakers from Cambodia, Ethiopia, Egypt, Japan, the Gold Coast, India, and elsewhere reiterated this theme throughout the gathering, which the *Christian Science Monitor* said was "perhaps the great historic event of our century." Using words with which few delegates would have disagreed, President Carlos Romulo of the Philippines declared, "We have known . . . the searing experience of being demeaned in our own lands, of being systematically relegated to subject status . . . politically and economically and . . . racially." According to Romulo, the western white man, to bolster his rule and to "justify his own power to himself," assumed his superiority lay "in his very bones, in the color of his skin," and this racism had served as a driving force in the development of nationalist movements in many of the lands represented at the conference.[49] It was not surprising that events in Bandung captured the attention of American race reformers.

Having occupied his position as NAACP head for less than a week, Roy Wilkins wired leading figures in Bandung, informing them of the association's interest in the conference and expressing hope on behalf of the organization's 250,000 members that the gathering might allow the world's peoples to work out their destinies free of the pressures exerted by the imperial powers. The association's journal also spoke hopefully about the meeting, observing that it was no longer possible for Europe alone to decide the fate of Asians and Africans. According to *The Crisis*, the diverse peoples represented at Bandung had at least one thing in common, the memory of western colonialism and the "scars of [the] white man's arrogance and humiliation." Asia and Africa were moving toward emancipation, *The Crisis* asserted, and were liberating themselves from the legacy of "white tutelage and exploitation."[50] The black press also covered the gathering, paying particular attention to the highly public activities of Harlem Congressman Adam Clayton Powell, Jr., who had journeyed to Bandung to tell anyone who would listen about the many freedoms black Americans enjoyed. Upon his arrival, Powell reported that to "be a Negro [in America] is no longer a stigma. It is a mark of distinction." The Harlem leader cited a variety of developments indicating that racism and second-class citizenship for blacks were "on the way out." If Powell's motives were difficult to understand—some called him a publicity hound—it is clear that Bandung helped draw attention to conditions in the developing world and to the idea of its emerging sense of unity. According to Brenda Gayle Plummer, Bandung "marked a turning point in the psychological awareness of formerly colonized peoples," and by conferring legitimacy on peoples of color, it helped to inaugurate a "new period of cultural interest in Africa" during the mid-1950s.[51] By the second half of the decade, it was clear that the continent stood on the threshold of epochal change, which would lend it added significance for the American race reform community.

As midnight struck on March 5, 1957, Kwame Nkrumah, adorned in colorful African robes, proclaimed to his people, "The battle is ended. Ghana, our beloved country, is free forever." As the British colonial flag came down and the Ghanaian flag arose in its place, the crowd of more than half a million thundered, "Freedom! Freedom!" Among the enthusiastic spectators were several leading black figures from the United States, including A. Philip Randolph, Ralph Bunche, Adam Clayton Powell, and Martin Luther King, Jr., who was abroad for the first time. Vice President Richard Nixon, representing the United States, was there as well, and when King crossed paths with him at a reception, the young minister remarked, "I want you to come visit us down in Alabama where we are seeking the same kind of freedom Ghana is celebrating." The men shook hands, and Nixon suggested that they should meet in Washington sometime.[52] A. Philip Randolph, who had long been drawn to the strivings of colonial peoples, spoke at the Ghanaian independence celebration, emphasizing the global significance of the event. Setting Africa's quest for self-rule in the context of the world struggle against totalitarianism, Randolph observed that these were perilous times and reminded his listeners of the "brute terror" the Soviets had used to crush the Hungarian quest for freedom. The Ghanaians, he noted, were fortunate to have escaped such a dreadful fate. Invoking the internationalism of the American race reformer, he conveyed to the Ghanaians the greetings of black Americans, whom he described as "your brothers and sisters of color," a people "fired" in their own struggle by the crusade for African independence. Randolph then sounded a refrain he had often articulated in the United States, conjoining the Cold War with events in the developing world, while noting that American race activists sought sustenance and inspiration from Africa in order to advance their own reform agenda.[53]

The following year, Prime Minister Nkrumah journeyed to New York, where he was honored by the NAACP, the National Urban League, and the American Committee on Africa. Roy Wilkins and the Urban League's Lester Granger spoke of the links between the freedom crusades in Africa and the United States, with Granger pointing to the "close kinship" between those involved in each revolution. According to Granger, although eight thousand miles of ocean separated Ghana from the struggles unfolding on the North American continent, there was "no more than the whisper of a bird's breath between the hopes and aspirations" of black Americans and those of black Ghanaians, who now walked the streets of Accra as free citizens. Wilkins identified the power of the African example, claiming that the Ghanaian people had inspired those laboring to build a more just society in the United States. "Your struggles and your successes," he told the African leader, "have aided us in our trials and tribulations here," and just as other Americans looked with pride and affection upon their European homelands, so black Americans looked upon Ghana.[54]

Bearing the torch that his predecessor Walter White had carried for so long, in 1957, Roy Wilkins incorporated a different set of international images into his address at the final session of the association's annual convention. To a large crowd in Detroit's Olympia Stadium, the NAACP leader spoke about a wartime meeting held fourteen years earlier in the same city, when race activists had debated the most effective way to wage war against Jim Crow as the country battled Hitler in Europe. He reminded the delegates that the answer, so difficult to reach at the time, now seemed quite simple. It was necessary to fight Jim Crow, "whether of the Hitler variety or the Alabama variety," at all times in all places. Returning his gaze to the present, Wilkins looked to the challenges the movement faced in an era of anti-Communist hysteria and claimed it was ironic to label as "subversive" those who were working to provide the full range of freedoms to all Americans. Any who would destroy such freedoms, he observed—those "parading themselves as patriots"—were the true subversives.

The NAACP head then spoke more directly about international matters, particularly about the Hungarian Revolution, which the Soviet military had quashed the previous year. He recalled how Americans had cheered the heroic efforts of the valiant Hungarians, who had thrown "their rocks and their bare fists at the Soviet oppressors." While thousands of tanks had finally forced the Hungarians into submission, he said, Russian slavery had been exposed before the entire world. Constructing an analogy between Soviet oppression in Hungary and the oppression blacks faced in the American South, Wilkins offered an argument that mirrored those advanced by countless reformers we have encountered before. "Only in degree is there discernible difference between the dictatorship of skin color in . . . the southern states and the dictatorship of communism in Hungary." Wilkins wondered how Hungarians who resisted persecution could be considered heroes while black Americans who did the same were considered agitators. Even as the American government sent observers to Hungary, organized airlifts, established refugee camps, and opened the door to immigrants, it said nothing about racial oppression in the South. Wilkins asked if there had been a Civil War, if the Constitution applied to black Americans, and if slavery had been abolished. The association's delegates and the nation were left to draw the inevitable inference: if Americans believed it was indefensible to deny freedom to eastern Europeans, then surely it was indefensible to deny southern blacks their citizenship rights. The United States was obligated to abolish Jim Crow, Wilkins contended; without such change, it was reasonable to ask precisely how the American and Soviet systems differed.[55]

Two days before Wilkins spoke, the NAACP presented Martin Luther King, Jr., with the Spingarn Medal for his role in the bus boycott. King said he was proud to accept the award for the fifty thousand black citizens of Montgomery, who had realized it was "more honorable to walk in dignity than ride in humiliation." The minister discussed three distinct periods in the history of American race relations: the centuries of slavery; the period from emancipation to the *Brown* ruling in 1954; and the current period, in which the nation stood at the border of the "promised land of integration." Asserting that it was essential not to rest until segregation and discrimination had been abolished from every corner of American

NAACP chairman Roy Wilkins, who joined the association in 1931 after working as a journalist, is seen here raising funds for the organization in its domestic battle for freedom during the Cold War era. The photograph is likely from 1959, the NAACP's fiftieth-anniversary ("Jubilee") year.

life, King set the reform crusade against the backdrop of global developments. He propounded an argument heard innumerable times at past NAACP gatherings, declaring that throughout the world, American prestige, self-respect, and self-interest were at stake. According to King, it was "one of the ironies of present history that the Negro, in his struggle for freedom, is no longer struggling for himself alone"; he was, in fact, "struggling to save America." Peoples of color simply would not accept this country's global leadership as long as racial persecution persisted in the United States, King observed, noting that his recent travels and his discussions with leaders in the developing world had made clear to him that hundreds of millions of Asians and Africans were demanding that "racism and colonialism must go." He told the NAACP's delegates that the subject of colonialism and racism was central to nearly every conversation he had had while abroad and asserted that if America wished to be a "first-class nation, we cannot have second-class citizens." While none doubted that the youthful clergyman brought much that was new to the movement, his contention that it was necessary to construct a just society at home so as to gain the allegiance of peoples of color around the world had been advanced by leading reformers for quite some time.[56]

A few months later, in September 1957, in one of the movement's memorable events, Arkansas governor Orval Faubus decided to prevent nine black teenagers from enrolling at Little Rock's Central High, a school of some two thousand white students. In rejecting the school board's decision to accept a federal court ruling to begin the process of integration, Faubus claimed it would "not be possible to restore or to maintain order if forcible integration was carried out."[57] The story of the hate-filled confrontation in Little Rock, which would compel a reluctant President Eisenhower to order one thousand soldiers into the maelstrom of race and politics, has been told many times. In a televised speech to the nation, the president acknowledged the international dimensions of the domestic crisis. Linking domestic to world affairs, he asserted that events in Little Rock had made it "difficult to exaggerate the harm that is being done to the prestige and influence, and indeed to the safety of our nation and the world." According to Eisenhower, America's "enemies are gloating over this incident and using it . . . to misrepresent our whole nation." The foreign press also provided extensive coverage of the episode, which one scholar contends dealt a serious blow to America's prestige abroad and helped to accelerate the dismantling of Jim Crow.[58]

The race reformers agreed with the president about the international implications of the crisis, although they spoke with greater passion and eloquence about the relationship between Little Rock and America's place in the world. At the NAACP's annual conference in July 1958, Channing Tobias stated that the "disgrace of Little Rock" was the "shame of America," and claimed the event would tarnish the nation. This was no local disorder, he asserted; in the eyes of the world, it was a "national affliction." In the words of Roy Wilkins, the Arkansas drama was "so shameful . . . that it shocked the minds and consciences of men around the world," and the NAACP chief contended that southern resistance to the black freedom struggle was doomed to fail. It was far too late for the actions of a "band of little men" to succeed either at home or abroad where people of all races were "battling for freedom and equality." The reformers were fighting against the theories of Hitler, he declared, while others were fighting to maintain Hitlerism. Setting the episode in the context of the Cold War, Wilkins observed that "[w]e and our country fight against dictatorship; they fight to impose dictatorship."[59]

Those outside the immediate circle of reform leaders also raised the subject of Little Rock, placing it in a global context. Senator Jacob Javits of New York, who addressed the NAACP delegates in Cleveland that summer, called the civil rights crusade "a struggle for the soul" of America and observed that it was now possible to make civil rights gains unparalleled since the Civil War. Considering the international implications of the domestic struggle, Javits said that events in Little Rock were crucial to America's quest for world leadership, and sounding a frequent theme, he noted that peoples of color in Asia and Africa were looking to America to see if it was up to the challenge of constructing a just society. Javits implied that gaining their support should be a key concern of United States policymakers, and he asserted that the federal government's willingness to enforce civil rights guarantees at Little Rock had already provided America with goodwill throughout the world. In conclusion, the New Yorker declared, "We are struggling for all posterity. The very moral force—perhaps the peace—of our country and of the whole free world is at stake."[60] By the end of the 1950s, then, it had become clear that the quest for racial justice in the United States had been globalized, and in the eyes of race reform leaders and even key policymakers, the domestic campaign was now of signal importance in maintaining the country's preeminence in world politics. As Dwight Eisenhower observed in his final State of the Union address, the "primary work on civil rights must go on. Not only because discrimination is morally wrong, but also because its impact is more than national—it is world-wide."[61]

In the summer of 1959, Roy Wilkins penned a thank-you note to the premier of Eastern Nigeria, Nnamdi Azikiwe, who had just addressed the NAACP's fiftieth annual conference in New York. The NAACP leader told the Nigerian statesman that the twenty-thousand delegates who had heard him were thrilled by the chance to listen to a leading figure from the emerging continent, and he noted that black Americans had "awakened on the African question." Wilkins pointed to America's special role as the leader of the western democracies and decried the Soviet Union, the leader of the world's Communist dictatorships, which sought to bring other peoples under its control. For this reason, Wilkins wrote, the United States recognized the importance of Africa.[62] To be sure, Azikiwe's address to a crowd of twenty-three thousand activists at New York's Polo Grounds was a testament to the interrelationship American reformers had established long ago between global and domestic matters. Introducing the Nigerian, Ralph Bunche, whose internationalism stretched back some twenty years, told the crowd that he looked forward to a time when "every Negro, wherever he is in this land," would be free of racial persecution. The matter of "equality and human dignity" was a global issue, Bunche asserted, noting that today the world's nonwhite peoples were insisting on their "right to traverse the highways and byways of the world with all other men . . . with their heads held high." They must not fail in this quest, he insisted, "just as we must not fail in America."[63]

The words of the African leader Azikiwe, whom Bunche called a "valiant warrior in the general cause of Negro emancipation," lauded the historic goals and recent accomplishments of the NAACP, which, he claimed, had inspired him and his colleagues in their liberation struggle overseas. Azikiwe, who had studied in the United States from 1925 to 1934, told his listeners that he knew the bitter taste of life in black America, as well as the invigorating challenge of working to overcome "man-made barriers and to forge ahead to the stars." He described America as "the cynosure of the world," a place where every act of injustice and every error in judgment in race relations was scrutinized by peoples everywhere. This was true not because America was hated, but because of the "universal respect" people had for the United States. Thus, like Caesar's wife, America had to be "above board" with respect to human dignity. It was essential, Azikiwe maintained, for the American government to guarantee to every citizen the enforcement of fundamental rights, which included freedom of speech, association, assembly, movement, and the right to due process.

Perhaps the most striking aspect of Azikiwe's address—and one heard rarely if ever before—was the African's contention that the "spirit of the American Negro," exemplified in the NAACP's constitutional struggles, had fired the imagination of "the sleeping African giant," which was arising to take its place in a world of free nations. If American reform leaders had long used the anticolonial struggles to inspire their followers in the United States, here a leading African freedom fighter told thousands of American reformers that they in fact had energized those working for change in Africa. According to Azikiwe, black Americans, by helping their own nation to "reconcile the theory of democracy with its practice," had inspired the freedom struggles outside America. And this, he proclaimed to the NAACP's committed members, was "a glorious victory for the American Negro!" In concluding his address to this annual gathering of race activists, Azikiwe highlighted the unity of aspirations that linked the crusade in black Africa to the crusade in America. "We struggle towards the same ultimate objective: to revive the stature of man so that man's inhumanity to man shall cease."[64] In an important sense, color-conscious internationalism had come full circle, with the achievements of black Americans providing inspirational energy to their brethren in Africa.

By any measure, the 1950s was a decade marked by historic progress in the campaign for racial justice. The movement's leaders could point to a momentous victory in the nation's highest court and to the sense that millions of Americans had come to recognize the black struggle as the nation's preeminent domestic challenge. By the end of the fifties, in the wake of *Brown*, Montgomery, and Little Rock, and with the emergence of new leaders and strategies, the country's attention was riveted to the civil rights movement. And there it would remain for the next ten years. While few doubted that there was still much work to be done, American race reformers could look to the years ahead with considerable optimism. If the coming decade, with its grand triumphs and wrenching tragedies, would not provide everything the reformers were hoping to accomplish, their conviction that the movement stood on the threshold of great achievements was not unfounded. It was ironic, therefore, that American globalism, which had contributed to the movement's steady progress since the end of World War II, would lead, by the mid-1960s, to grave tensions among reform leaders when they looked outside the United States and reflected upon their country's role in the world.

Eight

"I'VE SEEN THE PROMISED LAND"
Triumph and Tragedy in the 1960s

A CIVIL RIGHTS reformer who came of age in the early 1960s would have joined a struggle with no clear center of gravity. In the 1940s or 1950s, a young person committed to building a society free of racial persecution would have likely joined the NAACP, but during the 1960s, this was no longer the case. While the association continued to play a leading role in working for change, other organizations, with younger, more dynamic leaders, evolved or emerged. The influence of Martin Luther King, Jr., and the Southern Christian Leadership Conference continued to expand; the Student Nonviolent Coordinating Committee (SNCC) was established in 1960; and the Congress of Racial Equality (CORE), founded during World War II, assumed a greater degree of influence than before. The committed activist of the sixties would have been exposed to a variety of approaches to reform, and he or she would have heard a chorus of voices that was more discordant than harmonious.

Not surprisingly, such developments would eventually influence the way some race activists looked at international events and America's place in the world. Early in the decade, a young activist would have heard traditional reformers responding to world affairs as they had before, but a few years later, when the Vietnam War had come to occupy center stage, a new understanding of global developments would come to the fore. By the mid- to late sixties, many in the reform community had become severe critics of America's international role, and this caused their perspective on overseas affairs to assume different patterns from those we have encountered. The war in southeast Asia would transform the movement's distinctive internationalism, which had long helped shape the reformers' understanding of the world. And as the decade unfolded, it would become increasingly difficult and at last impossible to identify the United States as a beneficent force in international politics.

Flipping through the pages of *The Crisis* in 1960, one could read about the slaughter perpetrated by white policemen against dozens of unarmed black South Africans who were engaged in a peaceful protest against the oppressive laws of the minority white regime. The barbarity of the Sharpeville massacre surely stunned readers young and old. But the coverage and commentary resembled what older *Crisis* readers had encountered for decades: the perspective of the world press; the reaction of a world leader (Nehru); and an editorial that compared rebellion against racial oppression in the developing world to the revolt sweeping across the American South. Readers learned, too, that the world was shrinking, that "what happens in one corner affects the welfare and the destiny of people everywhere." A riot in the Congo, an election in Nigeria, and a North Carolina sit-in all shaped the future of mankind, *The Crisis* asserted. Subscribers thus confronted the proposition—heard many times before—that "American Negroes [could] take courage" from events in Ghana, Guinea, the Congo, and South Africa.[1]

A race activist who traveled to St. Paul, Minnesota, to attend the NAACP's annual conference in the summer of 1960 would have heard discussions about the sit-ins spreading across the South. Calling the new approach, which began at a Woolworth's lunch counter in Greensboro, North Carolina, "the most inspiring action" that had occurred in the civil rights field since the turn of the century, one speaker claimed that the "American Negro [was] now an equal partner in the decisions regarding his fate." Roy Wilkins told the delegates about the threat of "godless communism," about Soviet satellites that had been "gobbled up," and about the emergence of new nations in Africa whose loyalties were crucial to the West in the Cold War, which, he claimed, made it essential to abolish Jim Crow. Such words were not new, for race leaders had shared similar reflections on global affairs for some time.[2]

Two years later, a *Crisis* essay might have led readers to contemplate America's place in the world. Franklin Williams, an official with the newly formed Peace Corps (and formerly of the NAACP), wrote about the constitution, the law, and human rights in America, and considered the gap between America's professed belief in democratic values and its deficient record on human rights at home. While Williams painted a largely positive picture of the workings of the American system, which he believed could serve as an example for the world's new nations, he also ruminated on the damage done to American power and influence when it failed to uphold freedom and individual rights. While the Voice of America (a government propaganda organ) was proclaiming the country's commitment to freedom and democracy, wrote Williams, Moscow Radio was assailing the United States with the charge that American "freedom" permitted white supremacists "to victimize Negroes and deprive them of the basic human rights." The disjunction between American preachments and American racial practices presented by *The Crisis* in 1962 was worth pondering, though such discussions had first appeared some fifty years before in Du Bois's writings on the Great War.[3]

The spring of 1963 saw the start of a well-planned campaign in Birmingham, Alabama, which sought to abolish Jim Crow in one of the

South's most inhospitable and dangerous cities. Under the direction of the Reverend Fred Shuttlesworth and the Alabama Christian Movement for Human Rights, along with the participation of King and the SCLC, the movement initiated a nonviolent direct action campaign that aimed to produce a public confrontation with Commissioner of Public Safety Eugene "Bull" Connor in order to garner sufficient national attention to energize the reform process. And this caricature of a southern lawman did not disappoint the movement's leaders. The unforgettable pictures of singing children, snarling dogs, and fire hoses aimed full force at peaceful demonstrators would be branded into America's collective memory, and to the country's chagrin, much of the world was witness to those same images. In Washington, Los Angeles, London, and Moscow, people were horrified by the viciousness of southern race relations. As a result, President John F. Kennedy decided it was essential to support federal legislation aimed at sweeping institutionalized racial oppression from the South.[4]

Given the public character of the Birmingham campaign, it is not surprising that global considerations played a part in the way it was described and understood by policymakers and participants. And again, Cold War concerns and the reputation of the United States remained central to the domestic crusade. When the president addressed the nation about the Birmingham crisis on June 11, 1963, he noted—in language that echoed Walter White and Harry Truman,

> We preach freedom around the world, and we mean it. And we cherish our freedom here at home. But are we to say to the world—and much more importantly, to each other—that this is the land of the free, except for Negroes . . .? Now the time has come for this nation to fulfill its promise. The events in Birmingham . . . have so increased the cries for equality that . . . [we cannot] choose to ignore them.[5]

In discussing events in Birmingham, Martin Luther King noted that the views of the developing world were important to American policymakers, an argument race leaders had propounded throughout the postwar era. "The United States is concerned about its image," King told the congregation at Birmingham's St. John's Church. "When things started happening down here, Mr. Kennedy got disturbed. For Mr. Kennedy . . . is battling for the minds and hearts of men in Africa and Asia—some one billion men in the neutralist sector of the world." To a crowd of two thousand, King observed that people would not respect the United States if it continued to deprive "men and women of the basic rights of life because of the color of their skin."[6] An American race leader had again pointed to the competition the United States was waging to gain the support of the world's peoples of color and highlighted the notion that America's place on the international stage and its capacity to lead depended upon creating a genuine democracy on the home front.

A few months later, on a late August afternoon, the largest demonstration America had ever seen took place in the nation's capital, in the shadow of the Lincoln Memorial. Some quarter of a million Americans—black and white—had come to the city to proclaim their belief in human equality and to demand that America realize its historic promise. Amidst the "gentle army" that occupied Washington on that summer day, the movement's great figures discussed the aspirations of a people: Randolph, Wilkins, and then King, who, in the words of reporter James Reston, "full of the symbolism of Lincoln and Gandhi, and the cadences of the Bible," would touch "all the themes of the day, only better than anybody else."[7] Roy Wilkins told the throng about the death of Du Bois in Ghana the day before, and young activists learned, if they had not known it already, that Du Bois—more than anyone—had paved the way for black advancement. (As *The Crisis* noted a few weeks later, Du Bois was "the prime inspirer, philosopher and father" of the movement, "an impassioned and eloquent spokesman for equal rights, a fierce and uncompromising foe of colonialism," a promoter of Pan-Africanism, and a distinguished scholar.)[8]

With the passage of the Civil Rights Act in 1964 and the Voting Rights Act in 1965, the movement gained two of its greatest victories. These twin pieces of legislation, along with the *Brown* decision of 1954, made real many of the legal goals for which race reformers had been fighting throughout the twentieth century. The wide-ranging legislation of 1964 guaranteed equal access to public accommodations and gave the attorney general the authority to protect persons against discrimination in voting and education. In addition, the 1964 act established the Equal Employment Opportunity Commission and authorized the Office of Education (which was part of the Department of Health, Education, and Welfare) to help communities around the nation to desegregate their schools. The following year, the Voting Rights Act gave the attorney general the power to order federal examiners to register black voters in places where local officials refused to do so and banned literacy tests and other tactics states and counties had used to prevent blacks from voting. By the end of the year, almost two hundred and fifty thousand new blacks had registered to vote, and black officials soon began to win seats in the state legislatures and city councils of the South. These two monumental pieces of legislation would in time transform the status of black Americans, providing them with equality in law to live, eat, sleep, pursue an education, and vote, wherever they wished. This marked a change of epochal dimensions, not just in the life of black America, but in the life of the entire nation.[9]

As the civil rights campaign moved toward the realization of these historic goals, one of the more consequential—and controversial—figures to emerge in these years was the black nationalist Malcolm X, who boldly challenged the message advanced by more traditional reform leaders. According to Manning Marable, the religious group in which Malcolm would play a key role, the Nation of Islam, emphasized the separation of the races, the eventual "creation of an all-black nation state," and "capitalist economic development along racial lines," while it unambiguously repudiated the nonviolent, integrationist approach advocated by mainstream reform organizations. Malcolm's belief in separatism was clear. "Coffee is the only thing I like integrated," he was heard to say.[10] While his ideas fall outside the movement's mainstream, Malcolm's distinctive contribution to the reform dialogue in this period calls for a brief consideration of his perspective on overseas matters, which, intriguingly, was not entirely dissimilar from the views that have been encountered throughout these pages.

Born Malcolm Little in Omaha in 1925, Malcolm X experienced an unsettled childhood. His formal education was over by the eighth grade. At fifteen, he went to live with a half-sister in Boston, where he engaged in petty crime, sold drugs and alcohol, and became involved in other illicit activities. Convicted of burglary, Malcolm was sent to prison in 1946, where he became a follower of the Nation of Islam (the Black Muslims), a sect that appealed to northern working-class blacks and emphasized racial pride and the belief that white people were responsible for the oppression of peoples of color.[11] By the early 1960s, Malcolm had achieved considerable recognition as a Nation of Islam minister, establishing temples across the country and demanding to know why the persecution of black Americans persisted. Time and again, he scathingly rejected Martin Luther King, Jr.'s path to reform.[12]

Increasingly, Malcolm looked overseas, particularly after his journeys to the Middle East and Africa in 1964, which propelled him to advance a more temperate message. But even before that, his reflections on international matters were noteworthy. In 1963, he considered the transnational unity that peoples of color had demonstrated eight years earlier at the Bandung Conference. Pondering its lessons for black America, Malcolm contended that the key to Bandung was the exclusion of the white man, which led those in attendance, whether "black, brown, red, or yellow," to conclude "that they could get together." With the white man kept out, "everybody else fell right in . . . line." Peoples of color throughout the world understood that "where the dark man was being oppressed, he was being oppressed by the white man. . . . So they got together on this basis—that they had a common enemy." Black Americans should do likewise, Malcolm claimed. It was essential for blacks "to stop airing [their] differences in front of the white man," he said; instead, they should "sit down and talk shop with each other."[13] For Malcolm, the Bandung moment pointed not merely to the global unity of oppressed peoples of color, but also to the tactical necessity for racial separation in the United States, a theme he would emphasize repeatedly.

As was true of many activists who preceded him, Malcolm was drawn to the notion that transnational institutions could help improve the plight of black America. In a wide-ranging speech delivered in a Cleveland church in April 1964, he reflected upon the potential of the United Nations, offering an incisive distinction between civil and human rights. He spoke of the necessity for raising "the civil rights struggle to a higher level—to the level of human rights." The difference was crucial, he argued, for a civil rights struggle meant the outside world could not come to the aid of black America, which had limited itself to "the jurisdiction of Uncle Sam." A human rights struggle, however, meant oppressed peoples throughout the world might become involved; and more significantly, so could the United Nations, with its human rights charter. A campaign for human rights would enable black America to take its case before the General Assembly, Malcolm insisted. "You can take Uncle Sam before a world court. But the only level you can do it on is the level of human rights. Civil rights keeps you under his restrictions." The civil rights crusade, he told his listeners, meant black Americans were relying on "Uncle Sam to treat you right," whereas a human rights struggle was entirely different since "[h]uman rights are something you were born with." They were God-given and recognized by "all nations." And of course, black Americans could not rely on the United States to guarantee their rights because "Uncle Sam's hands are . . . dripping with the blood of the black man."

In the same address, Malcolm also alluded to America's Cold War posture and to a global community of oppressed peoples of color, two themes reformers had enunciated throughout the postwar era. Uncle Sam was the "earth's number-one hypocrite. . . . [I]magine him posing as the leader of the free world. The free world!" By taking black America's case before the United Nations, it would be possible to "let the world know how bloody his hands" were and how pervasive was American hypocrisy. At the United Nations, Malcolm asserted, "Our African brothers [could] throw their weight on our side," as could "our Latin American brothers" and "800 million Chinamen." The time had come to take Uncle Sam to court—not in Washington, but "before the world."[14] The power of Malcolm's rhetoric no doubt moved his Cleveland audience, even as the minister's bold language reflected ideas that had long been part of civil rights discourse. The notion that America's domestic practices were inconsistent with the nation's international stance was not new; nor was the claim that transnational institutions like the United Nations or the League of Nations might improve the plight of black Americans. As the

words of Du Bois, Trotter, and many others attest, such ideas had permeated internationalist discourse since World War I.

Race activists had long ventured overseas, but perhaps none was as
deeply affected by his travels as Malcolm. He acknowledged the impact
the journeys had upon his understanding of race relations and admitted
that such experiences had transformed his approach to reform. In his
Autobiography, Malcolm observed that his trips to the Middle East and
Africa in 1964 had caused "a radical alteration" in his perception of white
people; clearly, his international experiences had softened his rhetoric. Of
the Muslim world, he said, "I had seen that men with white complexions
were more genuinely brotherly than anyone else had ever been." Moved
by the "*sincere* and *true* brotherhood practiced by all colors" among Muslim peoples, Malcolm knew that some would find his observations shocking. He had been forced to "*re-arrange*" many earlier "thought-patterns"
and "*toss aside*" previous conclusions. Having eaten, slept, and prayed
with peoples of all colors, he realized "we were *truly* all the same," linked
by a shared belief in God. He hoped this might have implications at home,
for if white Americans could accept the "Oneness of God," they might
someday accept "*in reality* the Oneness of Man."[15] Admitting that in the
past he had made "sweeping indictments of *all* white people," he wrote,
"I will never be guilty of that again—as I know now that some white
people *are* truly sincere, that some truly are capable of being brotherly
toward a black man." Changed by his travel experiences in the Holy
Land, he had witnessed "brotherhood between all men, of all nationalities
and complexions."[16] Shortly after Malcolm had entered this new phase,
which hinted at a convergence between his views and those of more traditional reformers, he was murdered in a Harlem mosque in February 1965,
a victim of internecine violence. Although Malcolm had been silenced,
his influence would persist, and his potent example would animate those
pursuing a similar goal, "the decolonization of the black mind."[17]

By the mid-1960s, American actions in southeast Asia had begun to
attract the attention of the race reform community, and for the remainder
of the decade, the war in Vietnam would expose and create fissures in
the movement, just as it did throughout American society. Indeed, the
country's growing military commitment in southeast Asia would prove
more divisive than any issue the movement had confronted in decades.
For those following the trajectory of Martin Luther King, Jr.'s thinking
on Vietnam, the summer of 1965, when the minister began to express his
opposition to the conflict, was a critical time. In early July, at an SCLC
rally in Petersburg, Virginia, King said he was not prepared to "sit by and
see war escalated without saying anything about it." He was as concerned
about the spread of Communism as anyone else, he told the crowd. "We
won't defeat communism by guns or bombs or gases. We will do it by

making democracy work." The war must be stopped, King insisted. We must "even negotiate with the Viet Cong," he said, noting that Americans should support an immediate end to the war. King said his SCLC colleagues had considered holding "peace rallies just like we have freedom rallies."[18] At the SCLC's annual convention the following month, King again advocated a negotiated settlement to the war and a halt to the bombing, and expressed his willingness to contact North Vietnamese leader Ho Chi Minh, along with Russian and Chinese leaders, in order to end the war. Explaining the background of his decision, King said he did not intend to place blame on any party, stating that neither "the American people nor the people of North Vietnam is the enemy. The true enemy is war itself."[19]

In the months ahead, King continued to discuss the war in interviews, sermons, and speeches. At a Los Angeles forum in February 1967, he shared the platform with four antiwar senators—Ernest Gruening, Mark Hatfield, Eugene McCarthy, and George McGovern—and spoke out powerfully against American policies in southeast Asia. Physical injuries were not the only casualties of the war, King observed. America's "declining moral status in the world," self-determination in the developing countries, and the initiatives of President Lyndon Johnson's Great Society program were also imperiled. American support for South Vietnam's military regime represented a "new form of colonialism" and demonstrated "our lack of sympathy" for oppressed peoples. America, long the embodiment of the revolutionary spirit, was now "cast in the mold of being an arch anti-revolutionary" and was attempting to turn back the clock of history so as to "perpetuate white colonialism." Guilty of committing atrocities, the American military was no different from the Viet Cong, King contended, and the policies of the United States revealed the paranoid anti-Communism of Lyndon Johnson and "the deadly western arrogance" that had long poisoned the atmosphere of world politics.[20] The decades-old view, embraced by many in the reform community, that America was a potential force for good in the world, had begun to weaken. American actions on the international stage were now worthy of condemnation.

While King's remarks in Los Angeles received widespread coverage, his address some six weeks later on April 4, 1967, in New York's Riverside Church was still more significant. Before three thousand people, King linked America's prosecution of the war to the struggle for racial justice, declaring that those who doubted the connection did not understand King's commitment, his calling, or the world in which they lived. For several reasons, it was essential for those dedicated to the movement to speak out against American actions in southeast Asia, he said. First, the war drained scarce resources away from the nation's poverty programs, drawing men, skills, and money like "some demonic destructive suction tube." The war also took young black men away from home to die in disproportionate numbers, and King noted—as had countless race reformers since 1917—that the black soldier was fighting far from home for liberties he did not have in his own land. He claimed, too, that his credibility as a proponent of nonviolence was unsustainable as long as he remained silent on the war. After presenting an overview of western imperial duplicity and brutality in southeast Asia over the previous generation, King attempted to see the war and the West through Vietnamese eyes, a perspective that led him to conclude that the hostility and suspicion that the Vietnamese had for America was not surprising. The "madness" must cease, he said, claiming to speak not just for the "suffering poor of Vietnam," whose land and culture were being destroyed, but for the "poor of America," who were paying "the double price of smashed hopes at home and death" overseas. Tellingly, King identified himself as a "citizen of the world."

After setting out several actions he believed the United States government ought to take (an end to the bombing, a unilateral cease-fire, acceptance of a role for the Communist opposition in a future Vietnamese government, establishing a timetable for the removal of foreign troops from Vietnam), King offered a blistering critique of American actions in world politics and of American society. The war represented a "symptom of a far deeper malady within the American spirit," he said, quoting an American official who had observed that the nation was "on the wrong side of a world revolution." Driven by the need to maintain social stability for its overseas investments, the country practiced "counter-revolutionary" policies throughout the world, and by "refusing to give up the privileges and the pleasures" derived from the immense profits from our foreign investments, King argued, the United States had assumed an international role that made peaceful revolution impossible. If we are to get on the "right side of the world revolution," we must readjust our values and shift from a "thing-oriented" to a "person-oriented" society. Otherwise, it would be impossible to vanquish "racism, materialism, and militarism" from American life.

In such words, one could hear echoes of Du Bois on World War I, or of *The Messenger* writings that Randolph and Owen had authored fifty years before. Although a young activist might not have perceived such antecedents in King's critique of 1960s America, the minister's contention that the West was investing its energies in the developing world in order to extract material gain had deep roots in the discourse of American race reform and was consistent with the ideas some reformers had long embraced concerning the role of the West in world politics. But as King touched on olden themes in the Riverside address—he spoke of peoples struggling for justice against the forces of oppression and exploitation—

he also looked ahead. America had a choice between "nonviolent coexistence or violent co-annihilation." And finally, he called for the country to find "new ways to speak for peace in Vietnam and justice throughout the developing world." King asked his listeners to join him in the bitter and beautiful struggle for a new world, a struggle in which America could play an active part.[21]

The reaction to King's Riverside speech was generally hostile both inside and outside the movement. The repudiation of King by members of the Johnson administration was not surprising. Less predictable was the cool response of figures like Randolph, Wilkins, the Urban League's Whitney Young, and of leading black newspapers and magazines. The *Pittsburgh Courier* argued that King, though sincere, was "tragically misleading" black Americans on issues "too complex for simple debate."[22] The NAACP board adopted a resolution that labeled King's proposals a "serious tactical mistake" and claimed his efforts to join the peace movement and the civil rights movement would serve neither cause. The resolution's language would surely have stunned Walter White or Du Bois: "Civil rights battles will have to be fought and won on their own merits, irrespective of the state of war or peace in the world. We are not a peace organization or a foreign policy association. We are a civil rights organization." Ralph Bunche, a member of the association's board and someone who had long wedded foreign to domestic concerns, also repudiated King, stating that the minister ought to "positively and publicly give up one role or the other. The two efforts have too little in common." Responding to Bunche, King called on the organization to take a stand on the "rightness or wrongness" of the war and asserted that "no one can pretend that the existence of the war is not profoundly affecting the destiny of civil rights progress."[23] At another time, Bunche might have supported such sentiments, but a critique of American foreign policy, which had rarely been part of the reformers' internationalism, was inconsistent with the aims of the mainstream reform community.

Despite growing discontent concerning Vietnam among some activists in the years before King's 1967 address, NAACP leaders were reluctant to engage the issue, believing it would imperil their program, which the Johnson administration had energetically supported. In July 1965, for example, in the wake of King's Petersburg, Virginia, speech, Roy Wilkins had declared, "We have enough Vietnams in Alabama." According to the NAACP director, when "you mix the question of Vietnam into the questions of Mississippi and Alabama and getting registration and the vote and all the things . . . Negroes want . . . you sort of confuse the issue." Wilkins later observed that the black American's "first thought ought to be to strengthen his position as an American. If he's a third-rate citizen his opinions on South Africa or Vietnam will have no effect." The possi-

With the United Nations in the background, the Reverend Martin Luther King, Jr., speaks at a peace rally in 1967. King's stance on the Vietnam War was repudiated by many traditional civil rights leaders, who believed opposition to the Johnson administration's policies in southeast Asia would harm the domestic cause.

bility of alienating Lyndon Johnson, who had assumed significant political risks in backing civil rights legislation, was simply unacceptable to NAACP officials; consequently, they remained silent on American policies in southeast Asia.[24]

But others were speaking out about Vietnam. At a July 1965 conference that explored merging the peace and civil rights movements, CORE director James Farmer noted that despite his opposition to the war, he did not believe his organization should become part of the peace movement, since it would divert too much energy from CORE's principal focus.[25] A few days later, at CORE's annual convention, even as Farmer spoke out strongly against the war, he asserted that the organization should remain separate from the peace movement. Although it was "impossible for the Government to maintain a decisive war against poverty and bigotry in the U.S. while it is pouring billions down the drain in war against people in Viet Nam," Farmer maintained that CORE's task was to "mobilize as many people as possible" to back the civil rights struggle. If CORE established organizational ties to the peace movement, he worried, it risked losing support from elsewhere; such decisions, he said, should be made as individuals. As reform leaders assessed America's role in the world, pragmatism often won the day because they were convinced little could be gained by speaking out against the war.[26]

At its 1966 convention the following summer, a more radicalized CORE, now directed by Floyd McKissick (Farmer had resigned earlier in the year), voted to oppose American involvement in southeast Asia and to support those who had decided not to serve in the armed forces. As August Meier and Elliott Rudwick have written, CORE had become "deeply affected by the ebb and flow of sentiment among militant blacks," and the 1966 convention met amidst the excitement of the burgeoning "Black Power" movement. A CORE statement on the war discussed the conflict's racial dimensions, noting inequities in the draft and in combat casualty ratios, as well as its negative impact on government spending to eradicate poverty. The statement also rejected the language race reformers had long deployed in evaluating American foreign policy, declaring that the war contradicted "the philosophical base upon which this country was founded. It denies to the inhabitants of this South Asian country the right of self determination." Finally, the document considered America's place in the world and deplored "the loss of prestige the United States ha[d] suffered by its unilateral military intervention in Southeast Asia."[27] From CORE's perspective, the United States was no longer an exemplar on the world stage; instead, it had become the object of an emerging critique that would lead many in the reform community to condemn American policies in Asia.

By mid-decade, some of the movement's leaders had begun to establish important parallels between the freedom struggle in the United States and the conflict in southeast Asia. Speaking to an audience of ten thousand at a Berkeley, California, rally in May 1965, SNCC's Bob Moses identified a link between events in Vietnam and life at home. Calling himself a member of the "Third World," Moses spoke about his reaction to a photograph of what the press described as an American "Marine capturing a Communist rebel soldier." According to Moses, what he saw "was a little colored boy standing against a wire fence with a big huge white Marine with a gun in his back." But most Americans, he said, saw a "Communist rebel." And this led Moses to conclude that there were two realities in America. It was necessary to understand that part of the Third World existed within the United States, he told the crowd, and when people grasped this, they would better comprehend the struggle in the American South. To do anything about the war, Moses declared, one had to understand the South. He compared American actions in Vietnam to life in southern towns where white murderers of blacks went free, which, he claimed, said "something about a whole society." You can "learn when it is that a society gets together and plans and executes and allows its members to murder and then go free. And if you learn something about that, then maybe you'll learn something about this country and how it plans and executes murders elsewhere in the world." To do something

about the nation's involvement in Vietnam, Moses asserted, it was necessary to create a more just society in America.[28] Here was something new
in the language of race reform: American oppression abroad was comparable to American oppression at home. For some, it was no longer necessary to look to fascist or totalitarian systems to understand American race
relations; one could now point to American actions overseas.

In January 1966, the murder of Sammy Younge, a black Tuskegee Institute student who had worked for the Student Nonviolent Coordinating
Committee registering voters in Alabama, catalyzed SNCC's decision to
speak out against the war. In Clayborne Carson's words, the death of
Younge, who was attempting to use a "white" restroom at a Tuskegee
gas station, symbolized for SNCC's staff "the racism and hypocrisy that
infected the nation."[29] On January 6, SNCC issued a statement that condemned American involvement in Vietnam and questioned the commitment of the United States government to freedom abroad and at home.
The statement called for Americans to refuse to serve in the military and
declared that service in civil rights or similar organizations was a "valid
alternative to the draft." According to the document, Younge's murder
was "no different from the murder of people in Vietnam, for both Younge
and the Vietnamese sought and are seeking to secure the rights guaranteed
them by law. In each case, the U.S. government bears a great part of the
responsibility for these deaths. Samuel Younge was murdered because
U.S. law is not being enforced. Vietnamese are being murdered because
the United States is . . . [violating] international law." There was an inextricable link between domestic events and developments in southeast
Asia, SNCC believed. As James Forman asserted in 1968, "a clear relationship [existed] between racism and the Vietnam war," though at the
time many people (white and black) did not see the connection.[30]

Among NAACP leaders and other black officials, there was considerable opposition to SNCC's position on Vietnam, which points to the divisive effect the war was having on the movement.[31] More than any single
factor, the war opened fissures in the reform campaign—fissures that
would be impossible to close. In the judgment of people like Wilkins,
Bunche, and Randolph, opposing the war would prove counterproduc-
tive. Or as Wilkins observed in 1965, joining the civil rights and peace
movements risked dissipating the energies and resources of the former.
Still more crucial for understanding why NAACP leaders, in particular,
were reluctant to oppose the war was their concern that this would antag-
onize Washington policymakers (especially in the Johnson administration), who had energetically supported civil rights. As Ralph Bunche had
written after King's Riverside speech, that kind of approach was "bound
to alienate many friends and supporters of the . . . movement and greatly
weaken it." Clearly, some reformers were not willing to accept that risk.[32]

If it is important to understand why segments of the movement refrained from opposing the war, it is no less important to consider why those who rejected American policies in southeast Asia did so—for this marked a significant departure from the way race activists had perceived overseas matters in decades past. For those willing to speak out against the war, Vietnam represented the bankruptcy of American values and made manifest the immoral international conduct one would expect from a nation engaged in immoral practices at home. It is apparent that some in the movement looked at American policies overseas in order to understand and make a public point about American policies in the United States. For such leaders, American lawlessness in Vietnam was consonant with American lawlessness on the home front. As the 1960s unfolded, it would become unnecessary to equate Jim Crow with European fascism or Soviet totalitarianism; instead, some in the reform community would compare America's misdeeds overseas with its domestic malefactions. For many younger reformers, pointing to American actions abroad provided a potentially effective way to clarify the character of American domestic life. And this rhetorical strategy would necessarily drain color-conscious internationalism of much of its saliency. The days of fighting "to make the world safe for democracy" were no more, as were the years of the Double-V campaign. In the Vietnam era, a segment of the reform community could no longer claim, as reformers had for decades, that because the United States was spending blood and treasure to uphold the democratic cause overseas, it was essential to construct a genuine democracy at home.

Despite this crucial change, color-conscious internationalism did not disappear completely from the discourse of reform. On April 3, 1968, Martin Luther King, Jr., spoke in Mason Temple in Memphis. Noting that he was happy to be alive at this moment in history, and recognizing that it was a time of trouble and confusion, he claimed that only when it was dark enough could one see the stars. Something was happening in the world. In South Africa, Kenya, and Ghana, and in Georgia, Mississippi, and Tennessee, the cry was always the same: "We want to be free." And in language that harkened back to that of past reformers, he spoke of a human rights revolution, in which the "colored peoples of the world" were struggling to free themselves from years of poverty and neglect. His words echoing an earlier time, King told his listeners about the promise of America, about those things that distinguished it from China, Russia, or "any totalitarian country." The next day he planned to go to court to challenge an injunction banning a mass protest, observing that "somewhere I read of the freedom of assembly. Somewhere I read of the freedom of speech. Somewhere I read of the freedom of the press. Somewhere I read that the greatness of America is the right to protest for right." Though difficult days would follow, the young preacher seemed unconcerned. "Like anybody, I would like to live a long life. Longevity has its place. But I'm not concerned about that now. I just want to do God's will. And He's allowed me to go up to the mountaintop. And I've looked over. And I've seen the promised land. I may not get there with you. But I want you to know tonight, that we, as a people will get to the promised land."[33]

The next day, as he stood on the balcony outside his room at the Lorraine Motel, Martin Luther King, Jr., was cut down by an assassin's bullet. In the aftermath of his death, cities exploded in violence, a presidential candidate was murdered, and the Vietnam War would continue to tear at the social and political fabric of the nation. The race reformers could no longer contend that America had a constructive role to play on the world stage, and for many in the reform community, the immorality of the United States overseas had become an inevitable consequence of the immorality of the United States at home. By the end of the decade, the conviction that America was capable of doing constructive work in the world had practically vanished, and none could say when (or if) it would reappear.

Postlude

WORLD AFFAIRS AND THE DOMESTIC CRUSADE

In surveying the twentieth-century world, American race reformers beheld a series of titanic political, ideological, and racial struggles, which they believed possessed special significance in their quest to build a genuine democracy in the United States. As they worked to advance their cause early in the century, race leaders heard Woodrow Wilson speak of a battle pitting democracy against autocracy, which compelled the nation to take up arms to promote freedom and self-determination. Driven by these goals, the country went to war and helped to defeat Germany. The victory, it was hoped, would make democratic governance overseas more likely and war less probable. In the wake of the Great War, the reformers looked expectantly to the birth of a new institution, the League of Nations, which they hoped could maintain the peace and, at the same time, improve the lives of peoples of color in the colonial world and at home. In the postwar decade, the reformers continued to ponder international developments, training a watchful eye, for example, on the Soviet experiment, in the belief that Russia could serve as a model for building a more just society in America. In the 1930s, the menace of fascism proved extraordinarily meaningful for race reform leaders, who were persuaded that the oppression of Jews, Ethiopians, and Spaniards made clear the stark dangers that unchecked violence and aggression posed to all peoples—not least to black Americans. And a few years later, the reformers again heard the call to arms, as dictators in Europe and Asia, partly motivated by racialist ideas, shook the foundation stones upon which democratic civilization rested. This war, too, ended in victory for the United States and its allies, and according to American leaders, democracy had once more been saved, though millions had died to preserve it.

With hardly a chance to catch their breath after the triumph of 1945, the reformers considered the start of still another battle, in which two ideological foes would grapple with one another for more than a generation. Ultimately, the Cold War drew much of the world into a colossal and often brutally destructive competition spearheaded by the Soviet Union and the United States—a struggle that American leaders rather simplistically characterized as a conflict between those who believed in democratic rule and those who would quash it. And throughout the twentieth century, as two world wars and the Cold War shaped and scarred the historical landscape, the reformers scrutinized another transformative crusade, in which peoples of color in the hundreds of millions worked to free themselves from their imperial masters. These anticolonial campaigns possessed profound meaning for America's race leaders, who monitored the work of the oppressed in India, Asia, and Africa, and conveyed countless heroic stories to their followers in an effort to inspire those who were seeking racial justice in the United States.

This was the world the race reformers knew, and it was against the backdrop of such developments that they helped to direct the civil rights campaign. Indeed, it would be more accurate to understand their domestic quest as woven into the very history of the twentieth-century world, starting with the outbreak of the Great War, gaining strength during World War II, and gathering momentum and legitimacy as the anticolonial struggles and the Cold War came to dominate global politics after 1945. If the movement for racial justice was embedded in the epochal struggles of the twentieth century, it should be emphasized that this happened not by chance but by design. As I have contended, the reformers were utterly determined to make overseas affairs central to their cause, and for fifty years, with tenacity and skill, they communicated their distinctive understanding of international developments to their supporters, to policymakers, to the American people, and to the world. In conveying their message to these varied audiences, the reformers enmeshed their domestic campaign in the political and ideological struggles of the twentieth century, deploying affairs abroad in a purposive effort to advance their aspirations in the United States. By constructing a movement that gave primacy to the outside world, race leaders aimed to create a more just society in a country that for generations had denied justice to all Americans, even as it claimed to possess an exceptional devotion to freedom and democratic rule.

As the race activists worked for change, America's orientation toward the world underwent a striking transformation. Increasingly, the United States became energetically involved in international matters, a shift that emerged during World War II and gained undeniable momentum after 1945. In this period, American policymakers and the American people embraced the notion that events beyond the country's shores were critically important to America's well-being, and public officials asserted repeatedly that the nation's security could no longer be divorced from developments abroad. As I have discussed, this metamorphosis would have a notable impact on the race reform struggle after 1945, and the activists' long-standing effort to utilize global affairs to advance the reform agenda would interact powerfully with America's expanding influence on the world stage, injecting the domestic movement with heightened energy and legitimacy.

I have suggested that throughout the twentieth century, race leaders recognized an organic connection between their domestic aspirations and global developments, a perception that led them to forge a reform message based on internationalist ideals. In constructing that message, they fashioned a distinctive brand of internationalism—one they thought was particularly well-suited to promoting their agenda. That idiosyncratic worldview, color-conscious internationalism, was central to the discourse of twentieth-century race reform, and, as I have argued, for many decades, it helped shape the way the movement's leaders worked to attain their goals. In seeking to end the institutionalized oppression of black Americans and in framing their message, the race reformers were convinced that they could apply their unique internationalist outlook to a variety of epochal overseas matters: the democratization impulse of the Wilson era; the emergence of the Soviet Union; the necessity for crushing the rule of the dictators in the 1930s and 1940s; America's effort to contain the alleged Communist threat after 1945; and the liberation efforts waged by colonial peoples. The language of twentieth-century race reform thus reflected the reformers' deeply held belief that international developments could prove supremely helpful in advancing their agenda. This is significant, as I have noted, for in considering the history of reform movements, one cannot overstate the importance of language and rhetoric and message. Or as one student of race relations has observed, "words can have world-making and life-altering consequences."[1]

One is left, then, to ponder the implications of color-conscious internationalism for the history of the African-American freedom struggle. While I have argued that international affairs and American actions on the world stage gave shape, in a fundamental sense, to the reformers' message, it is reasonable to wonder to what extent the race leaders' worldview helped their cause. Color-conscious internationalism was, after all, more than an idiosyncratic view of the outside world; it was, at the same time, a set of interconnected ideas that race reform leaders believed would help them to advance their domestic agenda.

With respect to the conviction that the reformers were part of an "imagined community" of peoples of color working for justice throughout the world, the race leaders were convinced their supporters would be energized by the idea that they were participants in a global enterprise. In listening to the words of W.E.B. Du Bois, Walter White, Martin Luther King, Jr., or many others, countless thousands of men and women who were working for freedom and democracy in the United States heard repeatedly about the millions who were laboring in their own societies on behalf of similar objectives. For those toiling to reform a society deeply resistant and actively hostile to change, the notion that they were part of a noble international crusade surely helped to sustain and inspire their efforts during many arduous years. And NAACP resolutions that spoke of a fraternity between colonial peoples and black Americans suggest that such appeals indeed resonated with thousands of the movement's supporters, who embraced the idea embodied in a 1948 NAACP declaration that asserted, "In this common struggle we are not alone," for our allies include "the vast and unnumbered colored peoples of the world."[2]

The second element of color-conscious internationalism, the belief that transnational institutions might help reconfigure domestic race relations, seems, ultimately, to have achieved less than race leaders had hoped. Whether one reflects on William Trotter's efforts in Paris in 1919 and the conviction of leading reformers that the League of Nations could ameliorate the plight of black Americans, or ponders the faith placed in the United Nations after 1945, it is apparent that American policymakers would not permit such institutions to alter the character of domestic race relations. While the NAACP's 1947 petition did place the problem of American racial oppression on the list of malefactions that would need to be addressed in the postwar era, it is difficult to conclude that the reformers' United Nations–related activities helped to catalyze domestic change. The forces favoring Jim Crow were simply unwilling to heed the call of world public opinion to overturn life in the American South, and the United States government was not prepared to allow an organization largely composed of foreign peoples to reach into the American polity to end institutionalized racial oppression.

The third strand of color-conscious internationalism—that the United States had a leading role to play in the world, and that this role required America to harmonize its democratic preachments and overseas actions with its domestic practices—proved to be a constructive rhetorical device. This was especially so after 1945, as America's engagement in the world gathered momentum. Although some have argued that postwar American globalism and, more specifically, the domestic repression of the Cold War years weakened the movement, it is difficult to ignore the concrete achievements in this period. The desegregation of the military, historic victories in the Supreme Court, and the landmark legislation of the 1960s all came to pass during the height of the East-West conflict. To be sure, the Cold War exacted a heavy toll on American political culture, and, more pertinently, on figures in the civil rights movement. Nevertheless, the contention that, on the whole, America's conflict with the Soviet Union had a baneful impact on the civil rights struggle is difficult to sustain. What race reform leaders had been seeking for some five decades—the abolition of legally sanctioned segregation in the military, education, employment, public accommodations, and voting—came to pass during the Cold War.[3]

By enumerating such achievements, I am not suggesting that the United States had swept either racism or racial persecution from the American landscape, for it had done neither. Nor am I suggesting that the Cold War was solely responsible for progress on civil rights after 1945. Rather, a number of factors played a part, of which the Cold War was one. But in the post-1945 period, the pillars upon which an unjust and oppressive legal system rested were gradually removed, and the reformers' forceful internationalist rhetoric contributed to this transformative process. Some have argued that United States policymakers acted in what they perceived to be America's national interest vis-à-vis the Soviet Union (or in their own political self-interest), and that they were not, therefore, motivated by what was just. This may be so, for it is difficult to assess motivation with certainty. Moreover, at times (or even often) people's actions flow from a variety of impulses. Nevertheless, if calculations of national or political self-interest rather than more idealistic motives drove the actions of policymakers, one cannot ignore the fact that executive orders were signed, court cases were won, and legislation was passed. And in the eyes of civil rights leaders, those executive orders, courtroom victories, and laws marked the culmination of decades of toil and represented triumphs worthy of celebration. It was Roy Wilkins who described the day the *Brown* decision came down as "one of life's sweetest," and Martin Luther King, Jr., who called the 1964 Civil Rights Act a "monumental" piece of legislation and a "historic affirmation" of the truth that "'all men are created equal.'"[4]

While the debate on the implications of the Cold War will doubtless continue, it is clear that the epic struggle for racial justice in modern America was enmeshed in the international history of the twentieth century. The world wars, decolonization, the Cold War, Communism, fascism, the League of Nations, and the United Nations all played a critical part in the reformers' crusade to change American society. Whether one considers Spingarn, Terrell, Johnson, Bethune, Randolph, White, Wilkins, King, or, most obviously, Du Bois, it is apparent that they, along with many others, understood their quest in a global context. In working to transform America, the reformers looked beyond it, in the unshakable belief that developments in the outside world could help them to create a more just society.

NOTES

Introduction

1. *The Crisis* (May 1919): 7. David Levering Lewis writes that the trip "would achieve historic and enduring symbolism." Lewis, *W.E.B. Du Bois: Biography of a Race, 1868–1919* (New York, 1993), 564.

2. Peabody quoted in Clarence G. Contee, "Du Bois, the NAACP, and the Pan-African Congress of 1919," *Journal of Negro History* 57 (January 1972): 17. See also *The Crisis* (February 1919): 163.

3. Noting the similarity between the two, Lewis calls them "kindred intellects." *Du Bois: Biography of a Race*, 564. Each believed he could persuade the masses to accept his vision for reordering the world: Wilson would reform the practice of international relations, and Du Bois, the conduct of race relations worldwide. On Du Bois's aims in Paris, see *The Crisis* (January 1919): 111–12. On the proposed history of black Americans in the war, see Du Bois's report to the NAACP's board of directors. Minutes of the Board of Directors, November 11, 1918, NAACP Papers, Library of Congress, Washington, D.C., microfilm edition, pt. 1, reel 1.

4. The president's secretary, Joseph Tumulty, responded to Du Bois, promising the letter would be brought to his chief's attention, though he noted Wilson was currently too busy to meet with the reformer. Du Bois to Wilson, November 27, 1918 and Joseph Tumulty to Du Bois, November 29, 1918, Du Bois Papers, W.E.B. Du Bois Library, University of Massachusetts–Amherst, microfilm edition, reel 7. See also Du Bois to Secretary of War Newton Baker, November 27, 1918, in which Du Bois claimed it would be "a calamity" for 200 million black people to be "without voice or representation at this great transformation of the world." Ibid.

5. On the subject of narrative in historical writing, see Robert Berkhofer, Jr., *Beyond the Great Story: History as Text and Discourse* (Cambridge, MA, 1995), esp. ch. 2; and Alun Munslow, *Deconstructing History* (London, 1997), passim.

6. August Meier writes that in assessing the civil rights campaign, one can hardly overestimate the NAACP's importance. Meier, "Epilogue: Toward a Synthesis of Civil Rights History," in *New Directions in Civil Rights History*, Armstead L. Robinson and Patricia Sullivan, eds. (Charlottesville, VA, 1991), 212. See also August Meier and John H. Bracey, "The NAACP as a Reform Movement, 1909–1965: 'To Reach the Conscience of America,'" *Journal of Southern History* 59 (February 1993): 3–30.

7. Among the best grass-roots studies to emerge in recent years are John Dittmer, *Local People: The Struggle for Civil Rights in Mississippi* (Urbana, IL, 1994); and Charles M. Payne, *I've Got the Light of Freedom: The Organizing Tradition and the Mississippi Freedom Struggle* (Berkeley, CA, 1995). Note, too, J. Todd Moye, *Let the People Decide: Black Freedom and White Resistance Movements in Sunflower County, Mississippi, 1945–1986* (Chapel Hill, NC, 2004). An

illuminating work that employs a hybrid approach is Glenn T. Eskew, *But for Birmingham: The Local and National Movements in the Civil Rights Struggle* (Chapel Hill, NC, 1997). Sociological analyses of the movement's origins include Aldon D. Morris, *The Origins of the Civil Rights Movement: Black Communities Organizing for Change* (New York, 1984), which considers the period from 1953 to 1963; and Doug McAdam, *Political Process and the Development of Black Insurgency, 1930–1970* (Chicago, 1982).

8. Robert A. Divine, *Second Chance: The Triumph of Internationalism in America during World War II* (New York, 1967), 22–23. Divine also notes that the internationalists had little sympathy for those in the colonial world. It must be said that those who headed the race reform movement shared some important characteristics with the traditional internationalists. Like the latter group, race reform leaders (black and white) were well educated, often well traveled, and residents of urban areas. There was a convergence between the social background of white race reform figures and that of traditional internationalist leaders. This is manifested, for example, in the backgrounds of people like Mary White Ovington, Moorfield Storey, Oswald Garrison Villard, and even Joel and Arthur Spingarn. Concerning traditional black reform leaders, one sees what might be described as cosmopolitan types, Du Bois being an avatar among them. Other such black reform figures included William Monroe Trotter, James Weldon Johnson, Kelly Miller, William Pickens, A. Philip Randolph, Mary McLeod Bethune, Walter White, Roy Wilkins, and Martin Luther King, Jr., all well-educated members of a distinctive segment of African-American society. On the white race reformers' background in the movement's early days, see James McPherson, *The Abolitionist Legacy: From Reconstruction to the NAACP* (Princeton, NJ, 1975), esp. ch. 20 and app. A. On the traditional internationalists' background, see Divine, *Second Chance*, esp. ch. 1; and Sondra Herman, *Eleven against War: Studies in Internationalist Thought, 1898–1921* (Stanford, CA, 1969), ch. 1. The black reform leaders' backgrounds are sketched out in the pages that follow.

On the question of which Americans were drawn to international matters, see Ernest May, *American Imperialism: A Speculative Essay* (New York, 1968), which is suggestive. While May does not focus on reform figures, he identifies what he calls the "foreign policy public," a small segment of the population that maintained a keen interest in overseas developments in the late nineteenth century. The race reform leaders considered in this project (both black and white) were, in a sense, part of the public that was drawn to world affairs, albeit during the twentieth century.

9. On internationalism, see the following: Herman, *Eleven against War*; Frank Ninkovich, *The Wilsonian Century: U.S. Foreign Policy since 1900* (Chicago, 1999); Thomas J. Knock, *To End All Wars: Woodrow Wilson and the Quest for a New World Order* (New York, 1992); Akira Iriye, *Cultural Internationalism and World Order* (Baltimore, 1997); Warren F. Kuehl, *Seeking World Order: The United States and International Organization to 1920* (Nashville, IN, 1969); Charles DeBenedetti, *Origins of the Modern American Peace Movement, 1915–1929* (Millwood, NY, 1978); DeBenedetti, *The Peace Reform in American History* (Bloomington, IN, 1980); and Warren F. Kuehl, ed., *Biographical Dictionary of Internationalists* (Westport, CT 1983). On the link between internation-

alism and America's world leadership role, in particular, see Warren F. Kuehl and Lynne K. Dunn, *Keeping the Covenant: American Internationalists and the League of Nations, 1920–1939* (Kent, OH, 1997); xvi–xvii.

10. For an examination of the way African Americans sought to mobilize international public opinion against American slavery, see R.J.M. Blackett, *Building an Antislavery Wall: Black Americans in the Atlantic Abolitionist Movement, 1830–1860* (Baton Rouge, LA, 1983).

11. Herman, *Eleven against War*, ix; Kuehl, *Biographical Dictionary*, ix.

12. The term is from Benedict Anderson, *Imagined Communities: Reflections on the Origins and Spread of Nationalism* (New York, 1991; orig., 1983). Anderson writes that the national community is "imagined" because its members will never know or meet their fellow members, yet the "image of their communion" lives in the minds of each (6). Much the same can be said of the transnational community of reformers.

13. Henry Moon's 1959 address at the NAACP's annual conference considers this question explicitly, noting that the association had to appeal to different audiences: the black minority, which the organization had to inform and inspire, and the white majority, which had to be convinced the cause was just. Moon's address, July 16, 1959, NAACP Papers, pt. 1 (supp.), reel 11.

14. The Du Bois quotation is from his October 28, 1914, letter to Joel Spingarn. Du Bois Papers, reel 4.

15. On the utility of analogies for learning and persuasion, see Elliot Zashin and Phillip Chapman, "The Uses of Metaphor and Analogy: Toward a Renewal of Political Language," *Journal of Politics* 36 (1974): 290–326. On analogical reasoning, see Stella Vosniadou and Andrew Ortony, eds., *Similarity and Analogical Reasoning* (New York, 1989), esp. the introduction and ch. 15. See also Mark T. Keane, *Analogical Problem Solving* (New York, 1988), ch. 6. To understand how policymakers use historical analogies (often badly), see Ernest R. May, *"Lessons" of the Past: The Use and Misuse of History in American Foreign Policy* (New York, 1973); and Yuen Foong Khong, *Analogies at War: Korea, Munich, Dien Bien Phu, and the Vietnam Decisions of 1965* (Princeton, NJ, 1992).

16. On the racial dimension of the Pacific war, see John Dower, *War without Mercy: Race and Power in the Pacific War* (New York, 1986).

17. The war helped delegitimize institutionalized racism in the United States as Hitlerism made it increasingly difficult to defend racialist ideas. See Walter A. Jackson, *Gunnar Myrdal and America's Conscience: Social Engineering and Racial Liberalism, 1938–1987* (Chapel Hill, NC, 1990), esp. ch. 6.

18. On the significance of freedom in American history, see Eric Foner, *The Story of American Freedom* (New York, 1998). Note Daniel T. Rodgers on the importance of the word "freedom" in the United States during World War II and the way freedom-centered rhetoric informed civil rights activism during the Cold War. Rodgers, *Contested Truths: Keywords in American Politics since Independence* (Cambridge, MA, 1998, orig., 1987), 213–19.

19. Akira Iriye, "Culture," *Journal of American History* 77 (June 1990): 99–107. See also Iriye, "Culture and Power: International Relations as Intercultural Relations," *Diplomatic History* 3 (Spring 1979): 115–28; Frank Ninkovich, "Interests and Discourse in Diplomatic History, *Diplomatic History* 13 (Spring

1989): 135–61; and Robert David Johnson, ed., *On Cultural Ground: Essays in International History* (Chicago, 1994), passim.

20. Among the recent works that examine the link between African Americans and foreign affairs, see the following: Brenda Gayle Plummer's pioneering study, which presents a sweeping treatment of the subject, *Rising Wind: Black Americans and U.S. Foreign Affairs, 1935–1960* (Chapel Hill, NC, 1996); Plummer, ed., *Window on Freedom: Race, Civil Rights, and Foreign Affairs, 1945–1988* (Chapel Hill, NC, 2003); Carol Anderson, *Eyes off the Prize: The United Nations and the African American Struggle for Human Rights, 1944–1955* (New York, 2003); Thomas Borstelmann, *The Cold War and the Color Line: American Race Relations in the Global Arena* (Cambridge, MA, 2001); Borstelmann, *Apartheid's Reluctant Uncle: The United States and Southern Africa in the Early Cold War* (New York, 1993); Mary L. Dudziak, *Cold War Civil Rights: Race and the Image of American Democracy* (Princeton, NJ, 2000); Penny M. Von Eschen, *Race against Empire: Black Americans and Anticolonialism, 1937–1957* (Ithaca, NY, 1997); Marc Gallicchio, *The African American Encounter with Japan and China: Black Internationalism, 1895–1945* (Chapel Hill, NC, 2000); Michael L. Krenn, *Black Diplomacy: African Americans and the State Department, 1945–1969* (Armonk, NY, 1999); and James H. Meriwether, *Proudly We Can Be Africans: Black Americans and Africa, 1935–1961* (Chapel Hill, NC, 2002). See also the symposium in the Fall 1996 issue of *Diplomatic History*, entitled "African Americans and U.S. Foreign Relations." Note the work of political scientist Azza Salama Layton, *International Politics and Civil Rights Policies in the United States, 1941–1960* (New York, 2000). A notable earlier work is Thomas J. Noer's *Cold War and Black Liberation: The United States and Black Rule in Africa, 1948–1968* (Columbia, MO, 1985). More broadly, Paul Gordon Lauren brilliantly links world affairs to racial questions in *Power and Prejudice: The Politics and Diplomacy of Racial Discrimination* (Boulder, CO, 1988).

Beyond its broader temporal scope, this book differs from the above works in significant respects. Briefly, in the works of Borstelmann, Dudziak, Krenn, and Layton, the state (i.e., the U.S. government) occupies a central place in the analysis as each examines the interconnection between race and foreign affairs. (Note the following paragraph of this introduction.) Gallicchio's work considers African-American attitudes toward Asia and Japan, while Meriwether's focuses on African-American perceptions of Africa. Carol Anderson's book on the United Nations, the NAACP, and the African-American freedom struggle from 1944 to 1955 considers the tension between human and civil rights, and the implications of that dichotomy for black advancement in the postwar period. Penny Von Eschen's study focuses on the changing anticolonial discourse articulated by a variety of black figures and organizations from 1937 to 1957. As I have noted, my book examines how mainstream race reformers understood twentieth-century international affairs and America's changing role in the world, and employed their distinctive worldview in a purposive effort to advance their domestic program.

21. On the possibility of moving beyond a state-centered focus in the study of twentieth-century international history, see Iriye, *Cultural Internationalism*; and Iriye, *Global Community: The Role of International Organizations in the Making of the Contemporary World* (Berkeley, CA, 2002).

22. Iriye, *Cultural Internationalism*, 178–81.

23. As Eric Foner has observed, "global embeddedness" has shaped the country's past. See his presidential address to the American Historical Association, "American Freedom in a Global Age," *American Historical Review* 106 (February 2001): 1–16. See also Thomas Bender, ed., *Rethinking American History in a Global Age* (Berkeley, CA, 2002). Among the works that consider the domestic-international intersection in a variety of ways, see Michael Sherry, *In the Shadow of War: The United States since the 1930s* (New Haven, CT, 1995); Elaine Tyler May, *Homeward Bound: American Families in the Cold War Era* (New York, 1988); Daniel T. Rodgers, *Atlantic Crossings: Social Politics in a Progressive Age* (Cambridge, MA, 1998); James Kloppenberg, *Uncertain Victory: Social Democracy and Progressivism in European and American Thought, 1870–1920* (New York, 1986); Stephen Whitfield, *The Culture of the Cold War* (Baltimore, 1991); and Margot A. Henriksen, *Dr. Strangelove's America: Society and Culture in the Atomic Age* (Berkeley, CA, 1997).

24. The remarks, made by Henry Lee Moon, NAACP director of public relations, at the annual convention in 1959, illustrate the crucial importance NAACP leaders placed on the public message presented to the American people. Moon identified the association's long-standing concern with such matters and referred to the 1909 founding conference at which Oswald Garrison Villard discussed the importance of informing the public of the NAACP's programs and activities and the need to rally support for its goals. Moon also looked at the organizational challenge of informing, educating, clarifying, and inspiring the black community and the nation. Moon's address, July 16, 1959, NAACP Papers, pt. 1 (supp.), reel 11. In his 1909 address, Villard spoke of devising the "most efficient means of appealing to the conscience and hearts of the American people." See the Papers of Oswald Garrison Villard, Houghton Library, Harvard University, box 120 (1), NAACP.

On the significance of persuasive language in social reform movements, see John Wilson, *Introduction to Social Movements* (New York, 1973). Wilson describes how leaders of social reform movements direct such language at external and internal audiences. They speak to the former to increase awareness of and to legitimize the movement's ultimate aims, and they address the latter (internal) audience to rally support and inspire the rank and file. According to Wilson, such efforts occur at regular meetings, ceremonies, demonstrations, and in the organizations' printed publications (319–23). See also Gene Sharp, *The Politics of Nonviolent Action* (Boston, 1973), ch. 3, which identifies a variety of methods of nonviolent protest and persuasion used by organizations engaged in nonviolent action, including speeches, letters of opposition, signed public statements, group petitions, leaflets, pamphlets, books, journals, newspapers, radio messages, group lobbying, processions, public assemblies, and protest meetings. See also Gerard A. Hauser, *Introduction to Rhetorical Theory* (Philadelphia, 1986), esp. ch. 2.

25. On the importance of rhetoric and persuasive language, Hauser writes that those employing rhetoric choose their language carefully so as to connect with the intended audience in "ways that will be consequential"; rhetoric itself is concerned "with the specific audience [and] . . . the special concerns most appropriate" at a particular time with particular people on a particular matter. Hauser,

Introduction, 27–28. According to Terry Eagleton, rhetoric is concerned with "pleading, persuading, [and] inciting." Eagleton, *Literary Theory: An Introduction* (Minneapolis, 1996), 179. In studying the relationship between conditions in antebellum America and the way abolitionists framed their message, Ronald Walters writes of wanting to know what there is "in a social and cultural situation that [gives] a reform its style, its particular set of concerns," and notes that the social and cultural context can vitalize "long-standing issues," providing them with "special prominence at particular historical moments." Walters, *The Antislavery Appeal: American Abolitionism after 1830* (New York, 1978), vii–xii.

PRELUDE

1. On Wilson's departure from New York, see the *New York Times,* December 5, 1918. See also the diary of Wilson's physician, Dr. Cary Grayson, in Arthur S. Link, ed., *The Papers of Woodrow Wilson* (Princeton, NJ, 1986), 53:313–15. The letter to Wilson is quoted in Gene Smith, *When the Cheering Stopped: The Last Years of Woodrow Wilson* (New York, 1964), 35.

2. On the scene in Brest, see the *New York Times,* December 14, 1918; and Smith, *When the Cheering Stopped,* 35–37.

3. The description of Paris and the words of Clemenceau are from Smith, *When the Cheering Stopped,* 38–40. See also the Grayson diary in Link, *Papers of Woodrow Wilson,* 53:378–79.

4. Link, *Papers of Woodrow Wilson,* 53:386–87.

5. On Trotter's confrontations with Washington and Wilson, see Stephen R. Fox, *The Guardian of Boston: William Monroe Trotter* (New York, 1970), chs. 2, 5.

6. On Trotter's French adventure, see the *Christian Science Monitor,* July 25, 1919. For additional details of Trotter's trip, see *The New York Age,* June 28 and September 6, 1919. For a full discussion of Trotter's activities in Paris, see Fox, *Guardian of Boston,* ch. 7.

7. Trotter's letter is printed in *The New York Age,* September 6, 1919.

CHAPTER ONE

1. On the Springfield riot, see Charles Flint Kellogg, *NAACP: A History of the National Association for the Advancement of Colored People, 1909–1920* (Baltimore, 1967), 9–11. The assessment of the black population is from the *Illinois State Journal,* quoted in ibid., 11; the critique of Springfield's white residents was penned by William English Walling, a white reformer with a strong commitment to the cause of racial justice. Walling is quoted in Kellogg, *NAACP,* 11. Portions of this chapter appeared previously. See Jonathan Rosenberg, "For Democracy, Not Hypocrisy: World War and Race Relations in the United States, 1914–1919," *International History Review* 21 (September 1999): 592–625.

2. On the NAACP's founding, see Kellogg, *NAACP,* esp. chs. 1–3; David Levering Lewis, *W.E.B. Du Bois: Biography of a Race, 1868–1919* (New York, 1993),

ch. 14; and Mary White Ovington's first-hand account in *The Walls Came Tumbling Down* (New York, 1947), ch. 4. The following year saw the establishment of the National Urban League. Other organizations working for racial advancement from the late nineteenth to the early twentieth centuries included William Trotter's National Equal Rights League (which went through several incarnations in the early 1900s), the Afro-American League (founded in 1890), the National Association of Colored Women (founded in 1896), and the National League for the Protection of Colored Women (founded in 1906). On the Urban League, see Nancy J. Weiss, *The National Urban League, 1910–1940* (New York, 1974). See also Weiss's essay, "From Black Separatism to Interracial Cooperation: The Origins of Organized Efforts for Racial Advancement, 1890–1920," in *Twentieth-Century America: Recent Interpretations*, Barton Bernstein and Allen Matusow, eds. (New York, 1972), 52–87. On Trotter's group, see Stephen R. Fox, *The Guardian of Boston: William Monroe Trotter* (New York, 1970). See also James M. McPherson, *The Abolitionist Legacy: From Reconstruction to the NAACP* (Princeton, NJ, 1975), esp. chs. 16–20; and August Meier, *Negro Thought in America, 1880–1915* (Ann Arbor, MI, 1963), esp. chs. 8–9.

3. According to James McPherson, several groups came together to found the NAACP, including black activists whose organizations were failing, white neo-abolitionists, social justice progressives, and socialists. See McPherson, *The Abolitionist Legacy*, 386–93.

4. On the racial attitudes of the NAACP's founders, see Victor Glasberg, "The Emergence of White Liberalism: The Founders of the NAACP and American Racial Attitudes" (Ph.D. diss., Harvard University, 1971).

5. Oswald Garrison Villard was the son of Henry Villard, who came to America in the wake of the German Revolution of 1848. Henry became a newspaperman and a railroad and shipping magnate. Oswald's maternal grandfather was William Lloyd Garrison, one of the key figures in the movement against slavery. See D. Joy Humes, *Oswald Garrison Villard, Liberal of the 1920s* (Syracuse, NY, 1960).

6. Text of the 1909 address in the Papers of Oswald Garrison Villard (hereafter cited as Villard Papers), Houghton Library, Harvard University, box 120(1), NAACP.

7. For the 1912 speech, see the Villard Papers, box 120(1), folder 7. On Villard the foreign policy critic, see Michael Wreszin, *Oswald Garrison Villard: Pacifist at War* (Bloomington, IN, 1965).

8. Daniel Walter Cryer, "Mary White Ovington and the Rise of the NAACP" (Ph.D. diss., University of Minnesota, 1977), 259–60.

9. On Ovington's early life, see Cryer, "Ovington," chs. 1–3. See also Carolyn Wedin, *Inheritors of the Spirit: Mary White Ovington and the Founding of the NAACP* (New York, 1998). See Ovington's autobiography, *The Walls Came Tumbling Down*; and Ovington, *Black and White Sat Down Together: The Reminiscences of an NAACP Founder*, Ralph E. Luker, ed. (New York, 1995), 3–55.

10. See Villard, *Fighting Years: Memoirs of a Liberal Editor* (New York, 1939), 192.

11. On Storey's early years, see William B. Hixson, *Moorfield Storey and the Abolitionist Tradition* (New York, 1972), ch. 1. During the imperial surge at the

turn of the century, Storey was a critic of American foreign policy, comparing America's oppression and subjugation of the Filipinos after the Spanish-American-Filipino War to the oppression of blacks in the United States. On the African-American response to American expansionism at this time, see Willard Gatewood, *Black Americans and the White Man's Burden, 1898–1903* (Urbana, IL, 1975).

12. From Storey's *Autobiography* in manuscript form in "Addresses, Articles, Writings" in the Moorfield Storey Papers, Massachusetts Historical Society, Boston.

13. Storey to Ellen F. Mason, March 17, 1911, quoted in M. A. De Wolfe Howe, *Moorfield Storey: Portrait of an Independent* (Boston, 1932), 254.

14. On Spingarn's life and work, see B. Joyce Ross, *J. E. Spingarn and the Rise of the NAACP, 1911–1939* (New York, 1972). On his contribution to the field of comparative literature and the problems at Columbia, see ch. 1.

15. Ross, *J. E. Spingarn*, 3. Spingarn quoted in ibid., 10.

16. On Spingarn's early years in the NAACP and his deep commitment to race reform, see Ross, *J. E. Spingarn*, ch. 2.

17. The literature on Du Bois is vast. Numerous works will be cited throughout this book. Here I mention a few of the more standard studies. The most distinguished recent project is David Levering Lewis's two-volume biography: *W.E.B. Du Bois: Biography of a Race, 1868–1919* (New York, 1993); and *W.E.B. Du Bois: The Fight for Equality and the American Century, 1919–1963* (New York, 2000). A solid, reliable account is Manning Marable, *W.E.B. Du Bois: Black Radical Democrat* (Boston, 1986). On the literary aspects of Du Bois's work, see Arnold Rampersad, *The Art and Imagination of W.E.B. Du Bois* (Cambridge, MA, 1976).

18. On the significance of Du Bois's editorship, see Elliott Rudwick, "W.E.B. Du Bois in the Role of 'Crisis' Editor," *Journal of Negro History* 43 (July 1958): 214–40. On how the magazine got its name, see the 1914 NAACP pamphlet, *How the NAACP Began*, Villard Papers, box 120 (1), folder 7.

19. George A. Towns to Du Bois, February 20, 1918, Du Bois Papers, W.E.B. Du Bois Library, University of Massachusetts–Amherst, microfilm edition, reel 7.

20. Many examples of this appear in the personal correspondence between the two: an especially fine illustration is the exchange of lengthy and candid letters in October 1914. See Spingarn to Du Bois, October 24, 1914, and Du Bois's October 28 reply. Du Bois Papers, reel 4. On their friendship, see Ross Posnock, *Color and Culture: Black Writers and the Making of the Modern Intellectual* (Cambridge, MA, 1998), 147–61.

21. See Robert L. Zangrando, *The NAACP Crusade against Lynching, 1909–1950* (Philadelphia, 1980), 21.

22. On the early initiatives against discrimination undertaken by the NAACP, see Kellogg, *NAACP*, esp. ch. 9.

23. George Orwell, *Coming Up for Air* (New York, 1950), 144.

24. The literature on Wilson and the war is vast. Two works that are critical for understanding the subject are Arthur Link, *Struggle for Neutrality* (Princeton, NJ, 1960); and Ernest R. May, *The World War and American Isolation, 1914–1917* (Cambridge, MA, 1959). See also John Milton Cooper, *The Warrior and the Priest: Woodrow Wilson and Theodore Roosevelt* (Cambridge, MA, 1983),

esp. chs. 17–20; and Patrick Devlin, *Too Proud to Fight: Woodrow Wilson's Neutrality* (London, 1975).

25. Villard quoted in the *New York Times*, April 25, 1915.

26. Oswald Garrison Villard, *Prophets True and False* (New York, 1928), 162–65. For a discussion of Villard's views on American neutrality and the decision to intervene, see Wreszin, *Oswald Garrison Villard*, 48–55.

27. While it is difficult to generalize about the reformers' views of the war, those committed to race reform were by and large deeply opposed to American intervention and were mainly pacifists. See Charles Chatfield, "World War I and the Liberal Pacifist in the United States," *American Historical Review* 75 (December 1970): 1920–37. Several of the liberal pacifists were also committed to race reform, including Jane Addams, John Haynes Holmes, and Lillian Wald. See also John A. Thompson, *Reformers and War: American Progressive Publicists and the First World War* (Cambridge, Eng., 1987).

28. Ovington, *Walls Came Tumbling Down*, 134.

29. Ovington, *Black and White*, 84–85.

30. On Ovington's pacifism, see Cryer, "Ovington," 355–63.

31. Ovington, *Black and White*, 85.

32. Ovington, *Portraits in Color* (New York, 1927), 140.

33. For Storey's view of the war, see Hixson, *Moorfield Storey*, 82–90. Not a pacifist, Storey held Germany responsible for starting the war. Just after the war he predicted that "Negroes will come back [from Europe] feeling like men and not disposed to accept the treatment to which they have been subjected." Quoted in ibid., 162. Holmes quoted in Ray H. Abrams, *Preachers Present Arms: The Role of the American Churches in World Wars I and II* (Scottsdale, PA, 1969; orig., 1933), 198–99.

34. See Thomas J. Knock, *To End All Wars: Woodrow Wilson and the Quest for a New World Order* (New York, 1992), ch. 4.

35. Spingarn quoted in the *Cleveland Gazette*, January 23, 1915. On Spingarn's attitude toward the war, patriotism, and service, see Ross, *J. E. Spingarn*, 81–84.

36. Du Bois, "The African Roots of the War," *Atlantic Monthly* (May 1915): 707–11.

37. Ibid., 712–14.

38. Dewey quoted in David M. Kennedy, *Over Here: The First World War and American Society* (New York, 1980), 50.

39. *Atlantic Monthly* (May 1915): 707–14. David Levering Lewis calls the essay "one of the analytical triumphs of the early twentieth century." See Lewis, *Du Bois: Biography of a Race*, 503–4. In October 1915, Du Bois spoke about the war's significance before the Mu-So-Lit Club (an organization composed of prominent members of Washington, D.C.'s black community), expressing ideas similar to those he had advanced in the *Atlantic* article. See *The Decennial Brief of the Mu-So-Lit Club*, November 12, 1915, Moorland-Spingarn Research Center, Howard University.

40. *The Crisis* (November 1914): 28.

41. *The Crisis* (November 1914): 29–30. For a classic Du Boisian statement on war, see his editorial for the previous month, which evokes war's heroism, sorrow, and futility. "Of the Children of Peace," ibid. (October 1914): 289–90.

42. *The Crisis* (December 1914): 80.

43. *The Crisis* (June 1915): 81.

44. See the September 1916 *Crisis*, in which Du Bois writes of "The Battle of Europe," mentioning gas attacks, raids on undefended towns, and "Zeppelins dropping bombs on women and children." He contrasts the ideals of this barbaric culture of the Occident with the "warm, golden hue that harks back to the heritage of Africa and the tropics" (216–17).

45. Du Bois to Joel Spingarn, October 28, 1914, Du Bois Papers, reel 4.

46. "Military Training Camp for Colored Men: An Open Letter from Dr. J. E. Spingarn," February 15, 1917, Joel Spingarn Papers, Moorland-Spingarn Research Center, Howard University, box 13, folder 534. Spingarn's open letter appeared in Baltimore's *Afro-American*, February 24, 1917.

47. Spingarn's speech published in the *Washington Bee*, March 24, 1917.

48. Spingarn's letter to Pickens published in Baltimore's *Afro-American*, March 10, 1917. Pickens was a supporter of the camp; his letter to Spingarn is published in the same issue. See also Pickens, *Bursting Bonds* (Bloomington, IN, 1991; orig., 1923), 73–74.

49. *Chicago Defender*, April 7, 1917; the Cleveland *Gazette*, March 24, 1917; and Baltimore's *Afro-American*, February 24 and March 17, 1917. See also *The New York Age*, March 1 and 22, 1917.

50. Joel Spingarn to Du Bois, February 26, 1917, Du Bois Papers, reel 5.

51. *The Crisis* (April 1917): 270–71. See also ibid. (June 1917): 60–61, in which Du Bois wrote a strongly worded editorial about the need for the camp and excoriated those in the black press who were critical of the NAACP's white leadership for advocating the facility. So as to spare the association criticism, Spingarn was prepared to separate the NAACP from the plan and even offered to resign as NAACP chairman. See his exchange of letters with Archibald Grimké, head of the NAACP's Washington, D.C., branch: Spingarn to Grimké April 3, 1917; Grimké to Spingarn April 4, 1917, Joel Spingarn Papers (Moorland-Spingarn): box 5, folder 179. See also Dickson D. Bruce, *Archibald Grimké: Portrait of a Black Independent* (Baton Rouge, LA, 1993), 248–49. Although the question of the camp aroused strong opposition among some in the black population, certain prominent black figures besides Du Bois supported the idea, including the nation's highest ranking black soldier, Lieutenant Colonel Charles Young. On the reaction within the black community, see Ross, *J. E. Spingarn*, ch. 3; and Kellogg, *NAACP*, 250–56. For Young's views, see his letter to the Cleveland *Gazette*, March 31, 1917. William Pickens also expressed support for the idea. See his letter to Spingarn, which was printed on the front page of the *Afro-American* and Spingarn's published response. Pickens to Spingarn, February 27, 1917, Joel Spingarn Papers (Moorland-Spingarn), box 9, folder 354. Pickens's letter and Spingarn's response in the *Afro-American*, March 10, 1917. See also Pickens to Joel Spingarn, November 13, 1917, Joel Spingarn Papers (Moorland-Spingarn), box 9, folder 365. Despite her profound misgivings about the war, even Mary White Ovington came to support the camp. See Mary White Ovington to Joel Spingarn,

February 28, 1917, Joel Spingarn Papers (Moorland-Spingarn), box 9, folder 352. Among potential recruits, reaction to the plan was overwhelmingly positive. At Howard University, Hampton Institute, and other black institutions, young black men showed great enthusiasm for the idea. See "Howard University in the War—A Record of Patriotic Service," *Howard University Record* 13 (April 1919): 159–78. For a comprehensive discussion of the camp issue and camp life, see Arthur E. Barbeau and Florette Henri, *The Unknown Soldiers: African-American Troops in World War I* (Philadelphia, 1974), 56–69; and Gerald W. Patton, *War and Race: The Black Officer in the American Military, 1915–1941* (Westport, CT, 1981), 32–79.

52. *The Crisis* (June 1917): 61.

53. NAACP Board of Directors meeting minutes, May 14, 1917, Du Bois Papers, reel 5.

54. Joel Spingarn to Du Bois, October 17, 1917, Du Bois Papers, reel 5.

55. Before joining the NAACP, Johnson was associated with the camp of Booker T. Washington, which made his decision to join the NAACP in 1916 a significant move. See Eugene Levy, *James Weldon Johnson: Black Leader, Black Voice* (Chicago, 1973).

56. *The New York Age*, June 3, 1915.

57. *The New York Age*, February 15, 1917.

58. Ibid.

59. See Johnson's "Views and Reviews," in *The New York Age*, March 29, 1917.

60. For studies on the decision to intervene, see n. 24, above, as well as John A. Thompson, *Woodrow Wilson* (London, 2002), chs. 5–6; and Robert Osgood, *Ideals and Self-Interest in America's Foreign Relations* (Chicago, 1953), chs. 10–11.

61. Arthur S. Link, ed., *The Papers of Woodrow Wilson*, 41:519–27.

62. Wilson's speeches are replete with the rhetoric of assistance and transformation; the president believed American actions ought to be guided by a commitment to help the world and, ultimately, to transform world politics. On Wilsonian language, see my 1997 Harvard University dissertation, "How Far the Promised Land?" 64–65, n. 41.

63. *The Crisis* (May 1917): 8.

64. Ibid.

65. Minutes of the Board of Directors, April 9, 1917, NAACP Papers, Library of Congress, Washington, D.C., microfilm edition, pt. 1, reel 1.

66. For the conference announcement, see *The Crisis* (May 1917): 7. The resolutions were published in the June issue, 59–60.

67. Ibid.

68. NAACP, *Seventh Annual Report* (New York, 1917).

69. On Wilson's policy toward blacks, see Nancy J. Weiss, "The Negro and the New Freedom: Fighting Wilsonian Segregation," *Political Science Quarterly* 84 (March 1969): 61–67; and Desmond King, *Separate and Unequal: Black Americans and the U.S. Federal Government* (Oxford, 1995), 28–30.

70. *The Crisis* (July 1917): 115–16.

71. Villard's speech, Philadelphia, January 9, 1918, Villard Papers, box 136 (speeches). In early 1918, Villard published a lengthy piece on the relationship between the war and racial persecution. The essay, which appeared in *The New*

World, a publication geared to a white audience, touched on themes the reformers frequently raised in these years: the war's potential benefit for black peoples in America and throughout the world, and the notion that by fighting abroad for rights it denied its citizens at home, the United States placed itself in an awkward position. Villard, "The Negro and the War," *The New World* (January 1918): 17–19. Twenty years later, Villard considered the irony inherent in "the drafting of our Negroes to save the world for democracy when all over the South they were denied every vestige of democracy." Villard, *Fighting Years*, 340.

72. *The New York Age*, May 10, 1917. A few weeks later, Johnson criticized America's war mission, charging that its treatment of the black population left the country unsuited for the Wilsonian mission. He described the notion of fighting "to make the world safe for democracy" as "a bit of high-sounding phraseology" because America (and England) did not understand the meaning of democracy. Johnson concluded optimistically, noting that the "direct result" of the war would be the defeat of Germany, while the "indirect result" would be "a fuller degree of liberty for the peoples of the world, especially the darker peoples." Ibid., May 24, 1917.

73. *The New York Age*, May 3, 1917.

74. "What the Negro Is Doing for Himself," *The Liberator* (June 1918): 29–31. One finds similarly hopeful sentiments expressed repeatedly in black periodicals. For a typical example, see Kathryn M. Johnson, "The Negro and the World War," *Half Century Magazine* (June 1917): 13.

75. The best way to get a sense of the frequency and character of Du Bois's *Crisis* editorials is to read the journal during this period. Of the many such pieces he wrote during the war, two from 1918 include: "Liberty and Democracy" (July): 124; and "A Philosophy in Time of War" (August): 164–65.

76. *The Crisis* (August 1917): 165.

77. *The Crisis* (June 1918): 60.

78. *The Crisis* (September 1917): 216–17. The most controversial episode in which Du Bois was involved during the war concerned his "Close Ranks" editorial, which appeared in the July 1918 *Crisis*. The editorial, which caused a firestorm within the reform community and among African Americans generally, argued that blacks had a special interest in the war's outcome. Du Bois wrote that what Germany represents "spells death to the aspirations of Negroes and all darker races for equality, freedom, and democracy. Let us not hesitate. Let us, while this war lasts, forget our special grievances and close our ranks shoulder to shoulder with our own white fellow citizens and the allied nations that are fighting for democracy. We make no ordinary sacrifice, but we make it gladly and willingly" (111).

Du Bois's reasons for writing the editorial have been the source of debate. According to Mark Ellis, it is "highly probable" that Du Bois wrote the editorial in an effort to obtain a position in military intelligence, which Joel Spingarn had attempted to secure for him. Ellis writes that the editorial "crucially influenced" the War Department's decision to offer Du Bois a commission. Ellis, " 'Closing Ranks' and 'Seeking Honors': W.E.B. Du Bois in World War I," *Journal of American History* 79 (June 1992): 96–124. William Jordan has written that Du Bois's actions during the war, including the "Close Ranks" editorial, were part of the wartime accommodationism that the editor and others quite reasonably pursued, given the "dilemma" faced by race activists during the "nadir of black history in the United States." Du Bois's wartime position should be placed in proper "historical context" and in the context of his past pragmatism. William Jordan, " 'The Damnable Dilemma': African-American Accommodation and Protest during World War I," ibid. 81 (March 1995): 1562–83; quotes from 1564 and 1565. Note Ellis's response in the same issue, Ellis, "W.E.B. Du Bois and the Formation of Black Opinion in World War I: A Commentary on the 'Damnable Dilemma,' " ibid. (March 1995): 1584–90. I consider this debate in my dissertation (78–80, n. 58), but here would emphasize my central point, that the editor believed the war possessed unlimited potential for advancing the cause of racial justice in the United States and abroad. See also Jordan's more sweeping treatment of the challenges faced by the black press during the war. *Black Newspapers and America's War for Democracy, 1914–1920* (Chapel Hill, NC, 2001).

79. *The Crisis* (August 1917): 163–64. See also a letter from "The College Alumnae Club" of Washington, D.C., to President Wilson, which reminded him that while black Americans had always served honorably in the country's wars, segregation persisted. Ibid., 164–65.

80. Joseph Seamon Cotter, Jr., "A Sonnet to Negro Soldiers," *The Crisis* (June 1918): 64.

81. Du Bois to Emmett Scott, April 24, 1918, Du Bois Papers, reel 7. Scott, Booker T. Washington's successor at Tuskegee, had been tapped to join the War Department as special assistant to the secretary of war in the fall of 1917. On the significance of his appointment, see Scott, "The Negro and the War Department," *The Crisis* (December 1917): 76.

82. NAACP, *Ninth Annual Report* (New York, 1919): 19–21.

83. Note, for example, a June 1918 address by Moorfield Storey. He told the Wisconsin Bar Association that black Americans, while deeply devoted to their country, remained the victims of domestic violence. Storey went on to state, "We owe it to [black Americans]—we owe it to ourselves—that while they are giving their lives abroad to make the world safe for democracy we should do our part to make this country safe for their kindred at home, or, to quote a better phrase, we should 'make America safe for Americans.' " Moorfield Storey, *The Negro Question: An Address Delivered before the Wisconsin Bar Association* (N.p.), June 27, 1918.

84. Archibald Grimké to Woodrow Wilson, July 1, 1918, Archibald Grimké Papers (Moorland-Spingarn Research Center, Howard University), box 27, folder 549.

85. One of black America's most arresting speakers in this period, William Pickens of Morgan College, considered the conflict's potential for improving the plight of black Americans. See his speech from early 1918, "The New Year," Pickens Papers, Schomburgh Center for Research in Black Culture, New York Public Library, New York, microfilm edition, reel 4, box 7. Note, too, a Morgan College address, in which Pickens embraced the American mission and asserted that the black commitment to the war rested on the belief that America and the allies represented "the best hope for . . . democracy." He concluded with a grand vision, stating that black Americans welcome "the opportunity to lift the 'Negro ques-

tion' out of the narrow confines of the Southern United States and make it a world question. . . . [O]ur domestic race question, instead of being settled by Mississippi and South Carolina, will now seek its settlement largely on the battlefields of Europe." Pickens, "The Kind of Democracy the Negro Race Expects," May 30, 1918, Pickens Vertical File, Schomburgh Center for Research in Black Culture, New York Public Library, New York. See Sheldon Avery, "Up from Washington: William Pickens and the Negro Struggle for Equality, 1900–1954" (Ph.D. diss., University of Oregon, 1970).

86. For Miller's August 4, 1917, letter to Wilson, see Miller, *The Everlasting Stain* (New York, 1968; orig., 1924), 136–60. On the East St. Louis riot, see Elliott M. Rudwick, *Race Riot at East St. Louis, July 2, 1917* (Carbondale, IL, 1964); on the Memphis episode, see Barbeau and Henri, *Unknown Soldiers*, ch. 2. On Kelly Miller, see Bernard Eisenberg, "Kelly Miller: The Negro as Marginal Man," *Journal of Negro History* 45 (July 1960): 182–97; and August Meier, "The Racial and Educational Philosophy of Kelly Miller, 1895–1915," *Journal of Negro Education* 29 (Spring 1960): 121–27.

87. In 1918, Miller wrote *An Appeal to Conscience*, which argued that the war would lead to a "re-adjustment of the social structure [that] will be more radical than that effected by the French Revolution" and claimed its transformative impact on black America would be greater than that produced by the Emancipation Proclamation. According to Miller, world democratization would become a reality, and hereafter, "no nation . . . [would] be permitted to override a weaker neighbor by sheer dominance of power." Miller then focused on domestic matters, noting the "Negro will emerge from this war with a redoubled portion of privilege and opportunity." *An Appeal to Conscience* (New York, 1969; orig., 1918), 82–86.

88. Eulogy, April 12, 1918 in *The Works of Francis J. Grimké*, Carter Woodson, ed. (Washington, DC, 1942), 1:169–74.

89. See an August 1918 diary entry in which Grimké suggested that the war effort itself might benefit from progress made on the domestic racial front. Ibid., 3:50–51.

90. Quoted in Fox, *The Guardian of Boston*, 217. See also *The New York Age*, September 20, 1917.

91. 65th Cong., 2nd sess., *Congressional Record* 52 (June 29, 1918): appendix, 502. Representative Frederick Gillett of Massachusetts read the petition into the record.

92. Theodore Kornweibel, *No Crystal Stair: Black Life and the Messenger, 1917–1928* (Westport, CT, 1975), 30. On the intellectual influences of the two men, see ch. 1.

93. *The Messenger* (January 1918): 23–24. To understand what *The Messenger* thought of Du Bois, see the July 1918 issue, which included a critical profile. *The Souls of Black Folk* is described as a "mass of labored alliterations," which is filled more with "literature than information." The journal criticized Du Bois for his "scientific shortcomings," a consequence of the era in which he was educated: "Greek, Latin, and classicism were stressed at Harvard. None of the older Negro leaders have had the modern education" (27–28).

94. Kornweibel, *No Crystal Stair*, 3–4. See the special agent's report, which describes their activities (said to be in violation of the Espionage Act), arrest, and

detention in the A. Philip Randolph Papers, Library of Congress, Washington, D.C., microfilm edition, reel 23. In August 1971, Randolph requested copies of these documents, which the Department of Justice furnished to him. See the U.S. Attorney's letter to Randolph, August 10, 1971, Randolph Papers, reel 23. On the federal campaign against *The Messenger*, see Theodore Kornweibel, *Seeing Red: Federal Campaigns against Black Militancy, 1919–1925* (Bloomington, IN, 1998), ch. 5.

95. *The Messenger* (January 1918): 6. For a fine example of Randolph's and Owen's thoughts on the war's origins, which are strikingly similar to those of Du Bois, see their "Terms of Peace and the Darker Races" (New York, 1917). They conclude their discussion on the exploitative nature of capitalism by describing America's mission to "make the world safe for democracy" as "a sham, a mockery, [and] a rape on decency."

96. "Peace," *The Messenger* (November 1917): 7.

97. *The Messenger* (January 1918): 17, 20. Paula Pfeffer writes that Randolph's leadership was different from that of other black leaders for a variety of reasons, two of which are relevant here: his adherence to socialist rather than capitalist economic doctrine and his fusion of a labor orientation with a militancy on racial issues. Pfeffer, *A. Philip Randolph, Pioneer of the Civil Rights Movement* (Baton Rouge, LA, 1990), 3.

98. *The Messenger* (November 1917): 9. A September 1917 letter that Randolph and Owen had written to a supporter (published in November) could well have been written by more mainstream figures. Randolph and Owen to Lela Faye Secor, September 8, 1917, printed in *The Messenger* (November 1917): 10–11. On the relationship between *The Messenger*, radical journalism, and a new militancy among black Americans, see Kornweibel, *No Crystal Stair*, ch. 2.

99. John H. Hawkins, "14 Articles for Home Democracy," *Washington Bee*, November 16, 1918; Baltimore *Afro-American*, November 15, 1918; see also the editorial, "The Fourteen Articles," in ibid. Wilson had delivered his Fourteen Points address on January 8, 1918. Its key elements were support for "open covenants of peace, openly arrived at," freedom of the seas, the removal of economic barriers between nations, armaments reduction, the impartial adjustment of colonial claims based on self-determination, and the establishment of an association of nations. Link, *Papers of Woodrow Wilson*, 45:534–39. See also Knock, *To End All Wars*, ch. 8.

100. *The Crisis* (November 1918): 10.

CHAPTER TWO

1. Arthur Link, ed., *The Papers of Woodrow Wilson* (Princeton, NJ, 1966–94), 53:34–43. Portions of this chapter appeared previously. See Jonathan Rosenberg, "For Democracy, Not Hypocrisy: World War and Race Relations in the United States, 1914–1919," *International History Review* 21 (September 1999): 592–625.

2. James Weldon Johnson, "The Battle Begins," *The New York Age*, November 16, 1918; *Half Century Magazine* (January 1919): 11; "The Coming of Peace," *The New York Age*, November 16, 1918.

3. The most comprehensive study is Florette Henri, *Black Migration: Movement North, 1900–1920* (New York, 1975), 68–69. Note Emmett Scott's classic, if outdated, account, *Negro Migration during the War* (New York, 1969; orig., 1920).

4. On the war's impact on black labor, see the address by George E. Haynes, director of Negro economics in the Labor Department, who spoke at the Reconstruction Conference given by the American Academy of Political Science. *The New York Age*, December 14, 1918.

5. Powell quoted in Arthur E. Barbeau and Florette Henri, *The Unknown Soldiers: African-American Troops in World War I* (Philadelphia, 1974), 9.

6. At the founding meeting in March 1919, the "Purpose of the Conference" stated: "The preaching of world democracy and the disturbance attending the world war has given rise to 'Great Expectations' "—white expectations that blacks will return with an "impossible" attitude, and black expectations "that democracy in all its implications is coming immediately." Commission on Interracial Cooperation Papers, Atlanta University Center Archives, Atlanta, microfilm edition, series 2, reel 20.

7. The solicitation was sent to Du Bois. See the Du Bois Papers, W.E.B. Du Bois Library, University of Massachusetts–Amherst, microfilm edition, reel 8. See also an ad for the Southern Aid Society, which ran frequently in *The Crisis*. The ad, headed "Reconstruction," notes that the war and its aftermath have "opened the eyes" of black people. *The Crisis* (August 1919): 213. See "The Negro and the New Social Order: Reconstruction Program of the American Negro," *The Messenger* (March 1919): 3–11.

8. Kelly Miller, "The Negro in the New Reconstruction" (Washington, DC, undated). Context suggests Miller wrote the essay just after the war ended.

9. William Pickens, *The Negro in the Light of the Great War: Basis for the New Reconstruction* (Baltimore, undated). This pamphlet, parts of which resemble speeches Pickens gave in this period, was probably written just after the war. See also a lecture given just after the war by NAACP President Moorfield Storey. "Race Prejudice" in Moorfield Storey, *Problems of To-Day* (Boston, 1920), 104–6.

10. *The Crisis* (February 1919): 169–73. In referring to Wilson's Fourteen Points, Ovington referred to the Reverend John Hawkins's address (see ch. 1), which linked the Wilsonian formulation to black domestic aspirations.

11. On the manner in which Progressive reformers employed the notion of "reconstruction" in postwar discourse, see David M. Kennedy, *Over Here: The First World War and American Society* (New York, 1980), 245–48; and John A. Thompson, *Reformers and War: American Progressive Publicists and the First World War* (Cambridge, Eng., 1987), 247–51. On black perceptions of post–Civil War Reconstruction, see Leon Litwack, *Trouble in Mind: Black Southerners in the Age of Jim Crow* (New York, 1998), xiii; and August Meier, *Negro Thought in America, 1880–1915* (Ann Arbor, MI 1988; orig., 1963), 3–16.

12. *The Crisis* (May 1919): 10–11.

13. *The Crisis* (January 1919): 111–12. One gets a sense of Du Bois's activities in France from his memoranda written to the board while he was abroad. See his "Memorandum to the Chairman and Acting Chairman of the NAACP," December 24, 1918, NAACP Papers, Library of Congress, Washington, D.C., microfilm edition, pt. 11B, reel 18; the report from Paris to the Board, January 4, 1919, NAACP Papers, pt. 11B, reel 18; and the "Report of the Director of Publications and Research," December 1, 1918–April 1, 1919 (written after his return), Du Bois Papers, reel 8.

14. *The Crisis* (February 1919): 164; (March 1919): 215–16; and (April 1919): 268–69.

15. *The Crisis* (March 1919): 215. David Levering Lewis notes the irony in Du Bois's viewing the scene so uncritically. The honors bestowed on a black man by his colonial master might, after all, have engendered some measure of discomfort in the greatest race reformer of his generation. As Lewis writes, this reflected Du Bois's "eccentric Eurocentrism and radicalism-from-above." Lewis, *W.E.B. Du Bois: Biography of a Race* (New York, 1993), 566–67.

16. *The Crisis* (May 1919): 7–9.

17. According to Imanuel Geiss, Pan-Africanism is an "intellectual and political movement among Africans and Afro-Americans" who see Africa and people of African descent as "homogeneous." Geiss writes that this view leads to feelings of "racial solidarity and a new self-awareness" and causes African Americans to regard Africa as their real homeland, though they do not necessarily want to return there. Geiss, *The Pan-African Movement: A History of Pan-Africanism in America, Europe and Africa* (New York, 1974), 3. On the 1919 meeting, see ch. 12. For a discussion of Du Bois at the London meeting in 1900, see Lewis, *Du Bois: Biography of a Race*, 248–51.

18. Prior to the congress, Du Bois had prepared a document, "Memorandum on the Future of Africa," which outlined his thoughts on postwar Africa, including the disposition of the German colonies and the modernization of the continent, which he argued demanded the education of young Africans. Du Bois sent the memorandum to the American Secretary of State Robert Lansing, along with a letter seeking Lansing's approval to travel to Paris for the Pan-African Congress. Du Bois to Lansing, November 27, 1918, Du Bois Papers, reel 7; the memorandum is in ibid., reel 6. On Du Bois's preparations for the congress, see his memorandum to Blaise Diagne of January 1, 1919, Du Bois Papers, reel 8.

19. Imanuel Geiss, *Pan-African Movement*, 238.

20. "Résolutions Votées par le Congrès Pan-Africain." NAACP Papers, pt. 11B, reel 18.

21. *The Crisis* (April 1919): 271–74. Other Americans in attendance included John Hope, president of Morehouse College; Addie W. Hunton, a member of the YWCA in France, who addressed the congress and pointed out the importance of women in the world's reconstruction; Ida Gibbs Hunt, a leader in the women's movement; and Rayford Logan, a black soldier in France (and future historian).

22. *The Crisis* (January 1919): 112.

23. NAACP, "Africa in the World Democracy" (New York, 1919). On the distress within the association regarding diverting the organization's efforts from domestic matters, see Archibald Grimké's remarks at a December 1918 board

meeting. Minutes of the Board of Directors, December 9, 1918, NAACP Papers, pt. 1, reel 1.

24. On black soldiers in the world war, see Barbeau and Henri, *Unknown Soldiers*; Gerald W. Patton, *War and Race: The Black Officer in the American Military, 1915–1941* (Westport, CT), esp. chs. 4–5; and Bernard C. Nalty, *Strength for the Fight: A History of Black Americans in the Military* (New York, 1986), ch. 8.

25. *The Crisis* (May 1919): 16–18. Du Bois vouched for the document's authenticity in a letter to the NAACP Board of Directors, January 4, 1919, NAACP Papers, pt. 11B, reel 18. See Lewis, *Du Bois: Biography of a Race*, 571–72.

26. *The Crisis* (March 1919): 222.

27. *The Crisis* (July 1919): 128. Other examples of racial prejudice and maltreatment made their way into *The Crisis*. In the May 1919 issue, Du Bois sought to quash the unsubstantiated charges of rape levied against black soldiers by publishing a detailed account of French mayors' responses to questions about black conduct in their towns and cities. *The Crisis* (May 1919): 12–13.

28. *The Crisis* (February 1919): 167–68. The story, written by a French woman, first appeared in a French newspaper.

29. *The Crisis* (June 1919): 63. The scene is described in a lengthy piece written by Du Bois, "An Essay toward a History of the Black Man in the Great War," 63–87.

30. Ibid., 64.

31. *The Crisis* (March 1919): 222–23.

32. Ovington to Du Bois, April 11, 1919, Du Bois Papers, reel 7.

33. *The Crisis* (May 1919): 7.

34. The government asked Moton to investigate alleged difficulties concerning black soldiers in France, where he would examine charges concerning the behavior of black troops overseas. (It was rumored they could not control their "brutal instincts.") Moton also looked into the matter of black fighting efficiency, about which doubts had been raised. Moton's investigations demonstrated that the allegations concerning a high incidence of rape committed by black units were fraudulent and that American military authorities had maligned black soldiers unfairly. See Patton, *War and Race*, ch. 5; Barbeau and Henri, *Unknown Soldiers*, chs. 7–8; and Felix James, "Robert Russa Moton and the Whispering Gallery after World War I," *Journal of Negro History* 62 (July 1977): 235–42. See also Robert Russa Moton, *Finding a Way Out: An Autobiography* (College Park, MD, 1920), ch. 11. Moton's troubles began with his remarks to black soldiers in France, in which he praised their bravery and encouraged them to return home and quietly resume their lives. By suggesting that the black soldier should return to America and slip unnoticed into his former place in an oppressive society, Moton raised the ire of many. See Moton, *Finding a Way Out*, 262–63. *The Crisis* was especially harsh, as Du Bois lit into Moton for his lack of concern about the true conditions black soldiers had endured overseas. Moreover, *The Crisis* noted that Moton had been offered the opportunity to address the peace conference on the problems of the black world, an opportunity he had failed to seize. *The Crisis* (May 1919): 9–10. Defending himself, Moton claimed he had told white servicemen in France that their black compatriots had risked death in order "to make democracy safe for mankind, black and white." He also told them that with the war over, it was the

white man's "duty and sacred obligation" to give black Americans a "fair" and "equal chance." Despite the questionable message Moton had conveyed to the black soldier in France, it would appear that he believed the war had the potential to improve African-American life. See Moton, "Negro Troops in France," *The Southern Workman* (May 1919): 224.

35. See Leila J. Rupp, *Worlds of Women: The Making of an International Women's Movement* (Princeton, NJ, 1997), esp. ch. 3.

36. Mary Church Terrell, *A Colored Woman in a White World* (New York, 1980; orig., 1940), 331–32. See also Terrell, "My Experience Abroad," *The Competitor* (January 1920): 38–39. The quotations come from both sources, which cover the same material with only slight differences between the two. To understand how Terrell came to be invited to the conference, see *A Colored Woman*, ch. 33.

37. In a fine evocation of postwar internationalism, Terrell spoke of the spirit of "good feeling" that existed between the French and German women who attended the conference, which she believed demonstrated their "sincerity of purpose and . . . determination to heal the breach between them." *A Colored Woman*, 332.

38. Ibid., 332–35.

39. Ibid., 334–35. After the conference, Terrell spent five weeks in France before returning to the United States. Her admiration for the French was enormous, she wrote, because France treated its black subjects with dignity and fairness. Moreover, the French sang "the praises of the colored soldiers," who had served in their country. Terrell, *A Colored Woman*, 340–41. Noting the distance separating America's profession of democracy from its practice, she pointed out that other peoples were far more advanced than were the Americans in matching rhetoric with reality. Note, too, the 1920 volume by two women who had served as welfare workers under the auspices of the YMCA during and after the war. The book movingly describes relations between black soldiers and French citizens. Addie W. Hunton and Kathryn Johnson, *Two Colored Women with the American Expeditionary Forces* (Brooklyn, NY, 1920), 182. The women also suggested that the war afforded blacks, particularly soldiers, opportunities for postwar gains. Ibid., 253–55.

40. For example, the Reverend Francis Grimké reminded a group of returning black soldiers of their duty to the cause of reform. The French had treated them well, he said, but their experience would mean little unless they returned with the love of liberty and equality "burning in [their] souls and the determination to set other souls on fire with the same spirit." Grimké concluded with a familiar but powerful refrain: "If it was worth going abroad to make the world safe for democracy, it is equally worth laboring . . . to make it safe at home." Grimké's address, Washington, D.C., April 24, 1919, NAACP Papers, pt. 7A, reel 2. Note his November 24, 1918, speech in *The Works of Francis J. Grimké*, Carter G. Woodson, ed. (Washington, DC, 1942), 1: 559–77.

41. On the theme and aims of the conference, see NAACP press release, May 12, 1919, NAACP Papers, pt. 11A, reel 10. Its aims included the vote, equal educational opportunities, the right to due process, antilynching legislation, and an end to Jim Crow.

42. Pickens, June 22, 1919, NAACP Papers, pt. 1, reel 8.

43. Scott, June 22, 1919, NAACP Papers, pt. 1, reel 8; Gregg, June 25, 1919, ibid. Note board member Charles Edward Russell's address, which considered the black soldier's wartime contribution and the country's democratizing mission. Russell, June 26, 1919, ibid; and Joel Spingarn's address, June 23, 1919, ibid. For the resolutions passed at the Cleveland conference, see NAACP Papers, pt. 11A, reel 10. For a review of the conference, see *The Crisis* (August 1919): 189–93.

44. For an overview, see John Hope Franklin, *From Slavery to Freedom: A History of African Americans*, 7th ed. (New York, 1994), 348–52. See also Henri, *Black Migration*, ch. 10. Detailed studies include Arthur I. Waskow, *From Race Riot to Sit-In, 1919 and the 1960s: A Study in the Connections between Conflict and Violence* (New York, 1967); and William M. Tuttle, *Race Riot: Chicago in the Red Summer of 1919* (New York, 1984). See also Mark Ellis, "J. Edgar Hoover and the 'Red Summer' of 1919," *Journal of American Studies* 28 (1994): 39–59.

45. John Hope Franklin writes that "unrest . . . seized a considerable portion of the African-American population. . . when it became clear that many whites were seeking to deprive them of some of the gains they had made during the war." *From Slavery to Freedom*, 349–50. Tuttle makes a similar point, describing a collision between postwar aspirations and a white determination "to reaffirm the black people's prewar status." *Race Riot*, 21. James Weldon Johnson wrote of the emergence of a "spirit of defiance born of desperation." Johnson, *Black Manhattan* (New York, 1991; orig., 1930), 246.

46. Franklin, *From Slavery to Freedom*, 352.

47. "If We Must Die," *The Messenger* (September 1919): 4.

48. *The Messenger* (July 1919): 5.

49. *The Messenger* (September 1919): 4.

50. *The Messenger* (March 1919): supplement, 3–11. Note Chandler Owen's piece, "What Will be the Real Status of the Negro after the War?" (March 1919): 13–17, which is less sanguine. As part of their program proclaiming the birth of a "New Negro," Randolph and Owen regularly penned scathing critiques of everything from the League of Nations to Du Bois and the "Old Crowd" of black leaders. While the editors looked toward the postwar reconstruction with a measure of optimism, they did not view the proceedings in France with favor. See *The Messenger* (March 1919): 5. For a lengthy critique of the settlement, see Owen's "League of White Capitalist Governments," *The Messenger* (May–June 1919): 14–17. To get a sense of the criticism *The Messenger* directed at traditional black leaders, see "New Leadership for the Negro" (May–June 1919): 9–10; "A New Crowd—A New Negro," ibid., 26–27; and "The Crisis of *The Crisis*" (July 1919): 10–12.

51. Franklin, *From Slavery to Freedom*, 362. Reliable estimates of black opinion on the war are difficult to obtain. Theodore Kornweibel writes that 10 percent of the black population actively opposed the war, 40 to 50 percent supported it, and the remaining 40 to 50 percent were either oblivious, apathetic, or cynical about it. See Kornweibel, "Apathy and Dissent: Black America's Negative Responses to World War I," *South Atlantic Quarterly* 80 (Summer 1981): 322–38.

52. Norvell quoted in "Views of a Negro during the 'Red Summer' of 1919," *Journal of Negro History* 51 (July 1966): 209–18; Jones's letter reprinted in *The Crisis* (October 1919): 304–5. See Dr. John Hugh Reynolds's letter to the *Little*

Rock Gazette, which spoke of "a new Negro," who had "come back from the war changed" and "deeply move[d] by the democratic and humanitarian addresses of our President." Reprinted in *The Crisis* (January 1920): 142.

53. *The Correspondence of W.E.B. Du Bois*, Herbert Aptheker, ed. (Amherst, MA, 1973), 1:234–35. The idea that black soldiers would return to America as changed men was a common theme during this period. As Moorfield Storey wrote to John Shillady: "The negroes will come back feeling like men, and not disposed to accept the treatment to which they have been subjected." Storey to Shillady, January 10, 1919, NAACP Papers, pt. 1, reel 24.

54. "Reflections Written during a Quiet Hour 'Somewhere in France,'" October, no year (probably 1918), Du Bois Papers, reel 7. For additional examples, see Sgt. Percy Jones to Du Bois, August 6, 1919, ibid., reel 7; and Soldiers of America to the NAACP, undated, NAACP Papers, pt. 9, reel 1.

55. On the domestic debate over the treaty, see John Milton Cooper, *Breaking the Heart of the World: Woodrow Wilson and the Fight for the League of Nations* (New York, 2001); and William C. Widenor, *Henry Cabot Lodge and the Search for an American Foreign Policy* (Berkeley, CA, 1980).

56. Japan had introduced a "racial equality" clause to the treaty at Versailles the previous spring. It was rejected. See Paul Gordon Lauren, "Human Rights in History: Diplomacy and Racial Equality at the Paris Peace Conference," *Diplomatic History* (Summer 1978): 257–78.

57. On the internationalists and the League debate, see Warren F. Kuehl, *Seeking World Order: The United States and International Organization to 1920* (Nashville, TN, 1969), ch. 13.

58. U.S. Senate, *Treaty of Peace with Germany, Hearing before the Committee on Foreign Relations, United States Senate*, 66th Congress, 1st Session (August 28, 1919): 679–98.

59. Ibid. Charles Sumner Williams, head of the International Association for the Freedom of Africans, also spoke about amending the treaty so as to protect the black American in the United States. Ibid., 696–98. On Trotter's admirable presentation, see John Milholland of the NAACP board to Moorfield Storey, August 29, 1919, NAACP Papers, pt. 16A, reel 1.

60. *The Crisis* (May 1919): 10–11. For a critical assessment of the League, see Chandler Owen's piece in *The Messenger* (May–June 1919): 14–17.

61. *The Crisis* (May 1919): 14.

62. "Report of the Director of Publications and Research and Editor of *The Crisis* for the Year 1919," 7, Du Bois Papers, reel 9.

63. To follow the NAACP's rapid growth, see the following issues of *The Crisis*: (August 1918): 172–74; (October 1918): 274; (January 1919): 122; (April 1919): 284–85; and (August 1919): 190. See also the Minutes of the Board of Directors, September 8 and November 10, 1919. NAACP Papers, pt. 1, reel 1. See also Charles Flint Kellogg, *NAACP: A History of the National Association for the Advancement of Colored People, 1909–1920* (Baltimore, 1967), 135–37.

64. *The Crisis* (July 1919): 127.

65. Alain Locke, ed., *The New Negro: Voices of the Harlem Renaissance* (New York, 1992; orig., 1925), 3.

66. Spingarn's June 27, 1921, letter to James Weldon Johnson is quoted in B. Joyce Ross, *J. E. Spingarn and the Rise of the NAACP, 1911–1939* (New York, 1972), 105. NAACP official Walter White expressed the flip side of this new spirit in a 1919 letter: "[T]he new spirit of bitterness and resentment against wrongs has permeated, to a larger extent than most of us realize, the masses of colored people." Quoted in Carl Stanley Matthews, "After Booker T. Washington: The Search for a New Negro Leadership, 1915–1925" (Ph.D. diss., University of Virginia, 1971), 185–86.

CHAPTER THREE

1. On the Women's International League for Peace and Freedom (WILPF), see Leila J. Rupp, *Worlds of Women: The Making of an International Women's Movement* (Princeton, NJ, 1997), 26–33. The WILPF was established just after the war; its immediate predecessor, the International Committee of Women for Permanent Peace, had been established at the Hague Conference in 1915.

2. James Weldon Johnson, *The Race Problem and Peace* (New York, 1924). The speech is from May 1924. In this speech, Johnson also declared that America had "played the same game" in Haiti. On Haiti, see note 5 in this chapter. On the postwar decade, Akira Iriye writes that the "ideology of peace" drove the quest for global cooperation at this time. Iriye, *The Globalizing of America, 1913–1945* (New York, 1993), esp. ch. 7. Iriye writes that during the 1920s, peace was "elevated to the position of a privileged concept" (104). Note an address Johnson gave on August 12, 1920, in which he set the black struggle against the backdrop of contemporary international developments. Johnson, "The Negro's Place in the New Civilization," NAACP Papers, Library of Congress, Washington, D.C., microfilm edition, pt. 11B, reel 35.

3. Beginning publication in 1923, *Opportunity* was edited by Charles S. Johnson, the league's director of research and investigation. A wide-ranging monthly that focused on research with which the league was involved, *Opportunity* also presented the cultural works of the Harlem Renaissance. See Nancy Weiss, *The National Urban League, 1910–1940* (New York, 1974), ch. 14; and Richard Robbins, *Sidelines Activist: Charles S. Johnson and the Struggle for Civil Rights* (Jackson, MS, 1996), ch. 3.

4. On the relationship between overseas travel and racial and ethnic identity, see Paul Gilroy, *The Black Atlantic: Modernity and Double Consciousness* (Cambridge, MA, 1993), ch. 1.

5. In 1920, five years after the 1915 occupation of Haiti by the U.S. Marines, the NAACP sent James Weldon Johnson there to investigate reports of American brutality on the island. He spent six weeks in Haiti and upon returning published reports in *The Crisis*, *The Nation*, and elsewhere. The reports were highly critical of American policy on the island and attributed the intervention and occupation to American imperialism, which Johnson contended was no different from that practiced by the Europeans. He asserted that the benefits Americans had brought to the island were minimal and were outweighed by the brutal character of the occupation and the injustice of American oppression. The "United States has

failed in Haiti . . . [and] should get out as . . . quickly as it can and restore to the Haitian people their independence and sovereignty." Black Americans, especially, should want to see this done, Johnson wrote. Johnson, "The Truth about Haiti," *The Crisis* (September 1920): 217–24. See also his autobiography, *Along This Way* (New York, 1933) 344–60; and his four articles, titled "Self-Determining Haiti" (note the Wilsonian language) that appeared in *The Nation* in August and September of 1920, *The Nation* 111 (1920): 236–38, 265–67, 295–97, 345–47. For Johnson's view of the Haitian situation, see his speech (undated, probably 1920) given in New York's Commodore Hotel, ibid. See also the NAACP's *Eleventh Annual Report* (New York, 1920), "The Haitian Investigation," 9–12. The NAACP's *Twelfth Annual Report* (New York, 1921) also demonstrates the association's continuing interest in Haitian matters (85–86), as does a resolution from the 1922 annual conference, which demanded that America restore self-rule to the island, NAACP Papers, pt. 1, reel 8.

Later in the decade, *The Crisis* published additional material on Haiti. See the article on Haitian leader Dantes Bellegarde in (April 1926): 295–96; and two pieces by Clement Wood, "The American Uplift in Haiti" (May and June 1928): 152–53, 189–91. Wood's phrase, "American uplift," was meant ironically. Du Bois spoke out against what he believed to be the injustice of the American occupation. See his December 21, 1929, remarks to the Foreign Policy Association, in which he asserted that if the United States did not withdraw from Haiti, it will be because it is "willing to do to Negroes what it would never consent to do to white people." Du Bois Papers, W.E.B. Du Bois Library, University of Massachusetts–Amherst, microfilm edition, reel 80. *The Messenger* also covered Haitian affairs. Note the descriptions of American oppression in "America's Corea [*sic*] and Ireland" (March 1922): 367–68; and "America's India" (June 1922): 418–19. As the preceding material demonstrates, the reformers believed that the exploitation of black peoples anywhere—in this case, at the hands of the American government—deserved close attention. It is worth emphasizing, moreover, that the Haitian situation was an early and unusual example of the race reformers' willingness to offer a forceful critique of American foreign policy. Secondary accounts include Mary Renda, *Taking Haiti: Military Occupation and the Culture of U.S. Imperialism, 1915–1940* (Chapel Hill, NC, 2001), 188–96; and Mark Robert Schneider, "*We Return Fighting": The Civil Rights Movement in the Jazz Age* (Boston, 2002), ch. 6.

6. See James Weldon Johnson to editors of the black press, October 21, 1921, NAACP Papers, pt. 11A, reel 18, which outlines the association's interest in the conference.

7. On the conference, see Iriye, *Globalizing of America*, 75–84; and Warren F. Kuehl and Lynne K. Dunn, *Keeping the Covenant: American Internationalists and the League of Nations, 1920–1939* (Kent, OH, 1997), esp. ch. 7.

8. Seligmann's nine articles, written in November and December 1921, entitled "The Armament Conference," can be found in NAACP Papers, pt. 11A, reel 18. The first Seligmann quotation comes from the first article; the final quotation from the last.

9. *The Crisis* (January 1922): 103–4. See also Du Bois's *Crisis* editorial written after the signing of the Locarno Pact, in which he wrote that real disarmament

would not be possible while the "white nations" continued to hold "yellow and black folk in chains." (March 1926): 215–16. Other examples in which *The Crisis* placed the peace ideology in a racial context include Jessie Fauset's "To the Pacifists" (December 1924): 56. Note an exchange of letters between Du Bois and a reader on disarmament, which Du Bois published in *The Crisis* (September 1927): 240. *The Messenger* also weighed in on disarmament, though without discussing the question of race. The magazine based its analysis on its antipathy for the great-power diplomacy of the capitalist states. See *The Messenger* (November 1921): 279–80; (December 1921): 298; (January 1922): 328–29; and (February 1922): 352–53. William Pickens linked the peace idea to the race question in "Armistice," a talk given on WEVD-radio (New York), November 11, 1927, William Pickens Papers, Schomburgh Center for Research in Black Culture, New York Public Library, New York, microfilm edition, reel 28; and "Exploitation and Peace," another WEVD radio talk, May 12, 1928, ibid. Note a 1925 essay in *Opportunity* that linked the 1920s "ideology of peace" to the elimination of racial oppression. "Race and World Peace," *Opportunity* (September 1925): 259–60.

10. *The Crisis* (March 1921): 199–200.

11. *The Crisis* (November 1923): 7. For another example illustrating how the editor linked the League to race reform, see ibid. (January 1927): 130–31. Note Mabel Byrd, "The League of Nations and the Negro Peoples," ibid. (July 1928): 223–24.

12. James Jackson to Du Bois, July 15, 1924, Du Bois Papers, reel 13.

13. Peter G. Filene, *Americans and the Soviet Experiment, 1917–1933* (Cambridge, MA, 1967), 3. See also Paul Hollander, *Political Pilgrims: Travels of Western Intellectuals to the Soviet Union, China, and Cuba, 1928–1978* (New York, 1981), esp. ch. 4, which considers the question of equality and social justice; and Christopher Lasch, *The American Liberals and the Russian Revolution* (New York, 1962).

14. *The Crisis* (April 1922): 247.

15. *The Crisis* (July 1921): 102–3.

16. *The Crisis* (October 1921): 246.

17. On McKay's visit to Russia and his complex relationship with the Communist Party, see Wayne F. Cooper, *Claude McKay: Rebel Sojourner in the Harlem Renaissance* (Baton Rouge, LA, 1987), ch. 6. Note McKay's evocative account of the trip in his memoir, *A Long Way from Home* (New York, 1937), chs. 14–19. See also McKay's letter to Leon Trotsky, written while he was in Moscow in 1922, in which the poet tells the Russian leader of the disillusionment of black soldiers whom he met in London after the war. McKay to Trotsky, February 20, 1922, in *The Marcus Garvey and Universal Negro Improvement Association Papers*, Robert A. Hill, ed. (Berkeley, CA, 1983–), 9:351 (hereafter cited as *Garvey Papers*).

18. *The Crisis* (January 1924): 114–18.

19. *The Crisis* (December 1923): 61–65.

20. "Travel," *The Crisis* (December 1926): 63–65.

21. The preceding impressions of Russia appeared in two issues of *The Crisis*: See "Russia" (November 1926): 8; and "Travel" (December 1926): 63–65. Note another Du Bois piece on Russia that appeared in *The Crisis* (February 1927): 189–90, which focused on the relationship between labor and capital in Bolshevik

Russia and on the Soviet system's prospect for success. See also Abram Harris's essay, "Lenin Casts His Shadow upon Africa," *The Crisis* (April 1926): 272–75, in which Harris, who would become a key figure in the debates of the 1930s, discusses Communism's attraction for black Americans.

22. Du Bois address, "No Race Prejudice in Russia," June 24, 1927, Du Bois Papers, reel 22.

23. *The Crisis* (December 1927): 348.

24. For the biographical material on Pickens, see Sheldon Avery, *Up from Washington: William Pickens and Negro Struggle for Equality, 1900–1954* (Newark, DE, 1989), chs. 1–3.

25. The NAACP announced Pickens's trip in an October 1926 press release, Pickens Papers, reel 17. For Pickens's discussion of the Brussels Conference, which was held in February 1927, see his speech at the Fourth Pan-African Congress, New York, August 21, 1927, Pickens Papers, reel 17. Note his "Interdependence of the Oppressed," Pickens Papers, reel 27. It is not clear where or whether this two-page speech was delivered; context suggests it was written shortly before the February conference. The statement linked African-American aspirations to those of oppressed peoples throughout the developing world. On his journey across Europe, see "London to Moscow," in which Pickens writes that it "is interesting to a black man to be in a territory where the white folks hate each other and not him." (Paper 7), Pickens Papers, reel 27.

26. Sheldon Bernard Avery, "Up from Washington: William Pickens and the Negro Struggle for Equality, 1900–1954" (Ph.D. diss., University of Oregon, 1970), 165–69. (I consulted Avery's dissertation and the book that he published in 1989, which is cited in note 24, above.)

27. Pickens's *Daily Worker* article of August 2, 1926, quoted in Avery dissertation (see note 26, above), 170. According to Pickens, the trip was not funded by the Soviets or by American Communists. The NAACP paid most of his expenses, with Moorfield Storey, English Quakers (for his speaking fees), and several black newspapers (through the Associated Negro Press) paying for the remainder of the European trip. Pickens, "My Journey to and from Russia in 1927," Pickens Papers, reel 27.

28. William Pickens, "Russia" (Paper 8), Pickens Papers, reel 27.

29. William Pickens, "My Journey to and from Russia," Pickens Papers, reel 27. Pickens quotes the woman in a January 7, 1927, document on the meeting with Trotsky, ibid., reel 4. This document also provides some detail on the interview with Trotsky, in which the Russian leader spoke about black-white relations in American civil rights organizations, noting that whites "will never do any good until they come in simply as equals and comrades together and not as superiors looking downward at the colored people." On the Trotsky meeting, see also "Russia" (Paper 10), ibid., reel 27.

30. Pickens, "Russia" (Paper 9), Pickens Papers, reel 27.

31. Pickens, "Russia" (Paper 11), ibid.

32. William Pickens, " 'Bolshevism' as Seen by Representative of Oppressed American Group," 3–5. Pickens Papers, reel 27.

33. Ibid., 1–2.

34. "Russia" (Paper 8), Pickens Papers, reel 27.

35. *The Messenger* (July 1918): 9.

36. On the invasion of the Soviet Union by foreign troops, see David S. Foglesong, *America's Secret War against Bolshevism: U.S. Intervention in the Russian Civil War, 1917–1920* (Chapel Hill, NC, 1995).

37. *The Messenger* (March 1919): 7–8.

38. *The Messenger* (September 1919): 26–27. In a similar vein, see Domingo, "Will Bolshevism Free America?" *The Messenger* (September 1920): 85–86.

39. See, for example, "Why Negroes Should Study about Russia," which explored the significance of Soviet developments for black Americans and suggested that similarities between the conditions of Slavs and black Americans might prove instructive in the African-American struggle. *The Messenger* (October 1920): 109–11. See also "Soviets Recognize No Color Line!" ibid. (March 1919): 20.

40. On the changes at *The Messenger,* see Theodore Kornweibel, *No Crystal Stair: Black Life and the Messenger, 1917–1928* (Westport, CT, 1975), 205. Other examples of *The Messenger*'s positive assessment of Russia include two pieces on the Russian famine that appeared in 1921. See *The Messenger* (September 1921): 243; and (October 1921): 258.

41. *The Messenger* (May–June 1919): 8. The magazine was highly critical of America's unwillingness to recognize Russia. In an April 1923 editorial, which advocated immediate recognition, the editors asserted that the refusal to establish diplomatic relations was a consequence of a capitalist fear that oppressed workers throughout the world might interpret recognition as countenancing revolution (656–57).

42. Although Soviet matters fascinated certain race activists, Communism per se did not prove attractive to more than a handful of black Americans during the 1920s. By decade's end, black membership in the Communist Party stood between 150 and 200 (out of a total membership of approximately 10,000) and the Party, realizing its appeal for black participation had failed, would shortly adopt a new strategy ("Self-Determination in the Black Belt") to woo black members. See Wilson Record's two strongly anti-Communist works, *The Negro and the Communist Party* (New York, 1971; orig., 1951); and *Race and Radicalism: The NAACP and the Communist Party in Conflict* (Ithaca, NY, 1964). This new approach asserted that American blacks had the right to self-determination and, as a distinctive racial and cultural group, constituted a separate nation. See also Mark Solomon, *The Cry Was Unity: Communists and African Americans, 1917–1936* (Jackson, MS, 1998), chs. 1–5; Mark Naison, *Communists in Harlem during the Depression* (New York, 1983); and Philip Foner and James S. Allen, eds., *American Communism and Black Americans: A Documentary History, 1919–1929* (Philadelphia, 1987).

43. Kelly Miller expressed views on Bolshevism more cautious than those examined here. But even Miller found aspects of life in the new Russia germane to those interested in the American race question. See "Common Cause of Aggrieved Groups," in Kelly Miller, *The Everlasting Stain* (New York, 1968; orig., 1924), 21–24.

44. John B. Kirby, *Black Americans in the Roosevelt Era: Liberalism and Race* (Knoxville, TN, 1980), 6.

45. Figures from Theodore Kornweibel, "An Economic Profile of Black Life in the Twenties," *Journal of Black Studies* 6 (June 1976): 307–20; and Harvard Sitkoff, *A New Deal for Blacks: The Emergence of Civil Rights as a National Issue: The Depression Decade* (New York, 1978), 30–31. While the significance of the migration cannot be gainsaid, blacks found the North to be less than a land of milk and honey. If they escaped the tenantry and terror that marked rural life in the South, northern blacks encountered bigotry, substandard housing, and obstacles in employment and labor unions. But tangible benefits characterized northern black life, and owing partly to the migration, the black death rate dropped significantly during the 1920s, infant mortality declined by half, life expectancy rose dramatically, illiteracy declined, and school attendance and college enrollment rose. And northern blacks could vote: in 1928, the first black American in the twentieth century was elected to Congress. See Sitkoff, *New Deal for Blacks*, 31.

46. On the Harlem Renaissance, see Nathan Huggins, *Harlem Renaissance* (New York, 1971); and David Levering Lewis, *When Harlem Was in Vogue* (New York, 1981). The classic primary text of the movement is Alain Locke, ed., *The New Negro: Voices of the Harlem Renaissance* (New York, 1992; orig., 1925), which includes James Weldon Johnson's quotations on Harlem, 301–11. The Rampersad quotation is from the introduction to the 1992 edition (xxii–xxiii).

47. On the battle for federal anti-lynching legislation (which never passed), see Robert L. Zangrando, *The NAACP Crusade against Lynching, 1909–1950* (Philadelphia, 1980). From 1919 to 1929, the number of blacks lynched declined from seventy-six in 1919 to seven in 1929. According to Zangrando, the decline in the number of lynchings in these years was, in part, a consequence of the NAACP's efforts, which, along with economic, cultural, and political factors, reduced the southern propensity for mob violence (5–11). On the NAACP in the 1920s, B. Joyce Ross considers the transition from organizational to institutional status and the diminished influence of white liberals within the organization. Ross, *J. E. Spingarn and the Rise of the NAACP, 1911–1939* (New York, 1972), ch. 4.

48. On *Moore v. Dempsey*, see Schneider, *"We Return Fighting,"* ch. 14. On the Sweet case, see ibid., ch. 20; Kevin Boyle, *Arc of Justice: A Saga of Race, Civil Rights, and Murder in the Jazz Age* (New York, 2004); and Eugene Levy, *James Weldon Johnson: Black Leader, Black Voice* (Chicago, 1973), 282–84. See also James Weldon Johnson's story in *The Crisis* (July 1926): 117–20. Note Du Bois's appeal to the Russian people for financial support in the Sweet case. That Du Bois believed his appeal would receive a sensitive hearing in Russia says a good deal about his perception of racial attitudes there. Du Bois to *Pravda*, January 15, 1926, Du Bois Papers, reel 19. In 1927, in *Nixon v. Herndon*, the Supreme Court struck down a Texas statute that excluded blacks from voting in the state's Democratic primary. See Levy, *James Weldon Johnson*, 286–87.

49. See Sudarshan Kapur, *Raising Up a Prophet: The African-American Encounter with Gandhi* (Boston, 1992), chs. 1–2. On a 1929 questionnaire, Du Bois placed Gandhi first on his list of the people who "wield the most influence for world peace." Questionnaire dated November 27, 1929, Du Bois Papers, reel 29.

50. Du Bois frequently suggested a sympathy between black Americans and Indians. See his literary recommendation, which advised blacks to read Savel Zimand's "Living India" because the author "has had wide experience in the prob-

lems of oppressed peoples." *The Crisis* (May 1929): 161, 175. Note Du Bois's letter to the editor of an Indian publication, *The People*, on the death of Lajpat Rai, the Indian nationalist, in which Du Bois observed that "the people of India, like the American Negroes, are demanding today things . . . which every civilized white man has so long taken for granted." January 10, 1929, Du Bois Papers, reel 29. Correspondence between Indians and Du Bois also suggests his belief in the interconnectedness between the respective struggles. See letters to Du Bois from the following: B. Chaturvedi, November 9, 1924, Du Bois Papers, reel 13; Abdur Raoof Malik, undated, but 1927, ibid., reel 22; and Shripad Tikekar, December 23, 1927, ibid., reel 23.

51. Such interest on Du Bois's part predated the 1920s and reached back some two decades to his classic declaration in *The Souls of Black Folk* (New York, 1984; orig., 1903) that "the problem of the Twentieth Century is the problem of the color-line" (13). I am suggesting here that in the 1920s Du Bois began to bring Indian affairs to the attention of large numbers of people committed to race reform, mainly in *The Crisis*. An early example in which Du Bois discusses western oppression in the developing world, including India, is "The Color Line Belts the World," *Collier's Weekly*, October 20, 1906, 30.

52. Du Bois, "To the People of India," October 15, 1925, Du Bois Papers, reel 15. The editor, Benarsidas Chaturvedi, had written to Du Bois exactly one month earlier, ibid.

53. *The Crisis* (August 1921): 170. The open letter was originally published in *Young India*, which Gandhi edited. See also "India's Saint," which considered Gandhi's earlier methods of nonviolence in South Africa. *The Crisis* (July 1921): 124–25; "The Woes of India," ibid. (May 1921): 27; and an untitled piece, ibid. (October 1921): 270–72.

54. *The Crisis* (March 1922): 203–7. In August 1922, *The Crisis* published a poem, "Gandhi," which portrayed a similarly heroic figure and compared the Indian leader to Jesus Christ (177).

55. *The Crisis* (March 1924): 213–14.

56. *The Crisis* (June 1924): 58–59.

57. Du Bois to Mahatma Gandhi, February 19, 1929, Du Bois Papers, reel 29. Gandhi to Du Bois, May 1, 1929, ibid. *The Crisis* (July 1929): 225. Du Bois published another "Message to the American Negro," from the distinguished Indian writer, Rabindranath Tagore, who had won the Nobel Prize for Literature in 1913. *The Crisis* (October 1929): 333–34. In February, Du Bois had sought a message from Tagore, writing that he wanted "the Negroes in this land to hear directly from a great leader of the Indian people." Du Bois to Tagore, February 19, 1929, Du Bois Papers, reel 30. Tagore responded to Du Bois, sending his message to the editor on July 12, 1929. See A. C. Chakravarty to Du Bois, July 12, 1929, ibid. At the conclusion of Tagore's hopeful message, Du Bois told *Crisis* readers about the universality of the Indian's philosophy: "We are all of us black, red, white or yellow."

58. *The Messenger* (July 1919): 6–7.

59. *The Messenger* (April 1922): 394–95. On nonviolent resistance, see ibid. (May 1922): 405–6. On Gandhi's arrest, see ibid. (March 1922): 368–69. *Oppor-*

tunity also considered the Indian campaign. *Opportunity* (February 1925): 40–42.

60. John Hope Franklin, *From Slavery to Freedom: A History of African Americans*, 7th ed. (New York, 1994), 356–59. On Garvey, see Edmund David Cronon, *Black Moses: The Story of Marcus Garvey and the Universal Negro Improvement Association* (Madison, WI, 1955). For an incisive study, see Judith Stein, *The World of Marcus Garvey: Race and Class in Modern Society* (Baton Rouge, LA, 1986). For contemporary discussion of Garvey and Garveyism, see William Pickens, "Africa for the Africans: The Garvey Movement," *The Nation*, December 28, 1921, 750–51; E. Franklin Frazier, "Garvey a Mass Leader," ibid., August 18, 1926, 147–48; and Charles S. Johnson, "After Garvey: What?" *Opportunity* (September 1924): 284–85. For Du Bois's view, see the following *Crisis* pieces: (December 1920): 58–60; (January 1921): 112–15; and (September 1922): 210–14.

61. Kapur, *Raising Up a Prophet*, 16–17.

62. Garvey to Mahatma Gandhi, August 1, 1921, in *Garvey Papers*, 3:587; Garvey to Gandhi, August 3, 1924, ibid., 5:645. Other examples of Garvey speeches include January 8, 1922, *Garvey Papers*, 4:332–34; and January 4, 1925, ibid., 6:74–76.

63. Speech by Garvey, March 12, 1922, *Garvey Papers*, 4:567–68.

64. Kapur links developments in these years to later events, observing that the discussion of Gandhian principles during this period "helped to establish a viable basis for the successful adoption" of nonviolent methods later. See Kapur, *Raising Up a Prophet*, 4.

65. "The Transvaal," *Opportunity* (December 1928): 360.

66. *Opportunity* (January 1924): 6–9. Locke's essay provoked a response from René Maran, assistant editor of *Les Continents*, which was published there on June 15. *Opportunity* published Maran's letter (and Locke's response) in its September 1924 issue, 261–63. Maran, a black man, rejected Locke's assessment of race relations in France, asserting that the American had been deceived. Locke responded to Maran, noting that his objective was not to evaluate French policy in Africa, but to contrast, through observation and experience, the treatment of men of color in the French army with the treatment of African-American soldiers. Note a similar *Opportunity* piece by Maran, "Harriet Beecher Stowe of France," (August 1925): 229–31. In 1929, *Opportunity* looked at the relationship between America and Europe, or what it described as the "Americanization of Europe." Apparently, America had exported a number of things to the Old World, including machinery, mass production, and race prejudice. France, the magazine claimed, was historically untainted by racial and religious intolerance and was an unlucky recipient of American prejudice, which American tourists brought to its shores after the war. *Opportunity* (September 1929): 271.

67. In applying the term "Leninist" to *The Messenger*'s worldview, I have relied on Eric Hobsbawm's discussion of imperialism in *The Age of Empire, 1875–1914* (New York, 1987). According to Hobsbawm, Leninist analysis (as set out in Lenin's 1917 work, *Imperialism, the Highest Stage of Capitalism*) was based on the idea that "imperialism had economic roots in a . . . new phase of capitalism, which, among other things led to the territorial division of the world among the

great capitalist powers." Hobsbawm notes that such analysis posited that the "exploitation of the overseas world [was] crucial for capitalist countries" (60–61).

68. One must also consider *Messenger* articles that claimed racial categories were relatively less important than class categories for analyzing world affairs. See "Africa for the Africans," in which the editors write that "oppression is not racial; and that no particular race has absolutely clean hands." *The Messenger* (September 1920): 83–84. For the magazine's analysis of imperialism, see "Economic Value of the Philippines," which argued that America retained the islands strictly for economic reasons. *The Messenger* (May 1926): 137–38. For an illustration of the magazine's view of world politics, see "Three Schools of International Thought" (December 1920): 169–70.

69. *The Messenger* (December 1927): 353.

70. See the following 1927 articles, which also incorporate racial imagery into their commentary on Chinese affairs. *The Messenger* (March): 82; and (June): 207. In covering Africa, *The Messenger* regularly grafted a muscular anti-imperialism onto a well-developed sense of color-consciousness. See "Political Storms in Africa," a piece that described Britain's imperial "exploitation" and "hypocrisy," while employing the language of racial assertiveness. *The Messenger* (August 1925): 294, 306. Other examples in *The Messenger* that suggest the significance of race in the struggle against imperialism include "Revolt in South Africa" (March 1922): 369–71; "Look Out! England Is Up to Her Old Tricks Again!" (October 1922): 504–5; and "Black Trade Unionism in Africa" (November 1924): 348–49.

71. *The Messenger* (January 1926): 12. For another Rogers piece, see "The Negro's Reception in Europe," which appeared in *The Messenger* (November 1927): 320. Here he noted that the black man received different treatment in Europe than in Europe's colonies or in America. See also "Americanism in France," ibid. (September 1922): 477.

72. *The Messenger* (January 1927): 15, 26.

73. To get a sense of the scope of its international coverage, one can look at Du Bois's "Wide World" column in *The Crisis* (which later became "As the Crow Flies"), in which the editor provided his readers with a *tour d'horizon* of that month's international events. On the magazine's first page, one could read brief descriptions of events in Africa, Europe, Asia, and the western hemisphere. Imperialism, racial oppression, and the progress of international socialism were frequent themes. Another feature, "Along the Color Line," often considered African developments.

74. See Cullen's work in the 1929 *Crisis*: (April): 119; (June): 193; (August): 270; and (November): 273. It is clear that he moved comfortably in a variety of European worlds.

75. *The Crisis* (August 1926): 191–92.

76. Du Bois also wrote luminously on Africa in his 1920 book, *Darkwater: Voices from within the Veil*. See the Dover reprint (Mineola, NY, 1999), ch. 2. Sounding a frequent theme, he discussed Europe's exploitation of Africa's peoples of color. Chapter 2 ("The Souls of White Folk") presents a sweeping discussion of global developments, emphasizing World War I.

77. On the three congresses held during the 1920s (in 1921, 1923, and 1927) and their ultimate significance, see Imanuel Geiss, *The Pan-African Movement: A History of Pan-Africanism in America, Europe, and Africa* (New York, 1974), esp. ch. 12. Geiss considers Du Bois's shortcomings in directing the movement, suggesting that his romantic tendencies impeded his capacity to realize the lasting achievements he might otherwise have accomplished.

78. For a superb expression of Du Bois's belief that racial oppression could only be understood in a global context, see his essay, "The Negro Mind Reaches Out," which returned to evaluate his earlier declaration that "the problem of the twentieth century is the problem of the color line." Du Bois concluded the 1924 essay, which was published in Alain Locke's *New Negro* and in the quarterly *Foreign Affairs* (a forum for internationalist thought), with a restatement of the same idea. With respect to the notion of community (an element of color-conscious internationalism), the following assertion is telling: "Led by American Negroes, the Negroes of the world are reaching out hands toward each other to know, to sympathize, to inquire." Du Bois wrote of a "great human force" of peoples of color that extended to "all lands and languages." Locke, *The New Negro*, 412–13. Note also Robert T. Kerlin's piece in *World Outlook*, which Du Bois reprinted in *The Crisis* (January 1928): 21. Kerlin writes that the "enlightened American Negro is identifying his interests with the interests of all the peoples of African descent. . . . [H]is horizon encompasses the five continents and seven seas."

79. *The Crisis* (December 1923): 57–58. Despite four congresses (including the 1919 gathering) and a continuing interest in the idea by peoples throughout the world, there was no central unifying belief that could hold the movement together. As Imanuel Geiss has written, the movement lacked a "common denominator" that might unite its disparate peoples. Geiss, *The Pan-African Movement*, 258.

80. *The Crisis* (March 1924): 203–5. On the trip to Africa, see David Levering Lewis, *W.E.B. Du Bois: The Fight for Equality and the American Century, 1919–1963* (New York, 2000), 118–28.

81. *The Crisis* (April 1924): 247–51. Du Bois explained the circumstances leading up to his mission, describing how the U.S. Senate blocked an American loan previously promised to Liberia. As a "gesture of courtesy," the U.S. government sent him to Liberia on the occasion of the inauguration of the Liberian president; his mission was to convey from America "a word of encouragement and moral support." Throughout the decade, *The Crisis* covered African developments, typically focusing on Europe's exploitation of the continent and African efforts to free itself from European oppression. "Revolution in South Africa" (March 1926): 246–48, assessed the black struggle against white rule. Note that Du Bois published excerpts from the Brussels Conference against Colonial Oppression and Imperialism in (July 1927): 165–66.

CHAPTER FOUR

1. Du Bois to Gandhi, August 19 and October 30, 1931, Du Bois Papers, W.E.B. Du Bois Library, University of Massachusetts–Amherst, microfilm edition,

reel 36. Apparently, Gandhi did not respond to either letter. Du Bois penned similar requests to Liberian President Barclay and to Ethiopia's Haile Selassie.

2. *The Crisis* (April 1930): 113. Du Bois also described Gandhi as the world's only "living maker of miracles." Ibid. (November 1932): 342. The same issue contained a large photo of Gandhi with a short piece, "Satyagraha," on his hunger strike (351).

3. *The Crisis* (July 1930): 246. Note also the following *Crisis* pieces: (August 1930): 281; and (January 1931): 29.

4. Du Bois, "Europe in India," *Amsterdam News*, October 14, 1931. That same month, two other Du Bois columns explored the Indian situation. See ibid., October 7 and 28, 1931. Note Du Bois's "The Clash of Colour," *The Aryan Path* (March 1936).

5. William Pickens, "Incarcerating the Spirit of Liberty," address given at Temple Beth-El, January 12, 1932, William Pickens Papers, Schomburg Center for Research in Black Culture, New York Public Library, New York, microfilm edition, reel 28; Pickens, "United Front Against Prejudices," address given at Carnegie Hall, November 12, 1933, ibid. Pickens's pieces on India include "Gandhi and 'Jimmie,' " September 16, 1931, ibid.; and "Gandhi-ism and Prayer," *Amsterdam News*, February 10, 1932.

6. Sudarshan Kapur, *Raising Up a Prophet: The African-American Encounter with Gandhi* (Boston, 1992), ch. 3. On the experiences of others whose meetings with Gandhi influenced their understanding of the relationship between both struggles, see ch. 4.

7. Kelly Miller, "Passive Resistance of Gandhi," *Amsterdam News*, April 2, 1930.

8. See Raymond Sontag, *A Broken World, 1919–1939* (New York, 1971), 287–91.

9. George Schuyler, *Pittsburgh Courier*, November 23, 1935. On black America's response to events in Ethiopia, see William R. Scott, *The Sons of Sheba's Race: African-Americans and the Italo-Ethiopian War, 1935–1941* (Bloomington, IN, 1993); Joseph E. Harris, *African-American Reactions to War in Ethiopia, 1936–1941* (Baton Rouge, LA, 1994); and James A. Meriwether, *Proudly We Can Be Africans: Black Americans and Africa, 1935–1961* (Chapel Hill, NC, 2002), ch. 1. Ethiopian matters received an enormous amount of coverage in the black press during this period. My reading included the *Norfolk Journal and Guide*, *The New York Age*, the *Chicago Defender*, the *Amsterdam News*, and the *Pittsburgh Courier*. Robert L. Vann of the *Pittsburgh Courier* sent J. A. Rogers to the front to cover the story, making it the only black paper to have a correspondent there. See Andrew Buni, *Robert L. Vann of the "Pittsburgh Courier": Politics and Black Journalism* (Pittsburgh, 1974), 244–48.

10. On White's background, see his autobiography, *A Man Called White* (Athens, GA, 1995; orig., 1948); and Kenneth Robert Janken's first-rate study, *White: The Biography of Walter White, Mr. NAACP* (New York, 2003).

11. White to Hull, March 20, 1935, NAACP Papers, Library of Congress, Washington, D.C., microfilm edition, pt. 11A, reel 30; White to Hull, April 11, 1935, ibid. White to Selassie, May 23, 1935, ibid. The association also cabled its views on Ethiopia to the League of Nations Council. Ibid.

12. Resolutions of the Twenty-sixth Annual Conference, June 1935, NAACP Papers, pt. 1, reel 9. Note the memorandum from White to the NAACP's board, which sought a meeting with the president and the secretary of state, as well as a statement from the U.S. government opposing Italian policies in Ethiopia. July 8, 1935, NAACP Papers, pt. 11A, reel 30.

13. Makonnen Haile, "Last Gobble of Africa," *The Crisis* (March 1935): 70–71; George Padmore, "The Missionary Racket in Africa," ibid. (July 1935): 198–214; "Ethiopia Thrown to the Wolves?" ibid. (February 1935): 48; and Reuben S. Young, "Ethiopia Awakens," ibid. (September 1935): 262–63.

14. Du Bois, "Inter-racial Implications of the Ethiopian Crisis: A Negro View," *Foreign Affairs* (October 1935): 82–92.

15. Charles H. Wesley, "The Significance of the Italo-Abyssinian Question," *Opportunity* (May 1935): 148–51; and Wesley, "And Ethiopia Shall Stretch Forth Her Arms," ibid. (August 1935): 230.

16. *Opportunity* (September 1935): 276.

17. *Pittsburgh Courier*, October 12, 1935; *Chicago Defender*, October 26, 1935.

18. "An Appeal from Haile Selassie," *Pittsburgh Courier*, October 19, 1935; William Pickens, "Hot Air versus Airplanes" (undated article written shortly after the Italian invasion), Pickens Papers, reel 28.

19. See J. A. Rogers, *Pittsburgh Courier*, May 9, 1936.

20. "War Clouds Gather," *Opportunity* (September 1935): 263.

21. "At Geneva," *Opportunity* (July 1936): 197. David H. Bradford, "The Failure at Geneva," *The Crisis* (September 1936): 270–71. See also "The Failure of the League of Nations," *Opportunity* (May 1936): 133; Charles H. Wesley, "The Significance of the Italo-Ethiopian Question," ibid. (May 1935): 148–51; "Sad Spectacle," *The Crisis* (September 1935): 273; Dorothy Detzer, "Ethiopia at Geneva," ibid. (December 1935): 361; "Not a Pretty Picture," ibid. (August 1936): 241; and George Padmore, "Abyssinia Betrayed by the League of Nations," ibid. (June 1937): 166–68. Note William Pickens's letter, "What Is an Aggressor Nation?" *Norfolk Journal and Guide*, October 12, 1935.

22. *Opportunity* (January 1936): 19–21.

23. "Civilization Is Taken to Ethiopia," *The Crisis* (November 1935): 337.

24. Marthe Beaudry, "A Modern King Arthur," *The Crisis* (February 1936): 54.

25. Quoted in Scott, *Sons of Sheba's Race*, 131.

26. Only Italy had the resources and means to buy and ship arms from the United States; thus, an impartial ban would have adversely affected Italy and would not have harmed the Ethiopians. In late 1935 and early 1936, the NAACP supported the successful effort to defeat a congressional amendment that would have watered down the legislation and benefited Italy. See Robert Dallek, *Franklin D. Roosevelt and American Foreign Policy, 1932–1945* (New York, 1979), ch. 5.

27. For a detailed discussion of the NAACP's actions during the debate and during these months generally, see Scott, *Sons of Sheba's Race*, 132–35.

28. White's address at Madison Square Garden, September 25, 1935, NAACP Papers, pt. 11B, reel 36; *Pittsburgh Courier* editorial reprinted in *The Crisis* (October 1936): 307. After Ethiopia's defeat, Du Bois wrote in the *Courier* of the "inevi-

table program" of the world's people of color, who were struggling for freedom and autonomy, May 2, 1936.

29. In areas that provided relief, blacks received smaller payments each month than did whites, and white charities and soup kitchens often denied aid or food to black southerners. See Harvard Sitkoff, *A New Deal for Blacks: The Emergence of Civil Rights as a National Issue: The Depression Decade* (New York, 1978), 35–37.

30. Ibid., 37.

31. Ibid., 38.

32. Relief in Philadelphia was inadequate to sustain a sufficient diet, and Detroit, before running out of funds, paid out fifteen cents per day per individual. Sitkoff, *New Deal for Blacks*, 38–39.

33. The literature on the New Deal is vast. See David M. Kennedy, *Freedom from Fear: The American People in Peace and War, 1929–1945* (New York, 1999), chs. 4–12; and Alan Brinkley, *The End of Reform: New Deal Liberalism in Recession and War* (New York, 1995). An excellent one-volume treatment is William Leuchtenburg, *Franklin Roosevelt and the New Deal* (New York, 1963).

34. Agencies like the Farm Security Administration and the National Youth Administration furnished assistance and employment opportunities, and the Public Works Administration and Works Progress Administration were also helpful. Though the agencies' records in assisting blacks was mixed (discrimination marred the provision of aid, especially in the South), blacks benefited from such programs. See Patricia Sullivan, *Days of Hope: Race and Democracy in the New Deal Era* (Chapel Hill, NC, 1996), chs. 2–3.

35. According to John Kirby, blacks "identified New Deal concern for minorities with . . . Eleanor Roosevelt." Kirby, *Black Americans in the Roosevelt Era: Liberalism and Race* (Knoxville, TN, 1980), 76. See also ch. 4. Carol Anderson offers a less charitable view of Mrs. Roosevelt, calling her a master of "symbolic equality." Anderson, *Eyes off the Prize: The United Nations and the African American Struggle for Human Rights, 1944–1955* (New York, 2003), 3.

36. Beyond such actions, the First Lady's public statements demonstrated concern for the race question. See Kirby, *Black Americans in the Roosevelt Era*, ch. 4; and Nancy J. Weiss, *Farewell to the Party of Lincoln: Black Politics in the Age of FDR* (Princeton, NJ, 1983), ch. 6. Another indication of the heightened importance of racial matters during the Roosevelt years was the emergence of the "Black Cabinet," an unofficial group of professional blacks that exerted influence indirectly. The increasing importance of this group of talented and well-educated blacks suggests that African Americans were gaining a voice in government during the Roosevelt years, and it indicates a willingness on the administration's part to consider black concerns. See Weiss, *Farewell*, ch. 7.

37. While the electoral results are incontrovertible, explanations for the shift are not. Harvard Sitkoff writes that civil rights issues, rather than strictly economic concerns, were of primary importance to blacks. Sitkoff, *New Deal for Blacks*, 96–97. Nancy Weiss claims that economic concerns were the key reason blacks voted for FDR. Weiss, *Farewell*, xiv.

38. "The Fascisti in America," *The Messenger* (June 1923): 733. Note a second piece there (August 1923): 781.

39. *The Messenger* (October 1923): 832; ibid. (December 1923): 919. For additional *Messenger* stories on fascism in 1923, see (September): 806; and (November): 861.

40. White, "Nazism and the Negro," radio address (WMCA New York), September 21, 1936, NAACP Papers, pt. 11B, reel 36.

41. Pickens to Thyra J. Edwards, November 22, 1933, Pickens Papers, reel 10.

42. On the Kalisch family, see Pickens to Joseph Hyman, May 3, 1935, Pickens Papers, reel 12. Note the letters between Pickens and Hans Albrecht of Hamburg: Albrecht to Pickens, August 28, 1938; Pickens to Albrecht, September 14 and November 22, 1938, ibid., reel 12. The "General Correspondence" file (for the 1930s) in the Pickens Papers contains many letters on the refugee problem, in which people request help from Pickens, who seemed concerned about the plight of German Jews and progressive activists.

43. In a 1933 letter to Du Bois, Pickens noted the connection between the two groups. Pickens to Du Bois, July 25, 1933, Du Bois Papers, reel 39.

44. Pickens, "Hitlerism's Challenge to Human Brotherhood," September 16, 1934, Pickens Papers, reel 27.

45. Pickens wrote in a similar vein in 1939. In "Why the Negro Must Be Anti-Fascist," he compared the plight of German Jews to that of black Americans and claimed Hitlerism was "at least as much anti-Negro as it is anti-Jewish." *New Masses*, May 30, 1939, 29–30.

46. White's address at the NAACP's annual meeting, January 5, 1936, NAACP Papers, pt. 1, reel 14. See also his address at the NAACP's annual conference on July 5, 1936, ibid., pt. 1, reel 9.

47. White's statement to the *Amsterdam News*, November 15, 1938, NAACP Papers, pt. 11A, reel 1.

48. White, "The Nazi Terror: My Reaction," November 27, 1938, NAACP Papers, pt. 11A, reel 1.

49. For biographical details on Wilkins, see *Standing Fast: The Autobiography of Roy Wilkins* (New York, 1982).

50. *Amsterdam News*, September 4, 1937; ibid., February 5, 1938. See ibid., March 13, 1937, and June 24, 1939.

51. Wise's address was published in *The Crisis* under the heading, "Parallel between Hitlerism and the Persecution of Negroes in America" (May 1934): 127–29. *The Crisis* presented a piece on black-Jewish fraternity, a two-part essay by Jacob Weinstein published in mid-1934. Treating the subject historically and sociologically, Weinstein considered the shared experience of both groups, observing that they were beginning to recognize this convergence, which could be a "healthy omen" because it could lead to more effective means of combating prejudice in America. Weinstein, "The Jew and the Negro," *The Crisis* (June 1934): 178–79; "The Negro and the Jew," ibid. (July 1934): 197–98. See Mary van Kleeck's "Racial Conflict and Economic Competition: Some Observations on Hitlerism," ibid. (February 1934): 45–46, which explores Hitlerism from an economic rather than a racial perspective. Writing to Du Bois, Walter White called it "the ablest analysis" of Hitlerism he had ever heard, "especially in its relation to the Negro in the United States." White to Du Bois, October 17, 1933, Du Bois Papers, reel 41. The editorial page of *The Crisis* also linked the mistreatment of German Jews to the

racial oppression of black Americans. See, for example, a 1938 editorial that contended that black Americans sympathized more fully with German Jews than did any other group because "they have known the same type of persecution ever since the beginning of America." *The Crisis* (December 1938): 393. See also "Refugees and Citizens," ibid. (September 1938): 301.

52. As early as 1933, one sees NAACP leaders using the annual conference to comment on German developments. In June, Walter White asked Du Bois, who was drafting the resolutions for the annual conference, to include a "strong statement" opposing Hitler's discriminatory legislation toward minorities (Jews and blacks, specifically) in Germany. Under the subheading "The Hitler Government," the following statement appeared: "We denounce the vicious campaign of race prejudice directed against Jews and Negroes by the Hitler Government." White to Du Bois, June 9, 1933, Du Bois Papers, reel 40; "Memorandum to the Resolutions Committee" for the Twenty-fourth Annual Conference, June–July 1933, NAACP Papers, pt. 1, reel 9.

53. Spingarn, "The Second Quarter-Century of the NAACP," an address, June 25, 1935, NAACP Papers, pt. 1, reel 9. See also Spingarn's speech, February 23, 1938, NAACP Papers, pt. 11B, reel 35. In addition to the association's leaders, at the annual conferences others spoke about fascism. See Ralph Bunche, July 2, 1936, NAACP Papers, pt. 1, reel 9; Dr. Elmer Arndt, June 27, 1935, ibid.; Panel at the Twenty-seventh Annual Conference, July 2, 1936, ibid.; and Rabbi Edward Israel, July 2, 1936, ibid. Other race activists also deployed the fascist threat to advance the cause. *Opportunity* frequently compared the plight of Jews and blacks, and German and American racial practices. See the following sampling: an unsigned column (June 1936): 165; Joseph Roucek, "The Forgotten Man in Europe and America" (March 1933): 73–74; and Kelly Miller, "Race Prejudice in Germany and America" (April 1936): 102–5.

54. In this period, the *Courier*'s national circulation peaked at about a quarter of a million readers and then settled at a steady 149,000, making it the country's number-one black weekly. Figures from Andrew Buni, *Robert L. Vann of the "Pittsburgh Courier,"* 257.

55. Boas to Du Bois, April 22, 1936, Du Bois Papers, reel 45; Du Bois to Boas, May 5, 1936, ibid. In a May 11 letter to Du Bois, Boas worried that German officials might show him "Potemkin Villages" and pointed out that the German population was so terrorized that candor was impossible. ibid. A New Jersey man who wrote to Du Bois was amused by the proposed trip and wondered what possible benefit it could provide. Du Bois responded tartly, claiming he saw nothing amusing about "the search for truth" and noted that "sixty-three million people are always worth studying." Victor Lindeman to Du Bois, March 26, 1936, Du Bois Papers, reel 46; Du Bois to Lindeman, March 31, 1936, ibid.

56. Du Bois, *Pittsburgh Courier*, September 26, 1936.

57. Ibid., December 5, 1936.

58. Ibid., December 12, 1936.

59. Ibid., December 19, 1936.

60. Ibid., January 9, 1937. For other columns in the *Courier* on the German trip, see the following: October 17 and 24; and December 26, 1936; and January 2, 1937. After his return, Roy Wilkins criticized a lecture Du Bois had given about

the trip. Wilkins commented on Du Bois's remarks on Hitler's Germany, "the most amazing of which was that there is today, in some respects, more democracy in Germany than there has been in years past." Wilkins wondered if this was another of the race leader's "dry" jokes. *Amsterdam News*, January 30, 1937. See Du Bois's letter to Leo Stein of the American Jewish Committee in response to Stein's concern about an interview Du Bois had given on conditions in Germany. Du Bois claimed it was difficult to make a "direct comparison" between the plight of Jews and blacks because the Nazis had changed German law, thus making their racial policies legal, while American racial persecution directed at blacks was clearly illegal. In theory, Du Bois acknowledged, the Nazi attitude toward blacks was "just as bad as toward Jews," and if more blacks resided in Germany, this attitude "would be expressed in the same way." Du Bois to Stein, March 10, 1937, Du Bois Papers, reel 46. On the trip to Germany, see David Levering Lewis, *W.E.B. Du Bois: The Fight for Equality and the American Century, 1919–1963* (New York, 2000), 395–405.

61. Wilkins, *Standing Fast*, 163–64. See Walter White's letter to Owens, in which he expresses regret upon hearing that Owens had decided to participate in the Games. December 4, 1935, NAACP Papers, pt. 11B, reel 17.

62. *The Crisis* (September 1936): 273.

63. *Pittsburgh Courier*, October 24, 1936. (Du Bois was in France during the 1936 Olympics, though his column on the event did not appear until October.) Ibid., August 22, 1936.

64. On the war, see Sontag, *A Broken World*, 299–304.

65. Danny Duncan Collum, ed., *African Americans in the Spanish Civil War: "This Ain't Ethiopia But It'll Do"* (New York, 1992), 191. Note Robin D. G. Kelley's luminous introduction, which places the black volunteers' story in the context of 1930s black left-wing politics, 5–57.

66. Quoted in ibid., 26. Note Joe Brandt, ed., *Black Americans in the Spanish People's War against Fascism, 1936–1939* (N.p., undated).

67. *Amsterdam News*, November 28, 1936.

68. Pickens, "War in Spain," October 5, 1938, Pickens Papers, reel 28. The address also pointed to a recurrent theme in the writing on Spain, namely, that the international failure to respond to the Italian invasion of Ethiopia had led to the fascist challenge in Spain. See also Pickens, "What I Saw in Spain," *The Crisis* (October 1938): 319–21.

69. *Chicago Defender*, September 18, 1937; "Death to Men and Freedom," *The Crisis* (June 1937): 177.

70. Wilkins quoted in Raymond Wolters, *Negroes and the Great Depression: The Problem of Economic Recovery* (Westport, CT, 1970), 221. Wolters writes that the younger figures criticized the NAACP because, they claimed, its "insistence on political and civil liberties" had become inadequate to address "the desperate economic condition of the black masses." Ibid., 220. On this subject, Wolters's discussion is essential (see chs. 9–13). See Jonathan Scott Holloway, *Confronting the Veil: Abram Harris, Jr., E. Franklin Frazier, and Ralph Bunche, 1919–1941* (Chapel Hill, NC, 2002). See also James O. Young, *Black Writers of the Thirties* (Baton Rouge, LA, 1973), chs. 1–3. See also Beth Tomkins Bates, "A New Crowd Challenges the Agenda of the Old Guard in the NAACP, 1933–

1941," *American Historical Review* 102 (April 1997): 340–77. On Bunche, see Charles P. Henry's excellent biography, *Ralph Bunche: Model Negro or American Other?* (New York, 1999).

71. The words were those of Du Bois, chairman of the planning committee. Quoted in Wolters, *Negroes and the Great Depression*, 222. On Harris, Frazier, and Bunche, see Holloway, *Confronting the Veil*, chs. 2–4; Young, *Black Writers*, ch. 2; and Wolters, ch. 9.

72. See Wolters, *Negroes and the Great Depression*, 227. In 1934, the NAACP established the Committee on Future Plan and Program under the direction of the socialist economist Abram Harris of Howard University. Several figures worked with Harris, some of whom possessed a traditional orientation toward reform, while others held more radical views.

73. Wolters, *Negroes and the Great Depression*, 237. Du Bois quoted in Sitkoff, *New Deal for Blacks*, 251. On Du Bois's self-help program, see Wolters, ch. 10; and Lewis, *Du Bois: Fight for Equality*, ch. 9. On Du Bois's thought during this period, see Thomas C. Holt, "The Political Uses of Alienation: W.E.B. Du Bois on Politics, Race, and Culture, 1903–1940," *American Quarterly* 42 (June 1990): 301–23.

74. Among these factors, especially significant was the clash of personalities between Du Bois and Walter White, which exacerbated the ideological differences between Du Bois and NAACP officials. On cleavages in the NAACP, see Wolters, *Negroes and the Great Depression*, ch. 11; and Lewis, *Du Bois: Fight for Equality*, 334–48. See the following from Du Bois to the board, which helps clarify Du Bois's decision to resign: Du Bois to the board, May 21, 1934, Du Bois Papers, reel 42; Du Bois to the board, June 1, 1934, ibid.; and his letter of resignation, Du Bois to the board, June 26, 1934, ibid.

75. See Joel Spingarn to Du Bois, June 2, 1934, Du Bois Papers, reel 42. On the future character of *The Crisis*, see Wilkins's memorandum to Abram Harris, September 6, 1934. Wilkins wrote of "a vast circulation which can be reached . . . if the style and content of the magazine are changed to take in the interests of great masses of people whom it now ignores." James Weldon Johnson Correspondence, James Weldon Johnson Collection, Yale University, box 24, folder 544.

76. Between 1929 and 1939, membership increased from twenty-one thousand to fifty-four thousand and by 1940, the NAACP's budget was nearly twice what it had been seven years before. See Sitkoff, *New Deal for Blacks*, ch. 11; and Robert L. Zangrando, *The NAACP Crusade against Lynching, 1909–1950* (Philadelphia, 1980), chs. 5–7. The NAACP continued to fight for the passage of federal anti-lynching legislation, even though Franklin Roosevelt's support for the measure was lukewarm. Notably, the number of lynchings dropped during the 1930s. See also Elliott Rudwick and August Meier, "The Rise of the Black Secretariat in the NAACP, 1909–1935," in *Along the Color Line: Explorations in the Black Experience*, Rudwick and Meier, eds. (Urbana, IL, 1976), 94–127.

77. In noting the NAACP's apparent efforts to address the concerns of the young radicals, I am referring mainly to the Committee on the Future Plan and Program and the Harris Report and their reception by NAACP officials. On the Howard University conference, see Holloway, *Confronting the Veil*, 69–73; and Wolters, *Negroes and the Great Depression*, 354–58.

78. Randolph quoted in Lawrence S. Wittner, "The National Negro Congress: A Reassessment," *American Quarterly* 22 (Winter 1970): 885.

79. *Official Proceedings of the National Negro Congress* (Washington, DC, 1936), 3. Wilkins quoted in Wolters, *Negroes and the Great Depression*, 359. The best brief account is in Wolters, ch. 13. Note Wittner, "National Negro Congress."

80. *Official Proceedings of the National Negro Congress* (Washington, DC, 1936), 7. In addition to Randolph's address (ibid., 7–12), see those of Max Yergan and Lij Tasfaye Zaphiro, Haile Selassie's special envoy. Ibid., 12–13. See also the conference resolutions on Ethiopia (26–28), and the "Resolutions against War and Fascism," subheaded "The Significance of Fascism to Negroes" (28–29). On Ethiopia, see John P. Davis, "Let Us Build a National Negro Congress," January 1936, 27–28, National Negro Congress Papers, Schomburgh Center for Research in Black Culture, New York Public Library, New York, microfilm edition, reel 2. *Official Proceedings of the Second National Negro Congress* (Washington, DC, 1937).

81. Randolph's address printed in the *Official Proceedings of the Second National Negro Congress*. National Negro Congress Papers, reel 11. From the 1937 meeting, see also the "Resolutions on Ethiopia," ibid.; "Greetings to the Struggling Heroic Chinese People," ibid.; James W. Ford's speech, "John Brown's Body," ibid.; and "Resolutions on War and Fascism," ibid.

82. Bunche and Randolph quoted in Wolters, *Negroes and the Great Depression*, 375.

83. In assessing the reasons for the NNC's decline, Raymond Wolters emphasizes the influence of the Communists. *Negroes and the Great Depression*, 368–75. Wittner provides a more nuanced view, though he acknowledges the Communists' role. "National Negro Congress," 897–901. See also Kirby, *Black Americans in the Roosevelt Era*, 164–70.

84. An exception to this observation is Du Bois's description of the Soviet Union, which he visited in his round-the-world journey of 1936 and 1937. In several *Pittsburgh Courier* columns, Du Bois praised the achievements of the Soviet government, particularly in the economic and social spheres. See the following *Courier* columns from 1937: January 16, 23, and 30. For a far more circumspect *Courier* column, in which Du Bois pointed out the less appealing aspects of Soviet life, including curtailment of spiritual freedom and other individual liberties, see June 5, 1937. Note Lewis, *Du Bois: Fight for Equality*, 407–9. In *The Crisis*, Du Bois called the Russian Revolution "the greatest event in the world since the French Revolution." (September, 1931): 313. Several *Crisis* pieces from the 1930s commented positively on Soviet life, including: Henry Lee Moon, "Woman under the Soviets" (April 1934): 108; Langston Hughes, "Going South in Russia" (June 1934): 162–63; and Chatwood Hall, "Full Equality of Races and Nations" (September 1936): 268–69.

85. Spingarn, "Racial Equality," delivered at the Twenty-third Annual Conference, Washington, D.C., May 17, 1932, Joel Spingarn Papers, New York Public Library, box 17, folder "Printed Articles."

86. Sitkoff, *New Deal for Blacks*, 142. Sitkoff suggests that the initiative reflected Stalin's understanding of his own country's nationality problem. See ch. 6 in Sitkoff on the relationship between Communism and race reform in the 1930s.

Other works that explore this subject include Mark Solomon, *The Cry Was Unity: Communists and African Americans, 1917–1936* (Jackson, MS, 1998), esp. ch. 5; Solomon, *Red and Black: Communism and Afro-Americans, 1929–1935* (New York, 1988); and Mark Naison, *Communists in Harlem during the Depression* (New York, 1983). On the Party's efforts to make headway in the South, especially in labor unions, see Robin D. G. Kelley, *Hammer and Hoe: Alabama Communists during the Great Depression* (Chapel Hill, NC, 1990).

87. On the Scottsboro episode, see James Goodman's superb *Stories of Scottsboro* (New York, 1994). The case eventually wound up before the Supreme Court, where in a 5–4 decision the Court overturned the convictions on the grounds that the exclusion of blacks from Alabama juries constituted a denial of due process.

88. Sitkoff, *New Deal for Blacks*, 149–52. In 1937, after years of protest and legal wrangling, Herndon was freed when the Supreme Court overturned his conviction.

89. James Weldon Johnson, *Negro Americans, What Now?* (New York, 1938; orig., 1934), 7–12.

90. White, "The Negro and the Communists," *Harper's* (December 1931): 62–72. Note Asbury Smith, "What Can the Negro Expect from Communism?" *Opportunity* (July 1933): 211–12.

91. *The Crisis* (September 1931): 313–15. Other instances where Du Bois made this argument include his "Marxism and the Negro Problem," ibid. (May 1933): 103–4; and ibid. (June 1933): 141–42. To Mary White Ovington, who wrote in 1938 that her only hope lay with Communism, Du Bois responded: "Communism is the hope of us all but not the dogmatic Marxian program with war and murder in the forefront. Economic communism by the path of peace is possible." Ovington to Du Bois, March 11, 1938; Du Bois to Ovington, March 21, 1938, Du Bois Papers, reel 49. A wide-ranging discussion on the relationship between Communism and black uplift appeared in *The Crisis* in 1932. Seventeen leading black editors expressed their views on the subject, covering the spectrum from strong support to equally strong opposition. Du Bois also tackled the question, though he dismissed the idea that Communism could prove helpful to black Americans. "Negro Editors on Communism," *The Crisis* (April 1932): 117–19; ibid. (May 1932): 154–56. Du Bois's comment appeared in (June 1932): 190–91.

92. Pickens to Claude Barnett, September 17, 1931, William Pickens Papers, reel 8.

93. Despite the Communists' efforts, black Americans did not join the Party in great numbers during the 1930s. Black membership in the Party went from less than two hundred out of a total membership of ten thousand in 1928 to about twenty-five hundred out of twenty-five thousand total members in 1934. For the remainder of the decade, blacks continued to represent between 10 and 15 percent of the total membership in the Party, roughly equivalent to the black proportion of the total American population. See Wilson Record, *The Negro and the Communist Party* (New York, 1971; orig., 1951), 177.

94. "Soviet Russia Aids Italy," *The Crisis* (October 1935): 305.

95. White's address at the NAACP's Thirtieth Annual Conference (Richmond, VA), 1939, NAACP Papers, pt. 1, reel 10.

CHAPTER FIVE

1. *Pittsburgh Courier,* September 9, 1939.

2. On American diplomacy in the years before Pearl Harbor, see Robert Dallek, *Franklin D. Roosevelt and American Foreign Policy, 1932–1945* (New York, 1979); and Waldo Heinrichs, *Threshold of War: Franklin D. Roosevelt and American Entry into World War II* (New York, 1988).

3. For an illuminating look at the views expressed in the black press, which were largely anti-interventionist during the neutrality period, see Daniel W. Aldridge III, "A War for the Colored Races: Anti-Americanism and the African-American Intelligentsia, 1939–1941," *Diplomatic History* 28 (June 2004): 321–52.

4. "Defending Democracy," *The Crisis* (October 1939): 305. In the first wartime issue, an editorial, "The Great Betrayal," also criticized the Soviets for signing the Nazi-Soviet Pact. Ibid.

5. *Afro-American,* September 9, 1939; "Why We Are for War," ibid., September 16, 1939; Kelly Miller, "The Negro Faces the Second World War," *Amsterdam News,* September 23, 1939. See also a selection of editorials from the black press that *The Crisis* published (October 1939): 307.

6. For the conference resolutions, see *The Crisis* (September 1940): 295–96.

7. Address by Arthur Spingarn, June 18, 1940, NAACP Papers, Library of Congress, Washington, D.C., microfilm edition, pt. 1, reel 10.

8. Howard University Law School dean William Hastie considered war, peace, and the threat of Hitlerism in America. He discussed the impact such issues would have on blacks, examining the question of national defense and the black man's right to receive equal treatment in the service of his country. Hastie's address, June 21, 1940, ibid. On the military's policies regarding blacks in this period, see Richard M. Dalfiume, *Desegregation of the U.S. Armed Forces: Fighting on Two Fronts, 1939–1953* (Columbia, MO, 1969), chs. 2–3. See also Sherie Mershon and Steven Schlossman, *Foxholes and Color Lines: Desegregating the U.S. Armed Forces* (Baltimore, 1998), ch. 3.

9. White's address, June 23, 1940, NAACP Papers, pt. 1, reel 10. Another address that incorporated global affairs into the domestic struggle was given by Earl B. Dickerson, June 19, 1940, ibid. Note the association's annual conference in 1941, in which one sees the same phenomenon. The theme of the thirty-second meeting was "Defend Democracy at Home." See the NAACP's press release of June 6, 1941, ibid. Walter White's address again powerfully invoked the link between the war and race reform. White's address, June 27, 1941, ibid.

10. *The Crisis* (July 1940): 209. See also L. D. Reddick's poem, "Meditations upon the War and Democracy in America," in which readers encountered a poet's reflections on the European catastrophe and the suggestion that the key to victory had less to do with the production of armaments than with the fulfillment of America's unrealized values. *The Crisis* (August 1940): 263. Before Pearl Harbor, the Urban League's monthly often suggested that the war had implications for the movement. See, for example, "A New Era," *Opportunity* (January 1940): 2–3. The Urban League's annual reports for 1939 and 1940 also indicate how its leaders incorporated overseas events into its discussion of domestic reform. See "The

National Urban League's Work in 1939: Report of the Executive Secretary," February 14, 1940; and "The National Urban League's Work in 1940: Report of the Executive Secretary," February 19, 1941. See also "Effects of a Second World War on the Negro Discussed at Twenty-eighth Annual Conference of National Urban League," *The New York Age*, September 16, 1939.

11. Ralph Bunche to the Committee to Defend America by Aiding the Allies, June 12, 1940, Bunche Papers, Harvard University microfilm collection, reel 1. See also a memorandum that Bunche and Abram Harris prepared for the Committee to Defend America, which appeared as an advertisement in Washington, D.C.'s *Evening Star*, June 11, 1940. The title is telling: *Stop Hitler Now! The Negro Must Help*, ibid. Bunche to Harold Laski, January 24, 1941, ibid., reel 3.

12. Ralph Bunche, "The Role of the University in the Political Orientation of Negro Youth." The paper, delivered at Howard University on July 16, 1940, was published in the *Journal of Negro Education* 9 (October 1940): 571–79. For another expression of Bunche's view concerning the link between African-American life and the war, see "The Negro's Stake in the World Crisis," which argued that not since the Civil War had "a conflict meant so much to the Negro and his future as this one." *Proceedings, Association of Colleges and Secondary Schools for Negroes*, 1940. See Bunche's letter to Charles Dollard of the Carnegie Corporation, June 19, 1940, which considers the potential effect of totalitarianism on African-American life. Bunche suggested that the Carnegie-Myrdal study (a research project funded by the Carnegie Corporation), which led to the publication in 1944 of Swedish sociologist Gunnar Myrdal's classic volume on American race relations, *An American Dilemma*, would have to examine how world affairs affected black domestic life. Bunche noted that perhaps the "greatest weakness of all of us today is not being easily enough alarmed about what transpires in the outer world." Bunche Papers, Harvard University, reel 3. On Myrdal's iconic work, see Walter A. Jackson, *Gunnar Myrdal and America's Conscience: Social Engineering and Racial Liberalism, 1938–1987* (Chapel Hill, NC, 1990); and David W. Southern, *Gunnar Myrdal and Black-White Relations: The Use and Abuse of "An American Dilemma," 1944–1969* (Baton Rouge, LA, 1987).

13. "The Negro and Nazism," *Opportunity* (July 1940): 194–95. See also Vincent J. Browne's "Program for Negro Preparedness," ibid. (August 1940): 230–31.

14. L. D. Revoal to Pickens, January 2, 1941, and Pickens to Revoal, January 7, 1941, William Pickens Papers, Schomburg Center for Research in Black Culture, New York Public Library, New York, microfilm edition, reel 15.

15. Pickens, "Colored People Have a Stake in the War," undated column, Pickens Papers, reel 27; Pickens, "Britain Battles for Civilization," 1940, ibid. *Crisis* readers could also read essays that supported American aid to England. See Alfred Baker Lewis, "Dictatorship and Democracy," *The Crisis* (September 1940): 285.

16. Bethune, "The Negro on the Threshold of Tomorrow," October 26, 1941, National Negro Congress Papers, Schomburg Center for Research in Black Culture, New York Public Library, New York, microfilm edition, reel 23. On Bethune, see Rackham Holt, *Mary McLeod Bethune* (Garden City, NY, 1964). On Bethune's activities in government, see B. Joyce Ross, "Mary McLeod Bethune and the National Youth Administration: A Case Study of Power Relationships in

the Black Cabinet of Franklin D. Roosevelt," in *Black Leaders of the Twentieth Century*, John Hope Franklin and August Meier, eds. (Urbana, IL, 1982), 191–219.

17. "The Battle for Britain," *Black Worker* (September 1940): 8. See also Randolph, "Negroes Should Support 'All Out Aid' to Great Britain," *Black Worker* (February 1941): 4; Randolph, "National Defense," *Black Worker* (January 1941): 4. For Randolph's earliest reaction to the war, see his editorial, "War," in the *Black Worker* (September 1939), in which he supported American neutrality, though he noted the country's sympathies ought to lie with Britain and France because they represented "what Democracy there is still left in the world today."

18. Du Bois, for example, was not charitable to Britain during the neutrality period. See the *Amsterdam News*, August 30 and November 29, 1941. As late as January 1941, Du Bois could still describe Hitler's racial theories as "exactly the theories which we practice here in America." Ibid., January 25, 1941. Roy Wilkins also continued to write critically about Britain, noting that it refused to articulate its war aims because of an unwillingness to clarify its imperial policies. See his columns in ibid., December 14, 1940, and January 4, 1941. Worth noting is Randolph's April 1940 address to the National Negro Congress, which was delivered before the fall of France. It is quite different in tone from his later reflections on world affairs, especially regarding the gravity of the international situation and the need for a resolute American stance. While hailing Franklin Roosevelt as the champion of peace and democracy, Randolph did not support U.S. involvement in the war. His reluctance to acknowledge the perils posed by the war, which he would soon delineate, is likely attributable to the change in the international situation that emerged by the late spring and summer of 1940. Randolph, "The World Crisis and the Negro People Today," April 26, 1940, Randolph Papers, Library of Congress, Washington, D.C., microfilm edition, reel 31. On the third National Negro Congress and Randolph's reasons for leaving the organization, see Cicero Alvin Hughes, "Toward a Black United Front: The National Negro Congress Movement" (Ph.D. diss., Ohio University, 1982), 156–65; and Paula F. Pfeffer, *A. Philip Randolph, Pioneer of the Civil Rights Movement* (Baton Rouge, LA, 1990), 39–43. Note Ralph Bunche's superb account of the speech, the reaction to it, and the significance of the controversy in the context of the movement. See "Programs, Ideologies, Tactics and Achievements of Negro Betterment and Interracial Organizations." Bunche's analysis is from a June 1940 research memorandum prepared for the Carnegie-Myrdal study under the direction of Gunnar Myrdal. I read this source in the Bunche Papers, Harvard University, reel 1, 70–84. For Randolph's explanation for resigning, see "Why I Would Not Stand for Re-election for President of the National Negro Congress," *Black Worker* (May 1940).

19. On the March on Washington Movement, see Herbert Garfinkel, *When Negroes March: The March on Washington Movement in the Organizational Politics for FEPC* (New York, 1959). On the relationship between Randolph's group and the NAACP, see John H. Bracey and August Meier, "Allies or Adversaries? The NAACP, A. Philip Randolph and the 1941 March on Washington," *Georgia Historical Quarterly* 75 (Spring 1991): 1–17. See also Daniel Kryder, *Divided*

Arsenal: Race and the American State during World War Two (New York, 2000), 55–70.

20. White, *A Man Called White: The Autobiography of Walter White* (Athens, GA, 1995; orig., 1948), 186–87.

21. See White, *A Man Called White*, 187–88; and "White House Blesses Jim Crow," *The Crisis* (November 1940): 350–51. In December, the journal published Roosevelt's letter of regret to White, Randolph, and Hill, "F.D.R. Regrets That Army Policy Was Misinterpreted," 390. Jervis Anderson describes the episode in *A. Philip Randolph: A Biographical Portrait* (New York, 1972), 244–47.

22. To understand Randolph's thinking on this, see Jervis Anderson, *A. Philip Randolph*, 247–48.

23. Randolph, "How to Blast the Bottlenecks of Race Prejudice in National Defense," press release from the Brotherhood of Sleeping Car Porters, January 15, 1941, Randolph Papers, reel 34. See Randolph, "Let's March on Capital 10,000 Strong, Urges Leader of Porters," *Pittsburgh Courier*, January 25, 1941. Note the positive reaction in the *Chicago Defender*, February 8, 1941.

24. See Garfinkel, *When Negroes March*; and Lucy G. Barber, *Marching on Washington: The Forging of an American Political Tradition* (Berkeley, CA, 2002), ch. 4.

25. The Urban League's Lester Granger called Roosevelt's act "truly momentous." Granger, "The President, the Negro, and Defense," *Opportunity* (July 1941): 204–7; and "The Negro Marches," ibid., 194–95. Randolph's June 25, 1941, address at the NAACP's conference provides an overview of the movement. Randolph Papers, reel 28. For a firsthand account, see White, *A Man Called White*, 189–94.

26. There are countless examples between 1939 and 1941 in which the reformers linked the war to employment and military opportunities for blacks. See Walter White, "It's Our Country, Too," *Saturday Evening Post*, December 14, 1940, 27, 61; and columns by Roy Wilkins in the *Amsterdam News*, June 1, 1940, and March 22 and September 20, 1941. See Charles Edward Russell's address, "National Unity, National Defense, and the Color Line," January 26, 1941, given at a Washington, D.C., meeting called to protest discrimination in the military. NAACP Papers, pt. 16B, reel 19. See the "Program of Action," October 26, 1941, issued by the Negro Committee for United Action against Hitler and Hitlerism, an organization that linked defeating totalitarianism to vanquishing domestic racial persecution. National Negro Congress Papers, reel 27. For an early example, see William Pickens to Franklin Roosevelt, April 4, 1938, Pickens Papers, reel 13. The Commission on Interracial Cooperation (CIC) was also interested in employment in the defense industry and integration of the armed forces. See the resolutions from its 1940 meeting and Robert Weaver's address, "The Negro and National Defense," October 4, 1940. CIC Papers, Atlanta University Center Archives, Atlanta, microfilm edition, reel 22.

27. Johnson, "The Negro and the Present Crisis," *Journal of Negro Education* 10 (July 1941): 585–95.

28. On the attack, see Frank Freidel, *Franklin D. Roosevelt: A Rendezvous with Destiny* (Boston, 1990), 404–6. A black hero emerged from the Japanese attack. Doris Miller, a navy messman, shot down four enemy planes from the deck

of the battleship *Arizona* and was later awarded the Navy Cross for bravery. See John Hope Franklin, *From Slavery to Freedom: A History of African Americans* (New York, 1994), 448.

29. Freidel, *Franklin D. Roosevelt*, 406–7.

30. *Time*, December 15, 1941, 17.

31. "Board Action Re Segregation," December 8, 1941, NAACP Papers, pt. 16B, reel 12; Walter White, "Proposal to the Board of Directors, From the Secretary," December 8, 1941, ibid. A meeting was held in New York on January 10, 1942, in which the NAACP, the National Urban League, and other organizations participated. Many delegates expressed strong sentiments suggesting that blacks were not unreservedly in favor of the war, and the delegates passed a motion to this effect, though nearly one-third abstained. See "Reveal Race War Apathy," *Amsterdam News*, January 17, 1942.

32. See a December 9 emergency meeting of the executive board of the National Negro Congress, which led to the adoption of a resolution entitled "For Unity and Victory." The resolution spoke of America's just cause in the face of this "hideous threat to American democracy," asserted that blacks would fully support the war effort, and linked the fate of black Americans to that of the nation. Published by the NNC as part of a pamphlet, it established a clear relationship between Hitler's defeat in Europe and continued black advancement at home, declaring that the race reform program was "inseparable from America's fight for freedom." *Negro People Will Defend America* (Washington, DC, 1941). The pamphlet contains the December 9 resolution, along with a November report delivered to the NNC's board, which links winning the war to continued black progress.

33. Randolph, "The Negro Has a Great Stake in the War," *Pittsburgh Courier*, December 20, 1941. See also two Randolph pieces in the January 1942 *Black Worker*, a letter to union members and an editorial, "Negroes Should Demand Red Cross Accept Their Blood."

34. Randolph to Roosevelt, undated letter (but after Pearl Harbor), Randolph Papers, reel 3.

35. "Now Is the Time Not to Be Silent," *The Crisis* (January 1942): 7. See also "Fight for Liberties Here While Fighting Dictators Abroad, NAACP Urges," ibid.,

36. *Opportunity's* first editorial after Pearl Harbor, "The Fate of Democracy," linked American belligerency to race reform, observing that black Americans were now involved in a dual quest, battling for freedom abroad and in the United States. *Opportunity* (January 1942): 2.

36. "We Are Americans, Too," *Pittsburgh Courier*, December 13, 1941. The "Double-V" idea resulted from a letter to the editor sent by a young man, James Thompson, which the editors displayed prominently on January 31, 1942. Thompson spoke about a "Double V," in which the first V would mean "victory over our enemies from without," while the second represented "victory over our enemies from within" (i.e., racial prejudice and discrimination). On February 7, 1942, the newspaper began to display the "Double-V" banner across the top of the front page. The editors spoke of a "two-pronged attack against our enslavers at home and those abroad who would enslave us." See Lee Finkle, "The Conservative Aims of Militant Rhetoric: Black Protest during World War II," *Journal of American History* 60 (December 1973): 692–713.

37. "For Democracy and Unity," *Chicago Defender*, December 13, 1941. See also a front-page editorial in the *Amsterdam News*, which spoke of the enemy's "diabolic treachery." The battle for democracy must be fought as "one nation indivisible." "Win the War," *Amsterdam News*, December 13, 1941. Characterizations of the Japanese attack on Pearl Harbor in the black press ("cunning, dastardly, deceptive") suggest a degree of hostility toward Japan, which marks a break from the past. During the 1930s, black views of Japan were generally positive and were based on the notion that the Japanese were a "non-white race" that was thriving on the world stage. See Reginald Kearney, *African American Views of the Japanese: Solidarity or Sedition* (Albany, NY, 1998), ch. 5. Black readers encountered the positive reflections of Du Bois, who visited Japan on his round-the-world trip of 1936–37. His columns emphasized Japanese achievements, civility, and lack of race prejudice. See the following *Pittsburgh Courier* columns from 1937: February 13, March 13, 20, and 27, and September 27, and a Du Bois speech, "The Meaning of Japan," given at Morehouse College, March 12, 1937, Du Bois Papers, W.E.B. Du Bois Library, University of Massachusetts–Amherst, microfilm edition, reel 80. For divisions in black opinion on Japan during the war, see Kearney, *African American Views*, ch. 6. After Pearl Harbor, Roy Wilkins noted that white racism led Britain and the United States to discount Japan's capacity to conduct a successful large-scale attack. *Amsterdam News*, December 20, 1941. On the risk of characterizing the war in the Pacific as a "white man's war," see "White Man's War," *The Crisis* (April 1942): 111.

38. Immediately after Pearl Harbor, in a statement supporting the war effort, White considered the subject of the previous world war, advising blacks to proceed cautiously as the country embarked on another international crusade. White's statement was published widely in the black press and reprinted in *The Crisis* (January 1942): 36. In a September 1939 column supporting the maintenance of American neutrality, Roy Wilkins spoke of the "shameful story of the Negro in the last war," noting that the "Negro of 1939 is twenty years wiser than the Negro of 1919." *Amsterdam News*, September 16, 1939. For the reform journals' references to the black experience in World War I, see: "From the Press of the Nation," *The Crisis* (October 1939): 307; and "The Negro and War," *Opportunity* (May 1940): 130–31.

39. White's address at the NAACP's annual conference, June 23, 1940, NAACP Papers, pt. 1, reel 10. See also Rayford Logan's remarks at the business session of June 20, ibid.

40. Among the contributors to the Summer 1943 issue of the *Journal of Negro Education* were Du Bois, Walter White, Emmett Scott, Charles Houston, William Hastie, Robert Weaver, Kenneth Clark, Claude Barnett, Marion T. Wright, Ira De A. Reid, Lawrence Reddick, and Merze Tate. Du Bois wrote to Theodore Berry of the Office of War Information that black Americans had made progress since the past war, noting the present situation marks "a great improvement upon that of 1917 to 1920." Du Bois to Berry, June 23, 1942, Du Bois Papers, reel 54.

41. In the *Journal of Negro Education* 12 (Summer 1943), see Roscoe Lewis, "The Role of Pressure Groups in Maintaining Morale among Negroes," 464–73; Charles H. Houston, "Critical Summary: The Negro in the U.S. Armed Forces in

World Wars I and II," 364–66; and Ira De A. Reid, "A Critical Summary: The Negro on the Home Front in World Wars I and II," 511–20.

42. "Fascism Invades West Africa," *The Crisis* (October 1939): 297–98. In November 1939, *Crisis* readers encountered an idea that had gained currency during World War I, in an editorial asserting that the European states were fighting "to control and exploit the lands and destiny of hundreds of millions of black, brown, and yellow people." According to the editors, the British and French were waging war to protect their empires, and Hitler, not content with what he had gained in Europe, wanted a "share in the swag that flows from black and brown hands." This perspective on the origins of World War II echoed Du Bois's classic 1915 essay, "The African Roots of the War." "For the Right to Exploit Dark Peoples," *The Crisis* (November 1939): 337.

43. Occasionally, imperial developments had more tangible inspirational value, as in 1940, when Britain amended its colonial policy by lifting the color bar in the British military, allowing the admission of "non-European" British subjects. A *Crisis* editorial described how British military necessity led to the decision and discussed continued racial discrimination in the American military, despite the black soldier's historic loyalty. The headline topping the editorial, which focused on American racial practices, read: "War Crisis Forces Britain to Drop Army Color Bar." *The Crisis* (June 1940): 179. Note the way *The Crisis* looked at racial oppression in South Africa in two May 1943 essays: L. D. Reddick, "South Africa: A Case for the United Nations," 137–39; and Rayford Logan, "Smuts Speaks for South Africa, 1917–1942," 264–67. Reddick argued for intervention to wipe out fascism in South Africa by the states of the United Nations (a contemporary term for the Allies), while Logan argued that the policies and outlook of the South African leader Jan Smuts were similar to those seen in the American South.

44. Wilkins to Anup Singh, January 24, 1944, NAACP Papers, pt. 14, reel 11. On the India League of America, see Walter White's *Chicago Defender* column, February 24, 1945, in which he compared the two struggles.

45. *Amsterdam News*, March 21, 1942. It is worth bearing in mind that India was of great concern to Allied military leaders throughout the war. This was especially so during the spring and summer of 1942, when, as Gerhard Weinberg notes, nationalist stirrings on the subcontinent "rose to a new peak." In this period, military officials feared a change in India's status, which could have led to "a massive loss of Allied power," an eventuality that would have made it far more difficult to defeat Japan. Weinberg, *A World at Arms: A Global History of World War Two* (New York, 1994), 324–26.

46. "India Wants Freedom Not Promises," *The Crisis* (December 1939): 369. Additional *Crisis* editorials on India included "Time Is Not Ripe" (March 1940): 81; and "Britain Fumbles in India" (September 1942): 279.

47. S. Chandrasekhar, "I Meet the Mahatma," *The Crisis* (October 1942): 312–13, 331. On the American race problem, see Gandhi's message (written five years before) to black America, published in the *Pittsburgh Courier*, September 12, 1942.

48. Randolph, "The Negroes' Fight for Freedom on Two Fronts," *Chicago Defender*, September 26, 1942.

49. MOWM news release prepared by Peter Dana, "Philip Randolph Warmly Received at Boston Mass Meeting." Randolph Papers, reel 22. For an early mention of the MOWM's emphasis on civil disobedience, see "Non-Violent Disobedience May Be Used," *Chicago Defender*, January 9, 1943.

50. Randolph's *Chicago Defender* pieces appeared in six consecutive issues between June 12 and July 17, 1943. In particular, see "Randolph Tells Philosophy behind 'March' Movement," June 19, 1943, and "Randolph Tells Technique of Civil Disobedience," June 26, 1943. Regarding a distinction in means between the MOWM program and the Indian approach, Randolph claimed he had no desire to encourage blacks in the armed forces or in the defense industries to refuse to obey orders or stop work, two methods that might have been theoretically consistent with Indian practices. See two pieces in Baltimore's *Afro-American* that illuminate the differences between the approaches of Randolph and of Gandhi: "Movement Will Help Win War—Randolph," February 6, 1943; and "Randolph Explains His Civil Disobedience Project," May 29, 1943. Du Bois noted differences between the American and Indian situations and expressed reservations about the applicability of Gandhi's approach to domestic race relations. *Amsterdam News*, March 13, 1943.

51. See Sudarshan Kapur, *Raising Up a Prophet: The African-American Encounter with Gandhi* (Boston, 1992), esp. ch. 5. Note a *Pittsburgh Courier* poll published on October 10, 1942, in which 87.8 percent of ten thousand black respondents answered yes to the question: "Do you believe that India should contend for her rights and her liberty now?" "India Justified in Freedom Fight, Readers Declare." On the connection between Indians and black Americans, see R. Lal Singh, editor of *India News*, who spoke at the NAACP's conference on July 17, 1942. NAACP Papers, pt. 1, reel 11.

52. On the relationship between CORE and the MOWM, CORE's founding, and the influence of Gandhian ideas upon its founders, see August Meier and Elliott Rudwick, *CORE: A Study in the Civil Rights Movement, 1942–1968* (New York, 1973), ch. 1. See also Kapur, *Raising Up a Prophet*, 118–23. A look at some of the early CORE-related documents illustrates how reformers incorporated Gandhian principles into CORE's program. See, for example, "Summer (1945) Direct Action Campaign against Jim Crow." Congress on Racial Equality Papers, State Historical Society of Wisconsin, Madison, microfilm edition, reel 14; "Plan for a Two or Three Month Full-Time Campaign against Jim Crow," undated, ibid. See also Bayard Rustin, "The Negro and Non-Violence," Bayard Rustin Papers, Library of Congress, Washington, D.C., microfilm edition, reel 17.

53. Jervis Anderson, *A. Philip Randolph*, 262.

54. The MOWM demanded an end to Jim Crow; due process of law and anti-lynching legislation; full and free suffrage; integration of the military; an end to discrimination in employment and the establishment of a permanent FEPC; withholding of federal funds from agencies practicing discrimination in using such funds; Negro and minority representation in all administrative agencies; and Negro and minority representation on all missions that would be sent to the peace conference. See "8-Point Program, March on Washington Movement," undated, Randolph Papers, Library of Congress, Washington, D.C., microfilm edition, reel 22.

55. Randolph, "The Brotherhood Backs the War," *Black Worker* (February 1942): 4.

56. Randolph, "Keynote Address to the Policy Conference of the MOWM," Detroit, September 26, 1942, National Negro Congress Papers, pt. 2, reel 3.

57. To understand the character of the wartime message and the reform approach that Randolph and the MOWM advanced, see the following: Randolph's address, June 16, 1942, Madison Square Garden, New York, Randolph Papers, reel 22 (scheduling problems prevented Randolph from giving this address, but it was published in *Interracial Review* 15 [July 1942]: 101–3). Randolph's address, June 26, 1942, Chicago Coliseum, Randolph Papers, reel 28; and Randolph's address, "The Negro in the American Democracy," New York Federation of Churches, undated, ibid., reel 30.

58. Randolph's address, September 26, 1942, Randolph Papers, reel 22. The MOWM resolutions are stated in a "Message to the World": "The Negro can make no greater contribution to the cause for democracy and the United Nations [Allies] than to correct the evils and injustices heaped upon him by those people within his own country." Ibid.

59. Notwithstanding the all-black character of the MOWM, Randolph also sought to prick the nation's conscience. Note his letter to Interior Secretary Harold Ickes, in which he wrote of using the Lincoln Memorial as a highly visible meeting place to discuss the integration of the military and the defense industries. Randolph argued that such a meeting would help develop "a sounder national unity" for fighting and winning the war. Black Americans wanted the United States to win the war, "but the moral position of our country is greatly weakened when we profess to be fighting the cause of democracy and deny it to our own citizens because of color." Randolph to Harold Ickes, April 15, 1942, Randolph Papers, reel 20.

60. Wilkins's address at the NAACP's annual conference, July 14, 1942, NAACP Papers, pt. 1, reel 11. See also a July 16 radio address that Wilkins gave while in Los Angeles for the conference. Ibid. Walter White also made an especially powerful speech at the 1942 conference, in which he gave primacy to international issues. White, July 19, 1942, ibid. The conference resolutions illustrate how the association deployed war-related issues to advance its case for race reform. See "Resolutions of the Thirty-third Annual Conference of the NAACP," July 14–19, 1942, ibid.

61. The Detroit riot began on June 20 and lasted for three days, killing thirty-four people, twenty-five of whom were black. See A. Russell Buchanan, *Black Americans in World War II* (Santa Barbara, CA, 1977), 48–53; and Harvard Sitkoff, "Racial Militancy and Interracial Violence in the Second World War," *Journal of American History* 58 (December 1971): 661–81.

62. "Statement to the Nation Adopted by the Emergency Conference on the Status of the Negro in the War for Freedom Called by the NAACP," June 5, 1943. NAACP Papers, pt. 1, reel 11. Roosevelt articulated the "Four Freedoms" in his annual message to Congress, January 6, 1941. On the 1943 conference, note Walter White's June 3 keynote address, ibid. Langston Hughes, "How about It?" NAACP Papers, pt. 14, reel 9.

63. Marshall Field's speech, July 16, 1944, NAACP Papers, pt. 1, reel 11. The conference resolutions demonstrate the centrality of the war. See "Resolutions Adopted at the Wartime Conference," July 12–16, 1944, ibid. See also *The Crisis* (August 1944): 262–63.

64. White's address, July 16, 1943, NAACP Papers, pt. 1, reel 11.

65. For an overview of White's four-month trip to the Pacific theater from December 1944 to April 1945, see his *A Man Called White*, chs. 34–35; and Kenneth Janken, *White: The Biography of Walter White, Mr. NAACP* (New York, 2003), ch. 9. On his reasons for wanting to take the Pacific trip (and for going to the European theater), see the following correspondence: White to General A. D. Surles, September 18, 1944, NAACP Papers, pt. 14, reel 13; White to Colonel Falkner Heard, September 26, 1944, ibid.; and White to "Dear Folks" (NAACP colleagues), February 12 and March 23, 1945, ibid. Note some of White's *Chicago Defender* pieces written from abroad, including three from March 17, 24, and 31, 1945.

66. White to McCloy, September 3, 1943, NAACP Papers, pt. 17, reel 17. White to Roosevelt, September 20, 1943, ibid., pt. 17, reel 18. Note White's correspondence with Eleanor Roosevelt about the trip: White to Mrs. Roosevelt, November 1, 1943; Mrs. Roosevelt to White, November 3, 1943; and White to Mrs. Roosevelt, November 9, 1943, ibid., pt. 17, reel 17.

67. *Chicago Defender*, January 22, 1944. Walter White, *A Rising Wind* (New York, 1945). White's address over the CBS Network, April 30, 1944, NAACP Papers, pt. 17, reel 18. Note the following letters from White, written from abroad: White to *Crisis* editors, December 1943 (sent January 7, 1944), NAACP Papers, pt. 17, reel 17; White to "Dear Folks" (NAACP colleagues), January 15, 1944, ibid.; and White to Mrs. Roosevelt, February 13 and 23, 1944, ibid. See White, *A Man Called White*, 242–61.

68. White's radio address, April 30, 1944, NAACP Papers, pt. 17, reel 18. White's address at the NAACP annual conference, July 16, 1944, ibid., pt. 1, reel 11. For White's recommendations to the War Department, see "Observations and Recommendations of Walter White on Racial Relations in the ETO," February 11, 1944, ibid., pt. 17, reel 18.

69. Discussion of the experiences of the black soldier in World War II was common in the black press and in the reform periodicals. For the black soldier's voice, see Phillip McGuire, ed., *Taps for a Jim Crow Army: Letters from Black Soldiers in World War II* (Santa Barbara, CA, 1983). The secondary literature on the black soldier during the war is extensive. See Joyce Thomas, "The 'Double V' Was for Victory: Black Soldiers, the Black Protest, and World War II" (Ph.D. diss., Ohio State University, 1993); Kryder, *Divided Arsenal*, ch. 5; and Mershon and Schlossman, *Foxholes and Color Lines*, ch. 3.

70. White, *A Rising Wind*, 152.

71. Robert L. Zangrando puts the 1945 membership figure at 351,000. Zangrando, *The NAACP Crusade against Lynching, 1909–1950* (Philadelphia, 1980), 166–73. *The Crisis* stated that it exceeded 400,000 (February 1945): 53. See also "NAACP Annual Meeting Reports Reveal Greatest Year in History," January 4, 1945, NAACP Papers, pt. 1, reel 14.

72. On the complex reasons for Pickens's departure from the NAACP, see Sheldon Avery, *Up from Washington: William Pickens and the Negro Struggle for Equality* (Newark, DE, 1989), 172–80.

73. White's address, July 16, 1944, NAACP Papers, pt. 1, reel 11. On Du Bois's return, see David Levering Lewis, *W.E.B. Du Bois: The Fight for Equality and the American Century, 1919–1963* (New York, 2000), 497–99.

74. Du Bois to *Fortune* editor, May 21, 1942, Du Bois Papers, reel 53.

75. *Amsterdam News*, May 9, 1942. For other *Amsterdam News* columns by Du Bois on the relationship between the war and black progress, see March 14, 21, 1942, and September 11, 1943.

76. Wilkins quoted in *What the Negro Wants* (Chapel Hill, NC, 1944), 113, one of the more interesting publications to emerge during the war, which was edited by Howard University's Rayford Logan. The collection of essays by a distinguished group of fourteen black educators, writers, and journalists, united by a commitment to race reform, represented a broad spectrum of opinion in the reform community. Among the contributors were Mary McLeod Bethune, Charles H. Wesley, Du Bois, A. Philip Randolph, Langston Hughes, and several others.

77. Alain Locke, "The Unfinished Business of Democracy," *Survey Graphic* (November 1942): 455–59. The entire issue was devoted to the theme of Locke's essay and included pieces by leading reformers.

78. Langston Hughes, "Jim Crow's Last Stand," *Chicago Defender*, October 31, 1942. The quotation is an excerpt.

79. St. Clair Drake and Horace Cayton, *Black Metropolis: A Study of Negro Life in a Northern City* (New York, 1945), 760.

Chapter Six

1. Charles H. Studin to Du Bois, April 11, 1945, Du Bois Papers, W.E.B. Du Bois Library, University of Massachusetts–Amherst, microfilm edition, reel 57. Du Bois to Studin, April 13, 1945, ibid.

2. "NAACP Will Seek Bill of Rights, Race Equality, at San Francisco Parley," press release, April 19, 1945, NAACP Papers, Library of Congress, Washington, D.C., microfilm edition, pt. 14, reel 18.

3. Walter White, *A Man Called White* (New York, 1948), 294. For more on the train journey to San Francisco, see P. L. Prattis in the *Pittsburgh Courier*, "Conference Confetti," May 5, 1945. Along with Rayford Logan, Prattis reported on the gathering for the newspaper.

4. Wilkins to White, April 20, 1945, NAACP Papers, pt. 14, reel 18.

5. See, for example, Walter White's March 3, 1945, column in the *Chicago Defender*.

6. On the war's transformative impact on America's foreign and domestic policies, see James T. Patterson, *Grand Expectations: The United States, 1945–1974* (New York, 1996), ch. 4; and Alan Brinkley, "The New Political Paradigm: World War Two and American Liberalism," in *The War in American Culture: Society and Consciousness in World War Two*, Lewis A. Erenberg and Susan E. Hirsch, eds. (Chicago, 1996), 313–30.

7. White's statement at the NAACP's thirty-seventh annual meeting, January 7, 1946, NAACP Papers, pt. 1, reel 14.

8. *Opportunity* (June 1942): 162–63.

9. Johnson, "The Negro in Post-War Reconstruction: His Hopes, Fears, and Possibilities," *Journal of Negro Education* 11 (October 1942): 465–70.

10. Saville R. Davis, "The Task for the Future," *The Crisis* (May 1944): 161–63. Davis gave the speech at the NAACP's annual meeting, held in February 1944.

11. Du Bois to Rachel Davis Du Bois, June 11, 1943, Du Bois Papers, reel 55. On the plight of blacks in the postwar period, see Du Bois's *Amsterdam News* column of October 23, 1943, which suggests his belief in the prospect for racial progress. Far more pessimistic is his *Chicago Defende* column of January 6, 1945.

12. On the Dumbarton Oaks Conference, see Robert C. Hilderbrand, *Dumbarton Oaks: The Origins of the United Nations and the Search for Postwar Security* (Chapel Hill, NC, 1990). See also Robert Divine, *Second Chance: The Triumph of Internationalism in America during World War II* (New York, 1967), ch. 9.

13. On Du Bois's remarks in Washington, see the following: *The Crisis* (November 1944): 361; "Colonial Questions Ignored at Dumbarton Oaks Peace Session," the *Pittsburgh Courier*, October 28, 1944; Du Bois to American Friends Service Committee, et al., October 21, 1944, Du Bois Papers, reel 55. For Du Bois's most trenchant critique of the Dumbarton Oaks proposals, see ch. 1 of his *Color and Democracy: Colonies and Peace* (New York, 1945). Beyond asserting that the proposals neglected the rights of the colonial world, Du Bois claimed that the means by which the United Nations sought to maintain peace, that is, through the threatened use of force, would not be conducive to cooperation. See also Du Bois's December 15, 1944, speech, "Colonies in the Post-War World," given at Virginia's Hampton Institute. Du Bois Papers, reel 80. Note a November 15, 1944, radio address on WEVD (New York) on "The Negro and Imperialism." NAACP Papers, pt. 18, reel 12. Another critic of the proposals was Howard University's Rayford Logan. See "Dumbarton Oaks Proposals Ignore Colonial Problem," *Chicago Defender*, December 9, 1944; and his October 1944 speech to the National Council of Negro Women. See Kenneth Robert Janken, *Rayford W. Logan and the Dilemmas of the African-American Intellectual* (Amherst, MA, 1993), 175.

14. Resolution passed by the NAACP's board of directors, March 12, 1945, NAACP Papers, pt. 14, reel 6. See also the association's press release, "NAACP Adopts Resolutions on Colonial Issues for 'Frisco Conference," March 15, 1945, ibid., pt. 14, reel 18. In February 1945, Du Bois attended a Washington, D.C., conference on the Bretton Woods proposals (which aimed to reconstruct the international economic order), where he again expressed his concern that statesmen had neglected to consider the plight of colonial peoples. See Du Bois's *Chicago Defender* columns of March 17 and 31, 1945.

15. See Du Bois's invitation, "A Colonial Conference," Du Bois Papers, reel 57; and "Resolutions of the Colonial Conference in New York," April 6, 1945, ibid. On the attendees, see Du Bois's "Report of the Department of Special Research," March 12–April 9, 1945, ibid. See also Robert L. Harris, Jr., "Racial Equality and the United Nations Charter," in *New Directions in Civil Rights Stud-*

ies, Armstead L. Robinson and Patricia Sullivan, eds. (Charlottesville, VA, 1991), 133–34.

16. See the NAACP board resolution of April 9, 1945, which was forwarded to Franklin Roosevelt by Roy Wilkins, April 11, 1945, NAACP Papers, pt. 14, reel 9. See also Walter White's April 12 telegram to Roosevelt, concerning the association's distress over the U.S. government's failure to insist that the subject of colonial trusteeship be placed on the agenda at San Francisco, ibid. Roosevelt died that day.

17. For the NAACP's request to attend the conference as an observer, see Roy Wilkins to Clark M. Eichelberger (director, American Association of the United Nations), March 30, 1945, NAACP Papers, pt. 14, reel 19. For the State Department's invitation, see Edward R. Stettinius to George E. C. Hayes, April 12, 1945, ibid. See Du Bois's letter to the secretary of state, March 10, 1945, which discussed the possibility of African-American representation at the conference. Du Bois Papers, reel 58. On the NAACP's status in San Francisco, see Du Bois to Leo Pasvolsky, April 10, 1945, ibid.

18. The National Council of Negro Women, of which Bethune was president, requested and was denied observer status at the UN Conference, which led to Bethune's selection (after Eleanor Roosevelt interceded in her behalf) as one of the NAACP's assistant consultants. Neither Du Bois nor White was pleased with her selection, and they had little to do with her in San Francisco. Questions about who would pay Mrs. Bethune's expenses further exacerbated the situation. According to Brenda Gayle Plummer, Walter White tried to "sabotage her presence" at San Francisco, and White and Du Bois "privately impugned her competence to one another." Plummer, *Rising Wind: Black Americans and U.S. Foreign Affairs, 1935–1960* (Chapel Hill, NC, 1996), 135–37. See also Dorothy B. Robins, *Experiment in Democracy: The Story of U.S. Citizen Organizations in Forging the Charter of the United Nations* (New York, 1971).

19. On Du Bois's activities in San Francisco, see the "Annual Report of the Director of Special Research for the Year 1945," 4, Du Bois Papers, reel 57; for the NAACP statement of May 1, see the press release, "Formal Demand Made for Race Equality at San Francisco Parley," May 3, 1945, NAACP Papers, pt. 14, reel 18. On the May 1 proceedings, see the confidential May 1 memorandum from Walter White to Du Bois and Bethune, Du Bois Papers, reel 57. On White's activities at the conference, see *A Man Called White,* 294–99; and Kenneth Robert Janken, *White: The Biography of Walter White, Mr. NAACP* (New York, 2003), 297–301.

20. Bethune quoted in Plummer, *Rising Wind,* 135–36. Note Plummer's incisive discussion of Bethune's community-based activities in San Francisco, which were different from those of White and Du Bois, who had different black constituencies, 136–37.

21. "Mrs. Bethune Sees Frisco Issues Decisive," *Norfolk Journal and Guide,* May 26, 1945.

22. See Bethune's letter to Walter White, which includes a copy of the invitation, June 8, 1945, NAACP Papers, pt. 14, reel 17.

23. Memorandum to Stettinius from Walter White, May 15, 1945, NAACP Papers, pt. 14, reel 18. On the UN's authority to involve itself in the domestic

matters of states, see the NAACP's press release, "NAACP Sees Danger to U.S. Minorities and Colonials in Intervention Clause," May 17, 1945, ibid.

24. See the columns of White and Du Bois in the *Chicago Defender*, April 28, 1945. For insight into the wide-ranging message both men conveyed to their readers during these months in 1945, see the following columns on the conference in the *Defender*: May 19 and 26, and June 2, 16, and 23. Exemplifying the distinctive internationalism that was central to civil rights discourse at this time, the Urban League's monthly linked developments in San Francisco to African-American aspirations. Responding to the question, "what do we expect from this conference?" *Opportunity* intertwined international and domestic goals, including peace, security, a "comfortable home," and the "chance for a job." America also seemed to have a special role to play in leading the world toward a more humane future. Readers learned, too, that the plight of black Americans was inseparable from that of exploited peoples in China, Africa, and India. Alphonse Heningburg, "What the Urban League Expects for All Races as a Result of the San Francisco Conference," *Opportunity* (Summer 1945): 123. For a positive view of developments in San Francisco, see "Success at San Francisco," *Amsterdam News*, May 19, 1945. For a different perspective, see the editorial, "The Future Is Still the Thing," published at the close of the conference. *Amsterdam News*, June 30, 1945. Rayford Logan, who covered the meeting for the *Pittsburgh Courier*, was critical of the parley, noting that while two-thirds of those represented at the conference were peoples of color, nine-tenths of the delegates were white, and none was working class. See Logan, "The 'Little Man' Just Isn't Here," the *Pittsburgh Courier*, May 5, 1945; and his "Charter Will Not Prevent Wars," ibid., July 14, 1945. In general, the *Courier* was critical of the conference, claiming that it gave the world's oppressed little cause for hope. See the editorials of May 12 and 26, and June 2 and 23, 1945.

25. "President Truman Confers with NAACP's Walter White," NAACP press release, May 25, 1945, Du Bois Papers, reel 57. See also White, *A Man Called White*, 299–300.

26. For Bethune's opening statement, see the National Negro Congress Papers, Schomburg Center for Research in Black Culture, New York Public Library, New York, microfilm edition, pt. 2, reel 20. The meeting focused on civil rights legislation, educational concerns, postwar employment matters, veterans' affairs, and the right of colonial peoples to independence. See the "Findings of the Conference" in ibid.

27. "Testimony of W.E.B. Du Bois," July 11, 1945, Du Bois Papers, reel 58. For Du Bois's assessment of the conference and the charter, see Du Bois to Hamilton Fish Armstrong, July 9, 1945, Du Bois Papers, reel 57.

28. "Victory: Not without Sadness," *Amsterdam News*, August 18, 1945. On the reformers' response to America's use of the bomb, see "The Atomic Bomb," *The Crisis* (September 1945): 249; and Walter White, "Atom Bomb and Lasting Peace," *Chicago Defender*, September 8, 1945.

29. John Hope Franklin, *From Slavery to Freedom: A History of African Americans* (New York, 1994), ch. 21.

30. "A Different American Is Returning to the States," Herbert Seward's letter to the *Pittsburgh Courier*, May 19, 1945. See also "Soldier Predicts: Next War for

Freedom to be on Home Front," ibid., June 2, 1945; and letters in the *Amsterdam News*, September 8, 1945.

31. Beyond sheer numbers, black employment during the war was more occupationally diverse than ever. Byron R. Skinner, " 'The Double V': The Impact of World War II on Black America" (Ph.D. diss., University of California–Berkeley, 1978), ch. 4.

32. Ibid., ch. 3.

33. On the NAACP's struggle for equal educational opportunities, see Mark V. Tushnet, *The NAACP's Legal Strategy against Segregated Education, 1925–1950* (Chapel Hill, NC, 1987), chs. 6–8. On the Fair Employment Practices Committee (FEPC), see Merl E. Reed, *Seedtime for the Modern Civil Rights Movement: The President's Committee on Fair Employment Practice, 1941–1946* (Baton Rouge, LA, 1991).

34. On Roosevelt's death, see *The Crisis* (May 1945): 129; and Du Bois's *Chicago Defender* column, May 5, 1945.

35. *The Crisis* (August 1947): 233. See Michael R. Gardner, *Harry Truman and Civil Rights: Moral Courage and Political Risks* (Carbondale, IL, 2002), ch. 3.

36. On the September 19 meeting, see White, *A Man Called White*, 330–32; and Gardner, *Truman and Civil Rights*, 18–19. For an illuminating discussion of the report, see Steven F. Lawson's essay in his edited volume, *To Secure These Rights: The Report of Harry S Truman's Committee on Civil Rights* (Boston, 2004), 1–41.

37. Du Bois to White, August 1, 1946, NAACP Papers, pt. 14, reel 16. The idea for the petition was the product of a petition the National Negro Congress had submitted to the United Nations on June 6, 1946, which argued that the domestic problems of black Americans had not been satisfactorily addressed and which called on the United Nations "to mobilize the influence of all organized mankind" in order to confront the oppression of blacks in America. NNC's "Petition to the Economic and Social Council of the United Nations" (along with Herbert Aptheker's section on the "Oppression of the American Negro" and letters of transmittal from NNC president Max Yergan to President Truman and UN Secretary-General Trygve Lie) is in the NNC Papers, pt. 1, reel 18. For an illuminating treatment, see Carol Anderson, "Eyes off the Prize: African-Americans, the United Nations, and the Struggle for Human Rights, 1944–1952" (Ph.D. diss., Ohio State University, 1995), ch. 3.

38. See, for example, Du Bois's October 11, 1946, letter to William R. Ming, which describes the proposed petition. Du Bois Papers, reel 58.

39. Du Bois, "Statement to the Representatives of the Human Rights Council and Its Parent Bodies, the Economic and Social Council and the General Assembly," October 23, 1947, Du Bois Papers, reel 60.

40. For White's October 23, 1947, statement, see NAACP Papers, pt. 14, reel 16. Note the NAACP press release, "Petition on Treatment of Negroes by NAACP to United Nations," October 24, 1947, ibid.

41. The petition began with an introductory chapter by Du Bois, who described the "color caste system" in America and noted the hypocrisy of the American nation. Next, Earl Dickerson examined the denial of legal rights for American blacks from 1787 to 1914, describing how the absence of effective sanctions

against those who violated the law had created a gap between the "doctrinal idealism of constitutional guarantees and the practical realization of constitutional protection." Milton Konvitz then considered the legal inequalities blacks faced, a result of Supreme Court decisions and state laws, and William Ming's chapter on the current social and legal status of blacks explored the "appalling contrast" between the rights the law guaranteed every person and those that black Americans were allowed to enjoy. Leslie Perry's section presented sociological data documenting substandard black living conditions, and Rayford Logan tried to explain why the violation of black civil rights was the appropriate province of the United Nations. Du Bois concluded the document with a summation of the black historical experience in America and an appeal to the United Nations to "step to the very edge of their authority" in helping to protect the black minority in America, an action, he asserted, that would contribute to the peace of the world. The petition can be found in the Du Bois Papers, reel 86.

42. *Des Moines Register* and *New York Post* material is from "Press Reaction to the NAACP United Nations Petition," compiled by Hugh Smythe, Du Bois's assistant in the association's Department of Special Research. Du Bois Papers, reel 60. Saul K. Padover, "How about Democracy for Negroes Too?" *P.M.*, October 14, 1947. Capper introduced the petition abstract on December 4, 1947. "Rights of Certain Minorities," NAACP Papers, pt. 16B, reel 3. Arthur Schlesinger, Jr., to White, December 16, 1947, NAACP Papers, pt. 14, reel 16. The December 1947 *Crisis* provided an extensive overview. See Du Bois, "Three Centuries of Discrimination," *The Crisis* (December 1947): 362–64, 379–81; and the black press also noted the significance of the NAACP's dramatic action. See, for example, the *Chicago Defender* editorial, "An Important Appeal," November 1, 1947.

43. On the decision to present the petition to the United Nations, the following correspondence points to Du Bois's view that the organization was the proper forum before which to place African-American grievances: Du Bois to Trygve Lie (UN secretary general), September 11, 1947; Du Bois to John Humphrey (director, UN Division of Human Rights), October 6, 1947. Du Bois to John Humphrey, October 14, 1947; Du Bois to Trygve Lie, October 14, 1947; Du Bois to William Stoneman, October 16, 1947; Du Bois Papers, reel 60. On the UN's authority to address black grievances, see Du Bois to Logan, October 1, 1946, and Logan's October 12 reply in which he noted the difficulty he was having locating what power the organization possessed to address the situation. According to Logan, if no authority could be found, the NAACP petition would have to ask for a revision of the UN Charter or merely use the UN as a sounding board "to arouse [world] public opinion." Du Bois Papers, reel 58. As noted above, Logan examined this question in the petition and concluded that the UN did have the authority to apply its principles to the American race problem. For an illuminating discussion on the question of UN authority in this regard, with particular reference to the "domestic jurisdiction" clause, which appeared to preclude the organization's trying to influence domestic matters, see Carol Anderson, *Eyes off the Prize: The United Nations and the African American Struggle for Human Rights, 1944–1955* (New York, 2003), esp. 48–50, 86–88, and 95. Bert Lockwood writes that the UN Charter played a subtle but significant role in judicial decisions on civil rights matters in the ten years after World War II. Lockwood, "The United Nations

Charter and United States Civil Rights Litigation: 1946–1955," *Iowa Law Review* 5 (1984): 901–49.

44. See Divine, *Second Chance*.

45. Du Bois to Warren Austin, February 4, 1948, Du Bois Papers, reel 63.

46. Carey's address, June 26, 1946, NAACP Papers, pt. 1, reel 11. In accepting the Spingarn Medal, Thurgood Marshall mentioned the struggle of the "darker races of the world," who formed the majority of the world's peoples. NAACP Papers, ibid.

47. "Declaration of Principles" adopted by the thirty-ninth annual conference, June 26, 1948, NAACP Papers, pt. 1, reel 12.

48. Wilkins's address, July 12, 1949, NAACP Papers, pt. 1, reel 12. On the fortieth annual conference, see *The Crisis* (August–September 1949): 246–49.

49. Du Bois proclaimed Indian independence to be the greatest historical development of the nineteenth and twentieth centuries. Du Bois, "The Freeing of India," *The Crisis* (October 1947): 301–4. See Walter White's *Chicago Defender* column, August 30, 1947. On black views concerning post-1945 India, see Sudarshan Kapur, *Raising Up a Prophet: The African-American Encounter with Gandhi* (Boston, 1992), ch. 6.

50. Pandit's address, July 17, 1949, NAACP Papers, pt. 1, reel 12. From mid-1945 to 1949, *The Crisis* published some two dozen pieces on the developing world, which focused mainly on the activities of peoples of color. Rayford Logan's status as an NAACP consultant also reflected its interest in colonial affairs. See the 1949 "Preliminary Memorandum Suggesting Areas of Activity for Rayford Logan as Consultant on Colonial Matters and the UN," NAACP Papers, pt. 14, reel 10.

51. Note, for example, the fifth Pan-African Congress, which met in Manchester, England, in October 1945. Du Bois was the only black American to attend the conference and did so as a private person; his attempt to gain NAACP support for the meeting was unsuccessful. See the following Du Bois columns on the meeting in the *Chicago Defender*: September 1, 22, and 29, October 20, November 3, and December 22, 1945. See Imanuel Geiss, *The Pan-African Movement: A History of Pan-Africanism in American, Europe, and Africa* (New York, 1974), ch. 19.

52. A sampling from the *Chicago Defender* includes the following: April 7, 1945 (Poland); May 12, 1945 (South Africa); August 11, 1945 (the Pacific); August 18, 1945 (British socialism); August 25, 1945 (Asia); November 11, 1945 (Africa); January 12, 1946 (the atomic bomb); and July 7, 1947 (the international social benefits of atomic energy). Du Bois also wrote frequently on the United Nations. See the following examples in the *Defender*: July 19, 1947, and March 27 and April 3 and 10, 1948.

53. On the Universal Declaration of Human Rights, see Paul Gordon Lauren, *Power and Prejudice: The Politics and Diplomacy of Racial Discrimination* (Boulder, CO, 1988), 174–82; and John P. Humphrey's memoir, *Human Rights and the United Nations: A Great Adventure* (Dobbs Ferry, NY, 1984), 50–89.

54. *Chicago Defender*, September 4, 1948.

55. Ibid., October 2, 1948.

56. Ibid., December 11, 1948.

57. Ibid., November 13, 1948. White's piece linking developments in Paris to American racial oppression appeared in the *New York Herald Tribune* in December. White said it was ironic that America's vote in Paris supporting the UN's Declaration of Human Rights occurred almost at the same time a report was issued in Washington documenting the existence of segregation in the nation's capital. "U.S. Urged to Live Up to Human Rights Pledge," *New York Herald Tribune*, December 19, 1948. On the UN declaration, see "UN Adopts Civil Rights for the World," *Chicago Defender*, December 18, 1948.

58. On *America's Town Meeting of the Air*, see "Five Hundred Hours Old: America's Town Meeting of the Air, 1935–1948," bulletin published by the staff of Town Hall (New York, 1948); and " 'Good Evening Neighbors!' The Story of an American Institution: Fifteen Years of America's Town Meeting of the Air," bulletin published by the staff of Town Hall (New York, 1950). On the 1949 world tour, see 54–74. On *America's Town Meeting of the Air*, see also Barbara Dianne Savage, *Broadcasting Freedom: Radio, War, and the Politics of Race, 1938–1948* (Chapel Hill, NC, 1999), 206–22.

59. "Foreigners Bewildered by U.S. Race Problem," *Chicago Defender*, August 13, 1949. In her description of the tour, Mary Bell Decker noted that American race relations greatly interested peoples throughout the world. See Decker, *The World We Saw with Town Hall* (New York, 1950), 168–69.

60. "Foreign Peoples Curious about U.S. Race Question," *Chicago Defender*, September 10, 1949.

61. *Chicago Defender*, September 10, 1949. White also describes the encounter in *How Far the Promised Land?* (New York, 1955), 7–9. On the experience of Edith Sampson on the tour, see Helen Laville and Scott Lucas, "The American Way: Edith Sampson, the NAACP, and African American Identity in the Cold War," *Diplomatic History* 20 (Fall 1996): 565–90. Note Sampson's remarks on the September 13, 1949, Town Hall broadcast (the meeting was held August 17 in Delhi, India). "What are Democracy's Best Answers to Communism?" *Town Meeting: Bulletin of America's Town Meeting of the Air* 15 (September 13, 1949): 10–11, 16, 18–19.

62. *Chicago Defender*, September 3, 1949.

63. "How Can We Advance Democracy in Asia?" *Town Meeting: Bulletin of America's Town Meeting of the Air* 15 (September 6, 1949): 12. On White's optimism in this period, see his December 12, 1949, letter to Dewitt Wallace of *Reader's Digest*, which discusses "almost a revolution in the thinking of Americans on the world implications of race. . . ." Walter White Papers, Yale University, box 6, folder 171.

64. See White's observations in the introductory chapter in *How Far the Promised Land?* See also Poppy Cannon, *A Gentle Knight: My Husband, Walter White* (New York, 1956), 64–150.

65. "Good Evening Neighbors!" 74.

66. See White to Marian Anderson and Sol Hurok, December 12, 1949, Walter White Papers, box 1, folder 1. According to White, the tour's participants learned that "the most damaging weakness of the United States is its failure to abolish racial and religious discrimination."

67. See White's introductory chapter in *How Far the Promised Land?* and the *New York Times* story, "White Warns the U.S. Is Losing Prestige but His Respect for Her Rises on Trip," September 23, 1949.

68. The literature on the origins of the Cold War is extensive and highly contested. Some key works include John Lewis Gaddis, *The United States and the Origins of the Cold War* (New York, 1972); Walter LaFeber, *America, Russia, and the Cold War, 1945–1992* (New York, 1993), chs. 1–4; Melvyn P. Leffler, *A Preponderance of Power: National Security, the Truman Administration, and the Cold War* (Stanford, CA, 1992); and Lloyd C. Gardner, *Architects of Illusion: Men and Ideas in American Foreign Policy, 1941–1949* (Chicago, 1970).

69. On the Cold War's impact on domestic culture, see Stephen J. Whitfield, *The Culture of the Cold War* (Baltimore, 1991).

70. "Byrnes and the Balkans," *The Crisis* (December 1945): 345. Note another editorial on the same page, which offered a critique of western foreign policies that was similar to that expressed by revisionist historians years later in their analysis of the Cold War's origins. "Confusion for Christmas," ibid. See also Walter White's *Chicago Defender* column, July 7, 1945.

71. *Chicago Defender*, August 17, 1946.

72. Du Bois's statement to the National Council of American-Soviet Friendship, Inc., October 28, 1947, Du Bois Papers, reel 60.

73. Du Bois to the National Council of American-Soviet Friendship, Inc., "Get Together with Russia," November 16, 1946, Du Bois Papers, reel 59. On Du Bois's view of Russia ("the most hopeful country in the world"), see his letter to Anna Melissa Graves, July 9, 1946: When "socialism dominates the state it is under Communism for the benefit of the mass of the people. When [American and British] imperialism dominates the state it is for the benefit of the rich or the powerful. The difference between the two is the difference between heaven and hell. . . . [D]ictatorship in Russia has been for the uplift of the underdog." Ibid., reel 58.

74. *Chicago Defender*, March 2, 1946.

75. Ibid., March 23, 1946. In discussing Churchill's address, Walter White placed the Briton's words into an explicitly racial context, calling it the "most revealing evidence yet produced of abject fear on the part of the so-called Anglo-Saxon English-speaking white people of the world." *Chicago Defender*, March 16, 1946. White also criticized Secretary of State Byrnes. Ibid., September 21, 1946.

76. *Chicago Defender*, April 20, 1946. See also White's *Defender* column, February 22, 1947, in which he related developments in the Soviet Union to domestic racial persecution.

77. See the following pieces in *The Crisis*: "Democratic Elections—In Poland" (March 1947): 73; "Democracy Defined at Moscow" (April 1947): 105; and "Foreign Policy and FEPC" (May 1947): 137. On the message from overseas, see Mary L. Dudziak, *Cold War Civil Rights: Race and the Image of American Democracy* (Princeton, NJ, 2000), ch. 1; and Thomas Borstelmann, *The Cold War and the Color Line: American Race Relations in the Global Arena* (Cambridge, MA, 2001), 75–76.

78. On the Truman Doctrine, see LaFeber, *America, Russia, and the Cold War*, ch. 3; and Leffler, *Preponderance of Power*, ch. 4.

79. *Chicago Defender*, April 19, 1947.

80. Ibid., April 26, 1947.

81. Du Bois, "Aid to Greece," April 13, 1947, Du Bois Papers, reel 80.

82. *Chicago Defender*, April 12, 1947. Unlike Du Bois, White did not laud the Soviet system and claimed the threat to Greece and the Balkans created a choice between Russian or Anglo-American domination. Nevertheless, he believed the failure of the free enterprise system was responsible for the spread of Communism. White, "The Issue in Greece," March 17, 1947, written for release to other newspapers. NAACP Papers, pt. 14, reel 7. On aid to Greece and Turkey, see White's letter to the *New York Times*, April 9, 1947.

83. On the Marshall Plan, see Leffler, *A Preponderance of Power*, 157–64; and LaFeber, *America, Russia, and the Cold War*, ch. 3.

84. For White's testimony, see Congress, Senate, American Aid to the Peoples of the World, 80th Cong., 2nd sess., *Congressional Record* 94, pt. 9 (January 30, 1948): appendix, A525. White testified on January 27, 1948. Du Bois considered the Marshall Plan in his *Chicago Defender* columns of August 9 and November 8, 1947.

85. Wright's address, "The NAACP in 1946–47," June 24, 1947, NAACP Papers, pt. 1, reel 12.

86. On Randolph's activities in this period, see Paula Pfeffer, *A. Philip Randolph, Pioneer of the Civil Rights Movement* (Baton Rouge, LA, 1990), chs. 3–4. On the struggle for a permanent FEPC, see Reed, *Seedtime*, ch. 10. On desegregating the military, see Richard Dalfiume, *Desegregation of the U.S. Armed Forces: Fighting on Two Fronts, 1939–1953* (Columbia, MO, 1969), chs. 7–9. The idea of civil disobedience played an important role in Randolph's efforts to abolish segregation in the military. See his testimony before the Senate Armed Services Committee on March 31, 1948, in which he explained that his advocacy of passive resistance did not reflect support for the Soviet Union, toward which he was unwaveringly opposed. Testimony of A. Philip Randolph before the Senate Armed Services Committee, "Civil Disobedience," Randolph Papers, Library of Congress, Washington, D.C., microfilm edition, reel 28. See also "Civil Disobedience," *Black Worker* (April 1948).

87. Randolph, "Statement in Support of S-984," June 11, 1947, Randolph Papers, reel 30.

88. Randolph's address at Tuskegee, undated (context indicates late 1940s), Randolph Papers, reel 30.

89. Randolph, "In Quest for New Frontiers of Freedom," undated (context indicates he gave the address in May or June 1945), Randolph Papers, reel 30. See also Randolph's "Statement to Educational Political Conference in Chicago at the International House," undated, ibid.; Randolph, "Discrimination against Minorities," undated (context indicates it was written just after the war), ibid., reel 31. Randolph also blended the two themes, discussing the international battle against totalitarianism and the global struggle against racial oppression. See his Madison Square Garden address, February 28, 1946, ibid., reel 28.

90. "The New Year," *Black Worker* (January 1947). For pieces in the *Black Worker* that highlight the significance of the global struggle against racial oppression, see "The Old and New Years" (January 1946); and "The World of Color" (April 1946).

91. Truman's June 29, 1947, address was reprinted in *The Crisis* (July 1947): 200.

92. On the Truman administration's commitment to civil rights, see Michael Gardner, *Harry Truman and Civil Rights*, passim; and William C. Berman, *The Politics of Civil Rights in the Truman Administration* (Columbus, OH, 1970), chs. 1–3.

93. On the 1947 annual conference, see *The Crisis* (August 1947): 247–50. On the NAACP's belief that the conference had international significance, see "NAACP 38th Conference Held Internationally Important," press release June 13, 1947, NAACP Papers, pt. 1, reel 12. In an illuminating discussion about the negotiations between Walter White and the Truman administration, which preceded Truman's appearance, John Fousek shows that White suggested that the president link the international situation to the civil rights struggle. According to Fousek, White sought to convince Truman to make clear that the United States was determined to overcome its domestic shortcomings, a stance that could have positive implications for the country in the East-West competition. This suggests that the NAACP's argument that world affairs were inseparable from the domestic struggle had begun to influence policymakers. See Fousek, *To Lead the Free World: American Nationalism and the Cultural Roots of the Cold War* (Chapel Hill, NC, 2000), 133–36. See also Michael Gardner, *Harry Truman and Civil Rights*, ch. 3.

94. Truman quoted in Berman, *Politics of Civil Rights*, 72. Berman provides a full discussion of the document and its reception, 67–74. White quoted in his *A Man Called White*, 333. On the PCCR, see Robert L. Zangrando, *The NAACP Crusade against Lynching, 1909–1950* (Philadelphia, 1980), 177–86. See also Michael Gardner, *Harry Truman and Civil Rights*, ch. 4.

95. Dudziak, *Cold War Civil Rights*, 80–81. See also Azza Salama Layton, *International Politics and Civil Rights Policies in the United States, 1941–1960* (New York, 2000), 76–79.

96. Truman quoted in Dudziak, *Cold War Civil Rights*, 82. See also Gardner, *Harry Truman and Civil Rights*, ch. 6.

97. Dalfiume, *Desegregation of the U.S. Armed Forces*, 174. See also Sherie Mershon and Steven Schlossman, *Foxholes and Color Lines: Desegregating the U.S. Armed Forces* (Baltimore, 1998), 180–86; and Gardner, *Harry Truman and Civil Rights*, ch. 8. It should be emphasized that domestic political considerations—the 1948 presidential election was less than four months away—no doubt played a key role in Truman's decision. Roy Wilkins makes this point in *Standing Fast: The Autobiography of Roy Wilkins* (New York, 1982), 201–2.

98. Bunche's address, July 17, 1949, NAACP Papers, pt. 1, reel 12. See also Wilkins's address, "To Secure These Rights," June 22, 1948, NAACP Papers, pt. 1, reel 12. On the way East-West concerns were linked to the American race problem during White's 1949 Town Meeting of the Air tour, see "How Can We Advance Democracy in Asia?" *Town Meeting: Bulletin of America's Town Meeting*

of the Air 15 (September 6, 1949). See White's comments "What Are Democracy's Best Answers to Communism?" ibid. (September 13, 1949): 11–13; and Edith Samson's comments (10–11, 16, 18–19). See also White, *How Far the Promised Land?* 3–28; and "White Warns the U.S. Is Losing Prestige but His Respect for Her Rises on Trip," *New York Times*, September 23, 1949.

99. On America's use of the atomic bomb against Japan, see Walter White's column in the *Chicago Defender*, September 8, 1945; and "Who Won the War?" *The Crisis* (September 1945): 249.

CHAPTER SEVEN

1. "What Effect Do Our Race Relations Have on Our Foreign Policy?" *Town Meeting: Bulletin of America's Town Meeting of the Air* 15 (April 18, 1950): 4, 14.

2. Among those who argue that the Cold War had a positive impact on the movement are Gary Gerstle, *American Crucible: Race and Nation in the Twentieth Century* (Princeton, NJ, 2001), 249–50, 263–67, 277; Philip A. Klinkner with Rogers M. Smith, *The Unsteady March: The Rise and Decline of Racial Equality in America* (Chicago, 1999), chs. 7–8; John Fousek, *To Lead the Free World: American Nationalism and the Cultural Roots of the Cold War* (Chapel Hill, NC, 2000), ch. 5; Azza Salama Layton, *International Politics and Civil Rights Policies in the United States, 1941–1960* (New York, 2000), passim; Michael Sherry, *In the Shadow of War: The United States since the 1930s* (New Haven, CT, 1995), 208–12, 255–56; and Alexander Keyssar, *The Right to Vote: The Contested History of Democracy in the United States* (New York, 2000), 251–52, 268. Those who oppose this view include Penny M. Von Eschen, *Race against Empire: Black Americans and Anticolonialism, 1937–1957* (Ithaca, NY, 1957); Carol Anderson, *Eyes off the Prize: The United Nations and the African American Struggle for Human Rights, 1944–1955* (New York, 2003); and Ellen Schrecker, *Many Are the Crimes: McCarthyism in America* (Princeton, NJ, 1998), 389–95. Mary L. Dudziak occupies a middle position, arguing that "international pressures" would both "constrain and enhance civil rights reform." According to Dudziak, race reform was "*in part* [her italics] a product of the Cold War." See Dudziak, *Cold War Civil Rights: Race and the Image of American Democracy* (Princeton, NJ, 2000), 11–12.

3. Truman quoted in Ernest R. May, *"Lessons" of the Past: The Use and Misuse of History in American Foreign Policy* (New York, 1973), 81–82. On the Korean War, see William Stueck, *The Korean War: An International History* (Princeton, NJ, 1995).

4. "Korean War," *The Crisis* (October 1950): 586.

5. "Korean War," *The Crisis* (August–September 1950): 511.

6. *Chicago Defender*, August 5, 1950. White also linked the war directly to contemporary domestic events, asserting that the recent defeat of civil rights legislation would provide ammunition for America's Communist enemies. Ibid., September 9, 1950.

7. Ralph Bunche, July 1, 1951, NAACP Papers, Library of Congress, Washington, D.C., microfilm edition, pt. 1 (suppl.), reel 4. At the annual conference, sev-

eral others linked the Cold War, colonial matters, the Korean war, and domestic reform. Note the press report of a Bunche speech from earlier that year in which he linked the same issues. "Dr. Bunche Says U.S. Must Clean Own House," *Chicago Defender*, February 3, 1951. The NAACP's resolutions passed at the 1951 annual conference included a strongly worded statement supporting the American decision to fight in Korea. See *The Crisis* (August–September 1951): 491. The black soldier's experience interested the reformers as they reflected on the meaning of the Korean war. One example of discrimination concerned the courts-martial in 1950 of thirty-nine black soldiers for a variety of charges, including cowardice. The NAACP's Thurgood Marshall investigated the incident and found Jim Crow to be at the root of the allegations. The NAACP legal department's work resulted in reduced sentences or reversed convictions for the black servicemen. See "Smearing Negro GIs in Korea," *The Crisis* (December 1950): 215; "Mr. Marshall Reports," ibid. (March 1951): 180–81; and "Summary Justice—The Negro GI in Korea," ibid. (May 1951): 297–304.

8. White's address, June 25, 1950, NAACP Papers, pt. 1, reel 12. White expressed similar ideas at the annual conferences in 1951, 1953, and 1954. In an illuminating letter from White to NAACP President Arthur Spingarn written early in the decade, White argued that the Cold War and colonial developments were essential to the progress of domestic reform. Responding to criticism that he spent too much time "traips[ing] all over the world," White claimed the association's effectiveness had been enhanced by his foreign activities and asserted that the organization would grow "only as it recognizes that the problems of race and colonialism are world wide in their scope and, next to the question of US-USSR relations, the most important problem in the world today." White also rejected the idea that African Americans had little interest in world affairs and claimed his extensive contact with the black population suggested a deep concern for developments overseas. White to Arthur Spingarn, undated (context suggests early 1950s), James Weldon Johnson Collection, Yale University, box 6, folder 195. See also White's March 12, 1952, memorandum to Roy Wilkins on proposed speakers for the annual conference, in which White suggests selecting "people who will project the Negro question into the framework of national and world problems." White thought Dean Acheson and Kwame Nkrumah would be good choices. NAACP Papers, pt. 1 (supp.), reel 6.

9. The Reverend James H. Robinson, "International Implications of the Association's Work," June 26, 1952, NAACP Papers, pt. 1 (supp.), reel 6. Senator Hubert Humphrey of Minnesota offered themes similar to those of Robinson, telling the gathering (through a friend speaking on his behalf) that discrimination was the country's number-one problem at home and abroad. The speech knitted together North-South, East-West, and domestic themes. Hubert Humphrey, June 29, 1952, ibid. Numerous examples from the association's annual conferences between 1950 and 1960 suggest the extent to which overseas affairs, especially colonial developments and the Cold War, occupied a significant place in the language of race reform. In addition, throughout the decade, the NAACP's annual resolutions (passed at the annual conferences) indicate the extent to which overseas matters occupied the association's attention. Concerns about world affairs appeared under the heading "International and Colonial Problems"; a wide vari-

ety of areas and subjects was considered, including Asia, Africa, India, the Middle East, the Caribbean, imperialism, collective security, the United Nations, American foreign aid policies, and the Korean War. Beginning in 1952 and continuing throughout the decade, the association's resolutions included a prominent statement opposing the racist policies of the South African regime. See Walter White to Warren R. Austin, vice chairman, U.S. Delegation to the United Nations, December 5, 1952, NAACP Papers, pt. 14, reel 5.

10. An April 1953 editorial observed that while Americans spoke about the liberation of "enslaved peoples" behind the Iron Curtain, they paid little attention to the plight of unfree peoples in Africa and Asia. In fact, the "Free World" actually thwarted the longings of colonial peoples with a mixture of "broken promises, repression," and violence, and the United States often led the way in "upholding the imperialist viewpoint." According to the editors, American relations with the colonial world reflected a "mentality inherited from the traditions of the masters in a slave society." "Liberating 'Enslaved Peoples,' " *The Crisis* (April 1953): 228–29. In the same issue, see P. L. Prattis, "New Look at the World," 201–4.

In 1954, journalist William Worthy considered the relationship between imperialism and the East-West conflict and examined the deepening American commitment in French Indochina. He wondered what the country was defending in Indochina; in his view, the French colonial regime America supported was corrupt, oppressive, and without indigenous support. Presciently, Worthy asserted that the war waged by Vietminh forces against the French was a nationalist struggle that had little to do with ideology. These were not Communists, but nationalists, he argued, who wanted the French and Americans to go home. Worthy, "Our Disgrace in Indo-China," *The Crisis* (February 1954): 77–83. Note Worthy's second piece, an indictment of American foreign policy, which he said was driven by the search for markets and raw materials. Worthy, "Of Global Bondage," ibid. (October 1954), 467–74. According to a December 1954 memorandum from Herbert Hill to Roy Wilkins, the NAACP rejected the analysis offered by Worthy in his October piece. Hill noted that while the association identified with the movement against colonialism and supported the fight for national freedom, it repudiated the view of those who refused to question "the monstrous crimes of the rival imperialism of the Communist empire." In the future, Hill observed, the journal would express its support for "legitimate leaders" struggling against western imperialism, but will point out the dangers of the ideology that proclaims "its right to leadership in Asia and Africa" so as to lead the "masses onto the road of the most savage imperialism of our time, the road to Moscow and Peiping." Hill to Wilkins, December 9, 1954, NAACP Papers, pt. 14, reel 6.

11. Wilkins, "Undergirding the Democratic Ideal," *The Crisis* (December 1951): 647–51. Wilkins gave the address in New York in October 1951 at an award ceremony for the Catholic Interracial Council. See also Richard Deverall, "The Struggle for Asia," *The Crisis* (January 1951): 25–29.

12. As a 1951 piece observed, "Deny it as we will we cannot hide the fact that America's domestic racial policies create ill-will abroad." "Foreigners React to American Prejudice," *The Crisis* (February 1951): 103.

13. James Ivy, "American Negro Problem in the European Press," *The Crisis* (July 1950): 413–18.

14. Ibid. Note how *The Crisis* looked at French press coverage of the savage killing of Emmett Till in Mississippi and the sham trial of those accused of the crime. "French Reaction to Till Trial," ibid. (November 1955): 546–47; and "L'affaire Till in the French Press," ibid. (December 1955): 596–602. In 1951, novelist Richard Wright, who was one of about five hundred black Americans living in France, discussed French attitudes toward racial matters. Wright spoke of French open-mindedness, noting that the "American Negro in France goes about his daily routine with no anxiety of having to cope with arbitrary racial assaults." But it seemed change was in the air, for Wright described a phenomenon some had noted after the Great War, when American influence in France had adversely affected the character of Gallic race relations. According to Wright, as the United States sought to extend aid to Europe, American social practices had crossed the Atlantic, causing black expatriates to ask whether some Frenchmen, eager to please the Americans, would "accept racial doctrines alien to French traditions or customs." Wright, "American Negroes in France," *The Crisis* (June– July 1951): 381–83. On the Till case, see Stephen J. Whitfield, *A Death in the Delta: The Story of Emmett Till* (Baltimore, 1988).

In 1954, the journal presented a novel twist on the subject of foreign perceptions of the American race problem. Sociologist John Owen described teaching at the University of Helsinki, where Finnish students were interested in American race relations. Pointing to the international importance of the American race question, Owen claimed that ignorance of the subject might make foreigners susceptible to Soviet propaganda. It was essential to inform the world's peoples about the past and present achievements of black Americans. While many knew about American race riots and other acts of violence against blacks, the numerous "heartening changes" on the domestic front remained unknown. Owen believed it was now possible to answer yes to the question: "Does America have a better idea than the Russian idea?" Owen, "U.S. Race Relations—A World Issue," *The Crisis* (January 1954): 19–22. On European perceptions of American race relations, note John Hope Franklin's October 26, 1958, address, "America's Window to the World: Her Race Problem," delivered at a ceremony of the Catholic Interracial Council, in *Rhetoric of Racial Revolt*, Roy L. Hill, ed. (Denver, 1964), 201–11.

15. On Randolph's activities during the 1950s, see Paula Pfeffer, *A. Philip Randolph, Pioneer of the Civil Rights Movement* (Baton Rouge, LA, 1990), chs. 5–6.

16. Randolph to Dennis Wooding, June 14, 1950, Randolph Papers, Library of Congress, Washington, D.C., microfilm edition, reel 1. Several weeks later, after the war had begun, he wrote that the "only hope for democracy today is to start the march against Communism." Randolph to James M. Mead, August 17, 1950, ibid.

17. Randolph to Catherine Lealtead, January 22, 1952, Randolph Papers, reel 1. See also Randolph's January 7, 1952, letter to Lealtead on China, Communism, and the Korean War, ibid.

18. "Randolph Says Negroes, Other Minorities, Have Stake in Korean Struggle," *Black Worker* (July 1950).

19. "Back United States and United Nations on Korea," *Black Worker* (August 1950). On July 1, 1950, the *New York Times* published a letter from Randolph,

in which he supported American intervention in Korea. According to the labor leader, America's response was the only language Communist Russia would understand. Randolph wrote that he could not imagine any fate worse than the "domination of the world by Communist Russian arms and culture." Such a fate was worse even than atomic destruction. See "Attack on Korea Discussed" in the letters column.

20. Randolph's speech in Boston, undated (but early 1950s), Randolph Papers, reel 30.

21. Randolph, "My Trip to Asia" (written in 1952), Randolph Papers, reel 31. (It is not clear where he published the piece.) Note Randolph's address to the Catholic Interracial Council, October 28, 1956, ibid., reel 28; and the *Black Worker*, the organ of the Brotherhood of Sleeping Car Porters, which demonstrates how Randolph incorporated his view of overseas events into his reform rhetoric. Discussion of international developments permeated the publication, including reflections on the Korean War, African affairs, Randolph's foreign trips, and the global fight against Communism. A June 1953 letter to President Eisenhower, who was ready to depart for Bermuda to meet with British and French leaders, suggests how Randolph framed colonial developments. Telling the president that he wished to convey his thoughts on the current and future status of Africa, which might prove useful as Eisenhower prepared to meet with the leaders of the two leading imperial powers, Randolph encouraged the president to link foreign aid to Britain and France to their willingness to end colonial oppression in Africa. Randolph also discussed Communism, cautioning the president not to believe that the Kremlin was behind the unrest in Africa. Black Africans were moved by their own aims and were seeking to liberate themselves from their white oppressors in a crusade for "bread . . . freedom, justice and equality." The African people were moving toward self-determination, he assured the president, a crusade no earthly force could impede, and it was essential for these struggling millions to look for leadership not to the Soviet Union but to the United States. Randolph to Eisenhower, June 16, 1953, Randolph Papers, reel 1.

22. As has been noted, since the 1930s, many traditional reformers had come to believe that the Communist Party was less interested in advancing the aims of black Americans than it was in advancing its own agenda. For a thoughtful discussion on blacks and domestic Communism during the Cold War, see James H. Meriwether, *Proudly We Can Be Africans: Black Americans and Africa, 1935–1961* (Chapel Hill, NC, 2002), ch. 2. On the relationship between the Communist Party and the NAACP in this period, see Wilson Record, *Race and Radicalism: The NAACP and the Communist Party in Conflict* (Ithaca, NY, 1964), chs. 5–6. For the anti-Communism resolution, see Resolutions Adopted by the Forty-first Annual Conference, June 1950, NAACP Papers, pt. 1, reel 12.

23. For an excellent example, see Randolph, "Are Communists a Threat to Democratic Organizations?" undated speech, but early 1950s, Randolph Papers, reel 30.

24. Walter White, *How Far the Promised Land?* (New York, 1953), ch. 11. See also White, "Reported Red Plot to 'Take Over' the NAACP Is Discounted," *New York Herald Tribune*, December 21, 1947; White to Frederick Woltman, February 19, 1950, Walter White Papers, Yale University, box 6, folder 179;

White, "American Communists Had Good Opportunity; Fumbled the Ball," *Chicago Defender*, March 25, 1950; White, "The Negro and the Communists," *The Crisis* (August–September 1950): 502–6 (originally published in the December 1931 issue of *Harper's* magazine); and White, "Editor's Trip to Russia Found Both Fascinating and Heartbreaking," *Chicago Defender*, May 16, 1953.

On the traditional reformers' aversion to Communism, note the activities of the Civil Rights Congress (CRC), a legal defense group founded in 1946. Worth highlighting is one episode in the history of the organization, which helped establish numerous civil liberties rulings in the United States (particularly for minorities) during its ten-year existence. See Gerald Horne, *Communist Front? The Civil Rights Congress, 1946–1956* (Rutherford, NJ, 1988), 13. One of the organization's most significant projects was the petition "We Charge Genocide," which was submitted to the United Nations in 1951. The document detailed violence and discrimination against black Americans and claimed the treatment of blacks was a form of genocide, which the United Nations had outlawed in 1948. See William L. Patterson, *The Man Who Cried Genocide: An Autobiography* (New York, 1971), chs. 12–13. See Horne's illuminating assessment in *Communist Front?*, ch. 6. Those in the NAACP thought the organization that produced the petition was in league with the Communists. Walter White responded to a State Department request to evaluate the petition by claiming that most of its allegations of racial persecution were well-founded; nevertheless, he doubted the integrity of its authors. In embracing the message and repudiating its messengers, White could decry the persistence of racial oppression in America, while speaking in favor of a traditional approach to reform. According to White, the NAACP had chosen to do its work within the "framework of a free society" that allowed people of all races and colors to criticize, protest, utilize legal processes, and appeal to their fellow citizens for redress. White's statement (undated, but undoubtedly from November 1951) is in NAACP Papers, pt. 14, reel 16. For more on the CRC, particularly its relationship with the NAACP, see Earl Ofari Hutchinson, *Blacks and Reds: Race and Class in Conflict, 1919–1990* (East Lansing, MI, 1995), 198–214.

25. Herbert Hill, "The Communist Party—Enemy of Negro Equality," *The Crisis* (June–July 1951): 365–71.

26. Robert Alan, "Paul Robeson—The Lost Shepherd," *The Crisis* (November 1951): 569–73. According to Gerald Horne, Robert Alan was a mole working in the service of the FBI, which sought to discredit Robeson and other black dissenters. See Gerald Horne, *Black and Red: W.E.B. Du Bois and the Afro-American Response to the Cold War* (Albany, NY, 1986), 207. On the torrent of abuse Robeson had to endure at the hands of the United States government during the 1950s, a result of his alleged unpatriotic activities and ties to the Soviet Union, see Martin Duberman, *Paul Robeson* (New York, 1988), esp. chs. 17–21.

27. See Arnold Rampersad's luminous discussion of this episode. Rampersad, *I Dream a World: The Life of Langston Hughes* (New York, 1988), 2:209–22.

28. "Langston Hughes Speaks," *The Crisis* (May 1953): 279–80. A transcript of the fascinating testimony that Hughes gave in executive session (as opposed to the public testimony quoted here) is available online at http://www.gpo.gov/congress/senate/senate12cp107.html

29. Horne, *Black and Red*, ch. 16.

30. The government, disturbed by Du Bois's work for the Peace Information Center (an organization that asserted it was working for world peace) and angered by his professed sympathies for the Soviet Union and its supporters, tried to muzzle Du Bois, just as it sought to muzzle thousands of others in these years. On the stifling of dissent in the United States, see Schrecker, *Many Are the Crimes*.

31. *The Autobiography of W.E.B. Du Bois: A Soliloquy on Viewing My Life from the Last Decade of Its First Century* (New York, 1968), 379.

32. Du Bois quoted in Horne, *Black and Red*, 179. For a full account of the trial, including the NAACP's reluctance to support Du Bois, see ibid., ch. 14.

33. Du Bois, *Autobiography*, 394–95.

34. Harvard Sitkoff, *The Struggle for Black Equality, 1954–1992* (New York, 1993; orig., 1981), 14–15.

35. The preceding discussion is based on Sitkoff, *Struggle for Black Equality*, 14–15.

36. Warren quoted in "Text of United States Supreme Court Decision Outlawing Negro Segregation in the Public Schools," *The Crisis* (June–July 1954): 325–32. In the same issue, see "History of the Five School Cases," 337–42; and the editorial, "Segregation Decision," 352–53. The most comprehensive study is Richard Kluger, *Simple Justice: The History of* Brown v. Board of Education *and Black America's Struggle for Equality* (New York, 1976). For a genuinely enlightening account of the *Brown* decision, which argues that its significance has been overstated and its long-term impact not fully understood, see Michael J. Klarman, *From Jim Crow to Civil Rights: The Supreme Court and the Struggle for Racial Equality* (New York, 2004). For a highly readable and more personal study, see Charles J. Ogletree, Jr., *All Deliberate Speed: Reflections on the First Half Century of* Brown vs. Board of Education (New York, 2004). See also James T. Patterson, Brown vs. Board of Education: *A Civil Rights Milestone and Its Troubled Legacy* (New York, 2001), chs. 2–4.

37. Roy Wilkins, *Standing Fast: The Autobiography of Roy Wilkins* (New York, 1982), 214.

38. Tobias's address, June 29, 1954, NAACP Papers, pt. 1 (supp.), reel 10.

39. Marshall's address, June 30, 1954, ibid.

40. White's address, July 4, 1954, ibid. That same day, Ralph Bunche also identified a relationship between the decision and international matters. Ibid.

41. For Eisenhower's statement, see "45th Annual NAACP Conference," *The Crisis* (August–September 1954): 421.

42. Gerstle, *American Crucible*, 250. In a genuinely illuminating examination of the intersection between the Cold War and *Brown*, Mary Dudziak has shown that the global competition was very much at issue in the landmark case. The Department of Justice had filed an amicus curiae brief with the court in the bundle of desegregation cases of which *Brown* was a part, and that brief raised directly the issue of America's Cold War concerns. Utilizing the words of former President Harry Truman and former Secretary of State Dean Acheson, the Justice Department's amicus brief asserted that damage had been and would continue to be done to the country's overseas interests so long as racial discrimination persisted in the United States. Dudziak also speculates on the way Cold War concerns might have

contributed to the justices' decision in the case and considers the way the government, particularly the State Department, sought to use the decision striking down segregation to improve America's image overseas. In addition, Dudziak has shown that Cold War considerations likely played a part in several other key Supreme Court cases: *Shelley v. Kraemer* (1948), *Henderson v. United States* (1949), *McLaurin v. Oklahoma State Regents for Higher Education* (1949), and *Sweatt v. Painter* (1949). As in *Brown*, amicus briefs raised the issue of Cold War concerns. Mary L. Dudziak, "Desegregation as a Cold War Imperative," *Stanford Law Review* 41 (November 1988): 61–120. Note, too, Dudziak's *Cold War Civil Rights*, which explores the connection, ch. 3. Significantly, the NAACP also referred to the Cold War when *Brown* was reargued in 1953, pointing out that the "survival of our country in the present international situation is inevitably tied to resolution of this domestic issue." Quoted in Dudziak, *Cold War Civil Rights*, 102.

43. King and Parks quoted in Sitkoff, *Struggle for Black Equality*, 38. On the bus boycott, see David J. Garrow, *Bearing the Cross: Martin Luther King, Jr. and the Southern Christian Leadership Conference* (New York, 1986), ch. 1.

44. My discussion of the boycott's significance is based on Sitkoff, *Struggle for Black Equality*, 55–57. On the early days of the Southern Christian Leadership Conference, see Adam Fairclough, *To Redeem the Soul of America: The Southern Christian Leadership Conference and Martin Luther King, Jr.* (Athens, GA, 1987), chs. 1–2. On the degree to which religion, specifically "the prophetic tradition," influenced the movement, see David L. Chappell, *A Stone of Hope: Prophetic Religion and the Death of Jim Crow* (Chapel Hill, NC, 2004).

45. King's address, June 27, 1956, NAACP's annual conference, NAACP Papers, pt. 1 (supp.), reel 4. For Gandhi's influence on King, see Martin Luther King, Jr., *Stride toward Freedom: The Montgomery Story* (New York, 1958), ch. 6; King, "My Trip to the Land of Gandhi," *Ebony*, July 1959: 84–92; and King, *Strength to Love* (Philadelphia, 1963), 149–52. See also Clayborne Carson, ed., *The Papers of Martin Luther King, Jr.* (Berkeley, CA, 1997), 3:16–22; and William Robert Miller, "The Broadening Horizons: Montgomery, America, the World," in *Martin Luther King, Jr: A Profile*, C. Eric Lincoln, ed. (New York, 1970), 40–71.

46. King, "Facing the Challenge of a New Age," address at the first annual Institute on Nonviolence and Social Change, Montgomery, Alabama, December 3, 1956, in *Papers of Martin Luther King, Jr.*, 3:451–63. See also the following remarks made during the period of the bus boycott in which King incorporated discussion of the developing world into his message: "The Death of Evil upon the Seashore," sermon delivered in the Cathedral of St. John the Divine, New York City, May 17, 1956, ibid., 3:256–62; and "Non-Aggression Procedures to Interracial Harmony," address delivered at the American Baptist Assembly and American Home Mission Agencies Conference, Green Bay, Wisconsin, July 23, 1956, ibid., 3:321–28. For King's view of the developing world, see James H. Cone, "Martin Luther King, Jr., and the Third World," *Journal of American History* 74 (September 1987): 455–67.

47. See Numan V. Bartley, *The Rise of Massive Resistance: Race and Politics in the South during the 1950s* (Baton Rouge, LA, 1967). On southern efforts to obstruct the NAACP's work, see Sitkoff, *Struggle for Black Equality*, 25–36.

48. On White's death, see *The Crisis* (April 1955): 226–32. On the accession of Roy Wilkins, see ibid. (May 1955): 272–74. See also "10,000 Persons at White's Bier" and "The Wind Still Rises," *Chicago Defender*, April 2, 1955. Brenda Gayle Plummer makes a similar point about the accession of Wilkins. See Plummer, *Rising Wind: Black Americans and U.S. Foreign Affairs, 1935–1960* (Chapel Hill, NC, 1996), 253.

49. The Bandung material is from Paul Gordon Lauren, *Power and Prejudice: The Politics and Diplomacy of Racial Discrimination* (Boulder, CO, 1988), 210–11.

50. Wilkins's telegram, April 15, 1955, NAACP Papers, pt. 14, reel 6. "Bandung Conference," *The Crisis* (May 1955): 291. For an illuminating discussion, see Cary Fraser, "An American Dilemma: Race and Realpolitik in the American Response to the Bandung Conference, 1955," in *Window on Freedom: Race, Civil Rights, and Foreign Affairs, 1945–1988*, Brenda Gayle Plummer, ed. (Chapel Hill, NC, 2003), 115–40.

51. Powell quoted in "Significance of the Bandung Conference for Colored Americans," which also includes an overview of coverage in the black press and reaction to Powell's activities. *Spotlight on Africa* (May 1955): 16–22. This can be found in the NAACP Papers, pt. 14, reel 6. See also Adam Clayton Powell, "My Mission to Bandung," *Nation*, May 28, 1955, 455–56, in which Powell claimed his aim was to counter Communist propaganda at the conference. Plummer, *Rising Wind*, 255–56. Plummer is insightful on other aspects of the conference, 247–56. See also Thomas Borstelmann, *The Cold War and the Color Line: American Race Relations in the Global Arena* (Cambridge, MA, 2001), 95–97.

52. King quoted in Garrow, *Bearing the Cross*, 90–91. Randolph describes the scene in Accra in "Ghana Speaks to the World of Color," *Black Worker* (April 1957). See Roy Wilkins's February 1957 letter to Nkrumah and the NAACP board's resolution, published in *The Crisis* (April 1957): 208–9. Interestingly, Richard Nixon also linked the Cold War, the developing world, and domestic race relations, observing upon his return from Africa that those who "promote discrimination and prejudice in the U.S." were hurting the nation at home and abroad. The vice president even suggested that a lack of progress on the American racial front might cause Africa to fall to Communism. On Nixon, note "Sees Link between U.S. Race Relations and Africa," *Chicago Defender*, March 23, 1957. See Meriwether, *Proudly We Can Be Africans*, ch. 5.

53. Randolph's address at the Ghanaian independence celebration, March 2–10, 1957, Randolph Papers, reel 28. See also Randolph, "The World Challenge of Ghana," ibid., reel 30. In the *Black Worker*, see "President Randolph to Represent AFL-CIO at Independence Celebration in Africa" (February 1957); and "Ghana Speaks to the World of Color" (May 1957).

54. "Prime Minister of Ghana Honored," *The Crisis* (August–September 1958): 407–9; and Wilkins, "Ghana Heartens U.S. Negroes," ibid., 410–11. See also Meriwether, *Proudly We Can Be Africans*, 172–77.

55. Wilkins's address, June 30, 1957, NAACP Papers, pt. 1 (supp.), reel 6.

56. King's address, June 28, 1957, ibid. See also the following addresses, which advance a similar argument: Tobias, June 25, 1957, ibid.; and Charles C. Diggs, June 28, 1957, ibid. Note Roy Wilkins's July 1 address at the 1956 annual conference. NAACP Papers, pt. 1 (supp.), reel 4. On American prestige, see U.S. Ambassador to India Chester Bowles in "American Prestige," *The Crisis* (February 1957): 91.

57. Faubus quoted in Sitkoff, *Struggle for Black Equality*, 29.

58. See Robert F. Burk, *The Eisenhower Administration and Black Civil Rights* (Knoxville, TN, 1984), ch. 9. Eisenhower quoted in Gloster B. Current, "Crisis in Little Rock," *The Crisis* (November 1957): 525–35. On foreign coverage of Little Rock, see "English Press," *The Crisis* (November 1957): 555–58. See also Roy Wilkins, *Standing Fast*, 247–54. Note Cary Fraser's incisive treatment, "Crossing the Color Line in Little Rock: The Eisenhower Administration and the Dilemma of Race for U.S. Foreign Policy," *Diplomatic History* 24 (Spring 2000): 233–64; and Borstelmann, *The Cold War and the Color Line*, 102–4.

59. Tobias's address, July 8, 1958, NAACP Papers, pt. 1 (supp.), reel 8; and Wilkins's address, July 13, 1958, ibid.

60. Javits's address, July 9, 1958, NAACP Papers, pt. 1 (supp.), reel 8. A June 23, 1958, meeting on civil rights between Eisenhower, Randolph, Lester Granger, Martin Luther King, Jr., and Roy Wilkins indicates how leading reformers sought to convince government leaders that the persistence of racial discrimination was an international liability for the country. See "A Statement to President Dwight D. Eisenhower," Randolph Papers, reel 30. See Wilkins, *Standing Fast*, 255–58.

61. Quoted in Sherry, *In the Shadow of War*, 212.

62. Wilkins to Nnamdi Azikiwe, July 21, 1959, NAACP Papers, pt. 1 (supp.), reel 11.

63. Bunche's address, July 19, 1959, ibid.

64. Azikiwe's address, July 19, 1959, ibid.

CHAPTER EIGHT

1. South African material in the "Looking and Listening . . ." column, *The Crisis* (May 1960): 308–12; the editorial was entitled "Rising Tide of Color," 306–7. In the same issue, Thurgood Marshall compared apartheid to Jim Crow. "The Cry for Freedom," 287–90.

2. Donald Hoffman on the sit-ins, June 24, 1960, NAACP Papers, Library of Congress, Washington, D.C., microfilm edition, pt. 1 (supp.), reel 12; Wilkins's address, June 26, 1960, ibid. See also the convention resolutions 50 and 51, which relate to apartheid and imperialism, ibid. On the sit-in movement, see William H. Chafe, *Civilities and Civil Rights: Greensboro, North Carolina and the Black Struggle for Freedom* (New York, 1980).

3. Franklin H. Williams, "The Law and Human Rights—A Comment," *The Crisis* (January 1962): 11–17.

4. On the Birmingham campaign, see Glenn T. Eskew, *But for Birmingham: The Local and National Movements in the Civil Rights Struggle* (Chapel Hill, NC, 1997). On Kennedy and Birmingham, see Carl M. Brauer, *John F. Kennedy and*

the Second Reconstruction (New York, 1977), chs. 9–10. See also Jonathan Rosenberg and Zachary Karabell, eds., *Kennedy, Johnson, and the Quest for Justice: The Civil Rights Tapes* (New York, 2003), chs. 3–4.

5. Quoted in Taylor Branch, *Parting the Waters: America in the King Years, 1954–1963* (New York, 1988), 824. On the night of Kennedy's speech, civil rights leader Medgar Evers was assassinated in Jackson, Mississippi.

6. Quoted in Branch, *Parting the Waters*, 791.

7. Russell Baker wrote of a "gentle" army in the *New York Times*, August 29, 1963; the description of King's speech is from James Reston's piece in the same issue. On the march, see Lucy G. Barber, *Marching on Washington: The Forging of an American Political Tradition* (Berkeley, CA, 2002), ch. 5.

8. On the March on Washington, see the October 1963 issue of *The Crisis*. The quotation on the significance of Du Bois is from the NAACP board's resolution, September 9, 1963. Ibid., 472–73.

9. On civil rights legislation, see Hugh Davis Graham, *The Civil Rights Era: Origins and Development of National Policy* (New York, 1990), chs. 3–6; Robert D. Loevy, *To End All Segregation: The Politics and Passage of the Civil Rights Act of 1964* (Lanham, MD, 1990); David J. Garrow, *Protest at Selma: Martin Luther King, Jr., and the Voting Rights Act of 1965* (New Haven, CT, 1978); and Alexander Keyssar, *The Right to Vote: The Contested History of Democracy in the United States* (New York, 2000), 256–93.

10. Manning Marable, *Race, Reform, and Rebellion: The Second Reconstruction in Black America, 1945–1990* (Jackson, MS, 1991), 56. Malcom X quoted in David Burner, *Making Peace with the Sixties* (Princeton, NJ, 1996), 55.

11. David Howard-Pitney, *Martin Luther King, Jr., Malcolm X, and the Civil Rights Struggle of the 1950s and 1960s* (Boston, 2004), 6–9.

12. Note Malcolm's assessment of King's approach: "There is no such thing as a nonviolent revolution. The only kind of revolution that is nonviolent is the Negro revolution. . . . It's the only revolution in which the goal is a desegregated lunch counter . . . and a desegregated public toilet; you can sit down next to white folks—on the toilet. That's no revolution. Revolution is bloody, . . . revolution destroys everything that gets in its way." "Message to the Grass Roots," November 1963, in *Malcolm X Speaks*, George Breitman, ed. (New York, 1965), 3–17. On King and Malcolm, see James H. Cone, *Martin and Malcolm and America: A Dream or a Nightmare* (Maryknoll, NY, 1991).

13. Malcolm X, "Message to the Grass Roots," in Breitman, *Malcolm X Speaks*, 3–17. On Bandung, see "Twenty Million Black People in a Political, Economic, and Mental Prison," January 23, 1963, in *Malcolm X: The Last Speeches*, Bruce Perry, ed. (New York, 1989), 51–52; and "Not Just an American Problem, but a World Problem," February 16, 1965, ibid., 167–68. Malcolm also alludes powerfully to the notion of a global community of oppressed peoples of color in the 1965 speech. On this theme, note his June 28, 1964, speech at the founding rally of the Organization of Afro-American Unity in Malcolm X, *By Any Means Necessary: Speeches, Interviews, and a Letter by Malcom* (New York, 1970), 35–36; and his April 8, 1964, speech, "The Black Revolution," in Breitman, *Malcolm X Speaks*, 48.

14. Malcolm X, "The Ballot or the Bullet," in Breitman, *Malcolm X Speaks*, 23–44. On the United Nations, note Malcolm's "Appeal to African Heads of State," July 17, 1964, ibid., 72–77; and an address reprinted in *By Any Means Necessary*, 57.

15. *The Autobiography of Malcolm X* (New York, 1964), ch. 17. Italics in the original.

16. Ibid., ch. 18. See also Malcolm's "Letters from Abroad" in Breitman, *Malcolm X Speaks*, 58–63.

17. The phrase is from Peter Goldman's essay, "Malcolm X: Witness for the Prosecution," in *Black Leaders of the Twentieth Century*, John Hope Franklin and August Meier, eds. (Urbana, IL, 1982), 312.

18. "Dr. King Declares U.S. Must Negotiate in Asia," *New York Times*, July 3, 1965; and John Herbers, "Civil Rights and War," ibid., July 5, 1965. On King's response to Vietnam, see Adam Fairclough, "Martin Luther King, Jr., and the War in Vietnam," *Phylon* (March 1984): 19–39; and Herbert Shapiro, "The Vietnam War and the American Civil Rights Movement," *Journal of Ethnic Studies* 16 (Winter 1989): 117–41. See also Nick Kotz, *Judgment Days: Lyndon Baines Johnson, Martin Luther King Jr., and the Laws that Changed America* (New York, 2005), 345–55.

19. "Dr. King to Send Appeal to Hanoi," *New York Times*, August 13, 1965. See also "Dr. King May Make a Wider Peace Bid," ibid., August 14, 1965.

20. "Dr. King Advocates Quitting Vietnam," *New York Times*, February 26, 1967. King also quoted in David Garrow, *Bearing the Cross: Martin Luther King, Jr. and the Southern Christian Leadership Conference* (New York, 1986), 545–46.

21. King, "A Time to Break Silence," April 4, 1967, in *A Testament of Hope: The Essential Writings and Speeches of Martin Luther King, Jr.*, James Melvin Washington, ed. (New York, 1986), 231–43.

22. On the reaction to King's address, see Garrow, *Bearing the Cross*, 553–56. The *Pittsburgh Courier*, April 15, 1967. Note the *Amsterdam News*, April 15, 1967.

23. "NAACP Decries Stand of Dr. King on Vietnam," *New York Times*, April 11, 1967. The board's April 10 resolution was reaffirmed at the annual convention in July 1967. See *The Crisis* (August–September 1967): 358–59. "Bunche Disputes Dr. King on Peace," *New York Times*, April 13, 1967. Roy Wilkins also rejected King's position. See "King Spoke for Self, Not for Civil Rights Movement," *Los Angeles Times*, April 17, 1967.

24. Wilkins quoted in "Civil Rights and War," *New York Times*, July 5, 1965.

25. Farmer quoted in "Civil Rights and War," ibid.

26. "Civil Rights," *Time*, July 16, 1965; "CORE Reverses Call for Vietnam Pullout," *New York Times*, July 6, 1965. The convention initially passed a resolution condemning the Johnson administration's "immoral policy of racism abroad" and demanded "an immediate withdrawal of all American troops" from Vietnam. The resolution was reversed shortly thereafter, with Farmer urging the organization to avoid taking this "tactically imprudent" course of action. See August Meier and Elliott Rudwick, *CORE: A Study in the Civil Rights Movement, 1942–1968* (New York, 1973), 404.

27. See Meier and Rudwick, *CORE*, 414–16. "CORE Will Insist on Black Power," *New York Times*, July 5, 1966. "Position of the Congress of Racial Equality on the War in Vietnam," undated, Congress of Racial Equality Papers, State Historical Society, Madison, WI, microfilm edition (addendum), reel 13. On the NAACP's reaction to "Black Power," see "Wilkins Says Black Power Leads Only to Black Death," *New York Times*, July 6, 1966.

28. For Moses's speech, see James Petras, ed., *We Accuse* (Berkeley, CA, 1965), 148–53. SNCC's James Forman claimed that until 1965 the war had seemed "not irrelevant, but simply remote." Quoted in Clayborne Carson, *In Struggle: SNCC and the Black Awakening of the 1960s* (Cambridge, MA, 1981), 184.

29. See Carson, *In Struggle*, 188–89.

30. SNCC, "Statement on Vietnam War," January 6, 1966, in *The New Left: A Documentary History*, Massimo Teodori, ed. (London, 1969), 251–52. James Forman, *Sammy Younge, Jr.* (New York, 1968), 223.

31. Roy Wilkins, "SNCC Does Not Speak for Whole Movement," *Los Angeles Times*, January 17, 1966. See also "NAACP Disassociates Itself from Attack on Vietnam Policy," *New York Times*, January 9, 1966.

32. Wilkins, *Los Angeles Times*, July 19, 1965; and "Bunche Disputes Dr. King on Peace," *New York Times*, April 13, 1967. Note the letter from Randolph to Jerome Davis, in which Randolph writes, "Having long experience in the field of mass movements, I am aware that you cannot fight on two fronts at the same time without sacrificing one." Randolph to Davis, September 14, 1966, Randolph Papers, Library of Congress, Washington, D.C., microfilm edition, reel 2.

33. King's April 3 speech is published in Washington, *A Testament of Hope*, 279–86.

POSTLUDE

1. Michael Eric Dyson, *Making Malcolm: The Myth and Meaning of Malcolm X* (New York, 1995), 16.

2. "Declaration of Principles" adopted by the thirty-ninth annual conference, June 26, 1948, NAACP Papers, Library of Congress, Washington, D.C., microfilm edition, pt. 1, reel 12.

3. Carol Anderson argues eloquently that the Cold War transformed a movement for "human rights" into a movement for "civil rights." Anderson also contends that this proved "devastating" to the civil rights movement and the "fight for black equality," which, it seems to me, is more problematic. See *Eyes off the Prize: The United Nations and the African American Struggle for Human Rights, 1944–1955* (New York, 2003), 5, 7. See also the work of Penny M. Von Eschen, who writes that the Cold War had a harmful impact on what she identifies as "internationalist anticolonial discourse," particularly as propounded by activists like Paul Robeson and organizations like the Council on African Affairs. According to Von Eschen, this meant that questions pertaining to "political, economic, and social rights in an international context" were subordinated to questions emphasizing "domestic political and civil rights." *Race against Empire: Black Americans and Anticolonialism, 1937–1957* (Ithaca, NY, 1997), 2–3. Note,

too, Robert Korstad and Nelson Lichtenstein's essay on black workers, the labor movement, and the civil rights struggle, which contends that the East-West competition impeded the struggle for racial justice. "Opportunities Found and Lost: Labor, Radicals, and the Early Civil Rights Movement," *Journal of American History* 75 (December 1988): 786–811. Intriguingly, Malcolm X suggested a positive correlation between black progress and world affairs during the Cold War era, though, of course, he contended that such progress was limited. See his "An Appeal to African Heads of State," July 17, 1964, in *Malcolm X Speaks*, George Breitman, ed. (New York, 1965), 80–81; "To Mississippi Youth," December 31, 1964, in ibid., 141–42; and "The Second Rally of the OAAU," July 5, 1964, in Malcolm X, *By Any Means Necessary*, 85–86.

4. Wilkins quoted in *Standing Fast: The Autobiography of Roy Wilkins* (New York, 1982), 214; King quoted in *The Autobiography of Martin Luther King, Jr.*, Clayborn Carson, ed. (New York, 1998), 242. On the link between the Cold War and civil rights legislation, see Mary L. Dudziak, *Cold War Civil Rights: Race and the Image of American Democracy* (Princeton, NJ, 2000), 183–87, 209–14. On the connection between the Cold War and post-1945 Supreme Court civil rights decisions, see ibid., 90–114; Michael Klarman, *From Jim Crow to Civil Rights: The Supreme Court and the Struggle for Racial Equality* (New York, 2004), 183–84, 194–95, 210–11, 215, 299, 375–76; and Mark V. Tushnet, *Making Civil Rights Law: Thurgood Marshall and the Supreme Court, 1936–1961* (New York, 1994), 127–28, 172–73, 185, 188.

INDEX